Maximilian I

The Royal Facts of Life

Biology and politics
in sixteenth-century Europe

MARK HANSEN

The Scarecrow Press, Inc.
Metuchen, N.J., & London
1980

Library of Congress Cataloging in Publication Data

Hansen, Mark, 1956-
  The royal facts of life.

  Includes bibliographical references and index.
  1. Europe--Kings and rulers--Health and
hygiene. 2. Europe--Kings and rulers--Sexual
behavior. 3. Europe--Politics and government--
1492-1648. I. Title.
D107.H35   940.2'4   80-12557
ISBN 0-8108-1297-5

ACKNOWLEDGMENTS

For better or worse the Royal Facts of Life owes so much
to mentors, friends, and family that no acknowledgment
can be sufficient. That said, I would still like to thank the
following individuals for their contributions along the road to
publication, mentioning as many as possible within the context of their aid.

This book first saw the light as a gleam in Professor
P. David Lagomarsino's eye in the winter of 1977 at Dartmouth College. On a dull December morning he suggested
that I investigate the procreative activities of sixteenth-century
royalty for a seminar paper. Sensing a great deal of work,
I declined. He urged me to reconsider, and in the months
that followed I gave him ample cause to regret his idea, as
the professor found himself deluged with his student's questions, problems in research, and rather far-fetched theories--
most of which he dispatched with a gentle twist of the So-
cratic knife. Through it all--almost two years of regular
demands on his time and patience--Lagomarsino led his student with wit and scholarly brilliance. My debt to him is
immense, for the Royal Facts is as much his as mine--with
the exception of whatever errors of fact or emphasis can be
found, for all of which I take full credit.

During the course of research Michael Freeman and
the rest of the Baker Library staff at Dartmouth guided me
to useful materials and gave me wide leeway in using the library's fine resources. Dartmouth Professors Peter Saccio
of the English Department and Charles T. Wood, M. Leo
Spitzer, and H. Michael Ermarth of the History Department
gave freely of their time and counsel. And Ian Frank, a
medical student, clarified many questions of medical interpretation. Sony Lipton helped with the editing and preparation of the original manuscript, but it was Gail Patten of the
History Department who rescued the tired student in the final
hours and polished a slightly disheveled project into some-

thing with more sparkle if not a genuine shine. Of course, there are many others who gave aid and advice to the author at Dartmouth, and to them I offer my sincere thanks as well.

The persons truly responsible for the book you are holding are my father and mother, Charles and Carolyn Hansen. Each made a unique, crucial contribution. My father's strong mind and practical skills animated the project through days of doubt. His interest, support, and aid in the execution of almost every facet of the book stand as testimonial to his intellectual breadth and many talents. My mother worked still closer to the actual manuscript, blessing it with her editorial skills from the first page to the last, even performing the thankless labors of proofreading, typing, and preparing the index. Her knowledge of history and eye for style influenced each chapter greatly. Just as the Royal Facts would never have been completed without my father, it would never have been completed at all without my mother.

I would like to thank the people at Scarecrow Press for their patience, encouragement, and their judicious editing of the manuscript. John Neu, the Bibliographer for the History of Science at Memorial Library, University of Wisconsin/Madison, was very obliging in my search for pertinent illustrations of sixteenth-century medical procedures, and the entire staff of the University Libraries was most hospitable and well informed. The staff of the Milwaukee Public Library, main branch, also provided great assistance, as did the National Portrait Gallery, London, the Austrian National Library in Vienna, and the library at the Dartmouth Medical School, among many others. The photographic Media Center at the University of Wisconsin was most helpful with reproductions. Sam Crimi, Jr., an art student, designed and executed charts 1-12 with accuracy, clarity, and style.

Professor Michael MacDonald of the University of Wisconsin was kind enough to review the manuscript in preparation, to offer his detailed comments and suggestions, and to provide numerous insights into the political background of Tudor and Stuart England, which falls beyond the author's expertise. Professor Lagomarsino also viewed parts of the final draft. Nonetheless, all judgments and opinions in the book are the author's alone. Similarly, all errors of fact and interpretation reflect not on my mentors but on myself.

Finally, the author would like to mention the kindness and support provided by Sarah Jane Freymann of the Stepping Stone Literary Agency, New York, Dennis Dinan of the Dartmouth Alumni Magazine, David Boerke, Charles Prout, Richard Pugh, Merle Fleming, Lincoln and Gunnar Gundersen, Anne Samuels, and Melissa Hansen.

Mark Hansen
Fall 1979
Cambridge, Massachusetts

TABLE OF CONTENTS

	List of Illustrations and Charts	viii
1.	Introduction	1
Part I:	Royal Family Ways: The Major Dynasties of Sixteenth-Century Western Europe	5
2.	The Tudors: Uneasy Sits the Crown	6
3.	The Stewarts: Primus Inter Pares	43
4.	The Valois: The Price of Self-Indulgence	80
5.	The Habsburgs: Dynasty of Destiny	129
Part II:	Seasons in the King's House	199
6.	Birth	200
7.	Childhood and Adolescence	216
8.	Marriage	227
9.	Sex	247
10.	Health	265
11.	Death	287
12.	Afterword	294
	Endnotes	304
	Index	345

LIST OF ILLUSTRATIONS

Frontispiece: Maximilian I, portrait by Bernhard Strigel.
Reproduced by permission of the Kunsthistorisches
Museum, Vienna.

p.   90   Louis XII of France, from an anonymous engraving
of the eighteenth century.   Reproduced by permission of the Austrian National Library, Vienna.

170   Charles V, portrait by Christoph Amberger, c.
1532.   Reproduced by permission of the Staatliche
Museen PreuBischer Kulturbesitz, Berlin.

192   Rudolf II, Holy Roman Emperor, bust by Adriaen
de Vries.   Reproduced by permission of the Kunsthistorisches Museum, Vienna.

201   Title page of De Partu Hominis, by Eucharius
Roesslin, c. 1532.

204   Caesarian delivery, from Mercurio's La Commare
o' Raccolitrice, first published in 1596.

212   Roesslin's illustrations of fetal positions, from the
Latin edition of Der Swangern Frawen und Hebam-
men Rosengarten.

217   James I and VI of England and Scotland, age seven,
in 1574, by an unknown artist.   Reproduced by permission of the National Portrait Gallery, London.

267   A watercolor depiction of an operation, from Caspar Stromayr, Practica Copiosa, 1559.

289   Maximilian I, deathbed portrait, by an unknown
artist.   From a sixteenth-century compendium of
Austrian royal portraits.   Reproduced by permission of the Austrian National Library, Vienna.

292   Deathbed of Henry II of France, by Jacques Peris-
sin, 1559.   Reprinted from <u>Medicine and the Artist</u>
by permission of the Philadelphia Museum of Art.

LIST OF CHARTS

p.   8   1.   Pruning the Tudor Family Tree

38   2.   Tudor Birth Control

44   3.   Stewart Statistics

82   4.   The Valois Family Tree

126   5.   Henry of Navarre's Claim to French Throne

127   6.   Charles Emanuel's Claim to French Throne

130   7.   The Habsburg Family Tree in the Sixteenth
Century

230   8.   Inbreeding in the House of Habsburg

242   9.   Tudor Descendants of Henry VII

245   10.   Intermarriage in the Lineage of Spanish
Princes

268   11.   Porphyria in the House of Stewart

276   12.   Insanity in the Royal Families of Spain and
Portugal

Chapter One

INTRODUCTION

"The betterment of mankind stemmed from the will of princes"
--Henry VIII

Imagine, if you will, the sixteenth century: not the coronets
and noblesse oblige of Hollywood fantasy, but the bitterly
crude conditions of day-to-day life.   Place yourself in a large
building, where you are surrounded by the smell of open latrines and unwashed garments.   At the dinner table men
grasp large hunks of bland--even spoiled--meat firmly in their
hands and swill draughts of stale beer to wash it all
down.   A woman gives birth to her child beneath an oak tree,
a man dances crazily through the streets with a cloth sack
over his head, and a spiteful woman disfigures a pretty
young girl with a pair of blunt scissors.   A man lives for
seventeen years with a dripping abscess on the inside of his
thigh.   This outward manifestation of rampant venereal disease, the only extant souvenir of youthful pleasures, sometimes closes, sending the infection coursing through his
veins.   The screams and howls contort his ghastly, blackish
face and echo off the stone walls of his foul chamber.   Place
yourself in his position.   Vicariously experience the rages of
the unfortunates just cited.   Imagine the terror of those ex-
posed to such outbursts.   The life of the poor, you say, was
indeed difficult.   An undoubted truth, but then we are not discussing tenant farmers in Colyton, servants in London, or
even merchants in Genoa.   The man with the draining abscess on his leg is Henry VIII, King of England.   The woman under the tree is Louise, mother of Francis I, King of
France.   The man whose face peeks out from the sack is
Henry III, King of France, and the maniac with the scissors
is Juana, Queen of Spain.

1

Sixteenth-century monarchs undoubtedly had the best of everything: their larder was amply stocked, their lodgings were as comfortable as the age permitted, and their needs and wants were instantaneously serviced by an army of servants, mistresses, priests, conjurers, and physicians. Yet the glut of attention went for naught. The brimming cupboard fed unrestrained appetites, and gluttony took its toll on royal stomachs. Similarly, the easy virtue of court damsels spread virulent infection, and the ministrations of court physicians were themselves a plague.

As a result of these and other checks on the health of royal family members, the ruling houses of the sixteenth century were significantly less stable than other, seemingly less favored, population groups. The English aristocracy, for example, was subject to severe biological constraints from 1540 to 1660; only one third of these noble families maintained the male descent; 20 percent of their marriages were childless; and 30 percent produced no heir. Only two of three noble children lived to the age of fifteen.[1] But dismal as the record may appear, the English aristocracy was considerably more fortunate than their sovereigns. The Tudors were childless in almost 40 percent of their marriages; their male descent barely lasted two generations; and almost 87 percent of Tudor marriages produced no heir. Only one of three Tudor children lived to the age of fifteen. Although the Tudors were the most biologically blighted dynasty of their era, other houses were similarly unfit. Tudor males had a life expectancy of only ten years at birth, but Stewart children could expect little more, averaging about seventeen years of life. The relatively fit sixteenth-century Habsburgs averaged about twenty years in their second and fourth generation. Even the urban poor could match these figures. Thomas Malthus calculated the life expectancy at birth for mid-sixteenth-century city dwellers to be eighteen and a half years.[2] Malthus's sampling--the overcrowded and underfed-- lived in abject poverty, while the royal families presumably had the benefit of every advantage offered by their society. Yet demographic studies reveal that the rural European peasants averaged from four to five live births per marriage.[3] The Tudors, favored as they might have been, averaged fewer than two, the Valois produced fewer than three, and the Habsburgs had about four per marriage. Rural farm couples at minimum replaced themselves: leaving from two to two and a half children to carry on into the next generation. The Habsburgs alone among western European dynasties were able to duplicate this achievement.

The alarming inadequacy of this record was not lost on the sixteenth-century dynasts themselves; it was in fact their prime concern. The survival of each house was ever imperiled by physical collapse, and constitutional weakness overlapped with every other facet of monarchical life. These blighted individuals were, in effect, the state. As the Venetian Michiel noted, "the government of the kingdom, and the affairs of state likewise, all depend on the will of Kings, they having made themselves, as they are, masters and absolute lords."[4] But these absolute lords were never the masters of their own bodies, and thus their hegemony was dependent on the harsh uncertainties of the royal life cycle. Charles V's ambassador to England, Renard, asserted that "in this country the Queen's lying in is everything."[5] If not everything, reproduction was indeed an essential royal requirement. The effective governance of a monarchy necessitated the promise of continuity: legitimate and healthy heirs. In the absence of heirs, the barely repressed disaffections of varying factions surfaced with a vengeance: the struggle for the regency after the death of James V, for example. Disorder reigned, and each succession crisis stiffened the tasks of subsequent monarchs. The health and progeny of a king were more than mere preconditions of successful rule; they were a significant determinant of the health of the state. The personal biological problems of ruling families had the stature of political events.

The importance of royal biology--the essential events of life--was obvious to sixteenth-century observers, but from a twentieth-century perspective, such apparently mundane considerations pale before more "exciting" early modern developments: diplomacy, bureaucracy, the rise of the bourgeoisie, and the growth of "national" consciousness. As a result, recent texts have paid only lip service to the problems most distressing to the monarchs themselves. Historians laboriously detail Henry VIII's relations with Parliament, yet far more of King Hal's actions can be explained by his marital and reproductive difficulties than by his occasional tiffs with a body he considered to be largely irrelevant: a nuisance, in fact. What occurred in the royal bedchamber on the wedding night could facilitate an alliance, end civil strife, or consolidate a kingdom. Renaissance diplomacy existed in large part to bring two dynastic representatives together for just such an evening. The seeds of political success or failure were often the king's own seeds, so to speak.

The four major western European dynasties were subject to an entire range of afflictions, yet each seemed to have a special nemesis. The Tudors were visited with lung disease every generation and were seemingly inclined toward paranoia. The Stewarts lived in the midst of a sort of self-propagating chaos: early death and infant succession. A genetically transmitted disease known today as porphyria crippled every sixteenth descendant of Margaret Tudor, wife of James IV. This malady flared up under stress, causing the victimized monarchs to fall apart precisely at the most crucial junctures. The Valois were notoriously self-indulgent, watching their dynasty collapse from the fly-trap arms of their formidable mistresses. The Habsburgs' personal and family lives were for the most part carefully ordered to avoid the failures of their peers. Nonetheless, they fell victims to their own success; in order to maintain their extended family empire, they intermarried with a vengeance. By the end of the sixteenth century, the heirs of the three main family branches were unquestionably insane.

The victor of the early modern scramble for hegemony was the relatively healthy and fecund Habsburg family. Their biological success was an important component of their political achievement, as the once-minor Austrian house won a war of attrition: inheriting--through propitious marriages-- the kingdoms abdicated by decaying dynasties. We cannot forget that even the most favored individuals of the sixteenth century lived at the most visceral level. The basic concern of these early modern monarchs was personal and dynastic survival, and their perspective centered around the most basic components of existence: birth, sex, sickness, and death. These were the royal facts of life.

Part I

ROYAL FAMILY WAYS: THE MAJOR DYNASTIES OF
SIXTEENTH-CENTURY WESTERN EUROPE

Chapter Two

THE TUDORS: UNEASY SITS THE CROWN

"The near in blood, the nearer bloody"
                              --Shakespeare, Macbeth

The Tudors left an indelible mark on England.   That simple
fact stands up to any historical investigation.   But how much
Tudor lore stemmed from their actual accomplishments?
Were they in fact creations of the "white legend" propagated
by sycophantic contemporaries and later anglophiles?   Admittedly, the best years of Henry VIII and Elizabeth I stand as
evidence of a distinct Tudor character that was both shrewd
and pragmatic.   But at their worst, and they were at their
worst most of the time, they were petty, self-aggrandizing,
and ultimately self-destructive.   There was but a thin line
between the business of state and the personal condition of
the sovereign, and the personal condition of Tudor rulers
was such that it cast a shadow over their entire outlook.
These hard years for the Tudors were also difficult years
for their country as well; disease, infertility, mental derangement, and disappointment rendered the ruling house
highly unstable.   Out of personal trauma came political imprudence.

         Henry, Earl of Richmond, created the Tudor mon-
archy with a victory on Bosworth Field.   But two generations
later the house was bereft of a male heir, or even an heiress for that matter.   This decline owed nothing to civil war,
tyrannicide, or usurpation: the Tudors simply failed to reproduce.   Only one Tudor monarch produced a surviving child
in the sixteenth century.   Only two children born into the
direct line lived to see the age of sixteen, and both were
females.   With this scarcity of issue, there was no Tudor

male heir-apparent for eighty years of the sixteenth century, nor was there ever a truly undisputed female claimant.

This dismal reproductive record owed much to minds and ministers, but at base was the physical inadequacy of the Tudors themselves.   A propensity toward lung disease was a Tudor legacy for five generations, figuring in the death of three monarchs and significantly indisposing many other family members.   This, combined with sundry infections, menstrual irregularities, and the full complement of virulent diseases, undermined the health of every sixteenth-century English monarch.   On a statistical basis the expected life of a Tudor male was only 10. 3 years at birth and twenty-eight years if he reached adolescence.   Tudor females could expect eighteen years at birth and forty-two years if they lived through their childhood.   These were the shortest lifespans of any major dynasty in sixteenth-century western Europe. Still more telling was their rate of reproduction; on the average a Tudor marriage (defined as any marriage with a male or female Tudor descendant involved) produced only two pregnancies and less than one (0. 9) surviving child.   Only Elizabeth I's longevity enabled the dynasty to last the century, and at her death England had no recourse but to invite the scion of another country to be its sovereign.

Richmond:

Inter their bodies as become their births.
Proclaim a pardon to the soldiers fled
That in submission will return to us;
And then, as we have ta'en the sacrament,
We will unite the White rose and the Red.
Smile heaven upon their fair conjunction,
That long have frownde upon their enmity!
What traitor hears me and says not amen?
England hath long been mad and scarred herself;
The brother blindly shed the brother's blood;
The father rashly slaughtered his own son;
The son, compelled, been butcher to the sire:
All this divided York and Lancaster,
Divided in their dire division,
O now let Richmond and Elizabeth,
The true succeeders of each royal house,
By God's fair ordinance conjoin together!
And let their heirs (God, if thy will be so)
Enrich the time to come with smooth faced peace,
With smiling plenty, and fair prosperous days!

Chart 1

PRUNING THE TUDOR FAMILY TREE
Royal Descent in 16th Century

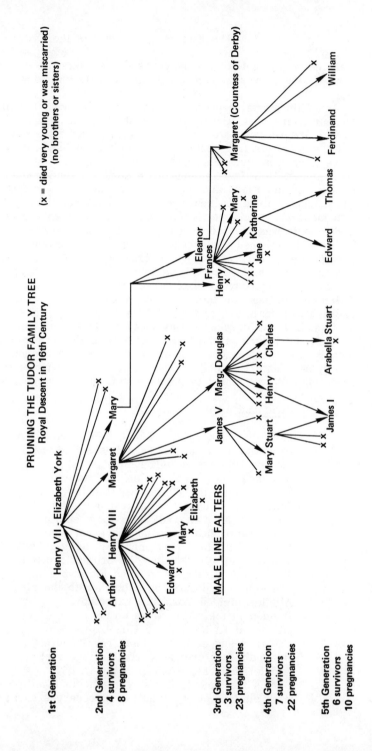

(x = died very young or was miscarried)
(no brothers or sisters)

1st Generation — Henry VII - Elizabeth York

2nd Generation
4 survivors
8 pregnancies

Arthur, Henry VIII, Margaret, Mary
Edward VI, Mary, Elizabeth

MALE LINE FALTERS

3rd Generation
3 survivors
23 pregnancies

James V, Marg. Douglas
Frances, Eleanor, Henry, Jane, Katherine, Mary
Margaret (Countess of Derby)

4th Generation
7 survivors
22 pregnancies

Mary Stuart, Henry, Charles
Edward, Thomas, Ferdinand, William

5th Generation
6 survivors
10 pregnancies

James I, Arabella Stuart

Abate the edge of traitors, gracious Lord,
That would reduce these bloody days again
And make poor England weep in streams of blood!
Let them not live to taste this land's increase
That would with treason wound this fair land's
   peace!
Now that civil wounds are stopped, peace lives
   again:
That she may long live here, God say amen!
                    --Richard III, V. v. 15-40

Such was, in great measure, the state of England in
1485.   But what is the Earl of Richmond, soon to become
the seventh Henry to mount the English throne, to do for an
encore?   Having just ended the century of civil strife occasioned by the Wars of the Roses and pledged--with God as
his co-signer on the note--prosperity and peace, the benevolent Richmond at the close of Shakespeare's Richard III fore-
shadows the reigns of his progeny, who, as fate would have
it, were also the great bard's major patrons.   Shakespeare's
Henry VII was an allegorical figure of major importance to
the Tudors.   As the cornerstone of the new dynasty, he
could only be portrayed as something of an avenging angel,
both a punishment and a reward for an errant monarchy.

In the Tudor approach to English history--a view
popularized by writers of the caliber of Shakespeare and
Pope--an evil spell had been cast upon the land after the
landmark deposition of Richard II in 1399.   Chaos was the
inevitable result of human interference with the divine ordina-
tion of sovereigns, and England was therefore punished by a
century of internecine warfare.   To simplify the message
Richard III was portrayed as the embodiment of his family's
accumulated evil.   In this context Richmond's own usurpation
of the crown on Bosworth Field became the avenging swoop
of God's "minister of chastisement"; the deposition of Richard was but a restoration of legitimate rule.   To complete
the fairy tale, the new regime, once again attuned to the
heavenly frequency, would unite royal Red and White, and
the land would prosper once again.

The mastery of Shakespeare breathed life into this
simple propaganda, but unfortunately for both the Tudors and
their patrimony the actors in the real life drama were not
avenging angels, divinely ordained rulers, or even solidly
established monarchs.   They were instead men and women
of widely variant caliber with a tenuous genealogical claim

to the throne and an even more precarious level of personal stability. Up from virtually the bottom of the aristocratic pile, Henry VII and his descendants struggled like alley cats to retain their dynastic windfall. Ever-mindful of his position as a self-made king, Henry and his successors were never comfortable on the throne. If all monarchs faced the threat of deposition, the Tudors were uniquely preoccupied with the possibility. Their tenuous monarchical roots haunted them. This was indeed unnecessary and unfortunate, for the Tudors were not a hearty lot, and the revolts they did encounter were largely a function of their inability to provide a male succession, an instance of biological and not genealogical failure. In fact, the members of the brief-lived dynasty were neither physically nor mentally capable of withstanding the strain imposed by their guiding obsession.

For those whose hearts are warmed by "rags to riches" stories, the career of Henry Tudor, Earl of Richmond, provides perhaps the most dramatic fifteenth-century example of this genre. Only in turbulent England could the insignificant son of a peripheral nobleman rise to claim--and hold--the scepter of king: God's partner in temporal affairs. Henry was not even a true Englishman, for his formative years were spent on Welsh soil, and his character owed much to this background. Royal blood ran relatively thin in the young Welshman's veins, and only the intrigues surrounding Richard III attached any importance to this dormant red rose. In the early fifteenth century, Henry's grandfather--a Welsh squire named Owen Tudor--had romanced the widow of Henry V and won her hand. This mismatch produced two sons, Jasper and Edmund. Both were acknowledged and given titles by the crown--their half-brother Henry VI. In 1455 Edmund married Margaret Beaufort, who descended from one of the bastards of the legendary John of Gaunt. Although Edmund died a year after this alliance, his thirteen-year-old wife nonetheless brought forth a son: Henry Tudor, the only remotely plausible Lancastrian heir, thanks to the entire male line's extermination in 1471. [1]

Although his lineage was not sufficiently royal to make him an obvious candidate for the throne, it did make life in England patently unhealthy after 1471. Thus, Henry spent his youth in transit. He was separated from his mother at the age of five and sent to Brittany. There the fatherless boy was shielded in the castles of a series of noblemen. This proved a rigorous life, long on dingy castles and short on education or human affection. But a spartan life without psychological pressure had its benefits for the prospective dynasty-builder. Henry became "tall, dark, athletic, and tough. "[2] He had also "learnt very early to keep his own counsel and to trust no confidant. "[3] Shrewd, strong, and aloof, Henry's hard early years prepared him well for later struggles. On the other hand, they left him with chronic consumption (lung disease has been postulated as a cause of his death) and a very low regard for human life: a coldness that would extend to his very children. Perhaps the stern and pragmatic young man was more of an avenging angel than we can appreciate.

By 1485 Richard III had alienated just about everyone, including those nobles he could least afford to offend. Henry the exile timed his return well. Disaffected nobles flocked to his ranks as he marched toward Bosworth, in Leicestershire. Here, in a land largely unfamiliar to him, fighting alongside new faces, Henry won himself a crown, while an astonishing number of would-be participants waited on the sidelines until the momentum swung decisively in his favor.

By all accounts Henry VII, crowned on the field at Bosworth, was as crafty a sovereign as Europe had ever seen. He was also ruthless in his efforts to entrench his family on the throne. Suffolk and Warwick paid the price for their marginally royal lineage, and who can be certain that Henry did not dispatch the heirs of Edward IV in the Tower? Add to this reputation for cruelty a noted taste for parsimony and a genuine love for the business of government. On top of all this, give Henry his due as arguably the most successful Tudor ruler. A more stable king than any of his successors, Henry increased crown coffers, ended once-rampant civil strife, and above all produced likely "heirs male. " Contemporaries revered "his yssue fayre and in good nombre"[4] mostly highly among his achievements.

Henry did not make any great changes in government. He used the medieval machinery left by his predecessors. The rise in government efficiency was primarily a function of Henry's personal efficiency. The king led something of a model life, never forgetting that he was king by de facto possession, not hereditary right. Prudence and cunning were the gems adorning his crown, and this bred in him moderation in all things--something his descendants regrettably failed to emulate. Avaricious, hard-working, and indifferent to pleasure, Henry "was a recluse and his court sombre"[5] noted one observer. After his victory on Bosworth Field,

Henry was beseiged with requests that he marry the Yorkist heir, Princess Elizabeth. This he was perfectly willing to do, but not before he had been proclaimed king in his own right. Suspicious Henry had little trust for his in-laws, and he made certain that the consolidation was accomplished on his terms. The delay was somewhat demeaning to Princess Elizabeth, but their eventual union satisfied the wishes of Parliament and strengthened the new dynasty's genealogical underpinnings.

At the rather advanced age of twenty-nine (Elizabeth was a similarly geriatric twenty-one), Henry began his family life. Here he brought the same single-mindedness to bear, making the political alliance more than a stagnant diplomatic formality. Contemporaries noted that Henry was "constitutionally indifferent to women,"[6] yet he and Elizabeth were flawless in the performance of their dynastic duty: eight infants were trundled in the royal nursery, and four survived to ensure the next generation of the house. Henry was apparently less than an ardent husband, and Elizabeth complained that her influence with him was inferior to that of his mother[7]--whom she detested. But these spats were less than major; for the most part Henry--who took no mistresses--and Elizabeth had an extremely stable family life by the standards of the age. In fact this domestic success was one of the few things about colorless Henry that was celebrated by contemporaries.

Henry was remarkable for his total concentration on the affairs of state. He ate small quantities, maintained an austerely religious lifestyle, and (reasonably enough) enjoyed the best health of any sixteenth-century Tudor monarch. This cannot explain his political achievement, but the simplicity and stability of Henry's personal and family life allowed him to consider external affairs to a degree unparalleled by less healthy monarchs. Henry was not seriously indisposed until his final illness--a boast no other sixteenth-century European sovereign could make.

Henry VII rightfully emerges as something of a hero in the establishment of the Tudor dynasty, but, like other heroes, Henry had his tragic flaw: he was a terribly insensitive man. In particular, his deployment of the royal children left much to be desired from both a personal and political standpoint. With two healthy sons the future of the dynasty appeared safe in 1500. But this framework for the future was composed of weak timber, and Henry's carpentry was hazardously slipshod and hasty.

A visitor to the royal nursery at the turn of the century would have encountered a most charming sight: fourteen-year-old Arthur, heir to the throne, would have been found learning his Latin and preparing for his impending marriage to the Spanish Princess Catherine of Aragon. Lively Henry was the brightest and most engaging of the children; he was training for a career in the church. Eleven-year-old Margaret awaited the day her mother would allow her to travel north for her marriage to Scotland's James IV. Her father was impatient to solder the alliance, but Elizabeth York--bearing in mind perhaps her own difficult experiences in childbed--was adamant about Margaret remaining in England until her fifteenth birthday. [8] The youngest child was two-year-old Princess Mary, her father's favorite. A delicate child, she was considered the most attractive offspring. [9]

This surface picture of the royal family, so warmly noted by ambassadors, was misleading to the extreme. Tudor child-raising (see Chapter 7) was a brutal business, and no father was less sensitive to the individual needs of his progeny than Henry VII. Grand schemes for the benefit of England's continental prestige were plotted, using each child as either bait or reward for foreign powers. Prevalent notions of child-rearing dictated that children were merely small adults, and as such were expected to act accordingly. Rigid education--enhanced by occasional beatings--was the program for the males, while the females were bound in impossibly uncomfortable clothing and trained in the intricate tedium of court ritual. In all events spontaneity and health were drilled out of the royal children by harsh tutors and demanding parents, and responsibility was yoked around their necks almost at birth. As one might imagine, the children of Henry VII were a far from happy lot.

The Prince of Wales, described as "slim, over-tall, and pale,"[10] had an especially severe upbringing and emerged from his training rather dispirited.[11] Healthy as a baby, Arthur became consumptive in his early teens. A more wooden young man could hardly be imagined. Arthur's frailty was apparent to all, but in his haste to further his dynasty Henry VII nonetheless negotiated a union with Spain. The responsibility of marriage to Catherine of Aragon weighed heavily on the fifteen-year-old prince, despite his jaunty attempts to live up to parental expectations. Although later evidence presented at brother Henry's divorce trial cast great doubt on the physical validity of Arthur's marriage, the prince felt compelled to boast "I have spent the night in Spain,

and it is a very hot region" following his wedding night. [12]
One wonders who might have ghostwritten this improbably
clever bit of ribaldry for the boy.   Life was enough of a
strain for Arthur without having to perform beyond his sexual
capabilities.   The added burden of this childhood marriage,
it was said, precipitated his demise, though he apparently
spent only seven nights with his Spanish bride during their
brief union. [13]   The Council had warned Henry VII of the
danger involved in Arthur's premature cohabitation, and Henry was distraught with the realization that he had been responsible for the boy's withering demise.   Characteristically,
Henry wrote Ferdinand of Spain a long letter indicating that
he had risked Arthur out of the great love he had for Catherine.   This, he hoped, would be a lever in the wrangling
over Catherine's dowry, causing the prudent king to up the
ante for Catherine's marriage to Arthur's brother.

    Arthur's death in 1502 signaled the beginning of a
period of disaster for the Tudors.   Crushed with grief, Elizabeth York went into childbed for the last time in 1503.   The
thirty-eight-year-old Queen did not have the will or the constitution to endure another such onslaught.   Her death snapped
something in wily Henry, who began to act strangely, to say
the least.   With Elizabeth gone, he whisked unhappy Mar-
garet--thirteen years of age--to the border himself for her
marriage to the promiscuous James IV of Scotland--seventeen
years her senior.   Margaret proved nothing but vexation for
the rest of her life, both to her family and her husband's
clan.   This accomplished, Henry turned to his own marital
prospects with uncharacteristic interest.   He considered
Juana, nominal Queen of Spain, despite detailed reports of
her madness.   Juana's troubled brain did not discourage the
king, since he was a great deal more interested in the queen
from the neck down, and reports told him she was still fecund.   Failing in this suit, he offered himself as a husband
for his son's widow--a rather distasteful proposition made
less than a month after the loss of his own queen.   Finding
Spain less than receptive once again, Henry instructed his
envoys to check into other prospects.   He demanded specific
information about the Queen of Naples: "to mark her breasts
and paps whether they be big or small, " "to mark whether
there appear about her lips any hair or not, " "to determine
her eating and drinking habits, " and also "that they endeavor
them to speak with the said young Queen fasting ... and to
approach as near to her mouth as they honestly may, to the
intent that they may feel the condition of her breath, whether
it be sweet or not, and to mark ... if they feel any savour
of spices, rosewater or musk by her breath or not. "[14]

Two children had been squandered, and the remaining
pair--Henry and Mary--bore the scars of rough handling.
Mary would flee the dynastic scene at first opportunity, and
Henry VIII would repress his fears with haughty bravado,
only to have them manifested unconsciously in his every action.   Henry VII's imprudence with his children notwithstanding, he left behind him a sparkling record at his death in
1509.   His twenty-four-year reign was one of unparalleled
peace, which prompted marked growth and development.   No
English sovereign, noted a Venetian ambassador, had ever
"reigned more peaceably. "15   Economic vitality was evident
everywhere, and in 1497 our Venetian observer hyperbolically
proclaimed England as the richest country in Europe.   Henry
VII's era was, by design, an era without cataclysmic events.
There were no crusades, great battles, or memorable occurrences at all--a lustreless oasis before the procession of
eminently colorful Tudor reigns.   Stability and prosperity
were the hallmarks of Henry VII, yet the temperate, stable,
and healthy monarch left an indelible stamp on his age.   His
was perhaps a greater contribution than the more flamboyant
doings of his successors.

The tragedy of Prince Arthur was mitigated by the
availability of the more regal Prince Henry.   Arthur's misfortune thrust the would-be cleric into the limelight, which
he welcomed.   Although perhaps a bit guilty at gaining his
windfall over poor Arthur's body, Henry basked undaunted in
the glow of sycophantic attention.   A direct contrast to his
cautious and saturnine father, Henry was flamboyant and
tumultuous--nor were their differences confined to mere appearances.   The father was a taciturn and traditional king,
while the son was a self-consciously Renaissance prince,
with all the trimmings.   Still, his color apparently delighted
his subjects.   Arthur had been a weakling, but Henry was
athletic and majestic.   Ascending to the throne two months
short of his eighteenth birthday, Henry VIII was described by
the Venetian ambassador as "the handsomest potentate I have
ever set my eyes upon: above the usual height ... and a
round face so very beautiful that it would become a pretty
woman. "16

Charm, intelligence, a robust physique, and a stable
and prosperous kingdom well disposed to the rule of his
dynasty--what blessings were not Henry's?   Yet not twenty
years later, Henry VIII was a melancholic tyrant, a bloated
mass of sickness, and an unpopular ruler.   Choosing to tilt
across the European scene like a chivalric hero, Henry's
attention to the cares of state was often subordinate to his

pursuit of court entertainments: dancing, hunting, games, music, and the rest of the pastimes that marked a fashionable royal household. Henry VII had embraced peace, but his blustering son sought to duplicate the achievement of Henry V with a conquest of French soil. Within three years of his accession Henry VIII had embroiled England in a war with France and had proved nothing except the impossibility of such a project. Truly a memorable individual, Henry VIII had a charisma that sparkled all the more for its contrast to Henry VII's rather dull persona. But Henry VIII was never to match his grand aspirations--he was never the king he wanted to be. This frustration intersected all areas of his life, from marriage to diplomacy.

Henry's transition from gifted prince to gutted monarch was something of an English tragedy, involving as it did so much hostility and internal strife. By the end of his reign a secure kingdom had turned into a virtual can of worms--with all of the worms moving in directions opposite to the sovereign's. Henry personally touched off many of the quarrels that dotted his era--most notably the break with Rome in 1536--through a solipsistic vision of English wellbeing. His most pressing concerns--even in his years of health--were always personal concerns: his body, his image, and his progeny. All three were inextricably linked. A domineering yet disturbed personality, Henry governed his patrimony (when Wolsey wasn't actually running it in his stead) in the most autocratic fashion. With his narcissistic focus, which cast the most superficial whims and disappointments in an inappropriately grandiose light, Henry's course was arguably set more in reaction to personal complaints than to external events. [17] During the final seventeen years of his life, he underwent a marked physical and mental deterioration, and in the process his rule became correspondingly arbitrary and cruel.

Henry's actions reflected the anger of an afflicted monarch, and afflicted he most certainly was. Beginning with an attack of a mysterious "pox" in 1512, Henry was yearly indisposed. The youthful Henry weathered the attacks and resumed his robust countenance, but each episode left a legacy of weakness and fear. Henry became a genuine hypochondriac, dabbling in pharmaceuticals and treatments as a hobby of sorts. Court lackeys celebrated Henry's remedy for "French Disease" (known in France as "English Disease," no doubt), but it is highly unlikely that a courtier would have disparaged the king's invention however much discomfort it occasioned. Whatever the talents of the physician-king, Henry was nonetheless unable to heal himself. Beginning in 1521 chronic sinus pain and seemingly malarial fevers were an annual visitation, and pounding headaches chipped away at the once magnanimous royal temperament. By 1532 gout hobbled Henry's formerly lithe frame, a bladder ailment burned in his abdomen, and an ulcer oozed a foul discharge from his leg. Occasionally, this ulcer would close, and Henry would "lay with blackened features and raging fever."[18] By 1537 the septic wounds had spread to both legs.[19] Able counselors took up the slack in government--as they had during Henry's hedonistic years--during the king's frequent indispositions, but the personal touch was sorely missed on occasion. Henry could not go north to quell an uprising in 1536, nor could he wage his French campaign in 1544. The king's armies must have taken little comfort with their general strapped into a trolley cart--instead of a prancing steed Henry rode a glorified wheelbarrow.[20]

Henry's reign was extremely lively from a political standpoint. Tumult was the order of the day, as the Church and the king went to war; Parliament tentatively flexed its muscles (particularly when Henry needed to pass a bill of succession); and continental powers took an ever-increasing interest in English affairs. Although much of this dynamism was a function of broad social change, a great deal of the ferment was Henry's own work. More specifically, many of the historically significant events of Henry VIII's reign were a function of his marital problems. Certainly, these difficulties were paramount in Henry's own mind, and he directed his subordinates to concentrate their energies on this matter as well; diplomats stalked the hands of continental princesses, clerics found canon-law rationalizations for Henry's illegal acts, and civil authorities made certain that no one on the streets cast aspersions on the validity of the maneuvers. Court seers and physicians--whose approaches were not wholly dissimilar--searched for the cause of Henry's inability to produce a fit male heir. King Hal was determined to leave a son on the English throne, even if it cost his realm a score of noble heads and the orthodox church he had supported so staunchly and with so much personal conviction.

Catherine of Aragon, the widow of Prince Arthur, was Henry VII's choice for his son, although she was six years his elder and had endured such unbearable strain after Arthur's death that her actual age probably surpassed her chronological years. "It is impossible for me any longer to endure

what I have gone through, " she wrote her father Ferdinand. [21]
In the same letter the twenty-three-year-old princess revealed the unpromising state of her health: "I have had so
much pain and annoyance that I have lost my health in great
measure; so that for two months I have had severe tertian
fevers and this will be the cause that I shall soon die. "[22]

Courageous as she may have been, Catherine was an
unlikely choice for a robust young prince desirous of a bevy
of sons to trumpet his masculinity to the world. But the
Spanish alliance had to be preserved, and obedient Henry
went about his conjugal duties with chivalric charm--taking
Catherine to wife within a year of his accession. Still there
is evidence that Henry was less than pleased about his mate;
she was first of all his brother's widow, and Biblical injunctions against such a marriage were clearly stated in Leviticus (which Henry would later claim as a basis for annulment). Henry, an amateur theologian, was doubtless aware
of these prohibitions, if only subliminally, at the outset.
More germane to the issue at hand, Catherine was also quite
unattractive. According to the Venetian ambassador she was
"rather ugly than otherwise, "[23] in 1515. Continental rival
Francis I of France gleefully twitted Henry on the subject,
claiming "he has an old and deformed wife. "[24] Proud Henry
was well aware of his wife's lack of allure, which was no
doubt exacerbated by her constant illness and by religious
observances so intense that the Pope himself commanded her
to stop lest they make her sterile. [25]

Sterile she was not. Within months of her wedding
in 1510, she was pregnant, and Henry's misgivings were for
the moment quieted. Quite naturally, he expected a son.
Perhaps the entire face of English history would be different
had Catherine delivered the hoped-for heir, but instead she
brought forth a stillbirth--a sign of divine disfavor to an
omen-conscious age. [26] For the next nine years, Catherine
was delivered of one grotesque disappointment after another.
A son lived fifty-two days in 1511, another boy saw a few
hours of light in 1514, and Mary (the future Queen Mary I)--
the only survivor out of eight pregnancies--arrived in 1516.
All were crushing blows to Henry. One of Catherine's miscarried sons was a veritable profanation of the human form,
leading Henry to think that God was punishing the couple. [27]
Only divine persecution could explain this personal and dynastic blight.

Catherine was pregnant for the last time in 1518, but

another dead child emerged from the womb of the thirty-two-
year-old Queen. Yet Henry sired a son by Elizabeth Blount
the very next year, and this he took to be proof of his virility, though his bastard son Fitzroy was but a sickly creature.
By 1522 Henry was discussing Catherine's inadequacy with
his confessor. Their cohabitation had ceased, as she was
all too clearly barren. [28] Ironically, it could well have been
Henry who was responsible for these obstetrical tragedies.
A number of medical historians suspect as much, claiming
that Henry contracted syphilis, infected his spouse, and thus
his offspring were congenitally diseased. [29] Although no firm
conclusion can be made on this point, the theory would certainly explain Henry's physical decline, Catherine's difficulties, and the obstetrical history of Anne Boleyn, as well.
In any event it was apparent in 1522 that there could be no
male heir with Catherine as queen, and the king was not taking his failure lightly.

Outwardly the very image of virility, Henry was inwardly seared with doubts. "Am I not a man like other
men?" he reportedly stormed. [30] At the time of his frustrated query only one spindly bastard son existed to prove
the King was indeed capable of siring an heir. Despite his
bluster Henry had not been particularly drawn to sexual in-
volvements during his years with Catherine, and it was hardly a fascination with her allure that kept him from straying.
Thus, his infatuation with Anne Boleyn proved a uniquely
disturbing episode. Beginning in 1527 Henry acted the part
of a love-sick adolescent in his pursuit of the determined
little merchant's daughter. Such flattering attentions went
essentially for naught, as Anne would not be a mistress.
This elusiveness only kindled kingly ardor, since the chase
and not the kill was Henry's favorite part of the hunt. Meanwhile, Queen Catherine had stopped menstruating, and the
best minds in the kingdom were set to work on the various
options available to the king. Anne was hardly a great beauty, "she in fact has nothing but the King's great appetite."[31]
But Henry was beyond reason on this matter.

He had instructed his envoys in Rome to ask for an
annulment on the grounds of "conscience" in 1527, the wheels
were put into motion in England, and the course was set.
Henry was determined to obtain his freedom to remarry.
Conscience and a belief in the validity of his grounds for
annulment prevented Henry from adopting a more expedient
solution--killing Catherine, for instance. But regardless of
the shaky merits of his case (Catherine, according to the

best evidence, never consummated her union with Arthur, and
was therefore not his lawful wife), the Pope was not likely to
do Henry's bidding on this matter; Charles V's sack of Rome
had placed the Pontiff squarely under the Imperial thumb, and
the disgrace of Charles's Aunt Catherine was not a project
Clement VII wanted to pursue. Henry's irresistible force
met an immovable object, and England would bear the brunt
of the crash.

The object of the king's autumnal attentions was a
shrewish and strangely formed creature plucked from within
the court circle--hardly a wise choice from either a personal
or a political standpoint. Anne had a sallow complexion, a
large mole on her neck, axillary nipples, and a rudimentary
sixth finger on her left hand--a mark that made the pious
cross themselves "to avoid the evil eye."[32] These deformities and a less-than-congenial disposition inclined court wags
to speculate on the paramour's involvement in witchcraft.
The Catholics were even less charitable; they called her "the
goggle eyed whore" in public, an epithet that caught on with
the Anglicans as well.[33] Anne's resistance to Henry's advances probably continued until sometime in 1532, when a
crown was in plain sight. Although Anne played her king
like a prize trout, her five-year defense of a questionable
chastity perhaps owed less to her cunning than her fear of
sex itself.[34] But Anne was pregnant early in 1533 and the
issue was decided; only a legitimate son could (thinking positively) inherit the throne. Church and Catherine cast aside,
Henry entered lawful, if un-holy, wedlock three months before the birth of Elizabeth.

Henry's ardor had cooled almost immediately after
the marriage--his "passion was overspent."[35] And the birth
of a daughter was a bitter setback, another divine reminder
that Henry was yet in disfavor. Anne knew all too well the
precariousness of her position--Henry had sent her a message
by his refusal to attend Elizabeth's christening. Beset by a
"chronic anxiety state,"[36] she "feigned a pregnancy" after
Elizabeth's birth in an attempt to recapture Henry's favor.[37]
Such was impossible, as the king had little time for his nagging, social-climbing wife. Her back to the wall, Anne delivered one miscarriage after another (four in all) over the
next two years--God's reminder to Henry that his second
marriage was in error as well. Searching for excuses,
Anne pointed to temper storms and concern over her husband's fall in a tournament as the cause for her failures,
but Henry was past the point of caring by 1536. His eye had

wandered to Jane Seymour, one of the queen's demure ladies-
in-waiting.   With Anne, Henry awaited the slightest provoca-
tion.   Such a spark was not long in coming.   In January of
1536 Anne miscarried a three-and-one-half-month-old boy,
and the condition of the tattered little body rekindled the
witchcraft rumors.   Meanwhile, palace gossip had Anne fro-
licking with her courtiers and, along with her imprudent
brother, gossiping about the king's dismal performance in
the royal bed. [38]   The loose-tongued pair were executed on
a trumped-up charge of adultery, causing Henry not one pang
of remorse.   Adulteress Anne was not, but casting aspersions on the king's virility was an equally deadly sin.

Jane Seymour was a far more sympathetic companion
for the king.   A calm and meek woman, Jane was yet another unremarkable--if distantly royal--lady of the court,
"no great beauty," in the words of the ambassador Chapuys.[39]
Another account describes her "pointed chin with a roll of
flesh beneath it."[40]   Unappealing though she may have been,
Henry was delighted by her modesty, a reticence that verged
on prudery.   She was the early Anne Boleyn without Anne's
ambition.   At forty-five, Henry was old, diseased, and tired,
yet he managed to sow his last seed in the twenty-seven-year-
old Jane.   A year and a half after their wedding, Jane began
her lying-in period--the last royal Tudor birth.   She lay for
over forty-eight hours in the throes of labor until the attending physicians ordered the child "torn from her womb."[41]
A caesarean delivery meant almost certain death for the
mother, but the alternative--allowing the protracted labor to
continue--was no more promising, and the child was of paramount importance.   Edward, the long-awaited heir, was thus
delivered in October of 1537.   Jane, her function behind her,
quietly passed on twelve days later, her death almost unnoticed in the rejoicing over Edward's birth.   Yet Henry appreciated the queen's supreme sacrifice; he made arrangements
to be buried beside her, which leads us to the rather cynical
opinion that the way to win the king's heart was to bear a
son and die in the process.   With the possible exception of
maternal Katherine Parr, conjugal familiarity bred nothing
but contempt in neurotic King Hal.

Having cast aside one wife, executed another, and
watched a third die after an agonizing childbirth, Henry
trotted once again into the marital lists of the continent.
His pride had been badly wounded in 1526 when the Emperor
Charles broke his marriage contract with Princess Mary, and
subsequent ventures into the marriage market reflected Eng-

land's--and its schismatic king's--lack of prestige and desir-
ability.   The best match Henry could avail himself of in 1540
was with Anne of Cleves, a second-line princess the king
agreed to espouse only after his advisers assured him of her
merits.   Heads would roll for this deceit, for Anne was a
veritable beast--"pock marked with a sallow complexion. "[42]
Henry dubbed her "the Flanders Mare" after her homeland
and physiognomy, and confided to Cromwell after his wedding
night that "by her breasts and belly she should be a maid;
which, when I felt them, struck me so to the heart that I had
neither the will nor the courage to prove the rest. "[43]   He
never went near her again, and the marriage was annulled
after only eight months.   Henry returned to his home ground:
young English noblewomen.

         Perhaps, as with Anne Boleyn, it was the aura of
sexual rivalry that drew aging Henry to twenty-year-old
Catherine Howard, for no more prudent reason can be found.
A "short, rather plump, vivacious and experienced girl, "[44]
Catherine had made the rounds.   At her eventual adultery
trial (this time no charges had to be invented), evidence
showed that Henry's "rose without a thorn"[45] first dallied
with her religious instructor, no less, at age fourteen and
"promised him her maidenhead though it be painful to her. "[46]
Chances are he got it.   But if he did not, many others had
their chance before the young girl caught Henry's attention.
She was no doubt inveterate, as even the most rudimentary
peek into her past would have indicated.   Catherine's maternal prospects were equally disturbing; physicians pronounced
her unable to bear children.   Rapturous over his plump child,
Henry cared not a fig.   After the wedding Catherine apparently found the rather decrepit king slow compared to previous, more confident, lovers.   Timidity in physical matters
was characteristic of Henry, as was rapid disillusionment.
In the past he had vented his disappointment on innocent
parties, but with Catherine he had good reason: the final
break was only a matter of acknowledging what everyone else
knew and what he certainly could have guessed.   Psycholo-
gists have speculated that Henry was actually fascinated by
the aura of sexual competition, but he could under no circumstances tolerate being mocked.   Catherine had been glar-
ingly obvious in her indiscretions.   To name but one, she
had probably been the common-law wife of Francis Dereham
before her marriage to Henry, and as Queen of England she
had the temerity to make Dereham her "private secretary. "
Rumors also circulated about her regular trysts with Thomas
Culpepper. [47]   Finally forced to come to terms with his be-

trayal after advisers precisely detailed the painful situation,
Henry's wrath was monumental. Catherine was quite understandably executed for treason, but the king was not appeased
until her entire clan had been very nearly exterminated.
There was a perverse delight in the ailing monarch's conduct
of the entire affair--almost as though he expected to be hoodwinked and thoroughly enjoyed exacting his vengeance.

Henry's tumultuous marital fortunes closely mirrored
the state of his health and the unease of his kingdom, and by
1543 the exhausted sovereign was looking to find a companion
suitable for a death-watch. This time no foolishness entered
into his choice. Katherine Parr was a "pleasant, cultured,
witty" widow of thirty-one. [48] There was no hope for more
children, for Henry was beyond the point of siring. Besides, Edward was doing as well as could be expected of a
sickly youngster. Still, Anne of Cleves was amused at the
thought of the grossly corpulent king on his honeymoon: "a
fine burden she had taken on herself, " was her verdict. [49]
This bon mot notwithstanding, the new union was sexless.

Throughout his career as difficult husband and sometime statesman, Henry grew increasingly afflicted. In 1538
a clot from his ulcerous leg apparently broke off and traveled
to his lungs, and "for several days he lay speechless and
black in the face. "[50] Both legs were now septic, leaving the
king incapable of walking, his bloated mass sprawling in bed
or in well-appointed chairs. The fits of fever returned in
1541, and Henry writhed once again "with blackened features
and raging fever. "[51] Interspersed with more mundane illnesses came another cataclysmic torrent in 1544, and by 1547
the final act of a marked seventeen-year decline was about to
unfold. Henry had from the very first viewed his disabilities
and marital frustrations as an admonishment from his heavenly partner, and now this divine sanction was coming in thun-
derbolts. Luckily for the king--and perhaps a boon for his
patrimony as well--age and disease had taken the edge off
his formerly facile and cruel mind. Henry was increasingly
forgetful and inward, except for the storms of frantic temper
occasioned by a particularly severe spell of pain. [52] In any
event the final years of Henry's reign were spent with one
of the king's feet firmly planted in death's camp. These
years were the apex of monarchical self-absorption, a characteristic of Tudor reigns in general.

Many had paid the price of the king's discomfort.
More, Rocheford, Cromwell, Buckingham, Courtenay, the

Duchess of Salisbury, the Poles, and the Howards all fell
victim to either his temper or his unreasonableness. Nor
was his vengeance confined to the great. In 1544 Henry was
informed of Scottish treachery, and an immediate dispatch
was sent to Hertford, the commander of the invading English
army. The charge:

> ... sack Leith and burn and subvert it and all the
> rest, putting man and woman and child to fire and
> sword without exception ... and extend the like ex-
> tremities and destructions in all towns and villages
> whereunto ye may reach conveniently, not forgetting
> among all the rest so to spoil and turn upside down
> the Cardinal's town of St. Andrews, as the upper
> stone may be the nether, and not one stick stand
> by the other, sparing no creature alive within the
> same.... Furthermore ... you shall take order
> with the Wardens that the borders in Scotland may
> be still tormented and occupied as much as can be
> conveniently, now specially that it is seed time,
> from the which if they may be kept and not suffered
> to sow their grounds, they shall by the next year
> be brought to such a penury as they shall not be
> able to live nor abide the country. [53]

Mentally disturbed, physically tormented, and temperamental-
ly immoderate, Henry VIII became the very model of a des-
pot--ruling almost totally on the basis of his own most visceral reactions. As Luther noted, "Junker Heinz will be
God, and does whatever he lusts."[54]

Henry VIII died in 1547, leaving as his replacement
the most tormented nine-year-old boy imaginable: Edward
VI. The "little manikin"[55] was sickly, stilted, and strange:
the result of a naturally cold temperament and the severe
pressures of his upbringing. With his mother dead and his
father a strange and formidable being seen only on state occasions, Edward was wholly raised by nursemaids until the
age of six, at which time he was turned over to zealous
Anglicans for his education. He, like many of his peers,
was beaten if he faltered in his recitations. [56] "There is almost nothing that is warm, spontaneous, or joyful in his
nature," wrote a foreign ambassador, who attributed Edward's priggishness to his being "too tightly disciplined and
trained."[57]

The strange character of the prince was but one of

his problems, for he was constitutionally weak and congenitally diseased. His repressive training only compounded matters. Henry VIII was acutely conscious of his heir's frailty; he imposed a near-quarantine on Edward's household and surrounded him with a staff of physicians. [58] At one point this retinue included eight surgeons and four physicians. [59] These misguided measures went for naught, as Edward was obviously undersized, short-sighted, and stoop-shouldered. [60] He inspired little confidence among the Anglicans, whose dominance rested on his uneven shoulders. The courts of Europe were similarly unimpressed. The Spanish ambassador characterized the supposed salvation of the Tudor house as "thin and delicate" and no longer a good marital catch, as he was "oppressed by responsibility and disappointment."[61] Although the young king lived past the age of fifteen, his marriage was rarely discussed, an unusual situation in European politics. This aberrant circumstance applied to his dishonored half-sisters as well, but in Edward's case his sexual immaturity made all such discussions of marriage academic. [62]

As king, Edward was notable only for his well-coached speeches (written by tutors Cheke and Cox) before the Council and his zealous Anglicanism. The actual power was wielded by his "Protectors," who in truth protected only their own position and sought further aggrandizement. Without a strong king to take the reins of state, competing factions engaged in constant bickering, and Lord Protector Somerset was insufficiently hard to bring the factions to heel. Edward had little love for his two Seymour uncles. He resented their shameless manipulation and their plots to enhance the standing of relatives in the order of succession. "It were better he should die," said Edward upon hearing that Somerset was in poor health. [63] When Somerset's enemy Dudley arranged to have his rival executed on false charges in 1551, Edward simply noted the execution of his closest adviser without comment in his diary. Although Somerset was indeed ambitious, he nonetheless possessed a certain "public spirit." Northumberland, né Dudley, was simply rapacious, and Edward was too weak, too bigoted, and too carefully controlled to exert much of a positive influence on his strong-willed Protector. The boy king was pleased with Northumberland's intolerant policies, and was only too happy to further Dudley's schemes to insure a Protestant succession--and raise his own heirs. Perhaps Edward knew his days to be numbered, for in 1552 Northumberland married his fourth son to Lady Jane Grey with the king's consent. This move solidified a Protestant claim to the throne in the likely event of Edward's

childless death.[64] But a female succession in lieu of Mary
Tudor would doubtless be disputed; Edward had to stay alive
at least until Jane could deliver a son. Here Northumberland's plan was flawed, for as much as the king wished to
participate in his dominating Protector's plans, Edward had
little control over his health.

　　　To provide some insights into the generally well-
known history of sixteenth-century England, we must concentrate our attention on the people involved. Diseased bodies
and tormented minds gripped the scepter with erratic strength
and the degree of their personal afflictions provided a constant limitation on monarchical effectiveness. This royal
suffering was shared with the public through cruel and vindictive monarchical actions. At no time was this syndrome
more evident than during the last few years of Edward VI's
reign. The year 1552 was the beginning of the end for the
fourteen-year-old king. In April he was attacked by measles
and smallpox, and although he warded off these common ailments, he never fully recovered his ever-precarious health.
During the next few months, court physicians puzzled over
the boy's decline, eventually deciding that Edward was beyond
the realm of medical science. After a "tough, strong, strain-
ing cough" developed in January of 1553--and yet another instance of the lung disease that was his paternal legacy--the
king was turned over to a woman charlatan, who dosed him
with poisonous stimulants. Edward appeared alert once
again. Although this measure quelled rumors of the king's
impending demise and thus gave Northumberland time to
hatch his plots, it did nothing to revive "his weakness and
faintness of spirit."[65] By the end of May, he was "steadily
pining away. He does not sleep except he be stuffed with
drugs," observed a young medical student attached to the royal household, who continued his recitation of the facts of the
case: "The sputum he brings up is livid, black, fetid, and
full of carbon; it smells beyond measure.... His feet are
swollen all over."[66] Edward's drug-induced alertness was
short-lived, and the remedies only deepened his agony as
the end approached. His arms and legs swelled to hideous
proportions, his skin darkened, his nails and hair dropped
from his feverish body, and his fingers and toes became
gangrenous. Edward's "extremis" was so disturbed by drugs
that the laundress who washed his shirts supposedly lost her
nails and the skin on her fingers.[67] Apparently, the charlatan had run the gamut of her remedies. Even these large
doses of poison failed to stir the king, who rode the toxic
wave into the final spasms of a gruesome death.

The combined efforts of Northumberland and Edward to effect a Protestant succession notwithstanding, Jane Grey was wholly unacceptable as a successor to the fallen king. Northumberland had his daughter-in-law crowned, but their nine-day charade ended summarily after virtually everyone rallied behind Mary. Legalisms, religion, and talk of bastard status aside, Mary, though a Catholic, was the credible heir to her half-brother's throne. Lady Jane was an obvious pretender. Biology would indeed dictate the course of England in this instance. Not that Mary was particularly popular or well qualified to rule; her psyche bore the scars of childhood disgrace, her health was suspect, and her attitudes were hardly in line with those of her countrymen. Mary's Catholicism was her lifelong escape from the disappointments of a bitter existence, but it led her to a zealous persecution of "heretics," which ultimately made "Bloody Mary" a name synonymous with tyranny and the most despised Tudor sovereign. The resistance she encountered--particularly Wyatt's Rebellion of 1554--only hardened her resolve.

The psychological torment of post facto illegitimacy and exile from the court undoubtedly crippled the sensitive child, and her status as an unmarried and unwanted middle-aged princess did little to repair the damage. This composite anguish provoked the queen to take a hard line, which also complemented and incited her physical ailments. "Every autumn she was liable to bouts of illness; she had lost many teeth; she suffered from indigestion and from racking headaches. Mental strain ... had perhaps been responsible, rather than physical defect, for the amenorrea from which she suffered, and from which she found relief in hysterical crying fits."68 She suffered with migraine headaches, frequent toothaches, and a heartbeat irregularity. Small wonder she was so often characterized as "melancholic" by foreign observers. Staid, demure, and withdrawn, in 1549 the thirty-three-year-old princess wrote the Council mindful of "the short time I have to live."69

There were many reasons why Mary found herself a spinster at her accession in 1553, and her own infirmities were by no means the most crucial of those reasons. "The King's Great Matter" left Mary a virtual orphan, and as such few European powers had been anxious to espouse this questionable princess or ally with her schismatic father. In any case, the dowries offered for the bastard princess of a second-rate power injured Henry's pride and were in no way commensurate with his own estimations, so Mary was

used only in the ballet of diplomacy. As the Archbishop of
Capua wrote to the Emperor Charles V: "In time of war
the English use of their princesses as they did of an owl,
as a decoy for alluring smaller birds. "[70] At Henry's death
the thirty-one-year-old Mary appeared doomed to spinster-
hood, as King Edward and his Protectors merely wanted to
forget the existence of his Catholic half-sibling, and she
certainly could not marry except through the agency of her
sovereign.

In 1553 the thirty-seven-year-old princess found herself in a totally unexpected position; she was Queen of England, and her subjects entreated her to marry--all but
Cardinal Pole, who realized what difficulties she would have
producing children. Having borne painful witness to the
matrimonial career of her father, Mary approached her own
union with great trepidation. She told the Imperial envoy
Renard that she had resolved to remain celibate, and he remarked that she had never been tempted by love. [71] The
decision to wed wrenched the queen for two days, during
which time she was physically ill. But having resolved to
marry, she pathetically entreated that defender of the faith
Charles V to find her a suitable husband--one who was "not
too young. "[72] Charles had a number of blind spots, but lack
of dynastic opportunism was not among them. He proposed
his son Philip, recently widowed and eleven years Mary's
junior. Such good fortune for Charles could hardly be believed; the English marriage--provided that it produced a
son--would unite still more of Europe under the Habsburg
aegis without costing the Emperor a great deal of money or
a drop of blood. Mary initially balked at the choice of the
dashing young prince, but as rumors of his beauty and virtue
filtered across the channel, she warmed to the match with uncharacteristic coquetry.

Philip of Spain was a dutiful son, young, virile, courteous, and in the prime of life. But the task ahead of him
was dismaying indeed. Arriving in 1554, he found his prospective bride "lacking all sensibility of the flesh, thin in
the wrong places, and without eyebrows. "[73] Dynastic duty
was clearly Philip's sole stake in the disagreeable business,
as his confidant Ruy Gomez related: "The king realizes
fully that the marriage was made for no fleshly consideration,
but in order to cure the disorders of this country and preserve the low countries. "[74] Gomez added a rather uncharit-
able postscript to his report: "it would take God himself, "
he mused, "to drink of this cup. "[75]

The semi-invalid queen made her charming paladin the center of her life, much to Philip's dismay. He wrote back to Spain complaining that Mary "almost talked love talk" to him. [76] The queen's autumnal passion apparently rendered her insensitive to her lover's unease; the marriage "maketh me happier than I can say" she wrote. [77] Mary was hopelessly in love with Philip, and only his eagerness to be off on continental ventures dampened her euphoria. Bitter experience warned her that only a son would restore Philip's flagging ardor. In this supposition Mary was only partly correct. As a Spanish gentleman wrote, "when she has had children of him, they say, he may go home to Spain. "[78] In any event the queen concentrated her energies on becoming pregnant--no mean feat for a sickly thirty-eight-year-old woman. But in this project she was destined to fail. All her life Mary had been plagued with menstrual difficulties. As Michiel noted, she suffered from "menstruous retention ... and suffocation of the matrix, to which she has been subject for many years. "[79] Michiel added that her "violent love" for Philip made her absolutely miserable during his absences.

Mary's "pathetically thwarted maternal instinct"[80] had an enormous power of suggestion. The first of her false pregnancies occurred in November of 1554, and her symptoms were so convincing that even the most careful observers were fooled. The poor woman happily pronounced that she felt the fetus kicking inside of her[81] and the usually reliable Renard wrote that "one cannot doubt that she is with child. A certain sign is the state of the breasts and that the child moves. There is an increase of the girth."[82] There was indeed a "swelling of [the] paps and emission of milk, " but it was only wishful thinking at work. [83] Nonetheless, Mary had the court earnestly preparing for the new arrival until well past delivery date. Her health was never better as she anxiously fingered her prayer book, consulting in particular the verses for women about to go into labor. But the symptoms were merely a combination of retained menstrual flow and the power of desperate hope. Skeptics were convinced once and for all of her barrenness. Yet not six months later she again believed herself pregnant. This time observers were more cautious. Renard dismissed this news as the symptoms of a tumor. But her problem was clearly gynecological in origin, for on May 7 the French ambassador Boisdaulphin reported that "the Queen was delivered of a mole or a lump of flesh, and was in great peril of death. "[84] With this failure Mary had ceased to be of political utility to Philip, who disliked--and was in turn disliked by--the people of his adopted realm. In August of 1555 he left for good, leaving a grief-stricken queen to her sleepless nights. The departure left Mary truly devastated; "she sleeps badly, is weak, and suffers from melancholy," wrote Count Feria. [85] Michiel noted that "she may be said never to pass a day without anxiety."[86]

The remaining three years of Mary's life were marked by a rapid decline, demonstrating once again the inextricably linked fortunes of royal mind and body. Having turned her country against her with a grossly unpopular Spanish marriage, the queen had nothing to show for it but wrinkles, myopia, and "a voice rough and loud, almost like a man's."[87] As Philip's advisors had noted, the preoccupied queen characteristically left her council to do most of the work: "the people who really govern are the Councillors ... and they are feared much more than the sovereign."[88] But Mary herself took the lead and vented her rage in the persecution of "heretics." Over three hundred Protestants were burned under Mary's official policy of intolerance. Harmless middle-class Anglicans bore the brunt of the queen's unhappy childhood, woeful health, reluctant husband, and inability to have a child. Mary made this purge her very own, rebuking reluctant prosecutors and even warning Cardinal Pole to avoid leniency. By the summer of 1558, Mary was gravely ill. Perhaps her ovarian tumor had run its course. But in the final stages of her malady the characteristic Tudor lung disease was most prominent, and the sputtering queen fell into a coma. On November 17, 1558, she finally died, regretfully leaving the forgotten Protestant princess Elizabeth to inherit the scepter.

For the sake of Elizabeth's well-being, it was quite fortuitous that she was largely ignored during the stormy years of her siblings' reigns. Mary had assured Renard that she would do all in her power to keep the popular young princess from succeeding her, as she held nothing but antipathy toward Elizabeth. [89] Such a crown posture placed the princess in constant danger. Only a deathly illness saved her life during Wyatt's Rebellion in 1554, when Mary ordered her to London. Had she actually arrived during the revolt she would have been identified with the rebels, and Mary would have had proper justification for executing her troublesome rival. But as luck would have it, Elizabeth was far too ill to travel. She was suspected of malingering, but Queen Mary's physicians certified the gravity of the girl's condition

when they arrived at the scene. [90]   By the time she eventually reached London, the revolt had been quashed and cooler
heads prevailed.   This was but one episode of crown hostility toward Elizabeth.   She had endured similar treatment
from her earliest years on, and her half-sister was no more
cruel than her father; in 1535 the Privy Council admonished
Henry VIII for his disregard of daughter Elizabeth.   Princesses, they wrote, ought "to be made of some estimation,
without which no man will have any great respect for
them. "[91]

The "concubine's little bastard, " as she was known in
some quarters, was raised in the country under less than
easy circumstances and was passed about like an unlucky
charm.   Taken in by the kindly Katherine Parr, Elizabeth
lived a seemingly sober life until her guardian married (after
Henry VIII's death in 1547) the irascible Thomas Seymour.
The Lord Admiral paid undue attention to the adolescent
princess, surprising her with visits to her bedchamber in
the morning, playing familiarly and undecorously with her,
and even going so far as to cut off all her clothes on one
lascivious occasion.   The pair frolicked under the benevolent
gaze of Katherine in an obviously sexual relationship, and a
scandal was ignited.   In its wake Elizabeth was disgraced
and Seymour was executed for treason.   The cool fourteen-
year-old princess was able to convince a court of nobles
that nothing truly improper had transpired and thus saved
herself from a still more ignominious fate.   She wisely escaped genuine censure by admitting the obvious; she had engaged in a great deal of foreplay with Seymour, if nothing
else.   But the proprietous Edward VI refused to receive
Elizabeth at court for two full years after the shameful episode. [92]   The importance of this adventure in Elizabeth's development cannot be overstated.   She demonstrated great
presence of mind in front of the court, but after the execution of Seymour in 1549, the petrified young girl faded into
nine full years of ill health.   Cool and collected on the outside, inside Elizabeth the most timorous creature cried to
be comforted.   "Almost in a day she changed from a strong
girl into a weak anemic one, who was never well again except for short periods. "[93]   This onslaught of invalidism
forced Elizabeth's guardians to discontinue her schooling,
and her enforced seclusion took on the tone of a stay at a
sanitarium.   Although isolated, Elizabeth was still of interest to foreign observers, but the only reports dealt with her
unchanging bad health.   In 1557 it was rumored that the
princess was suffering with jaundice, and her "swarthy" complexion was duly noted. [94]

Elizabeth's health did not improve appreciably after her accession, nor did she feel less threatened. Illness and suspicion exacted their toll; by 1560 Elizabeth "looked like one lately come out of childbed."[95] In 1562 she very nearly died of smallpox, and in 1564 her stomach was lanced with the spasms of an apparent gastroenteritis. In between these particularly dramatic attacks, Elizabeth suffered with a variety of other ailments, for the infirmities of her youth had doggedly followed her to the throne. Each year she was alternately visited with some combination of smallpox, "dropsy, colic, toothaches, chronic headaches, "nerve storms," melancholia, neuralgia, claustrophobia, rheumatism, bronchitis, pneumonia, insomnia, and other less specific ills. Foreign ambassadors characterized Elizabeth as "a Queen of no great good health or robustious and strong constitution."[96] Most distressing of all was the apparent dysfunction of her reproductive system; like sister Mary, Elizabeth's monthly periods were scanty and far between. Elizabeth reacted to sickness in a manner reminiscent of her father; she became a hypochondriac and showed an unusually avid interest in medicine. The indomitable queen of Tudor lore was actually a frightened and ailing woman who deferred completely to the men around her during frequent personal crises. Overwhelmed with a near-fatal attack of smallpox in 1562, Elizabeth deliriously called for Leicester, her current favorite. With a full coterie of witnesses, she appointed this shallow gallant Lord Protector of the Realm with an annual stipend of 10,000 pounds sterling in the all-too-likely event of her death. No choice would have been more explosive. The queen relied more frequently, and more prudently, on Lord Burghley, her ablest Councillor. Never among her paramours, Burghley was the man most responsible for the relatively efficient Elizabethan government. Although charismatic and talented, Elizabeth herself was anything but stable, and the affairs of state were constant and pressing. Ailing and preoccupied, Elizabeth could hardly give such matters her undivided attention.

If Elizabeth was, as her deputy in Ireland indicated, "ready to be-piss herself for fear of the Spaniards," she was still more anxious about the idea of marriage.[97] Her adamant refusal to name a successor--or better yet, marry and produce one--created great consternation. Despite vicious rumors of hermaphroditism and sterility, there was no physical reason why Elizabeth could not marry. In fact her doctors felt that marriage would do her good: "It may be good reasons maintained that by forebearing from marriage her majesty's own person shall be subject to such dolors and infirmities as all physicians do usually impute to womankind for lack of marriage, and especially to such women as naturally have their bodies apt to conceive, " wrote Burghley in 1579. [98] Nor were there compelling political injunctions. Sussex wrote to Cecil claiming that a "child of the Queen's body" was the supreme necessity, and he was even willing to see her marry his archenemy Leicester to accomplish this end. [99] The queen's reasons, then, were almost wholly personal, if reasonable in the light of her experience. Her reluctance stemmed from no aversion to men. On the contrary, she loved the sexual gamesmanship of the chase, much like her father. Up to the point of consummation, she was apparently all passion, as she confided to the Spanish ambassador Mendoza. "I wish to confess to you and to tell you my secret, which is, that I am no angel. "[100] She undoubtedly enjoyed the physical attentions of her long series of favorites, including Leicester, Hatton, and Raleigh. [101] But, if we are to believe contemporary sources, at the moment of capitulation she backed off. Perhaps, as one ambassador wrote, she was "too stately to suffer a commander. "[102] It is even more likely that she refused to place her fortunes irrevocably in male hands; the lessons of Henry VIII's wives and sister Mary were all too fresh in her mind. Sex for a reasonably fertile woman--in the unsophisticated days of the sixteenth century--resulted in children, and even the heiress of the barren house of Tudor could not risk an illegitimate pregnancy. If an unmarried Elizabeth had produced a child, she would have effected her own ruin. As for marriage, she told the French ambassador de Foix that whenever the subject crossed her mind she felt as though someone "were tearing the heart from her bosom. "[103] The future of England be damned! Elizabeth was determined to survive and trusted herself to no man.

It was clear that the suitors who thronged around the queen were hardly pierced with Cupid's arrow. The Duke of Anjou, long a potential husband and affectionately dubbed "my little frog" by Queen Bess, let fly a cruel sally in 1570; "the Queen, " he ungallantly sneered, was "not only an old creature but has a sore leg. "[104]

Elizabeth was indeed tormented by an open ulcer above her ankle, and her teeth were in frightful condition. Her physical allure--never great--was hardly compelling. With marriage out of the question, she saw to it that none among her retinue enjoyed what she herself was denied--favorites

and ladies-in-waiting fell immediately from grace if they
dared to marry. [105] But their punishment was lax compared
to the fury unleashed on royal relatives who had the impunity to wed without crown permission (see Chart 2, pp. 38-40).
The offspring of these unions would be claimants to the throne,
and Elizabeth was paranoically afraid of such a challenge. In
all such clandestine unions, she interceded before rivals
could be conceived and put the transgressors under literal arrest. The Safety Act, which Elizabeth helped Parliament to
draft, provided that anyone attempting to thwart the rightful
pattern of succession would be automatically disqualified from
their position in the order of precedence. This was Elizabeth's lynch law, and she interpreted it broadly, to say the
least. Her relatives found themselves victimized by a policy
of virtual extermination.

As a politician Elizabeth "left no doubtings whose
daughter she was. "[106] She was all too willing to execute
her rival Mary Stewart, and snarled fiercely when Mary's
jailor refused to do the evil deed without a proper warrant.
She also ordered hangings in every village green and market-
place where rebels had assembled after the northern rebellion of 1569--just about the time her leg became ulcerated.
A miserable childhood, constant fear, and ceaseless discomfort combined to make Elizabeth Tudor a very hard woman
indeed.

Committed to her own survival above all else, Elizabeth parlayed this instinct into forty-five years of solid rule.
Despite her frequent illnesses and her pathological insecurity,
she supervised--more actively at some times than others--
a stable and effective government. The Spanish threat was
repeatedly warded off (more the result of its own blunders
than plucky little England's martial might), and a penny-
pinching crown set the tone for the birth of "a nation of
shopkeepers. " Unlike Mary, Elizabeth's personal tendencies
were very much in accord with those of her subjects, and
hers was a remarkable reign. But even though her collapses
were covered by able ministers, Elizabeth as queen left
something to be desired--a successor. Such was her fear
of deposition that she wished for no one else to have a claim
to the crown while she lived.

Elizabeth of "White Legend" fame and the fearful, unhealthy, and often imprudent queen we come to know through
contemporary sources appear to be two different people.
Elizabeth was physically unable to be her country's true guid-

ing light; illness and personal preoccupations rendered her
susceptible to collapse and far too willing to pursue unwise
courses of action: notably the extermination of her relatives
and her refusal to provide for the succession.   Under these
volatile circumstances the Council and the growing corps of
bureaucrats took an ever-increasing part in the government,
pointing the way toward middle-class rule.

In 1603 the Queen was seventy years old, and for
seven years only her remarkable presence of mind had stalled
the grim reaper.   In only one position--lying on the floor
propped with pillows--was she able to escape pain, and her
finger was, according to observers, ever in her mouth to
massage her rotted gums.   The once-haughty queen was not
a pleasant sight in these last years.   Finally, in 1603 she
was beset with the bronchitis or pneumonia so characteristic
of her family.   She complained to Nottingham of "a heat in
her breasts" and was ultimately suffocated by "hard and dry
phlegm. "[107]   After only three generations the royal Tudors
were extinct, a testimonial to their poor health, vindictiveness toward their relatives, and dismal reproduction.

The Other Tudors

At varying times in the sixteenth century, it was literally
treasonous to marry a person of even peripherally royal blood
without crown permission, and this permission was rarely
forthcoming.   Given the dominating personalities of Henry
VIII and Elizabeth I, we tend to forget that there were in
fact "other Tudors. " These individuals themselves would for
the most part have preferred to be forgotten, or at least
shielded from the hostility of their sovereign relatives.
Neither was forthcoming, as the main branch of the family
kept its two subordinate branches in a state of suspension
and kept a particularly vigilant watch on their reproductive
activities.   These "other Tudors" descended from Henry
VIII's sisters in two distinct lines: the Stewart heirs of
Margaret Tudor and the Suffolk offspring of her sister Mary
(see Chart 1, p. 8).   These "other Tudors" accounted for
the survival of the family into the seventeenth century, as
eleven of the twelve surviving Tudor males born in the sixteenth century descended from either Margaret or Mary.

The ruling Tudors' distrust of their relatives extended
beyond mere suspicion to genuine persecution, a pathological
pattern unmatched by any other major sixteenth-century dy-

nasty. Elizabeth was perhaps the most vehement in her repression: "any claimant to the succession she branded as a potential traitor."[108] Whenever possible she trimmed these offshoots from the family tree. The career of Margaret Douglas provides a fine example of official Tudor policy toward royal cousins. The single daughter of troublesome Margaret Tudor and her rebel husband Angus, young Margaret was brought to England by her father after the failure of one of his protracted revolts against his wife Margaret, and her son James V. In England she was raised at court, and Castellon, a French ambassador, reported to Francis I that she was highly regarded. But all this changed dramatically after she privately contracted to marry Thomas Howard in 1536. On hearing this, Henry VIII burst into a blistering rage and had the miscreants cast into the Tower.[109] Howard died in captivity, and Margaret was released a year later. But in 1541 she returned to prison for her courtship of the queen's brother, Charles Howard. An eventual restoration to "favor" occurred only after Henry had engineered Margaret's legal illegitimacy, just as he had legislated the bastardy of his own daughters Mary and Elizabeth. The rationale for this disgrace was Angus's betrothal prior to his marriage to Margaret Tudor, but in truth Margaret was certainly no less legitimate than the future Edward VI, whose father had been fully wedded twice before and was a bigamist by the decree of Rome. Such fine points of law aside, Henry VIII ultimately decided to marry the safely dishonored Princess Margaret to Matthew Stuart, Earl of Lennox. Since both had strong claims to the Scottish throne (and more importantly both were in effect "birds in hand"), Henry schemed to bring the unreconstructed Scots into English orbit through a campaign on behalf of the couple's male heir.

This plan died with Henry, and Elizabeth I had other ideas about Margaret; she first made certain that the captive princess was excluded from the English succession by law, and then she added insult to injury with frequent references to Margaret's illegitimacy. Needless to say, Margaret had scant love for her royal cousin and was quite delighted when her son Darnley--long considered a possible husband for the queen--escaped to Scotland in 1565 and married Mary Stewart. Margaret was quite possibly involved in the caper, which left Elizabeth greatly embarrassed. But this brief revenge had a dear price; Margaret spent the remainder of the decade in the Tower. Yet no sooner had she returned from this captivity when, understandably bitter, she took part in still another forbidden marriage: this union involved her second son

Charles and Elizabeth Cavendish.   So. in 1574 the fifty-eight-
year-old princess returned to the Tower for the last time.
She had spent virtually her entire life in the bad graces of
her sovereigns.

Tudor rulers would have liked to control the rest of
their Scottish cousins in the same way, but distance proved
a frustrating impediment.   Attempts were nonetheless made;
Henry supported the insurgent Angus in his efforts to over-
throw the legitimate succession, and Elizabeth tried to block
the marriage of Mary Stewart.   Twice the Scots played right
into Tudor hands with disastrous invasions of English soil.
James IV was killed in the first of these aborted conquests,
and James V died a few miles away from the scene of the
second.   The internal affairs of Scotland were tangled beyond
comprehension, and the Tudors really had only to wait for
yet another Stewart--this time Mary--to make a rash move.
After she fled her disgruntled nobles in 1568 and threw herself on Elizabeth's mercy, the Stewart trump card was down.
As for the rest of the royal Stewarts: constant wars, early
deaths, late marriages, and the high rate of infant mortality
placed pseudo-Malthusian checks on the family population.

Although the Tudor sovereigns interfered at every opportunity, the royal Stewarts were nonetheless separated from
their ill-intentioned relatives.   No such distance protected
the heirs of Mary Tudor, whose family bore the full brunt of
their sovereigns' fear of deposition.   Mary herself had been
father Henry VII's favorite.   Nervous and emotional, she was
reputed to be both beautiful and graceful. [110]   According to
the Spaniard Fuensilada, she was "not learned," nor was she
of a particularly sanguine disposition; in fact she was given to
brooding and long fits of depression. [111]   Neither was Mary
religious or ambitious, and she quailed at her dynastic assign-
ment.   With her doting father dead, brother Henry VIII had
arranged a marriage between his eighteen-year-old sister and
the fifty-two-year-old French king Louis XII.   After much
wrangling Mary agreed to the distasteful match on the condition that she be allowed to choose her next spouse--an
unheard-of proposition that Henry had no intention of allowing.
Still, to speed matters along he gave Mary his meaningless
promise of free choice.   In France Mary found her old
satyr tottering on the verge of death; according to an observer, Louis was "red faced, bloated, and porcine; his posture gives the impression of an asthmatic invalid. "[112]   He
has "lost many teeth and dribbled when he spoke. "[113]   Within three months he was dead.

(continued on page 40)

Chart 2

TUDOR BIRTH CONTROL
Interference of Tudor rulers in the lives of relatives

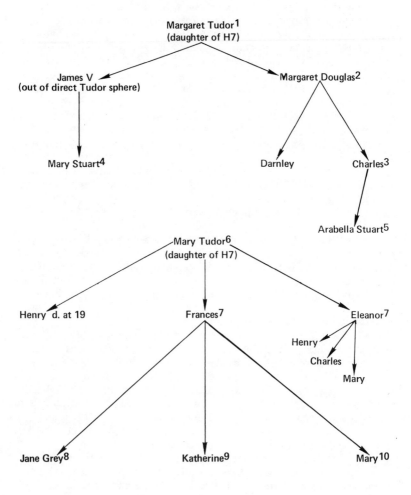

1. Forced to marry James IV at age thirteen. Not ready in view of mother. Her brother, Henry VIII, tried to interfere with her last two marriages--he allied with Angus (second husband) while Margaret was at odds with him.

2. 1536--put into Tower for contracting marriage with T. Howard, bastardized to eliminate her from succession, then released.
1541--sent to Tower again for courtship with C. Howard, brother of current queen, Catherine Howard.
1544--H8 arranges her marriage with Matthew Stuart in an attempt to bring Scot throne (to which they both are claimants) under his power. She is twenty-nine, only two of eight children survive infancy.

3. Secretly marries Elizabeth Cavendish in 1575 after impregnating her. Elizabeth calls all participants to Court, sends the mothers of the two to the Tower for allowing it to happen. Couple separated and confined. Charles dies of consumption within a year.

4. Executed 1587 by Elizabeth.

5. Virtually imprisoned for most of her life. Not allowed to marry--her name is linked with a series of Catholic plots, and Elizabeth despises her. She begs James I to be allowed to marry. He equivocates. She marries W. Seymour--descendant of correlate branch of family--in secret. After seventeen days of marriage, they are sent to prison, he to the Tower, she to Lambeth. Attempt to escape fails, she spends rest of life in prison.

6. Mary, at eighteen, forced to marry decrepit Louis XII (fifty-two). After Louis dies she marries Charles Brandon in secret, evoking choleric rage in H8. After some anxious months, he allows them to remain married and return to England, though he appropriates most of their wealth as a consolation.

7. By 1535 Brandon is again the king's crony, and is allowed to arrange noble marriages for his daughters. Family in favor with Henry--he has changed line of succession to give heirs of Mary precedence over heirs of older sister Margaret.

8. Married to Guilford Dudley, son of Lord Protector Northumberland. Northumberland had convinced dying Edward VI that Jane should succeed him. Power play also involved marrying Katherine to a relative. Marriage lasts two months, then both are captured and sent to prison. Jane executed in 1554 (January) after Protestant uprisings made her presence dangerous in Mary's view.

9. First marriage part of Northumberland plot--husband's family repudiates her after Jane's capture (marriage never consummated).
(continued on next page)

Henry had great plans in store for the eminently marriageable widowed Queen of France. But at this point Mary acted on the promise she had extracted. She married her confidant Charles Brandon, a man long on physical courage but short on brains. Mary had loved Brandon for some time, perhaps as much for the quiet country life he offered as for his personal charm. But Brandon, long a hunting partner of the king, as a condition of his visit to France had sworn that he would not propose to the queen. Far from English shores, Brandon all too quickly forgot the sanctions of promise and position.

But Henry did not forget them, for Suffolk and Mary had ruined his scheme for an Anglo-Imperial alliance. He raged and uttered such threats that the fearful Brandon wrote: "Alas that I ever did this."[114] But the evil deed could not be undone, so the penitent couple waited in France under the benevolent eye of the new king, Francis I, who was delighted at this turn of events; an encircling alliance had been foiled, and Mary--espoused to a mere English nobleman--posed no threat to his power. Henry was powerless to punish his recalcitrant sister while she remained in France, and a barrage of apologies led to the abatement of his wrath. Brandon wrote his friend and related that both he and Mary were ill with anxiety and suspense, and Mary wrote her brother with a threat to enter a nunnery if he tried to arrange a marriage for her. Henry chose to let the matter rest for the time being, and allowed them to return. But to make up for his affront, the king confiscated most of the pair's accumulated wealth, including some of the crown jewels of France.

Having carried off their amazing love match, Mary

1561--secretly marries Hertford, becomes pregnant (though they only spent a few hours alone together while hiding the marriage), and Elizabeth puts them both in Tower. While in Tower (summer 1562) they are allowed to cohabit, which resulted in another pregnancy. Elizabeth jails keeper of Tower for this breach; couple permanently separated. Katherine dies in prison six years later.

10. Although deformed, she secretly marries Thomas Keyes in 1565. Elizabeth immediately imprisons both of them. Keyes dies in prison six years later. Mary cannot marry again.

and Brandon settled into a quiet country life, keeping their
appearances at court to a minimum.   Brandon was once again
in favor with the king, and Henry magnanimously attempted to
raise the Suffolk heirs above the bothersome Stewarts in the
succession.   Mary's two daughters, Frances and Eleanor (a
son, Henry, had died at age nineteen), both married with the
consent of the crown during this grace period.   These halcyon
days ended abruptly.   Frances and Eleanor found themselves
out of favor, unwittingly swept into plots, and suddenly the
family was an enemy of the realm once again.

        Jane Grey, Frances's eldest child, was wedded to the
remaining bachelor son of Northumberland during his year
as Lord Protector.   With the full knowledge and consent of
Edward VI, Northumberland planned to place his daughter-in-
law on the throne after the demise of the sickly king.   But
support for this bold power play was not forthcoming, and
two months after the marriage both parties were captured
and imprisoned.   The seventeen-year-old Jane had not wanted
to be queen at all.   But in January of 1554, Queen Mary,
egged on by her advisors and fearful of the Protestant uprisings in the North, had the reluctant pretender executed.
Jane's sister Katherine had also been embroiled in the marriages pivotal to the Northumberland plot, but the union was
never consummated, and her husband's family repudiated her
after Lady Jane's capture.   In 1561 Katherine secretly married Hertford and became pregnant.   Elizabeth had the pair
tossed into the Tower for their license, and Katherine died
in prison six years later.   The third sister, Mary, was deformed, but she too "ate of the forbidden fruit."   After her
clandestine marriage to one Thomas Keyes, Elizabeth immediately imprisoned the two of them.   Keyes died in jail, and
Mary was kept in enforced widowhood the rest of her sad life.
Of the children of Frances's sister Eleanor, only Margaret
survived infancy.   Like her cousins, this princess was also
kept in a state of custody at court, and eventually vented
her frustrations by turning to witchcraft. [115]   Such was the
sorry state of affairs that befell Tudor relatives.

        It was in many senses a needless persecution.   By
closely incorporating--and perhaps marrying with--these relatives, Henry's children might have provided a lineal male succession, eliminated the ubiquitous plots involving royal blood,
and strengthened their position.   Instead, these relatives were
uniformly regarded as rivals.   As a result of this policy, by
1615 the Tudors had exterminated most of their cousins and
had downgraded the rest.   Rather than create a dynasty, the

ruling Tudors had almost deliberately destroyed one. These sovereigns were themselves--with the exception of Henry VII--biological failures, and in their paranoia all relatives became virtual enemies. From Henry VIII to Elizabeth I, Tudor monarchs resolved that the correlate branches of the family would fare no better than the sickly main line of descent. They committed dynastic suicide in the process.

Chapter Three

THE STEWARTS: PRIMUS INTER PARES

"Short summers likely have a forward spring"
                                    --Shakespeare, Richard III

Like their Tudor cousins Scotland's royal Stewarts had a
talent for escaping extinction, even under the most favorable
odds.   The Stewarts reigned in Scotland for over two centuries in an unbroken line of succession, yet paradoxically
the family had as grim a record as any in Europe.   From
the fourteenth century until the consolidation of Scotland and
England, no Stewart king acceded to the throne as an adult.
The great majority of these monarchs were, like James I
and VI, sovereigns in their infancy, rulers almost from the
very day of their birth.   Quite obviously such kings were
sovereign in name alone, which left the actual government,
such as it was in backward sixteenth-century Scotland, to an
unruly cabal of bastard uncles and rapacious cousins.   The
restless Lennox, Atholl, Tranquhair, Blantyre, and Ochiltree
Stewarts--all branches of the original family of actual stew-
ards to the monarchs of Brittany and Scotland--disputed and
contended each regency amongst themselves, but in these matters possession was indeed nine-tenths of the law; whoever
had the infant monarch in hand rendered such interfamily
arguments irrelevant.   Under these circumstances the rival
Stewart clans became adept at the art of kidnapping.   The
Earl of Angus, for example, made a fine end run with the
young James V, which made a shambles of the Scottish Parliament's plan to rotate custody of the king to all the great
nobles.   Such laws and agreements were only for the faint-
hearted; the strong nobles accepted no master, and the clans
made a cult of defiance.   The bastard sons of former kings
also forayed into these battles, for there was no stigma at-

Chart 3

Stewart Statistics

Royal Descent in 16th Century

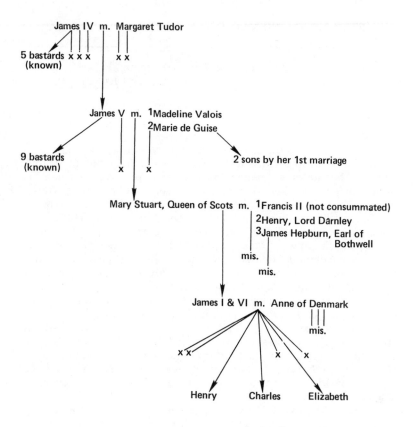

James IV m. Margaret Tudor

5 bastards x x x x x
(known)

James V m. ¹Madeline Valois
              ²Marie de Guise

9 bastards   2 sons by her 1st marriage
(known)   x   x

Mary Stuart, Queen of Scots m. ¹Francis II (not consummated)
                                  ²Henry, Lord Darnley
                                  ³James Hepburn, Earl of
                                                      Bothwell
                        mis.
                                mis.

James I & VI m. Anne of Denmark
                                  mis.

          x x   x   x

        Henry   Charles   Elizabeth

(x = died very young or was miscarried)

tached to illegitimacy.   Although bastards were not considered proper candidates for the throne, many of these individuals emerged victorious, if only for a moment, from the
fray; Moray, "natural" son of James V, became regent of
Scotland, and two other bastard sons occupied positions of
importance at Mary Stewart's court.   Under these conditions
monarchical authority was but a formality, for among their
entrenched and aggressive relatives the royal Stewarts were
no more than "primus inter pares" (first among equals).

With this chaos as a backdrop, the seven consecutive
minority successions plunged the characteristically carnivor-
ous nobles into an almost ceaseless civil war and severely
impaired the young monarchs themselves both physically and
mentally.   As David Lyndsay, poet and tutor to James V, lamented: "unhappy is the age which has o'er young a King."[1]
But the age was certainly no more unfortunate than the king.
Violence was undoubtedly the most distressing part of each
monarch's expectation; two of the four Stewart rulers in the
sixteenth century were murdered and both of the others nar-
rowly escaped a similar fate.   James I and VI, whose reign
was comparatively felicitous, always sported a bulky padded
doublet (protection against knife thrusts) even after he left
bloody Scotland and took residence in more civilized England.
This violence was far-reaching, perpetuating the unfortunate
cycle of early death and infant succession; orphaned monarchs
faced close and hostile scrutiny amidst fractious nobles, who
trained them to follow the same suicidal course that had ended
each father's life.   A perfect example of the pattern was
James IV, who rushed off to certain death on Flodden Field
with only a seventeen-month-old infant to succeed him.   The
child grew up as James V, but learned nothing from the example of his foolhardy sire.   This James left only an infant
daughter as he marched to repeat his father's debacle, this
time at Solway Moss.   With such uniformly unwise conduct,
each generation of the sixteenth-century royal Stewarts left
only one child to carry on in the face of a seemingly pre-
determined fate.

Locked into this pattern, the royal line barely survived
each decade.   The families of relatives, however, flourished.
In previous centuries Stewart kings had been relatively prolific; James I had produced seven surviving children; James
II, five; and James III, three.   These offspring had in turn
populated their own families, and by the sixteenth century it
seemed that virtually everyone was of royal blood.   But this
was only the proverbial tip of the iceberg.   A lusty brood

all, the Stewarts also fathered an incalculable number of bastards, which further complicated family relations. James IV kept five of his illicit offspring in the royal household, and James V was responsible for at least nine love children, each by a different woman.

With the lineal succession at best marginal, the destructive effect of this unharnessed fertility was obvious in every scrap of defiant behavior. Cousins and bastards gained in status through their association with the crown, but the royal family itself was only threatened by this untamed mob.

> Neither for King nor Queen's authority
> They strive, but for particularity [2]

wrote the Scottish poet Maitland. In this pursuit the Scottish aristocracy was primitive, unrestrained, and above all savage. Their internal feuds were pursued with limitless vengeance, particularly in the remote Highlands and Western Isles. Testaments to this brutality abound. In one instance Lachlan, chief of the MacLean clan, had married a daughter of the Earl of Argyll. After some years he grew tired of her and effected the most summary divorce imaginable; he placed the unfortunate wretch on a coastal rock at half-tide. Then, having successfully disposed of his unwanted spouse, he peacefully went off to bed. But unbeknownst to Lachlan, her brother had discovered her fate and had arrived at the rock in time to rescue her. To avenge this affront the Argylls proceeded to Lachlan's castle that very evening where they slit his treacherous throat while he slept. But the cruelty extended beyond family feuds. The regent Moray, bastard son of James V, took a peculiar delight in unusual executions; he was prone to hang women with babies still in their arms, and reportedly drove prisoners to the gallows like sheep--piercing them with spears while they ran.

Even the effeminate Darnley became infected with blood lust after a few months in the company of his wife's relatives. The boon companions broke into Mary Stewart's chamber and dragged David Riccio, her French secretary and confidant, from the queen's very skirts out to the antechamber, where they stabbed him over fifty times. Mary was six months pregnant at the time of the incident, and she correctly interpreted the murderers' real target to be herself and her unborn child. Darnley's gang of well-born thugs quite likely hoped to induce a miscarriage. The absence of an heir only strengthened their hand. Better yet, the miscarriage could

well have killed Mary, as miscarriages had ended the lives
of many other sixteenth-century queens. Darnley, whose
jealousy had been piqued, was an all-too-willing dupe for the
scheme. The Frenchman Fontenay, who evaluated Scotland
in 1584 at Mary's request, reported that the only matters of
importance to the Scottish nobility were "de biens et de
grandeur. "3

Under these trying circumstances Stewart kings had
effective possession of the throne for only about forty-eight
years in the sixteenth century, and even during those years
the sovereign's personal control was anything but absolute.
This endemic political instability was both a cause and a result of the ruling Stewarts' stark biological failure. Violence
and disease prevented all but one Stewart from attaining the
age of fifty during the sixteenth century. The average life
span was not even close to that figure; a royal Stewart male
could expect to live only 18. 4 years. This mortality insured
the blight of infant successions that was Scotland's main political problem. Still, the maintenance of Stewart family
rule on any terms was a remarkable achievement. But a
chimerical "family rule" would not alone suffice. The notable survival abilities of the five royal Stewarts who outlived
their infancy perpetuated the depleted dynasty, but did little
to alleviate the predominant disorder. The situation demanded superhuman strength, but these escapees were extremely unhealthy and unbalanced; physical and psychological
collapses negated the fleeting gains of their brief actual
reigns. Still there were moments of success. Both James
IV and James VI achieved at least a small measure of political stability until poor health, bad judgment, and idiosyncratic behavior effected their ruin. The procession of
infant successions, with its accompanying political atavism,
was all but impossible to interrupt.

To make matters worse, the Stewarts were a markedly imprudent family, and their ill-considered actions often
compounded the intrinsic problems they faced. Yet the com-
plexity of those native difficulties is difficult to imagine.
Sixteenth-century Scotland was impoverished, commercially
backward, and steeped in a tradition of internecine warfare.
In the estimation of other European countries Scotland was
"but the arse of the world, "4 though these more civilized
nations were only too happy to import the fierce Scotsmen to
serve in their armies. The Frenchman Estienne's desultory
report described the rustic countrymen as a suspicious race
"who consider themselves all to be cousins of the King, "5

which far too many of them were, and a common French phrase characterized a repeated stabbing as "poignarder a l'Ecossais." This patronizing French attitude was not far off the mark. Though sixteenth-century Scotland was not wholly medieval in the areas of trade and culture, it was nonetheless a country in which local clans enjoyed political autonomy and civil authorities were powerless and corrupt.

With fewer than half a million inhabitants, sixteenth-century Scotland had barely grown since the time of the legendary Robert Bruce, depopulated as it was by periodic wars. [6] To keep this kettle boiling, the contemporary English kings, ever eyeing their northern border, bribed Scottish nobles to subvert their crown. Henry VIII, for example, both supported the open rebellion of Angus and bought the loyalty of Matthew Stewart, Earl of Lennox. Such rebels enjoyed many tactical advantages; roads were largely impassable, communications poor, martial and feudal traditions still held the field, and the kingdom was partitioned by linguistic (half the population spoke only Gaelic) and cultural barriers. Scotland was but a step away from the state of nature. The process of political evolution was further impeded by the aggravating insurrections of the peripheral areas, as the Hebrideans and the "wild Scots" of the Highlands frequently rose in revolt. The crown, perennially short of revenue, had no control over these distant and savage tribes. But even the nobles in the court circle itself were uniquely independent; few felt compelled to serve the monarchy above clan interests. For the most part these individuals dressed like peasants and were illiterate; a stark contrast to their contemporaries at continental courts, who were at the very forefront of the renaissance in letters and sciences. The existence of a Scot noble had changed little over the centuries. Unrestrained by a coercive social fabric, these neolithic individuals had little need for paltry crown beneficence. What they desired they fought for, and their own power rendered them impervious to refinements, edicts, and laws. The Stewart monarchs were confronted with a group of peers who valued only money and family stature.

Erasmus, who served as a tutor to one of James IV's natural sons, described the king in glowing terms: "He had a wonderful force of intellect, an incredible knowledge of all things, and invincible magnanimity, the sublimity of a royal heart, the largest charity, the most profuse liberality." [7] Erasmus was of course somewhat beholden to the king, but

even the less partisan Ayala noted that "he is much loved. ...
James possesses great virtues and few faults worth mentioning."[8] Warlike, proud, and generous in temper, James
was an ideal prince in the Spaniard's estimation.

But the real character of James IV was much more
complex, containing as it did both great promise and hopeless morbidity. Although James was celebrated as a model
Renaissance prince he was more akin to medieval monarchs
in his superstitions, his extreme piety, and his unfathomably
melancholy temperament. The paradoxical king was a riddle
from the very beginning of his life; James was so sickly that
his parents named their next child "James" as well to ensure
that a James would live to succeed father James III. The
name "James," obviously enough, meant a great deal to the
royal family, as it had been the given name of Scottish sovereigns for over a hundred years.[9] Such caution proved unnecessary, as the younger brother predeceased the firstborn.
Still, James IV would later take the same precaution with his
own heirs; children, even royal children, were far more likely to die in their infancy than live through adolescence. Only
40 percent of the Stewart males escaped infant death. This
disconcerting fact had little bearing on James III's family, as
his three sons all grew to be adults. But instead of cele-
brating this triumph against the odds, James III was extremely upset. The king was of a superstitious ilk and a great
fancier of prophets and conjurers, and he had been warned
of "a lion ... devoured by its whelps."[10] The divine message was all too clear: his sons would kill him. The father
stiffened; ambitious Albany, the youngest son, was exiled,
and his brothers were treated with great hostility.

If the eldest of the whelps began his adulthood with
benign intentions, his filial feelings for the old lion rapidly
evaporated under the heat of James's paranoid measures. As
such, the prophecy was self-fulfilling. At the age of sixteen,
the long-estranged son took sides with one of the anti-crown
factions. Young James was undoubtedly eager for his throne,
but he entered their camp only after his cohorts had promised
that the old king would not be murdered in the coup. Even
the vicious Scots had some scruples regarding patricide. Unfortunately, James had been misled, and his father was indeed murdered to insure the success of the revolt. Guilt
was seared into the new king's very character. As penance
he wore a wrought-iron chain around his waist and increased
the weight by one link every third year "to awake remem-
brance of his sin when it hurt him."[11] His religious devotion

took on a slightly hysterical tone, and every hint of misfortune sent him racing for the shrine of St. Ninian. Of course these pilgrimages were hardly austere; he "set out for tain accompanied by a poet, three falconers, a horse laden with silver plate, four Italian minstrels, and a moorish drummer. "12 The king's stylish journey also included a stop in Darnaway, where he visited two mistresses. Such luxury notwithstanding, James IV was genuinely haunted by the ghost of his murdered father and fully expected to suffer the visitation of his own evil. During his frights he told confidants that he longed only for "a simple life without dread. "13

Morbidity was but one phase of James IV's paradoxical personality. He was also "profuse and generous, " a grand romantic, a sumptuously appointed king, and "handsome in complexion and shape. "14 Although he could ill afford it, he lived in the splendid style of continental rulers, to create the pretense of magnificence, and his subjects appreciated the display, much to the disdain of the Spaniard Ayala, who denounced the whole country as "vain and ostentatious by nature ... spending all they have to keep up appearances. "15 The Scots also approved of James's reckless courage. James III had preferred the company of artists, and was accused of effiminacy by clan leaders, but his son was well accepted by the martial nobles; on the subject of war and violence they were of one mind. James captured their bloodthirsty imaginations with his plans for a new crusade, although a minor country like Scotland was far too wretched to carry off such an endeavor. Still, the visions were grand and hypnotic. Through them he attained a popular following unequalled by any of his sixteenth-century successors.

James had yet another side to his character, that of the dabbler and dilettante. The mercurial king indulged in a series of whimsical pursuits, among them alchemy, astrology, education, and medicine. He was well versed in music, ships, clothes, and guns, and he filled his palaces with exotic splendor. Neither did he lack personal presence. The king was robust and performed admirably at many sports, but he nonetheless had a strange interest in disease. In fact he even fancied himself something of a physician; surgery was his favorite specialty, and the treasury accounts reveal that he paid twenty-eight shillings to be allowed to bleed a man and fourteen shillings for the privilege of pulling a tooth. There was a kind of distorted logic at work in his fee scale, for his own physician charged the king twenty-eight shillings for bleedings. 16

So many were James's varied pastimes that he all but
forgot to marry. The handsome and athletic king was certainly a prime candidate for the altar, but he had squandered
his youthful vigor on a procession of paramours. Some contemporaries found his unashamedly licentious behavior scandalous. "And sen thou art a king, thou be discreit," admonished the poet Dunbar. [17] But discreet he was not; bastards
and discarded mistresses littered the Scottish landscape.
Still, a king could not wench forever. James, nearing twenty, was ready to settle down with his favorite mistress Margaret Drummond, but such a love match was political anathema. Failing that, he obstinately resumed his extremist
lifestyle of alternately scheduled masochistic penance and unbridled lust; in fact, as mentioned above, to reconcile his
pleasures he often visited mistresses on the way to the
shrine. [18] Perhaps his dichotomous character merely reflected different sides of the same coin, since James had
little difficulty combining his excessive indulgence of both
tastes.

Henry VII saw in the Scottish king's bachelorhood an
opportunity, for he had a rather unpromising daughter to offer
in an alliance. Held back only by her mother's reluctance,
Margaret was without such protection after her mother's
death, and was rushed post haste to the Scottish border by
King Henry himself. There they parted for the last time.
Margaret was painfully alone at the age of thirteen. James
professed to be pleased by his young consort's arrival, but
his enigmatic personality was beyond the child bride's comprehension. The thirty-year-old king was set in his habits,
most of which were highly disconcerting. It was quite characteristic of James to visit, as he did, not one but two different paramours while the final preparations for his wedding
were being completed. [19] For her part Margaret acted like
the homesick child she was. From the very beginning she
was ill and unhappy; her primitive surroundings appalled her
and her dashing husband was no more to her than "this king
here," as she wrote her father. [20] Others would pay for her
hard luck, as the sickly and spiteful Scottish queen vented
her rage in constant tantrums and frequent skulduggery.
James foresaw political benefits from the union--Margaret
stood to inherit the English throne in the event of her brother
Henry VIII's childless death--and let it go at that. He had
not expected an Aphrodite; other women could serve that function. Still, James could not just ignore his "moon faced and
plump" spouse, shrewish as she was. More than anything
James needed legitimate heirs, and he had certainly proved

himself capable of siring them. Margaret was herself fertile; at the age of seventeen she began a seven-year odyssey of consecutive pregnancies. The yield was, however, discouraging. Five of their six children died shortly after birth. James and his physicians looked for the silver lining to this cloud and optimistically hailed such fertility as a portent of more resilient youngsters to come. It was all part of the progress toward a healthy family, they thought. Margaret hardly shared their high hopes. Twenty-one months had been her longest respite between arduous pregnancies, and on at least one occasion she conceived the very month after a delivery. Each confinement battered her, and the mounting toll had a cumulative effect; by her seventh delivery it took forty-eight hours of labor to bring forth the child. This effort so weakened Margaret that she was unable to rise from her bed for two months afterwards. [21]

These events worried him, and to mollify his troubled conscience--his philandering had continued, his children had died, and many fingers had been pointed at him--he undertook a number of barefoot pilgrimages to favorite shrines. Such was the remedial course of expiation. No one in sixteenth-century Scotland (of all places) could have pinpointed the nomadic lifestyle, filthy nurseries, dark castles, and improper diets truly responsible for the royal children's deaths. Under the circumstances there was little for James to do but shriek imprecations at the skies.

Among all his sins the sin of pride was perhaps nearest to the king's heart. Through his marriage to the Tudor princess, James had a reasonable chance at the English throne, and he was eager to announce it to the world in the defiant manner so beloved of his similarly unwise countrymen. "The Queen shall lose nothing for my sake," he proclaimed. [22] Such open gloating betrayed in him something of a death wish, for no neighbor of sound mind challenged the crafty Tudors so blatantly. But the gauntlet was thrown, unfriendly gestures were made, and tensions between the two countries elevated with each incident. Henry VIII was reportedly so piqued after the future James V was born--and appeared a good bet to survive--that he refused to pass on their father's bequest to Margaret. [23] James answered by openly gloating over each of Margaret's births--while Henry's wife delivered nothing but stillbirths and weak children who lived only a few heartbreaking moments. In the escalating battle of the wills Henry then arranged to have Margaret removed from the English succession. This roused James's

ire to frothing rage, and he marshalled his willing nobles into a war council.   With an anger completely disproportionate
to their military might the Scots prepared for no less a project than the invasion of England.

Battle plans laid, ten thousand men marched with
James across the English border.   Surprise was on their
side, but instead of advancing while their opponent lacked an
organized force, they dawdled among the border castles.
There, all too typically, squabbles, privations, and desertions
sapped the impetus behind the initial attack.   Meanwhile, the
Earl of Surrey, who was charged with the welfare of the
North in Henry VIII's absence, put together an army the
numerical equivalent of James's.   After much wrangling over
protocol, the two armies finally met for an apocalyptic battle in which the Scots were slaughtered to a man.   James
acquitted himself admirably on the field at Flodden, exhibiting
much of the vaunted courage that endeared him to his fellow
victims.   It was a monumental slaughter; an entire generation of warriors fell on Flodden Field; approximately 2 percent of the total population of Scotland (which was some half
a million).   The country was left with no more than a pretty
legend; James reportedly died while leading a wild charge
against the advancing enemy.   His panache was duly noted,
as was the futility of his entire venture.   Years before Ayala
had summarized James's fatal volatility in a military critique: "He is not a good captain, because he begins to fight
even before he has given his orders. "[24]

James IV was not a dullard, yet he led a quarrelsome
army into a country far more powerful and much better organized than his own and, once there, made a strategic
mockery of whatever advantage he might have had.   Surely
he was not laboring under the illusion that his rag-tag band
could conquer England?   Given James's background, the mo-
tive would seem to lie in his self-destructive instincts.   As
a chronically depressed man and a lover of grandeur, James
may have considered the invasion of England to be a noble
knight-like endeavor regardless of the practical consequences.
A more prudent and healthy monarch would never have attempted such a fiasco, but from childhood James had been
shaped to be rash and mentally unstable.   He was merely a
human being in the grip of overwhelming environmental pressures.   He, like Luther, was programmed for his fate: "Ich
kann nicht anders. "   The human failings of a monarch had
left the "golden age" of Scotland to a leaden future.

Margaret had been miserable throughout her decade in Scotland, and at the death of her husband she stubbornly set a course designed to salvage at least a few moments of personal happiness. After Flodden, she had been made her son James V's guardian on the condition that she remain unmarried, but almost immediately after the blood had drained from the field she married the Earl of Angus, a man "most lusty in the Queen's sight."[25] Margaret was a renowned shrew, and Angus was duplicitous and cruel; it was a marriage made in heaven. It was also an invitation to revolt. Angus's noble peers were livid with jealousy and spite, and could not bear the thought of his elevation. Civil war erupted. The romantic struggle of the two lovers against reprobate crown servants was moving indeed, until Angus decided in 1514 to enlist with his former cronies in the fight against his wife. However ungallant his decision, Angus had picked the winning side, for the rebels had Margaret on the run. The young James V was taken from his mother and thrown to the nobles, who proceeded to fight over his custody with unseemly relish. The revolt took a number of confusing turns, and at one point Angus was forced to flee to England, where he found sympathetic listeners and financial backing at court. He returned to woo Margaret once again, only to find that she still bore a grudge against him for his earlier betrayal. "If he had desired my company or my love," she sniffed, "he would have shown himself more kindly than he has done."[26] Angus of course wasn't interested in either her company or her love; it was her power he coveted. Could she truly have been so blind? "I took my Lord Angus against all of Scotland's will, whereby I lost the keeping of my son," she complained to Dacre. "Sith I took him at my own pleasure, I will not be bosted [browbeaten] into taking him now."[27] By 1519 Margaret wanted a divorce, which she eventually obtained on the basis of Angus's precontract with another woman--a suitably flimsy pretext to ease the Pope's mind. By 1524 she was indulging in "ungodly living" with Henry Stewart,[28] or so Norfolk wrote to Wolsey. Henry VIII was shocked by the unconscionable and frivolous behavior of his sister, and took many an opportunity to enlighten her on the error of her ways with sanctimonious missives. He particularly urged her not to bastardize her daughter.[29] Meanwhile, Henry was doing exactly the same thing, the only difference being that he believed himself justified while she was not. Such were the strange notions of the twisted individuals who ruled western Europe.

Admittedly, Margaret was an extremely silly woman.

Her conduct as Queen of Scotland was the height of folly, but
before passing judgment we must acknowledge the forces that
drove Margaret into such lunacy.   The queen was constantly
ill, and her response to pain was never stoic.   She was a
complainer, and each malady roused her to anger.   Her
pregnancies were horrible experiences, leaving her with,
among other ills, a "great and intolerable ache" in her right
leg. [30]   This was a frequent problem, and Henry VIII's spy
Dacre referred to it as a "sciatica" of the hip joint. [31]   In
1516 she contracted typhus, and was not expected to survive,
but her attack of smallpox in 1522 was still more severe; on
the borders she was thought to be dead. [32]   She wrote Wolsey
that "all my body be so full of smallpox that I neither write
nor sit, nor scarcely speak. "[33]   A pearl-sized growth covered
one of her eyes as a lasting legacy of the disease.   These attacks highlighted a lifetime of poor health, and when all her
symptoms were marshalled together, a convincing case for a
rare genetically transmitted malady known as porphyria can
be made (see Chart 11, p. 268).   Her hysterical "attacks, "
insomnia, difficulty in writing--"mine own evil hand, " Margaret called it[34]--and sensitive skin, among others, fit the
porphyric pattern.   Sufferers also tend to break down under
stress, which Margaret certainly did at every crucial juncture.   Under this circumstance Margaret's conduct was less
the imprudent folly of an incapable woman than the frantic
writhings of a horribly diseased victim.

Margaret and Angus were, of course, only stand-ins
for the baby king.   Their antics created a smoke screen
around the boy, but nonetheless the regency period was as
difficult for young James V as it was for his patrimony.   His
mother Margaret forfeited her position as tutrix to marry,
and thus relinquished her son.   She apparently found the allure of Angus more compelling than her maternal duties, and
the young king was left to the care of the great nobles before
he reached the age of two.   "Care" is perhaps a malaprop,
for the legion of uncles were not the caring type.   Although
logical, this solution was far from efficacious, and the interests of both Scotland and the king were not well served by
the arrangement.   As David Lyndsay wrote, "what great misrule in this region rang, when our younge prince could neither speak nor gang. "[35]   The surrounding turmoil of wars between factions and constant rotation among ambitious guardians
was hardly nutritive, yet James V apparently led a relatively
uneventful life in his earliest years. [36]   He was accompanied
in his travels by the poet Lyndsay, who assumed the role of
benevolent parent--his later reminders of this to James were

both mawkish and irksome--and tutor. It was he who attempted to educate the king and maintained a stable environment around him. But Lyndsay and the boy's official guardians had conflicting views on child care. The guardians, particularly his stepfather Angus, opposed the education of the king; for their purposes he was best kept distracted and ignorant. There was little poor Lyndsay could do, except to complain, "Imprudently, like witless fools, they took that young prince from the schools."[37] From the arid lessons of Aristotle and Plato, James moved to the real-life teachings of wenches and drink, and his noble servants were delighted by the young king's application to his new studies. Such debauchery prophesied that James was to be no more than a "roi faineant," leaving the actual government to his protectors.[38]

The plan would have been a brilliant success but for two unforeseen peculiarities: James's awareness--even as a twelve-year-old boy--of the manipulative schemes and his hatred for the duplicitous uncles. While still in their custody from the ages of twelve to sixteen, James developed a cold-hearted, arrogant, and "naturally suspicious" personality.[39] Well he might have, under the circumstances. He was among enemies, and he awaited only an opportunity to escape and proclaim himself king. This he did in 1528, at the age of sixteen. Choler permeated the king's very marrow, and once established on the throne, he embarked on a course of vengeance that would bring him almost universal enmity. His first target was Angus, but he too had made an escape and now resided at the English court. Lacking the culprit himself, James exacted his revenge from the entire Douglas clan (Angus was a Douglas): he ordered the execution of all Douglas males and the exile of their priests, women, and children.[40] The young king's vindictiveness was as pointless as it was cruel; the murders only united the clans in their hatred of the king. Foolish though it was, James could no more control his wild impulses than he could tame his vassals; "ill tempered and violent," he was deliberately tactless and arbitrary to intimidate his opponents. But instead of respect he evoked torrents of hatred from all quarters. "So sore a dread king and so ill beloved of his subjects was never in this land."[41]

Perhaps there was no proper solution to the political chaos in Scotland; had James been gentle he probably would have been discounted like his grandfather James III, and through his cruelty he became despised. Arguably, the only

safe course would have involved a strong stance without personal vindictiveness, and of this James was incapable.   He
bore far too many grudges, and had scores to settle.   In
any event, James certainly asserted his kingship, but the
realm of Scotland was not much to lord over.   The young
monarch found his kingdom impoverished, for the regents had
been extravagant.   The chance to recoup was minimal as
well: the value of money was falling, and Scotland had no
system of organized taxation. [42]   Nor was James the king to
lead Scotland out of the dark ages; he was himself too much
a creature of that era.

Once taken from his tutors, James had proved an apt
philanderer, surpassing even the legends of his wanton father.
"Most vicious we shall call him, " wrote Knox, who added
that "he spared neither man's wife nor maiden. "[43]   Such
conquests came so easily to James--though it certainly wasn't
his looks that mesmerized his partners--that he occasionally
donned peasant garments to carouse unrecognized in the countryside.   The sporting masquerade gave rise to a whole
series of colorful "jolly beggar" legends.   One of the best
of this genre was the story of James's pursuit of a saucy
scullery maid; she first defied him by pouring a vat of ale
on his head, then surrendered in the resulting puddle.

... would God the lady that lovit ye best
had seen you there sweating like twa swine

wrote Lyndsay. [44]   Along with these great oral traditions,
James left nine known bastards scattered across the landscape, sheer license even in a sexually indulgent age.   A
royal mistress or two was accepted practice, but the ceaseless yearnings of James were distracting and embarrassingly
barbaric to the more educated Scots.   "On ladronis for to
leap ye will not let" (You will not stop leaping on whores),
scolded Lyndsay. [45]   Yet like his father James had his one
great love: "the lady that lovit ye best" of Lyndsay's verse,
Margaret Erskine.   Such was his feeling for Margaret that
he seriously considered a marriage with this mere noblewoman, but financial and political considerations interceded.
James needed money more than love, so he stalked a rich
foreign dowry.   Fearful of Henry VIII's intentions, he
steered clear of an English alliance (he perhaps had the behavior of his own mother in mind as well) and sought to renew "the auld alliance" with wealthy France.   But the French
proved hopelessly intransigent in negotiations.   At this turn
of events, James decided that the spurned Margaret was his

fated spouse, though she had married in the interim. This
was not to be, for the Pope refused to dissolve Margaret's
marriage. 46 Negotiations with France resumed.

At the advanced age of twenty-five, James finally
turned to the business of marriage in earnest. Delicate
Madeline Valois had been offered to James just two years
earlier, but when the Scottish king arrived in France in 1536
he found the princess weak and consumptive. Yet the princess's pallor and frailty were in no way displeasing to James;
in fact a spark jumped between them. This struck Francis
I as sheer perversity. He had offered James any woman in
the realm except his sickly daughter to show his good faith.
The "auld alliance" was important to him. But the life of
Madeline hung by only a thread. With paternal concern he
urged James to reconsider his insistence on the princess:
"the princess Madeline was unhappily not in a state of health
to be removed from her native air to a cold climate like
Scotland." Her doctors were similarly gloomy. She would
never be able to withstand such hard conditions, they
warned. 47 The Scottish Council joined in the protest, having followed James to France to assist in the bargaining.
These nobles warned their sovereign that, as the last Stewart male, he was duty-bound to marry a princess capable of
bearing children, which the consumptive Madeline clearly
was not. 48 But Madeline and James were both stubborn and
smitten. The love match proceeded, to the dismay of all
but the principals. Theirs was a pyrrhic victory. True to
the prophecies Madeline was never well after her marriage.
As her companion Madame Montreul wrote: "The Queen has
no good days after she came to Scotland but was always
sickly, with a catarrh, which descended to her stomach."49
Madeline died forty days after reaching Scotland, as predicted.

Regardless of the interlude's romance, James had
nonetheless wasted a valuable year. His stubborn decision
to wed an obvious invalid appeared very unwise indeed. He
was still without an heir, and diplomatic banter took on renewed importance. France was willing to make good his loss,
but pickings were slim. After some hesitation James finally
accepted Francis's offer of Marie de Guise, whom he had
once declined, though he made it known to the French king
that he did not consider her the equal of his lost wife. Marie was not overjoyed either. She had been tantalized by the
prospect of marriage to Henry VIII, who, aware of plans for
her marriage to James, made tentative offers in the hope of

severing the "auld alliance." Francis, enraged by her independent thinking on the matter, ordered her to Scotland in
no uncertain terms. Henry VIII, a bad loser as always, almost had his revenge; Marie's ship was imperiled by a
fierce storm as it crossed the English Channel, and Henry
denied the wedding party sanctuary in an English port. The
ship weathered the storm, as it turned out, far better than
Marie weathered her stormy reception in Scotland. From
the reaction of her betrothed it might have been wiser to
anchor in England permanently. With great reluctance on
both sides, the nuptials were solemnized in 1538. Marie
was tall and robust, but her beauty inspired no poetry. For
one thing, her slightly deformed upper lip curled strangely
close to her nose. 50 James was nonplussed, and the rumor was that "the king sets not much store by the queen."51
He took his pleasures elsewhere, and after eighteen months
of marriage, the queen was conspicuously childless. Relatives on both sides of the channel were concerned. The
Duke of Guise contemplated a trip to expedite the problem
first-hand. After all, Marie was of proven fertility, with a
little son from her first marriage left behind in France.
James of course had even more compelling proof of his virility. Apparently, all that was needed was widespread concern to impress the couple with the necessity of their task,
and in 1540 Marie dispelled remaining doubts with the delivery of a son. The vindicated father fired off a dispatch
to cousin Henry VIII: "It has liked God ... to have sent us
... ane son and prince, fair and lifelike, to succeed us and
this our realm, we think it accord us well to make you participant with us of sic joyous good novelis and that we have
of our blood to this our realm, which hereafter do pleasure
to you and yours."52

The happy day gave reason to gloat, but almost immediately the need to bear more children fell on Marie. Under this pressure the queen mistakenly announced herself
pregnant a few months after the birth of James. This was a
grave error, as even her recent triumph could not erase
the stigma of her miscalculation. As her mother-in-law
Margaret Tudor wrote to Henry VIII, "She is not [pregnant],
whereat the subjects of Scotland much grudgeth against her."53
Within a year Marie delivered another son, Robert, and the
objections were answered. Or were they? Political stability
was only as secure as the lives of royal infants, and these
royal infants were never more than a hair's breadth away
from death. Two days after his birth, Robert was dead,
and shortly thereafter little James perished as well. This

complete collapse of the royal family reignited popular discontent with the king and queen, as Queen Mother Margaret
noted: "There hath been a great displeasure for the death of
the prince and his brother, both with the king my son and the
queen his wife."[54] Such a singular tragedy could only be a
sign of evil forces at work in the royal house.

Evil forces were indeed at work, but their true locus
was within the king's own body. Although he had yet to reach
his thirtieth year, James's health was failing, and observers
detected a corresponding decline in his spirit as well. The
king's final phase was, like most royal declines, both painful and protracted. Until 1537 there was little mention of
James's health. In fact, some sources effusively praised
the young king as a paragon of physical strength, although
this kind of flattery was "de rigueur" for sixteenth-century
chroniclers and diplomats. We can only be certain that
James was not seriously indisposed from his early years to
the age of twenty-five. But in 1537 the king suffered a serious hunting accident, and from then on his health was precarious.[55] The accident was only a trigger, for thereafter
the king was beset with unrelated ailments. He began to suffer chronic depression and nightmares, and treasury accounts
for this period show increased medical expenditures. Unusual measures were taken; in September 1539 £10 was spent
to send a Frenchman named Raphael to obtain rare drugs for
the king. Yet these and more conventional remedies seemed
to have no effect: James continued to languish. Under the
strain of his ailments James's behavior became increasingly
erratic. As early as 1536 a spy had noted his native instability: "I hear he is somewhat crased."[56] By 1540 this had
escalated to "feverish nights of insomnolency" at Linlithgow.[57] Though he had never been prudent, James now
seemed oblivious to the ramifications of his impulsive actions.

In 1542 James's mental and physical demons surfaced
in an unusually bold policy: the invasion of England. For
over a decade James had wisely avoided a confrontation with
Henry VIII. Now, almost overnight, he called his bitterly
divided nobles--Flodden still fresh in their minds--to war.
His commanders were initially unenthusiastic, having an unhealthy respect for James and a healthy fear of annihilation.
This unfamiliar reluctance was merely a "no confidence"
vote against the despised king, and was not even unique to
this particularly foolish plan; they had refused to follow him
into battle once before. Still the prospect of combat was

fetching. This time disdain for the king could not outweigh
the allure of war, and a sizable army was ultimately raised.
History mimicked itself, as James advanced on the English
border just as his father had thirty years before him. There
were important differences though. James IV had been widely respected, and had led his troops to a fighting end. James
V was surrounded with enemies, and still worse, on the eve
of the battle at Solway Moss, the king was inexplicably absent. Unbeknownst to his troops James had taken ill and
had retired to a nearby castle. Almost as the lines of battle
were being drawn, James's "minion" Oliver Sinclair came
forth with an authorization to command the troops signed by
the king. Quite predictably, no one cared to follow Sinclair,
who perhaps commanded more enmity than even James, and
the nobles all but forgot the English in the bickering amongst
themselves. At the critical moment confusion reigned in the
Scottish camp, the English seized on the opportunity, and
Flodden was reenacted--although in the absence of leadership,
the Scots were killed in ignominious flight instead of honest
battle. James's covert departure from his expedition without
so much as an attempt to make provision for his absence
sealed its fate. He later gave his only explanation to Queen
Marie in an extremely incoherent letter, claiming that "I
have been ill these three days past as I never was in my
life. "58

Far away from the king's deathbed at Falkland, Queen
Marie lay in a different sort of agony. The queen was pregnant, and the anxiety produced by James's impending death
brought on a hastened labor. In the very fortnight of the
king's death, his heiress, Mary Stewart, the Queen of Scots,
was delivered prematurely. James was past the point of
cheer at the news, and few expected the undersized infant to
succeed where her heartier brothers had both failed. Two
astute foreign emissaries, Chapuys and Lisle, disparaged
both mother and child's chance for survival. Even if Mary
lived, what solace was the birth of a sickly female when Scotland desperately required a strong king? King James V's
only recorded comment on his daughter's birth was the oft-
repeated and incorrect prophecy, "Adieu, it came with a
lass and it shall pass with a lass. "

Romantic legend has it that James died of a broken
heart over the defeat. Contemporaries could find no other
explanation for the precipitous demise of a superficially
healthy thirty-year-old king. Their confusion was understandable. It is quite true that James merely languished in

bed after the defeat, and perhaps his will to live was indeed broken. But in all probability this stress and disappointment only activated the underlying malady truly responsible for the king's failing health and ill-timed breakdown: porphyria, his mother's legacy. James had suffered for five long years, and this had no doubt unbalanced him. In the end the struggle with disease sapped him of all his living strength. This was more than a personal tragedy; in pain and anger James had been cruel and rash, and he left Scotland more unruly than he found it. With this foolish career a fait accompli, James issued a series of dire proclamations, the first being "I shall be dead," which no one questioned. [59] But his subsequent jeremiads showed more insight into his mistakes. He disparaged the future of Scotland: "King Harry (Henry VIII) will either take it by arms or by marriage," and mourned, "All is lost."[60] James knew better than anyone the ruin he had courted. The rout on Solway, his imminent death, and his lack of a male heir all placed Scotland in a pitiable negotiating position. Henry VIII freely dictated the settlement to his northern neighbors, pathetic as they were, and Scotland was subjugated as never before. [61] For this indignity the proud Scots could thank James, whose final years were a monument to misrule, a primer on the dangers faced by a country under an unhealthy monarch.

King James can be viewed as a character of sympathy; his cruel and vindictive streak the result of a bitter youth and ill health, his erratic behavior in part attributable to a chemical disorder. But his legacy to Scotland was no less bleak for its partial blamelessness. The nobles were more intransigent than ever, alienated in particular over James's ever-impinging personal covetousness[62] and his arrogance. James's career left his successor with an abysmal kingdom similar to, if not more complicated than, James's original patrimony. But of course James's only successor was the infant Princess Mary, born while he lay on his deathbed at Linlithgow. She was a mere bone for contention among the nobles, and there could be little hope of stable rule for decades. As Knox mourned, "All men lamented that the realm was left without a male to succeed."[63] Their gloom was well founded; Mary was both an infant and a female, two completely sufficient causes for political turmoil in a country already rife with discord. The perils of infant monarchs and their rapacious protectors were etched in blood across the pages of Scottish history, and twenty long years would pass before Elizabeth of England's reign proved the viability of female succession. At the time of Mary's birth, the evidence

was uniformly unfavorable, as the great majority of countries
left bereft of a male heir were subsumed under a foreign
prince. Yet Mary was all Scotland had. Thus cumulative
effects of the reigns of James IV and James V now settled
squarely on the shoulders of the baby princess. Even if she
lived to carry the burden, lamentation was indeed the order
of the day. The year 1542 was a most unpropitious time to
be an infant Queen of Scotland, and all manner of schemes
swirled around the baby. The issue of the regency provoked
a battle among the nobles, with Arran, described by Marie de
Guise as "the most inconstant man in the world," winning the
struggle. [64] Among other flaws, Arran was indecisive, exactly the wrong regent for the situation in which Scotland was
mired. From the South Henry VIII pressed for the immediate
marriage of his son Edward to Mary, hoping to seal irrevocably the two countries under the Tudor aegis. To this end
he sent a number of captured Scottish nobles as a public-
relations force to pave over any resistance to the idea. But
these victims of Solway Moss could not eradicate the deep
sentiment against the English, and the planned union met a
number of obstacles. Henry was in the catbird's seat as a
result of the victory at Solway Moss and the death of James V,
and he pressed his advantage with typical bellicosity. Mary
was to be raised at the English court under Henry's watchful
eye. This was unacceptable to the Scots, who promised to
send the queen on her tenth birthday. Deprived of her custody, Henry nonetheless imposed his misguided notions of
child-rearing; he demanded that she be taken from her mother and raised by an impersonal staff. In this he was satisfied; Mary was raised at a whole series of far-flung castles.
The baby's nomadic wanderings were the result of Henry's
annoyance with the resistance of some important Scottish
nobles. If the Scots were to be difficult, Henry had neither
the patience nor the need to employ gentle persuasion. With
armies massed at the northern border, Henry began a more
compelling declamation: a "scorched earth" policy designed
to strike fear into the Scotsmen's flinty hearts. Known as
"the Rough Wooing," this binge of terror only destroyed any
chance for a peaceful union and hardened the nobles' resolve
to wed the queen to the Valois heir. The Scots were vulnerable, but they were not easily intimidated. Henry's rage
had produced just the effect he least wanted: a Franco-
Scottish alliance. But after this defiance Scotland was not a
safe haven for the infant Mary; Henry was too close and ambitious peers maneuvered their own sons into her marital prospects. So, like a national treasure during enemy occupation,
at the age of five, the queen was sent to safety in France.

At the French court Mary found a home. Both Ron-
sard and Brantome praised her beauty, and King Henry II
himself diplomatically called her "the most perfect child that
I have ever seen."[65] Regal France was a direct contrast to
chaotic Scotland, and Mary reveled in her special treatment.
As dauphiness she was accorded much more respect than her
jealous uncles would have given her in Scotland, and in the
settled world of the French court, she and her little betrothed husband Francis were the main ornaments. Although
the condescending French found Mary's Scottish train motley,
the queen herself had been rescued from barbarism in time.
French became her natural tongue and her perspective on the
world. From the age of six until nineteen, Mary enjoyed the
happiest years of her life in an environment most antithetical
to her birthplace. Yet there were storm clouds hanging over
even this period of security and high esteem. Mary was beset with a plethora of physical complaints as early as 1548.
A great attack of measles led many to believe she had died
in that year, and in 1550 the "flux" imperiled her life. In
1555 her chronic stomach disorders were first noted, and in
1556 a series of fevers drained her strength. These bouts
were but a prelude to 1559, when the seventeen-year-old
Queen of Scots appeared on the verge of death. Mason wrote
Cecil that "the Queen of Scots is very sick and men fear that
she will not long continue."[66] Mundt wrote Elizabeth describ-
ing Mary "in a consumption," and Throckmorton characterized the ailing Mary as "very pale and green, and withal
short breathed."[67] Mary unconsciously added to these symptoms with a wishful pregnancy, though everyone at court knew
of little Francis's sexual immaturity. Quite understandably,
Mary was eager to establish herself in her adopted land as
the mother of an heir. Yet in 1560 this happiness was shattered with the death of King Francis II. (Henry II had been
mortally wounded in a joust the previous year.) Beside her
genuine grief over the death of her stunted husband was Mary's
sudden change of circumstances. As the childless wife of a
dead king, she had no function in France, but the prospect
of returning to Scotland was distasteful at best.

After negotiations for several prominent Catholic
princes proved fruitless, Mary's sole option was a return to
her inheritance. Her reluctance to pursue this course was
underscored by more than a touch of cultural chauvinism; she
had naively signed a secret marriage treaty completely unfavorable to Scotland, and its repercussions would be felt
across moor and heath. Under the terms of the contract,
the son of Francis and Mary would have inherited both Scot-

land and France. But in the event of her childlessness, both her right to the English throne and her Scottish birthright would revert to France--as a "forfeit for defense costs. "[68] If she had only a daughter, the girl would inherit only the throne of Scotland. On the bottom line, the contract was an attempt to make Scotland a French dominion, which Mary's countrymen took very badly. With her trunk packed with French prejudices, mementoes of civilized life, and this innocent act of treason, Mary headed for Scotland in 1561.

Although Mary was the nominal ruler of Scotland for three decades, she spent only six years of her adult life there, and these years began--just as they would end--with illness and squabbling. The nineteen-year hiatus between monarchs left the nobles entrenched and intransigent, and Mary's task required strength, diplomacy, and stability. She could muster none of these requisites. This challenge for the stalwart was oppressive for the weak, and Mary was indeed weak. She was in Scotland less than six months before her first collapse triggered the issue of her marriage. Upon her arrival she had been constantly entreated to marry, for in the words of Buchanon, Mary "took a husband to herself and gave a king to her people. "[69] But Mary retreated from this responsibility into illness: a severe attack of tertian fever that required prolonged convalescence. Her indisposition and tears stalled, as they would so many times, a decision about her future. In September 1561 Mary suffered a nervous collapse such as, according to contemporaries, "she is often troubled with, after any great unkindness or grief of mind. "[70] Mary's mental state was certainly akin to grief; she had neither the equipment nor the temperament for her current situation, and as for marriage her desires were equivocal. She had sought a match with Don Carlos of Spain, whose apparent madness was mitigated by his Catholicism and continental prestige. But such a match was impossible, since the formidable Catherine de Medici had foiled the negotiations. The issue of marriage was a moot point while Mary lay ill, but it was nonetheless a topic of great interest in both Scotland and England--where Mary stood squarely behind Elizabeth in the succession. Burghley had written Cecil in 1560 on "the menace of a foreign marriage by the Scottish Queen. "[71] The once-cossetted queen was now faced with some stiff, and irrevocable, decisions. And these were the decisions she was least capable of making.

The events of 1562 reiterated the importance of Mary's marital obligations. She was once again ill, this time with influenza, and an attempt was made to disgrace her. A suspected Huguenot, Chatelard, made valiant efforts to sneak into her bedchamber on two occasions, but was apprehended both times. Hysterical over this ploy, Mary immediately ordered his death, though wiser heads persuaded her to allow him a trial. Elizabeth made a number of "suggestions" to her cousin, although the eccentricity of her choices seemed a deliberate preventative measure. Still Mary felt compelled to take heed, as the English throne presumably hung in the balance. Knox and the Scottish Protestants further complicated the issue with their adamant opposition to a Catholic marriage. Through all of this profitless wrangling, Mary's physical condition steadily declined. In the autumn of 1563, she collapsed into fits of weeping and depression, which her French doctor treated with a new diet, and in December the chronic pain in her side was first noted. 1564 was also a hard year. Yet, during this time marriage plans had been laid. The choice of a husband--so crucial to Mary's future-- had been all but made. Henry Stewart, Earl of Darnley, traveled north from London early in 1565 to meet his future wife. Strangely enough, Elizabeth let him leave, although he was a potential heir to the English throne. Chances are that she suspected his errand as well, but no softness of heart guided her decision. Darnley was a vain and impudent fool. If Mary wanted him, so be it. This was to be, as Elizabeth probably hoped, just the rope Mary needed to make a hangman's noose for herself.

To Mary's discredit, Darnley was her own choice, though she had shown no interest in him during a previous encounter (arranged by his scheming mother). But in 1565 Mary became attracted to this "beardless and lady-faced" boy. [72] For all his many failings, Darnley was nonetheless more refined than the nobles who surrounded Mary, and in this rank environment he passed for a Renaissance prince. By all indications Mary fell madly in love, with "all care of common wealth set apart," as Randolph wrote to Cecil. [73] But now that she was finally inclined to wed, the nobles recanted; in less than a year Darnley had managed to offend all the important aristocrats, and once again hatred proved the only workable bond between noble Scots. With Darnley, their hatred was well founded. He was an effeminate egotist, at best "un gentil huteaudeau," as he was called by the Cardinal of Lorraine. [74] All practical considerations aside-- including the fact that the required dispensation had not arrived--Mary and her ill-chosen consort were secretly wed in July of 1565. The alienated nobles made their disapproval

known--former regent Moray went so far as to stage a re-
volt--and a protracted battle for control flared.

With the nobles in their characteristic state of disorganized hostility, Mary came to rely increasingly on foreign-
ers and middle-class civil servants, an example being her
Italian secretary David Riccio.   Darnley was no help at all;
loutish and arrogant, he swaggered with a group of similarly
shiftless cronies and wasted his time on gambling and sports.
Even those who cavorted with him on occasion took careful
measure of his throat.   "I know not, but it is to be greatly
feared that he can have no long life among these people, "
wrote Randolph. 75   By November of 1565 Mary was two and
one-half months pregnant with their first child, and the great
pain in her side left her unable to keep track of her prodigal
spouse.   He was, as usual, up to no good; a cabal of angry
court opponents persuaded him that Riccio's intimacy with the
queen did him public dishonor.   Of course, their real aim
was to intimidate Mary and destroy her new class of civil
servants.   Darnley was quite keen on revenging his imagined
slight.   In March, while ill health and advanced (six months)
pregnancy confined Mary to Holyrood castle, Darnley and his
cohorts broke into the queen's chamber and dragged the
screaming Riccio from her skirts.   Outside in the antechamber the conspirators stabbed the hapless Italian fifty-three
times. 76   In June, after escaping from the in-house arrest
arranged by the Riccio killers, Mary prepared to give birth.
A will was prepared--given the queen's state of health the
worst had to be expected--and Mary began her "long, painful,
and difficult" labor. 77   The result was a son born with an
unlucky caul over his head, but Mary was duly grateful.
Caul or not, James set off great rejoicing in Edinburgh and
bolstered Mary's weak political position.   The price of such
success was dear; Mary could not rise from bed for five
days, and she could barely speak to the well-wishers at her
bedside.   For the next year her health was a source of constant misery, and her two subsequent pregnancies were miscarried well before term.   Yet despite this incapacity her
acts following the birth of James were politically astute.
She loudly proclaimed Darnley the father in her public appearances with the infant, though by now she despised him and
there were rumors of her involvement with other men.   Before plunging into less prudent schemes, Mary did what she
could to cement public acceptance of James's legitimacy.

This was fine acting indeed, for there was no mistaking Mary's hatred for her husband.   Their cohabitation was

indeed less than the eighteen months of their marriage. "I
know for certain," wrote Randolph, "that this queen repenteth
of this marriage, that she hateth Darnley and all his kin. "[78]
Even as early as 1565, Bedford had suspected that "there is
some misliking between them. "[79] Maitland sympathetically
commented, "It is an heartbreak for to think that he should
be her husband. "[80] Darnley had long complained of Mary's
coldness with some cause, for Mary denied him conjugal
rights for most of their marriage, owing to her poor health.
Her martyrdom, she decided, would be saved for a different
cause. In February 1566 Drury wrote that Mary and Darnley
no longer slept together; the reason, he claimed, was too
horrible to put in a letter. [81] Even the public was apprized
of the couple's marital difficulties. According to a popular
ballad of 1568:

> For twelve month and a day
> The king and she would not come in one sheet. [82]

By the fall of 1566, Mary had lost all control of her
life and was swirling in a fog of disease toward an unhappy
end. In October she had an attack previously unequaled in
severity; she reportedly vomited over sixty times, fell into
convulsions, and was unconscious for days. "All her limbs
were so contracted, her face distorted, her eyes closed, her
mouth fast, and her feet and arms stiff and cold," wrote
Maitland. [83] According to the French ambassador du Croc,
Mary was past the point of endurance. "I could wish to be
dead," she sighed. [84]

Mary's illness left her dispirited and exceptionally
vulnerable, but the murder of Darnley in December of 1566
delivered the blow that pushed her over the edge of responsibility. Although the royal pair had long been estranged,
Darnley's brutal murder demonstrated once again the weakness of monarchical authority in the face of an untamed
aristocracy. Now more than ever Mary's fate rested in hostile hands. Some have speculated on Mary's involvement in
Darnley's murder, and there is even a theory that points to
Mary as an accomplice to the Kirk o' Field murder. But
given her physical condition, Mary could hardly have been an
active participant. She was past the point of action, and her
reactions were those of a frightened woman. Besides, the
Earl of Bothwell needed no encouragement or guidance. With
Darnley dead, the weakened queen was his for the taking,
as he well knew. Darnley's many enemies were eager to
spill his blood as well. But there was no joy in the murder

for Mary. "She hath been for the most part either melancholy or sickly ever since ... the queen breaketh much," wrote Drury. [85]

In the aftermath of the murder, Mary leaned, to a large degree involuntarily, on Bothwell, whose dynamic presence was impossible to ignore. Having won the consent of the other important nobles to press his suit on the queen, Bothwell's wooing in spring 1567 was no less rough than Henry VIII's earlier scorched-earth policy. He literally captured Mary on the open road and took her to the castle of Dunbar. There he raped her, according to Maitland, who accompanied them to the castle. This guaranteed the success of Bothwell's plan, for "the queen could not but marry him, seeing he had ravished her and lain with her against her will." [86] As Mary explained to the Bishop of Dunblane, "He has finally driven us to end the work begun at such time and such form as he thought might best serve his turn." [87] In this unfortunate episode, the queen was merely passive. Bothwell, despite his brutal, coarse, and ugly appearance, (an "ape in purple," claimed Brantome) had a will much stronger than Mary's weak resistance. She had no choice, in her condition of exhaustion and illness, but to acquiesce. Yet this irresponsible passivity did not prove a comfort; Mary had been used by the ambitious Bothwell, as she well knew, and her subjects thought very badly of her union with her husband's suspected murderer. Life with Bothwell was unpleasant enough by itself. In her misery Maitland overheard her asking for a knife with which to kill herself. [88] Drury reported that Mary's sorrow was the talk of the court, and her appearance mirrored her state of mind. [89] Unfortunately, her nadir was yet to come; in July 1567 Mary suffered her second miscarriage, losing a great deal of blood in the process. Observers were horrified by her swollen arms and legs, yellow-tinged skin, and horrible pustules for weeks afterwards.

The looming shadow of death was but one of Mary's problems. By the time of this miscarriage, she was imprisoned by her own nobles. If Mary believed that she had saved herself by submitting to Bothwell, the events of the four weeks immediately following their wedding proved just how wrong she was. Bothwell had merely gained the upper hand for a moment, and his enemies were awaiting the swing of the pendulum back to their cause. In perspective, her acquiescence proved fatal; by allying with Bothwell Mary linked her fortunes with his and lost the respect of her people.

What appeared the path of least resistance at Dunbar soon
became tortuous and overgrown, and now she was to discover
the long-range cost of her mistake. Bothwell's former cronies
turned against the pair, with popular sympathy behind them.
Bothwell himself fled at the first opportunity, never to see
Mary again, and the downtrodden queen was taken to Lochleven. There she remained for ten and one-half months in
a miserable state. Mary was not stoic in captivity; she was
restless, tormented, and without alternatives.

  With virtually everyone against her, there could be
no return to grace in Scotland. Nor could she stand further
confinement at Lochleven. The only solution, she decided,
was to flee to England and throw herself on the mercy of
Elizabeth. Mary had made another of her frequent miscalcu-
lations; Elizabeth had very little mercy to offer anyone, despite her sugar-coated assurances of safety. "I assure you
I will do nothing to hurt you, but rather honor and aid you,"
wrote the English queen after Mary's arrival in 1568. 90
Mary was far too ill to be more resourceful; she had surpassed the limit of human endurance and faced her fate with
uncharacteristic calm. Removed from Scotland, the twenty-
five-year-old Queen of Scots had the disposition of an old
woman; she was never again involved with a man, she lived
in simple confinement, and for nineteen years she made little
trouble for Elizabeth. Without the strains of rule, she endured fewer physical crises, but not one of her letters fails
to mention her constant sickness. Harmless as she was,
her mere presence was still anathema to Elizabeth. As long
as there were English Catholics, there would be plots involving Mary, and Elizabeth would not stand for this. In
1587 the execution order was signed with trembling hand
(Elizabeth wanted the deed done, to be sure, but did not want
official responsibility for it) and Mary's sad life came to an
end. A life of unending misery was concluded, and Mary
seemed to thank her executioners as she stood on the gallows.
"I forgive you with all my heart," she said, "for now I hope
you shall make an end to all my troubles."91 Elizabeth, to
justify the sudden murder of the dormant queen, wrote Mary's
son James VI, now the adult King of Scotland, "By saving of
her life they would have had mine. Do I not make myself
trow ye, a goodly prey for every wretch to devour? Trans-
figure yourself into my state, and suppose what you ought to
do."92 Mary wrote her own best epitaph in a letter to the
bishop of Dunblane, pointing to political chaos and personal
infirmity as the reasons for her failure. "This realm being
divided in factions as it is, cannot be contained in order,

unless our authority be assisted and forthset by the fortifi-
cation of a man who must take upon his person in the execution of justice ... the travail thereof we may no longer sustain in our own person, being already wearied, and almost
broken with the frequent uproars and rebellions raised against
us since we came in Scotland. "93

Rebellions and congenital illness effected Mary's personal collapse, and in a lethargic--even demented--state of
mind, she made blunders that ignited her intrinsically volatile position.

James VI of Scotland never knew his mother or his
father, not that such royal orphanage was rare. But James
was in a still more distressing situation; he was without protectors. Even his unfortunate predecessors had surrogate
parents and noble allies, but not James. He was to reap the
bitter seeds sown by his unwise mother, and his youth was
spent in the dark cloud Mary had left hanging over Scotland
after her precipitous departure in 1568. James was only
thirteen months old when he became the nominal king of Scotland, and unlike his mother there he remained for a desolate
and loveless childhood in the custody of hostile crown servants. The nobles used this intermezzo to retrench their
feudal prerogatives. While they ruled, the king was raised
in the strict household of the Earl of Mar. There a series
of harsh tutors trained him, with the primary lesson being
his mother's wickedness. The nobles doubtless hoped to in-
still their hatred of the absentee queen in her unhappy son,
and to further this end they taunted him with her failings as
punishment for misbehavior. If this failed to command
James's full attention, a whipping was ordered, which led
even the cold Countess of Mar to rebuke the tutor Buchanan
for "laying hands on the Lord's anointed. "94

These pedagogical exercises took root; James gradually
accepted the image of his mother as adulteress, murderer
(of James's father no less), and heretic. He would later
chill his failing parent to the bone with his refusal to deal
with her in anything but a strictly formal manner. To cap
his filial sins, he ultimately repudiated her. Other pressing
lessons shaped the young king's character as well. As a
five-year-old boy, he saw the bleeding body of his uncle and
regent Lennox carried from Stirling Castle, and the ceaseless, violent struggles among his cousins left their mark.
James emerged from childhood aloof, suspicious, and ever-
fearful of his safety. In the difficult world of sixteenth-

century Scotland, these were, unfortunately, useful traits, and they served him well. Yet they excluded him from normal human feeling, leaving his emotions twisted and confused. His childhood isolation was pathetic; not until the age of thirteen did he know affection, and then it came from his stylish French cousin Esme Stuart. This dalliance only confirmed James's inadequacy, for he was clumsy and ill-formed, his legs were disturbingly bowed (he was unable to walk until the age of six), and his tongue was too large for his mouth, among other defects. Esme, on the other hand, was gracious and sleek. James was dazzled by first love. Esme left a lasting mark on the impressionable boy, for even after he departed James was indifferent to women. An attractive man, however, never failed to catch the king's eye. In these young dandies James searched for the love he had been denied in childhood, but the wages of this particular sin were costly, both personally and politically.

From the outset James faced an uncertain future and many obstacles, not the least of which were his physical infirmities. A childhood bout with rickets--perhaps the Earl of Mar compounded ill treatment with a poor diet--left his legs weak, with one foot permanently turned out. The simple act of walking was difficult, and as an adult James leaned heavily on his favorite of the moment--motivated no doubt by the equal measures of affection and infirmity. Yet James walked far better than he ate; the dinner table was a constant embarrassment, owing to the unfortunate size of his tongue "which ever made him speak full in the mouth very uncomely, as if eating his drink, which came out into the cup on each side of his mouth. "[95] To be criticized for lack of refinement in an uncouth age was indeed a telling insult. The king's skin was similarly malformed; such was its sensitivity to touch that he could not bear to bathe, a flaw which could be overlooked in Scotland, but not in England. In short, his was a naturally deficient physique further battered by the ravages of childhood disease and harsh treatment.

James further demeaned his regal image with an entire range of idiosyncratic behavior. His movements were peripatetic, with "his fingers ever in that walk fiddling about his codpiece. "[96] Since, as James firmly believed, monarchs were divinely ordained, he felt little compunction to set a regal example for his people. Instead, he reveled in vulgarity and bawdry. Once, on a progress, the king was asked to allow his subjects to have a glimpse of him. After all, this was the intended purpose of the journey. James irritably replied "God's wounds, I will pull down my breeches and they shall also see my arse."[97]   Nor were men of God spared his rebukes.   At one particularly somnolent church service the king shouted, "I give not a turd for your preaching."[98] But even in crude jest, James occasionally flashed the quick intelligence lurking behind the swinish humor.   In reference to a cleric who objected to the phrase "with my body I thee worship" in the marriage service, James wryly remarked that "many a man speaks of Robin Hood who never shot in his bow."[99]

James, quite obviously, had a number of problems without even considering the hazards of his birthright, and these pitfalls were considerable indeed.   The political chaos of Scotland continued unabated while James endured his minority, and even after the death of the regent Morton gave the fifteen-year-old king a chance to assert himself, the nobles refused to relinquish their hard-won booty.   They fought many delaying actions, spreading the rumor that James was actually the son of one of his mother's confidants.   Mary's various indiscretions had left room for doubt, although the accusation never really caught on with the Scots.   Nevertheless, these jibes proved annoying as James went about the business of taming his aristocracy.   Henry IV of France congratulated James's kingship as the very image of Solomon's.   After all, laughed the French king, James too was the son of David.   Still, the gossip was far less distressing than the open defiance.   A new Earl of Bothwell laid siege to the castle of Holyrood in 1591 and nearly succeeded in capturing the king.   In fact his assault reached James's very chamber, where the raiders set fire to the door.   Only a counterattack by the townspeople saved the king.   Bothwell fled with a sizable bounty on his head, but he remained at large to trouble James for a number of years.   These and other episodes kept the king in a padded doublet, ever fearful of his life.   In the words of Weldon, "He was of a timorous disposition."[100]   This was only prudent in Scotland, although English observers later found it peculiar.

To face his personal inadequacies and the regnant disorder of his land, James had few allies, little money, and less prestige.   His sole blessing was his intelligence, which in his youth was quite a weapon.   Although his education was halted when he reached the age of fourteen, he was nonetheless regarded as something of a prodigy.   The Frenchman Fontenay, who had little regard for Scotsmen, found James very sharp and well educated on his visit in 1586.   Neither

was James possessed of the family streak of foolish bravado
and self-destructiveness.   Instead, he used his facile mind
to play faction politics; he expected disorder, and he used it
to his advantage.   His course of attack was simple; as long
as the factions fought each other they were incapable of fighting James with a unified front.   James was also, it should
be noted, in Scotland for thirty-six uninterrupted years, which
provided him with time to implement both his plan and himself.   By the end of the sixteenth century, most of the realm
was under royal control, and by 1597 even the Kirk--long a
sore spot--had been largely tamed.   Still, these victories
were but a beginning, as every stone hid a different conspir-
acy.   James was only too glad to leave in 1603, and he later
gave thanks to his English council "for bringing him into the
promised land, where he sat amongst grave, learned, and
reverent men, not as before, elsewhere, a king without state,
without honor, without order, where beardless boys would
brave him to his face. "101

Despite this modicum of political success, James had
not silenced his critics.   They merely shifted their focus.
Sexual peculiarities made him an easy target, for he was
known to be strangely uninterested in women.   This did not
sit well in an unsophisticated kingdom known for its roister-
ing masculinity.   According to an English report, James
"never regards the company of women, not so much as in
any daliance. "102   At the relatively advanced age of twenty-
three, he was still a bachelor, and this occasioned much
grumbling.   James himself admitted that "this my nakedness
made me to be weak and my enemies strong, and the want of
my succession bred disdain. "103   Perhaps the king, fearful
of failure to produce children, deliberately avoided the issue,
as many suspected.   James wrote, "my great delay bred in
the breasts of many a great jealousy of my inability, as if
I were of barren stock. "104   Of course James was of relatively barren stock; each generation of Stewarts had passed
on only one surviving child.   But it is far more likely that
James's postponement of dynastic duty was a function of his
involvement with male favorites.   Still the issue could not
be avoided indefinitely, and James reluctantly pressed his
suit for the fourteen-year-old princess Anne of Denmark.
The princess was a fine-looking girl, tall and slender, and
was sturdy as well.   With Scotland's continental reputation,
she was the most prestigious catch James could expect, but
still he was hesitant.   As Asheby wrote to Walsingham, "The
king is but a cold wooer.   He is not hasty of marriage. "105
Little did he know, but James had blundered upon a dynastic

treasure, for Anne proved truly fecund; she produced seven children and three miscarriages in twelve years.   Unfortunately, only three of the children lived past their infancy, by no means an unusual result.   On the face of it, Anne's achievement may seem trivial, until we consider James's sexual indifference and his open contempt for her company: he preferred to live apart from women whenever possible. For her part Anne was puzzled and ultimately bitter about her husband's strange predilections.   Empty-headed as she was, the concept of homosexuality was beyond her imagination.

For better or for worse, James's achievements in Scotland had been completed by the turn of the seventeenth century, and from a personal standpoint, the king was past the zenith of his powers as well.   Yet, James was on the verge of a new career far more significant than his reign in backward Scotland.   On the death of Elizabeth in 1603, the King of Scots was welcomed with open arms and great fanfare as James I, King of England.   The warmth of this greeting was a pleasant surprise to the thirty-six-year-old monarch, who was more accustomed to open defiance or, at best, sullen indifference.   In Scotland he had fought for every increment of control, but in England it appeared that control was to be handed to him on a silver service.   Gone were the days of barbarism.   Now James believed he could rule in the manner so longingly described in his book, The True Law of Free Monarchies.   But England was not Eden, and James was not the ideal monarch of his warmed-over melange of pilfered political wisdom; in fact James was run down, eccentric, and totally maladapted to the English throne.   After his jubilant entry into England in 1603, his health had taken a turn for the worse, leaving him "un vieux jeune homme," according to Fontenay. [106]   His physician Mayerne sketched a comprehensive medical profile of the king:

> He is easily and quickly disturbed ... sometimes he is melancholy from the spleen exciting disorders. Excreta--he blows his nose and sneezes often.... His stomach is easily made sick if he retains undigested food or bile....   He then vomits vehemently, so that for two or three days afterwards his face is dotted with red spots.   Wind from the stomach preceeds illness and he is constipated....
> Colic--Very frequently he labored under a painful colic with flautus (an affliction from which his mother also suffered) ... with vomiting and diar-

rhoea, preceeded by melancholy and nocturnal
rigors.... Fasting, sadness, cold at night produced it....

Diarrhoea--He has been liable to diarrhoea all
his life, attacks are usually ushered by lowness of
spirits ... pain in the chest, palpitation, sometimes hiccough. In 1610 his life was in acute danger with persistent vomiting. In 1612 after the
death of his son another fit of melancholy with the
same symptoms, and again in 1619.... In 1619 the
attack was accompanied by arthritic and nephritic
pains, he lost consciousness, breathing was labored, great fearfulness and dejection, intermittent
pulse, and his life was in danger for eight days.
It was the most dangerous illness the king ever had.
In 1623 an attack lasted only two or three days but
was very severe. It was followed by arthritis and
he could not walk for months. [107]

James was obviously a very sick man in England--
Mayerne's catalog of royal complaints extends far beyond the
brief sample noted above--and the evidence indicates that he
may have had porphyria, the same stress-aggravated condition
that quite likely wreaked havoc on his progenitors. Whatever
the medical diagnosis, the ailing king became highly self-
indulgent and carelessly imprudent. He had, it seemed, a
perverse desire to offend each of the estates. With Parliament he sneered, "I am surprised that my ancestors should
have allowed such an institution to come into existence."[108]
He alienated the nobles in bestowing the best plums of patronage on his lovers, and a noxious disregard for the remainder
of his subjects earned him reciprocal contempt. By far the
most glaring offense was his slavish devotion to favorites.
Although James's inclinations had not prevented him from siring heirs, his sexual preference was decidedly men. This
hedonistic pursuit had major political ramifications. With
his English lovers James believed in monogamy, if in seri-
atim, and here the king made the mistake he had avoided in
Scotland; he unswervingly raised one faction above the others,
and in so doing sparked bitter jealousy. He also placed, for
all intents, the scepter in the hands of men qualified only to
be the king's lap dog, while he himself tended to purely personal concerns. Such behavior had an impact on all observers, who were frequently treated to the sight of an aging
king's open displays of affection with androgynous young men.
This did little to repair James's diminishing esteem at court,
and it cost him the respect of his wife and his subjects. As

Fontenay commented, "His love of favorites is indiscreet and willful and takes no account of the wishes of his people."[109]

We can sympathize with the fading monarch's attempt to grasp the only human warmth he was able to respond to, but this visceral need proved political poison. By all indications James was past the point of caring what anyone thought as long as his lover was content. As he wrote his great love Buckingham, consenting to a course of action he knew to be unwise, "I cannot content myself without sending you this billet, praying God that I might have a joyful and comfortable meeting with you, and that we may make at this Christenmass a new marriage, ever to be kept hereafter; for, God so love me, as I desired to live in this world for your sake, and that I had rather live banished in any part of the world with you, than live a sorrowful widow life without you."[110]

Although perhaps the greatest, Buckingham was not the first of James's inamoratos. At the age of thirteen, his heart was captured by Esme Stuart, and after Esme's tenure an entire succession of royal paramours enjoyed spectacular ascents to power and fortune. Two of the most notable were Robert Carr and George Villiers. Carr cast his spell over James shortly after his ascent to the English throne, and unknowing English observers were stunned at the king's frolics with the effeminate young man. Osborne rather naively complained that "the love the king showed was as amorously conveyed as if he had mistaken their sex and thought them ladies; which I have seen Somerset [Carr] and Buckingham [Villiers] labor to resemble in the effeminateness of their dressings ... the king's kissing them after so lascivious a mode in public ... prompted many to imagine some things done in the tiring house."[111] Whatever actually transpired in the "tiring house" apparently created a strong bond between James and his male mistresses. When Somerset and his wife--who was known to be something of a trollop herself--were convicted of the murder of Thomas Overbury and sentenced to death, James pardoned them and allowed them to skulk into retirement. Overbury had been letting Lady Somerset's dark secrets out of the bag, the case was solid, and James's obvious tampering with justice nettled the other nobles and raised a general outcry across Britain. But for James the tragedy of the affair was the parting with Somerset at Roylston, when Carr left the king to stand trial. Apparently, the king "hung about his neck, slabbering his cheeks, saying, 'when shall I see them again? On my soul I shall neither eat nor sleep until you are come again.' The earl told him,

'On Monday.' 'For God's sake let me,' said the king. 'Shall I? Shall I?' Then lolled about his neck, 'Then for God's sake give thy lady this kiss for me.' In the same manner at the stair's head, at the middle of the stairs, and at the stair's foot."[112] Despite these touching histrionics James had the resilience of a young heart. "I shall never see his face more," he blandly remarked as the earl faded into the distance.

The true love of James's sad life was Villiers, made Earl of Buckingham by the smitten king. "Steenie"--dubbed for his supposed resemblance to St. Stephen--was the king's confidant, minister, lover, and in effect his substitute at the head of state for the final years of James's life. The ailing monarch was not the least bit discreet about his great romance, in fact he took many opportunities to trumpet it. To his Council he announced, "You may be sure that I love the Earl of Buckingham more than anyone else, and more than you who are here assembled." James was quite clever with a turn of phrase, and his justifications were at least glib. Who could question him when, as he pointed out, "Jesus Christ did the same." To complete the analogy, James explained, "Christ had his John and I have my George."[113] Of course, with a bit of pandering to the drooling sovereign, Buckingham could do whatever he chose and he took this power to its limit. In this he followed precedents; paramours at the head of state were not unheard of in sixteenth-century Europe; Diane de Poitiers was only the most notorious. But the arrogant rule of a preening sodomite went down hard in Scotland and was but slightly more felicitous in England. The French ambassador wistfully noted that James "wishes to be his [Buckingham's] friend rather than king."[114] This is truly what James came to be, if that, for after 1619 his physical deterioration set him free from any sense of responsibility. He traveled everywhere with "Steenie" by his side for comfort, and when he stirred it was only to legitimize Buckingham's self-aggrandizement. He proudly pronounced that "I desire to advance it [Buckingham's family] above all others."[115] But the rewards of such love were ever decreasing. In 1622 the French ambassador wrote that "his strength deserts him ... and he feeds his eyes where he can no longer content his other senses. The end of all is ever the bottle."[116] Still more insulting, for the last four years of his life James had to be carried around in a chair.

James was seized with one of his usual attacks in 1625, and his physicians treated the matter as purely routine.

But this time James took a sudden turn for the worse and
died.   An autopsy revealed none of the poison Buckingham
was said to have slipped to his "deare dad and steward, " but
it did disclose a right kidney less than an inch in length.   It
was hardly surprising to find that James had been as internal-
ly deranged as he had been superficially malformed.   His
last attack, like that of his grandfather James V, was suspiciously porphyric in character.   This was ironic enough,
for even after most of Scotland had been brought to heel, the
Stewarts were still faced with the stark biological insufficiency
of their line.   Their own bodies, not their willful relatives,
were the insurmountable obstacles to stable rule and family
prosperity.   In weakness they were their own worst enemy:
a collection of singularly unfit individuals.   James VI and I,
the most intelligent of the lot, justified his sufferings as
part of his monarchical duty and settled for an easy platitude
rather than face the true conundrum.   "Look not to find the
softness of a down pillow in a crown, " he wrote in his treatise Meditations of St. Matthew, "but reminders that it is a
thorny piece of stuff and full of continual cares. "[117]

Chapter Four

THE VALOIS: THE PRICE OF SELF-INDULGENCE

"Alexander the Great attended to women when he had no
business,
Francis attended to business when he had no women."
                                        --Tavannes

If historians attempted to categorize royal courts in botan-
ical nomenclature, the Valois's sixteenth-century circle,
known and imitated as Europe's most gracious, would be a
Venus's flytrap. Although outwardly inviting, the diversions
and entertainments of court life were rife with hazards both
personal and political, and the Valois sovereigns, when not
too diseased to be dissolute, drowned themselves in the revels, each through his own particular weakness. Here, the
French kings from Francis I through Henry III--encompassing
the years from 1515 to 1589--were seduced into voluptuous
exile, while the wearying demands of politics were relegated
to mistresses and favorites of a governmental bent. To
complete our garden imagery, the charms of sixteenth-century
voluptuaries were like the leaf apex of the insectivorous plant;
at their core was disease, distraction, and, for the smitten
monarch, dependence. For all the celebrated glamour of the
Renaissance court, underneath the glittering costumes was
filth no less foul than what caked the garments of "the great
unwashed." Perhaps court grime was all the more noxious
for the courtesan's attempts to hide her uncleanliness with
sweet scents. For what did France's monarchs surrender
their standing and even their dignity? Sadly enough, the
grand royal passions were spent on women who, for the most
part, "have no care to keep themselves clean except in those
parts that may be seen, remaining filthy ... under their lin-
en," according to a sixteenth-century handbook for young girls.

80

The entire situation left a great deal to be desired:
when French kings were not physically blighted, they were
voluntarily besotted, and when momentarily inclined to rule,
they were anachronistic braggarts, dogmatic bigots, or the
final evil of the dying royal house, cold-blooded murderers.
The reign of the sixteenth-century Valois might have set the
development of modern France back a full century. Less
than monarchs, sometimes less than men, these sovereigns
were veritable parasites.

What then, were the specific failings of the sixteenth-
century Valois kings? There were many, but perhaps most
glaring was the dynasty's noted sloth: the legendary courtier
Francis I never rose before noon, and only the most nimble
ambassador or secretary managed to bend his ear before he
was off to the hunt, either in the woods or in the boudoir.
The list continues: Henry II spent much of his time in his
mistress's lap or in melancholy meanderings; Charles IX followed the hunt all day in a frenzy and then collapsed into
bed at nightfall--not that anyone particularly desired his
counsel; and Henry III pranced the streets of Paris in drag
or occupied himself with clever games. Valois kings ruled
whimsically and infrequently.

This sort of lifestyle had actual, as well as figurative,
costs; each succeeding monarch left the crown deeper in debt,
finally reaching a level where the royal income was barely
enough to cover interest costs. On what was this fortune
squandered? The traps were embarrassingly sybaritic; far
too much French wealth was spent on bright costumes, fancy
balls, beautiful palaces, greedy favorites and mistresses,
bribes to cover imprudent policies (ransom for royal children
being one), magnificent feasts, and unwieldy retinues. The
kings themselves argued that such opulence was required of
them by their people, but this feeble rationalization barely
obscured the fact that the French monarchy was a hindrance
to economic development--something it had not been in the
fifteenth century. To keep the Valois from doing without,
financial institutions were coerced into making uncollectible
loans, taxes were raised, the coinage was debased, and offices both important and illusory were sold, all to keep
Henry III in the latest feminine fashions, so to speak.

Of course, someone had to give the orders, but that
person was less likely to be the king than his mother, his
uncles, his friends, or his mistress. It was an age of up-
starts, and the power of the parvenu reached new heights.

Chart 4

VALOIS FAMILY TREE

(x = died very young or was miscarried)

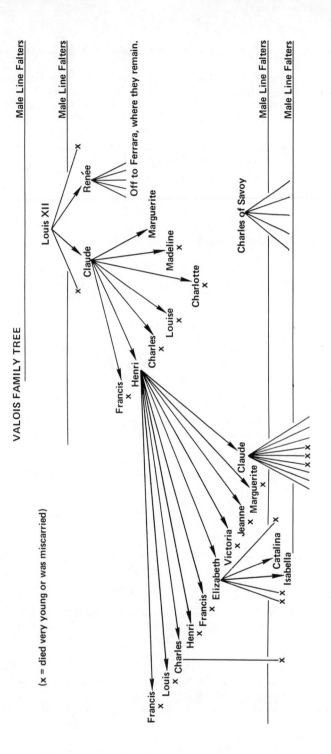

In the glamorous heyday of "Francois Premier," Queen Mother Louise of Savoy guided and protected her "chef d'oeuvre"
as though he were still attached to the umbilical cord. The
sovereigns who followed Francis I were themselves unweaned:
Diane de Poitiers dominated Henry II; the Guise uncles of
Mary Stewart--wife of Francis II--rode roughshod over the
stunted child-king; and with the exception of a few petulant
outbursts, Catherine de Medici absorbed the duties of her
sons Charles IX and Henry III. These female powers behind the throne were, in all fairness, clever courtesans, but
they were hardly capable of engendering stable, fruitful policy.
Their grasp of events was limited by the court vista, and
their practical education in intrigue lacked grounding in economic and social thought. Of course the kings were themselves narrow-minded, but a king had access to capable ministers and could usually muster enough respect to weight his
pronouncements. Paramours had no such advantages. If
the king's acquiescence was easily won, other battles proved
more challenging. Despite occasional triumphs, the bedroom-
regents labored in vain to maintain the royal prerogative in
their own bejeweled hands. Even when these women pursued
sensible courses of action--the moderate "politique" efforts
of Catherine de Medici in the religious wars, for instance--
their initiative was subject to the merest yawn of the hibernating king, and there were always other, contrary voices
whispering into a king's ear. Cardinal Wolsey, for one,
conferred so intimately with his prince that he was in fact
accused of infecting King Henry VIII of England's ear with
venereal disease. A king and a minister could certainly join
forces to good advantage, as Henry IV of France later did
with Sully, but without a politically active king, the power of
the monarchy was necessarily fragmented. It is easy to
blame the parvenues for this, and the women whose skirts
shielded the sixteenth-century Valois kings were often unwise,
but the errors were only part of the puzzle. As Henry IV
later, in a charitable mood, wrote of Catherine de Medici:
"I am surprised that she never did worse."

No matter what Catherine and her counterparts did,
it was liable to be insufficient. The sixteenth-century ideal
of monarchy required an absolute ruler. Even in an era of
rapid change and endemic turmoil, the conceptual underpinnings
of government were postulated as static absolutes. Michiel defined what he believed to be the English monarchy's structure:
"With the exception of judicial matters, the government of the
kingdom, and the affairs of state likewise, all depend on the
will of the kings, they having made themselves, as they are,

masters and absolute lords. " In France itself this construct
was advanced, if only in theory, by King Francis I, a man
whose attention to his responsibilities was whimsical at best:
"Every properly established monarchy and republic consists
of only two parts--the rightful rule of princes and superiors
and the loyal obedience of subjects, in which, if one of the
two is at fault, it is, as in the life of man, the separation
of the body and of the soul. "[2] This was the variety of government found in France at the beginning of the sixteenth
century. Machiavelli celebrated the arrangement in The
Prince, claiming that "there is a fine balance between the
crown, the nobility, and the people, which makes France one
of the best ordered kingdoms of the period. "[3]

These theories had a comforting internal logic, but
they hinged on the presence of Prometheans. In practice,
such consistent systems were impossible for the sixteenth-
century Valois, and thus France became a political arena in
which everyone but the king attempted to be king. The kings
attempted to be sportsmen, dabblers, debauchers, lovers,
even chivalric knights, and in all of these pursuits they attained some standing. Kingship, however, was not their forte. The people, the "body" of Francis's simile, were slow
to react to this absence of leadership. Popular opinion was
kind to the Valois until almost the bitter end; Francis I was
greatly admired despite his prodigality, and subsequent kings
were given at least the benefit of the doubt. But finally under Catherine de Medici's twisted offspring this patience
wore thin. Henry III was so offensive that he became something of a continental joke. While he restricted himself to
pleasure he was tolerated, but when he ventured into the political fray unaided by his mother a great deal of rhetoric
arose invoking the French people to depose him as an unfit
sovereign, which in fact he was. With his murder at the
hands of a zealot monk, Henry became the first modern
French king to die at the hands of his own subjects.

Other French dynasties had been known for their ineptitude; the early Capetians for example, but even this unfortunate house maintained a stable adult male succession.
The Valois, however, failed to match this achievement in the
sixteenth century. Let us begin at the close of the fifteenth
century, after Charles VIII failed to sire a single surviving
child. His death presented cousin Louis d'Orléans with the
monarchical opportunity, but as Louis XII he too was unable
to father a prince and reluctantly anointed cousin Francis of
Angoulême as his successor. Francis I, after sending two

of his three sons to Spain as security for his own release from the imperial prison (he had been captured at the battle of Pavia in 1525), lost one of the hostage sons and his beloved third son. The middle son, Henry, twisted and embittered by his captivity, became Henry II, but he was indeed a tortured king. One could hardly have imagined him his father's son, such was his saturnine disposition. Henry's first ten years of marriage to the Italian "arriviste" Catherine de Medici were conspicuously childless--the result of both the king's distaste for his wife and their mutual malformations. After some peculiar measures Catherine's maternal fount burst forth copiously, but its wellspring was curiously and tragically polluted. Her sons, three of whom sat on the throne in turn, were an abomination. The Valois were themselves a threat to the monarchy; the procession of sixteenth-century Valois rulers was less a succession than a degeneration.

The weak succession was only one indication of the family's inability to bear up under the strain of their responsibilities. Of the others, none was more distressing than their propensity to collapse under pressure. Louis XII succumbed to physical blight, but Francis I lost heart under mere discomfort. After his capture at Pavia, Francis was so miserable in prison that he signed a treaty he knew his country could never honor--in fact he had signed a covenant to the effect that all such agreements made under duress were invalid before marching off to Italy. This trickery was no salvation; Francis had to back his promise with his two eldest sons. The youths were exchanged for their father and were held as surety, an effective mortgage on the future of France. This done, the French king returned home and immediately broke his promise, war between Spain and France was renewed, and the Emperor--annoyed at the deception-- held the French princes for four years. The substitution of the princes for the king was a costly trade. France's welfare was not, as we have previously noted, dependent on Francis's steady hand to guide the tiller of state. Two princes, on the other hand, could sustain a dynasty for decades. The king's absence, then, was not keenly felt. Others conducted business, as they had for ten years. But the conditions of his return were debilitating. This was all the more unfortunate since an exhibition of stoic resolve on the part of Francis might well have forced the Emperor into a more reasonable settlement; Francis's value as bargaining chip declined with the length of his captivity. Endurance was not a Valois virtue. Francis's successor Henry was similarly volatile; on the delicate and threatening issue of religious dissent, he retreated into frothing anger and ordered burnings to crown his policy of widespread persecution. This policy irrevocably committed France to the disastrous Wars of Religion, a self-perpetuating struggle that crippled the country for the remainder of the century. Francis II did not even live long enough to make such a blunder: the pressures of kingship and congenital disease were sufficient to end his reign within a year of its inception. Charles IX, who personified the Valois decline from irresponsibility to insanity, had a veritable seizure when pressured by his mother and militant Catholics to allow a handful of assassinations. The upshot of this breakdown was the horrendous Massacre of St. Bartholomew's Day in 1572, in which thousands of Protestants were slaughtered while they slept in Paris. Henry III awoke from his lascivious nightmare life to find himself challenged by Henry of Guise, popular leader of the Catholic party. King Henry's actions in the face of this dilemma were, like those of his progenitors, miserably ill-considered; in a fright he ordered the murder of Guise--to be accomplished in his own chambers no less. This immediately touched off a furor in Catholic Paris, led into further civil war, and finally culminated in the king's own death at the hands of an assassin.

Unlike Stewart Scotland, where long-standing chaos existed to devour kings (and particularly queens), France was relatively tame and broken to the royal saddle. Nor can the dismal sixteenth-century performance of the French royal house be wholly attributed to pain and disease. The Valois unquestionably endured their share, but even in years of health they were preoccupied and simply ill-suited to their mission, in whatever terms that mission was defined. The Valois were, as the following pages will demonstrate, diseased and under-reproductive. But irresponsibility and imprudence were perhaps their telling traits. Sixteenth-century France witnessed the decline of a house of kings into what contemporaries labeled a race of idiots.

How incongruous it seems when we find that the most powerful countries in the Renaissance world were led by the most feckless of monarchs. Yet the most leonine men were either sovereign in a less significant state, one example being Henry VII of England, or were relegated to less important secular pursuits, as was the great thinker Erasmus of Rotterdam, who spent a number of years as a tutor for one of the Scottish king James IV's bastard sons. Of all these incongruities, France was perhaps paramount in paradox. At the end of the fifteenth century, France had the largest single-country land base in western Europe, a population larger than that of Spain, Scotland, and England combined, and a royal house whose male descent had been unbroken since the thirteenth century. For all these advantages France was no more than a hibernating bear, and its rulers were for the most part myopic and inattentive. If France lacked a single blessing, that was leadership, a lack that became most notable in the reign of Charles VIII, the last of the truly lineal successors to the French throne.

Charles was a royal aberration, a genetic mutation at the end of a long line of inbred Valois kings. He was described as "nightmarish in appearance, with an over-large head on a tiny, crippled body."[4] Besides this strange disproportion between Charles's ferret-like head and his homely hunchbacked body, his eyes appeared to be bulging out of their sockets, his hands had a spastic twitch, his face was flabby, and "he spoke haltingly through thick, wet lips."[5] Apparently, his drooping under-lip dominated his grotesque visage.

Guicciardini reported that

> his stature was short and his face very ugly--if you except the dignity and vigor of his glance. His limbs were so disproportioned that he had less the appearance of a man than a monster and not only was he ignorant of liberal arts but he was virtually illiterate. Though eager to rule, he was in truth made for anything but that. Hating business and fatigue, he displayed in such matters as he took in hand a want of prudence and a lack of judgment. His desire for glory spread rather from impulse than from reason. His liberality was inconsistent, immoderate, promiscuous. When he displayed inflexibility of purpose it was more often an ill-founded obstinacy than firmness.[6]

This was no princely countenance, nor was it the unfortunate heritage of a genuinely talented monarch. Charles, against all forces of nature, was by disposition a rake. Brantome tells us that "he loved women more than his slight constitution could bear."[7] This, not war or statecraft, was Charles's fondest pursuit. While he did govern, his was mainly a custodial reign. Certain misplaced chivalric instincts led him

on marches of conquest into Italy, but as a general he was
more remarkable for his frequent sorties in search of a willing wench than his charges against the enemy. Charles's
reign was, in short, status quo, and aside from his physical
decrepitude, monarchical life continued in the solid, lustreless tradition set by the previous two centuries of Valois
rulers. But there is still something to be said for continuity:
a stable succession was the best protection against civil war
and was similarly useful as a defense against foreign intru-
sion--Henry VIII, for example, did not send his armies into
Scotland until that country was without a valid adult monarch.
An unbroken succession was also an immense reassurance
to the population as a whole, for it signified that God's blessing was with them. Nothing but ill came of an interrupted
succession, and unfortunately for France, Charles VIII was
a likely candidate to end his long-lived line.

In 1498 the slender strand was snapped. At the age
of twenty-eight, Charles, a man quite understandably without
heirs, found a rare doorway that was shorter than he and
bumped his head rather sharply. Insignificant though this
may have seemed, within hours Charles was in raging convulsions and by nightfall he was dead, stretched out on the same
filthy straw pallet he had been laid upon after the accident.
This sudden and virtually unparalleled situation was alarming
in itself and for its implications. The strongest candidate to
replace Charles was clever and of royal lineage but was a
bona fide black sheep of long standing. This worrisome man
was Prince Louis d'Orléans, a rebellious nobleman whose
kingly blood flowed from Charles V, a fourteenth-century
monarch. His regal heritage notwithstanding, Louis's family
had remained in the shadows for two full centuries, except
for an occasional foray from their provincial base to cause
trouble for their lieges. French nobles were apt to do this
sort of thing periodically, but young Louis had been a particular discipline problem. Two of his most grating faux pas
were personal affronts to King Charles VIII himself; Louis
once refused direct military orders during a battle, and still
more brazen, had openly gloated upon hearing that Charles's
infant son had died. For these and other mildly treasonous
acts, Charles incarcerated the spirited young prince for a
number of years in the 1490s.

Still, the French crown, to its credit, had a much
greater respect for royal blood than the atavistic Scots or the
paranoid English sovereigns. The French kings would never
publically hang their relatives, as Elizabeth did with discon-

certing frequency and the Scots did in less humane ways.
Disruptive relatives were given veritable immunity, as the
French crown promoted the idea that royal blood was sacred
and under no circumstances was it to be shed as though it
came from a spigot.   Such barbarism was not proper for
the widely emulated French court.   This admirable advance
of civilization replaced open retaliation with that mainstay of
developed political cultures; cunning.   Valois attempts to restrain relatives were almost brilliantly subtle.

King Louis XI, Charles VIII's predecessor, had himself realized the roguish streak in young Louis d'Orléans,
and had concocted a marvelous plan to preclude any threat
from the Orléanist heir.   He arranged for the prince to marry his deformed daughter Jeanne, quite a novel solution.
For Louis it was roughly similar to being slapped with a velvet glove; he was undeniably shown royal favor with the compelling offer of the king's daughter, yet such a marriage--if
it lasted though Louis's virile years--would undoubtedly end
his line.   With Jeanne as his lawful spouse, he was effectively gelded, for the sorry cripple's maternal prospects were
bleak.   Pleased with his maneuver, Louis XI allowed himself
to gloat a bit; "it will not cost these two a great deal to rear
their children, " he wryly noted. [8]

If old King Louis was rather suspicious of young
Prince Louis's intentions, we can forgive him, for there was
definitely much to be suspicious of.   Born in 1462, the Orléanist was under something of a cloud from the outset.   His
very paternity was suspect, as rumor had it that he was actually the son of Charles d'Orléans's steward Robadange.
Those who evaluated him in his youth had mixed reactions,
particularly in regard to his personality.   In Trevisan's report Louis was described as "well conditioned, tall and thin,
abstemious, avaricious and niggardly. "[9]   Louis was also a
libertine in his youth.   The Frenchman Commynes slyly observed, "He was a young man and handsome of person, but
fond of his pleasures. "[10]   As for his appearance, the testimony was similarly equivocal.   Some commented on his
"big nose, thick lips, and low forehead, " and a Florentine
noted that "he has a small head with not much room for
brains. "[11]   He does not seem to have been a terribly winning
youth.

The fate saddled on Louis was certainly designed to
dampen what little charm and enthusiasm he had.   Cousin
Jeanne was almost unimaginably wretched.   Hunchbacked,

Louis XII of France

lame, one shoulder resting higher than the other, arms and
legs attenuated, head set awry, and lips "thick and unsight-
ly, "[12] Jeanne was "the sorriest cripple in the kingdom. "[13]
This distressing physiognomy might have been less unfortunate had Jeanne been able to bear children, for certainly an
occasional night with the poor creature would have done Louis
no harm.   But fruitful she was not.   Evidence at her divorce
proceedings based on a physical examination, along with a letter from her father to a confidant, indicate that she was
structurally incapable of conceiving.   Unhappy Jeanne paid
the full price of her deformity, as legend has it that even
her father refused to acknowledge his daughter's existence
except in the most perfunctory way.   Although he had never
seen his Jeanne as a child, he did not believe the reports of
her extreme beastliness, and so he arranged to have her
brought into a garden below a window from which he could
observe.   Viewing her from this distance to gauge the extent
of her deformity, he reportedly uttered a gasp of disbelief
at the sight: "I would not have believed that she was so
hideous. "[14]   But hideous she was, and Louis's she was.
The situation drove the prince to near-mania, but Jeanne
meekly accepted her misfortune.   She reveled in religion and
good works, and later admirers characterized her as a saint.
To Louis's dismay she was also quite fond of him, although
in her saintly way she understood his unhappiness.   "I am
not a fit wife for such as he, " she wisely acknowledged. [15]
Yet when Louis wanted a divorce, she tenaciously held to him
with less than beatific stubbornness.

     Throughout his marriage to Jeanne, Louis walked a
personal and political tightrope.   Happiness was not a term
that held great sway in the world of sixteenth-century royalty, but Louis was plainly unhappy.   In his frustration he
glutted himself with rebellion and debauchery--a wildness
totally eradicated after his divorce from Jeanne--and he forbade any of his companions to mention the name of his
twisted mate aloud in his presence.   But complain as he
might, the problem of Jeanne appeared insoluble; a mere
nobleman did not simply discard the daughter of a king, however ill-formed she was.   Louis later claimed that the marriage had never been consummated, and was thus invalid.
But the evidence presented at the eventual divorce trial--at
which Louis based his case on this argument--was equivocal.
Witnesses claimed to have heard Louis announce, "I have
mounted my wife three or four times during the night, "[16]
their wedding eve.   Well might Louis have forgotten the exact number, but it is far more likely that his boast was a

mere pro forma utterance. From what Jeanne's father wrote, sex was probably impossible for the gynecologically malformed princess, and it is likely that the marriage was never consummated.

Louis's case for annulment was probably just, but he never would have had the opportunity to present it had Charles VIII lived. But as luck would have it for Louis, Charles died suddenly, which left the Orléans's scion heir to the throne of France. With this immeasurable and unexpected reverse of fortunes, Louis took the scepter, and one of his first actions was to extricate himself from the knotty situation his royal relatives had engineered for him. Luck apparently ran in streaks; a Borgia sat in the Papal chair and desired a favor from the new King of France. Cesare Borgia, son of the Pope, needed a Duchy, which he received from the French king. In return Alexander VI agreed to help Louis with his divorce. It was a simple transaction, as Alexander admitted: "We are on the king's side, because of the love he bears to our Duke."[17] The trial was a great travesty, obviously rigged, and Jeanne's impassioned pleas won her much popular support. But she squandered her temporary advantage; she agreed, in a mistaken appeal to Louis's heart, to drop her objections if Louis testified in public that they had not lived as man and wife. She claimed that she wanted only to hear the charges from him. Distasteful as it was, Louis swallowed whatever gallantry he possessed and did just that. Almost instantly he was a free man and a king. It is indeed an ill wind that blows no one good.

Immediately after the divorce Louis pressed his suit on Anne of Brittany, the widow of Charles VIII. While a far cry from Jeanne, this rather unremarkable woman was no beauty herself. Apparently, Louis found something in her that was hidden from the rest of the world, for in the opinion of the Venetian ambassador Contarini, "She is small and thin in person, visibly lame in one foot, although she uses a false heel; very determined for her age, so much so, that if a wish enters her head, by smiles or tears, at any cost she will obtain it."[18] She was also a fierce advocate for Brittany, her home, an attitude that made her notably provincial even in the narrow-minded court circle. Although she claimed to love King Louis--some of her professions of love have survived in letters--Anne was foremost a zealous guardian of her personal interests, even when those interests ran counter to Louis's. When poor aged Louis appeared to be on his deathbed, Anne packed up her plate and jewels and headed for Brittany, fearful that after the king's death her possessions would be commandeered. While this demonstrated admirable foresight, Anne had nonetheless made a major miscalculation. Caught in her flight, she was apprehended and brought before her miraculously revived husband who, though not amused by the desertion, forgave her.

Whatever Anne's charm, it certainly blinded Louis to many important considerations, particularly the question of heirs. Anne had an obstetrical history of miscarriages and crib deaths, and her first marriage with Charles VIII produced not a single surviving child. Yet Louis was eager to have her try again, so eager that his passion surprised his prematurely aged twenty-three-year-old bride, "and this ardor, though it seemed to her to be a thing out of the ordinary, was in no wise displeasing to the queen."[19] These pleasurable frolics created a lasting bond, and Louis abandoned his noted profligacy shortly after the marriage. But the issue of the succession remained, and violent disagreements arose over Anne's inability to bear a son. Louis blamed his queen loudly, vehemently, and entirely. Anne had spawned heirs, but the two sons she delivered were stillborn, an unfortunate omen, and this unsatisfactory result set court tongues aflutter. Much bickering solved nothing, and no son was forthcoming. The royal couple and their retinue resolved themselves to the disappointment. In 1512 an observer wrote, "The Queen is in great pain, and her baby is expected at the end of the month or the beginning of the next. But there is not the fuss or the excitement here that was made over the others."[20] Such pessimism was well warranted, for Anne delivered still another dead boy. Two daughters were the only survivors of Anne's twelve years of almost continuous pregnancy, and in 1514 the exhausted thirty-five-year-old queen died. After centuries of lineal kings, France faced its second consecutive succession dilemma. Who was to be king?

Louis XII's reign set another unfortunate precedent, one that would plague each sixteenth-century French monarch: physical incapacity. King Louis was of borderline vitality throughout his reign. The robust and difficult youth rapidly gave way to a frail and testy king. In 1498, the year of his accession, the thirty-six-year-old king was elderly beyond his years. A biographer described Louis's decay: "His body though wiry from hard exercise, was already scorched and seared. His eyes were too bright and prominent, his lips

too thick and dry, his neck too goiterously swollen. He
quite possibly had Graves' disease. When he was worried
he became testy and explosive; generally he stayed on an
even keel; and, when his health permitted, he was friendly,
easy, open. "21 This ill health did not arrive in one single
onslaught when Louis reached the age of thirty-six. He was
sick while imprisoned in the 1490s, suffered an apparent attack of malaria while reveling in an unusually debauched wel-
coming festivity at Lombardy in 1494, and on his return to
France in 1499, "he was often shaken by agues, tormented
by sudden attacks of illness, and depressed by gloom. "22

This range of indisposition undoubtedly affected the
manner in which Louis conducted, or neglected to conduct,
business. Louis was known as a frugal king and preferred
to be disdained for his mundane court than despised for high
taxation. He was prudent, disciplined in his lifestyle, and
was apparently well regarded by the general populace, much
like his contemporary Henry VII of England. His reign saw
the abolition of the practice of selling offices and the restoration of quiet prosperity. Perhaps Louis deserved his sobri-
quet "pere du peuple. " On the other hand, Louis rushed into an expensive and unsuccessful campaign in Italy and characteristically avoided his tiresome duties. Others attended
to crown business. The bulk of the government work fell to
Georges, Cardinal d'Amboise. Louis was so often heard to
mutter "let Georges do it" when new business arose that the
refrain became a colloquialism. 23 Yet the king's inattention
to business was more the result of sickness than sloth.
Much of the time Louis was simply too ill to govern; although he lived until the age of fifty-two, the years of his
reign were spotted with episodes of near-collapse.

In 1504 Louis was "gouty and ailing";24 January found
him seriously diseased, and many doubted that he would rise
from his sick bed. The advisor Gie was so concerned that
he made provisions for the orderly transfer of power in the
event of Louis's death. Of course no one truly knew what to
do--with the exception of Louis's own accession there were
few precedents for the death of a king without a clear succession. To quell opportunistic princes and spare an anxious
populace, news of the king's illness was suppressed. To almost everyone's relief, Louis recovered from this battle, but
not until March 1504. Later in the same year he fell victim
to the same malady once again and was wracked with severe
sweating, constant fever, and an inability to sleep or eat.
After this attack abated Louis had yet another in February
1505, and all at bedside felt the presence of death.

Such dire illness could not be long hidden, and by 1505 most court observers were convinced of the sovereign's fragile hold on life. The Florentine Pandolfini noted in 1505 that "with so feeble a constitution the smallest ailment is of moment ... his constitution is thoroughly feeble and unsatisfactory."[25] The 1505 illness left Louis emaciated and alarmed; in his delirium his France had swirled out of control and a chaotic scramble for power had ensued. Potential heirs thronged to the center of government. The succession had to be settled, so acting on the advice of his counselors, Louis marked his return to relative health with the marriage of his eldest daughter Claude to Francis of Alençon, who, as Louis himself had once been, was the energetic progeny of another subordinate branch of the Valois family. Although Francis would mirror Louis with his undisguised pleasure over the queen's stillbirths, he was nonetheless the logical candidate to succeed, and Louis was now apprized of the need for a clearly designated heir-apparent in case of his sudden demise. Louis was not, however, ready to die. The brush with death made the aging king even more cautious and abstinent, and this apparently paid off: he outlived almost everyone's gloomy predictions and even some of the predictors themselves. In 1510 Henry VII of England and the ambassador Badoer discussed continental Europe, and Badoer wrote that Henry's estimation rested largely on the imminent death of Louis. But in fact it was Henry, not Louis, who receded into the pages of history that year. Louis's surprising tenacity caused the Venetian ambassador to write of his improved health in 1513, but such a resurgence was only temporary. In fact Louis had to be transported in a litter that very year.[26] Observers were shocked by his aged and ailing appearance. Louis himself admitted to the ambassador Dandolo that "this gout rather troubles me," and he confessed that his health precluded his involvement in monarchical business.[27]

Yet at precisely this point in his obvious decline, Louis rediscovered frivolity. Queen Anne died in 1514, and the king set out to replace her with the reknowned beauty Mary Tudor, aged eighteen. Such whimsical behavior was appreciated as a fine joke in diplomatic circles, and their descriptions of the new bride and groom were rife with suppressed snickers. The descriptions of Louis alone make it difficult to imagine that the king was once vital and young himself. An eye-witness called him "red-faced, bloated, and porcine."[28] Elephantiasis and a skin condition of a scrofulous nature rendered the king a repellent bridegroom, but unfortunately for Mary he felt better than he looked, and according to observers took full measure of her charms. This rambunctiousness took its toll; instead of a progress to Paris after the wedding night, as planned, Louis remained at Abbeville for three weeks of recuperation. Mary suffered the king's advances, but she exacted her revenge in the long days and nights of games and entertainments. Louis did what he could to please his young bride, but for the most part he witnessed her gambols from a chaise lounge. His ostensible purpose in this foolish last fling was to beget a son, but the Tudors had a more realistic appraisal of Louis's condition; in the marriage treaty they arranged to have the cost of Mary's return to England guaranteed in the event that the French king died without siring a child. They expected Mary back soon, and with good reason. But the man with the most interest in the strange union was the heir-apparent Francis. The sharp-featured youth shadowed the newlyweds, and his spies actually scrutinized the pair's conjugal performance. Their report was the best of news; as Francis told his friend Fleurange, "Adventurer, I am happier and easier in my mind than for twenty years past as I am sure, unless someone has lied to me, that it is not possible for the king and queen to beget children."[29]

As it so happened no one had lied to Francis on this particular issue. There would be no children, and Louis would be strained past his endurance attempting to recapture his youth. The played-out satyr died in a powerful fit of vomiting in January 1515, and a clever outsider headed for the throne once again. Louis had never been comfortable with Francis and had misgivings about the transition from the start. His gloom was evident as he watched the nimble Francis at play. "Ce gros garçon gatera tous," he muttered from his heavily cushioned chair.[30]

Francis I was certainly the "big boy" of Louis's description, but as to whether he would ruin everything France waited to see. Francis inherited, at the age of twenty-one, a most powerful country: France was the population center of Europe, and Paris was the continent's greatest city. The semi-feudal society structure was mitigated by inflation, and due to the debasement of coinages and the increased availability of precious metals, peasants' traditional dues were eased, and they were in fact able to purchase land. This, peace, and other economic developments were an invigorating force, and French commerce and industry was on the ascendant. There was much to ruin.

The man who took hold of this giant was himself
larger than life; born outside under a tree in the traditional
manner of French royalty, Francis of Angoulême grew to
manhood in an extremely unusual environment.   Although his
father died when Francis was three, his young mother (fourteen at the time of Francis's birth) and his father's former
mistress--close allies in a unique household--raised the boy
themselves with unstinting maternal solicitude.   Unlike most
of his contemporaries, who were taken from their parents and
raised by strict tutors, Francis was fiercely protected by his
women in the comfort of his home.   He grew up spoiled and
loved, which no doubt helped shape him into the magnanimous,
self-indulgent and supremely confident prince he became.   For
this blissful childhood Francis felt a lifelong debt to women,
a debt he paid in constant attention, courtliness, and all too
frequently in submission and deference to female wishes.
For her part Louise of Savoy certainly expected great things
of the prince she addressed as "mon roi, mon seigneur, mon
Cesar. "

No one could deny that Francis grew into a physical
marvel and a Renaissance courtier in every sense of the term,
save perhaps his superficial classical education.   Castiglione,
the sixteenth century's arbiter of court standards, heaped
praise on the young prince and saw in him the buds of a
truly gracious and mannerly king.   "So great ʌ majesty, "
he enthused, "accompanied nonetheless with a certain lovely
courtesy. "31   Besides this obiter dictum, in his masterwork
The Book of the Courtier, Castiglione had his characters dis-
cuss M. de Angoulême:

> When I was at that court not so long ago, I saw
> this prince; and, besides the disposition of his body
> and the beauty of his countenance, he appeared to
> me to have in his aspect such greatness that the
> realm of France must always seem petty to him. 32

These were considerable kudos, for the "petty" realm of
France was the greatest on earth in the estimation of Castiglione's courtiers.   Still, a certain accounting must be
made for courteous flattery, the deference due to all persons
of royal timbre.

Courtiers were not social critics, yet young Francis
was an unmistakably impressive sight; he was over six feet
tall, elegant and melodramatic, the best athlete at court, and
clever if not genuinely intelligent.   His personality was charm-

ing and his lifestyle was enchanting. Few escaped his spell,
and even the most astute observers were quite taken with
him. By all outward appearances Francis was the very picture of royalty, one of the few Renaissance kings who actually looked and acted the part. The Venetian ambassador Contarini described him in 1515 as "inexpressibly handsome and
generous."[33] But as always there were dissenting opinions,
even with this most prepossessing monarch. Another Venetian
faulted Francis for a disturbing lack of character; "pareva el
diabolo" was his verdict, and perhaps this intuition captured
Francis better than the sycophantic praise. A king could
certainly be an angel to his courtiers and a devil for the
country as a whole, and in fact it was this gracious, insular
court that distracted the king from his duties and made him
a parasite. Developing France paid a high price of Francis's
chivalric excesses, both in war and in pleasure.

Pleasure was Francis's business, and although he created a spectacular environment in which to enjoy himself, the
bare fact remained that all his vaunted youthful promise was
being squandered on epicurean pursuits. The French throne
was but his springboard to sybaritic excesses. These inclinations were known to be Francis's principal failing, and his
enemies made every use of them. When both Francis and
the Duke of Bourbon were discussing marriage with Eleanor
of Austria in 1525, Lursi, the duke's agent, told Eleanor
that "the king's amorous temperament would render her the
unhappiest woman in the world, and that he had been moreover and was much diseased with the pox, which malady the
late Queen Claude caught from him and died of it."[34] This
was unfortunately all true, except perhaps Claude's death of
venereal disease. No one doubted that the king had the
"pox"; even his doting mother admitted that her Caesar had
been "punished where he had sinned."

Francis took great delight in his conquests, especially
the more difficult ones. Certain accounts relate that he took
a judge's wife while the poor cuckold guarded the stairs,
raped a woman while holding her husband at bay with the
point of his sword, and even made shameful advances on his
own gentle sister.[35] Whether apocryphal or true, these vig-
nettes only enhanced Francis's standing at court and abroad.
Henry VIII was said to be insanely jealous of this Most
Christian King, an inappropriate title by which he was called.
This was undoubtedly the height of irony: the very qualities
most celebrated in Francis were the epitome of his weakness
as a king. Although his superficial affairs were mere virile

entertainments, Francis was completely and utterly beholden to the women in his life. They knew it and treated him like the irresponsible little boy he was. At the age of twenty-four, the king began his ten-year affair with Madame de Chateaubriant, which was followed by an even longer liaison with Anne d'Heilly, Duchess d'Etampes. Along with his iron-willed mother, these two women ruled the king in turn. They were his lovers, his closest friends, and his most trusted advisers. But if, as Francis supposedly remarked, a court without women was a garden without flowers, a country without a strong monarch was a garden overrun by weeds. The English ambassador Nicholas Wotton reported that Francis was king in title alone, so dominating were his women.[36] Lursi concurred and was particularly hard on Louise of Savoy, whom he called "una terribilisima dama."[37] Tavannes, a page at the French court, was more stylish in his critique: "Alexander the Great saw women when he had no business, Francis attended to business when he had no women."[38] Other ambassadors complained that it was impossible to state their business to the king; he slept until noon, traveled constantly, and was ever engaged in activities they dared not interrupt. But someone had to attend to business while Francis was otherwise engaged, and that someone was usually Louise of Savoy. As she instructed a papal legate, "address yourself to me and we shall go our way. If the king complains we'll just let him talk."[39] Women not only dominated the king, they occasionally deceived him and even betrayed him. In 1540 the Imperial ambassador related that Francis confided only in his women, but "of all these things I am perfectly aware having lately obtained reliable information from one of the said damsels."[40] Such treachery was only the tip of the iceberg. Proud Francis was cuckolded as well, for many of his mistresses had other lovers. Seemingly a commanding presence, Francis could not even control his lovers.

Although marriage was anathema to the chivalric love so rife at the French court, Francis did have a wife throughout his courtly adventures. Claude, daughter of Louis XII, had been a condition of his entrée into the royal house, but she was eminently forgettable. This suited Francis perfectly; Claude remained in the background and produced children at regular intervals without a hint of complaint. She was, sadly enough, the perfect royal wife.

Their union had been planned since Claude was seven and Francis twelve, but the consummation was delayed until

the young girl reached the age of fifteen, at which point
Louis could no longer wait. With commendable loyalty to
his house he realized that his dauther's marriage to his heir-
presumptive was an important step toward a smooth transition. The marriage was chimerical without consummation,
and Louis would not be alive to orchestrate the entire affair
if he waited much longer. The biological validation was accomplished in 1514, apparently without pain for the twenty-
year-old groom, who left Claude to follow the hunt the very
next day. Such a marriage was pure business for Francis,
and like all business he attended to it with reluctance. Yet
the total absence of conjugal affections between Claude and
Francis did not, happily enough for France, prevent them
from the accomplishment of their central dynastic mission:
the begetting of healthy male offspring. The year after the
marriage, Claude gave birth to a daughter, and another
girl followed the next year, but two years later a son was
born. Two more healthy sons followed in rapid succession,
and a fine family was amassed. Poor dutiful Claude had
performed admirably; from the age of fifteen to the age of
twenty-three, she delivered seven children--virtually a child
each year.

This amazing streak was a boon for France and a
blight for Claude. By 1523 the ambassador's dispatches referred almost constantly to her illnesses, and death loomed
on the horizon for the neglected twenty-four-year-old queen.
She had not, in truth, been a prepossessing physical specimen
from the outset. A limp and a permanent squint in her left
eye particularly marred her countenance, and less charitable
observers described her as "a fat, torpid, deformed child
with a limp."[41] Yet, no one could fault her for her children,
unsavory as she might have been. The king's friend Fleurange noted that "she has borne the king many beautiful children, the most beautiful I ever saw among rich or poor,
there were never lovelier children."[42] But in their aftermath Claude was exhausted, and as 1524 approached she had
to follow the peripatetic court on a specially constructed
river barge, instead of the usual cart or litter.

The death of Claude in 1524 shocked no one although
it prompted much speculation regarding the cause. Brantome and the ambassador Mezeray claimed that Claude fell
victim to venereal disease, a pox she had received from her
obviously infected husband. The evidence is less than convincing, for Claude's children all arrived without incident.
Whatever evil Francis had brought her, she held no bitterness

toward her profligate husband, or if she did, she inhibited her anger in a manner that would become a tradition among French queens.   In her will she bequeathed Brittany, her own possession, to "son seul tres aime mary."[43]

After the productive reign of Queen Claude, marriage was of little interest to Francis, for he suffered no lack of companionship.   He was mainly a dilettante king with no great desire to enter into the wranglings of diplomacy.   These matters he left to those who would have them: Louise, Bonnivet, Montmorency, Lautrec, and a few cardinals.   As for internal government, Francis, despite his glowing personal reputation, had indifferent success.   His constant wars won no bounty and depleted the treasury, the "taille" was raised to increasingly unpopular levels, and little effort was made to cultivate France's enormous economic resources.   To finance his wars and his excesses, Francis resumed the sale of offices, an unsavory business that created a large class of middle-class civil servants who gladly took a creeping hold on once-royal functions.   Worse still, he allowed his favorites everything that was in his power to bestow.   To his mother Francis gave the duchies of Anjou and Angoulême, the counties of Maine and Beaufort, and the barony of Amboise.   This magnanimity certainly reflected well on Francis the man, but it plainly demonstrated that Francis the king was unwise.   He had only so much to give, yet he continued to spend far beyond the level of his revenues.   Taxes mounted, and French bankers were pressed for loans; the king's magnificence was bankrupting his country, and for this Francis graciously apologized.   In 1523 he promised to trim his expenditures, "not including, however, the ordinary run of our little necessities and pleasures."[44]   These good intentions aside, there was no relief in sight, and the resources of France continued to be squandered.   One of the major drains for both men and money was Italy, where Francis advanced his claim to various principalities with minimal success.   But what was a major trap of long standing became a full-fledged tragedy in 1525, when Francis was defeated and captured at Pavia.   For this minor Italian state, Francis had become the Emperor's hostage, yet another stroke of good fortune for Charles.   The future of France was in the Emperor's hands; while Francis languished in an Imperial prison, France was without its titular head, and the cost of his freedom was bound to be steep.

Charles was content to let Francis feel the rigors of prison life, hoping that a few months of such treatment would bring the French king to the bargaining table in a suitably humble spirit. The Emperor's astuteness rivaled his luck, for Francis was completely unaccustomed to pain and humiliation, and captivity altered the very roots of his personality. Still more distressing to him was the onset of illness. When Charles was ready to dictate conditions for his release, Francis was ready to sign almost anything, which he essentially did; Charles demanded a veritable partitioning of France in which England would recover the areas it had held under Henry V and peripheral provinces would fall under the aegis of the Habsburgs or their allies. It was clearly an untenable settlement, and Francis had no intention of honoring it once his freedom was won. Yet Charles was not naive to the ways of negotiation; as a security for the French king's pledge his two eldest sons were to be hostages in Francis's stead. Without blinking, Francis accepted this crippling codicil, effectively mortgaging the future of France for his personal safety. At the actual exchange he was so overjoyed to be king again that he all but forgot that his sons faced the same misery he had been unable to bear. Francis was nothing if not irresponsible. The two boys, ages seven and eight, endured four full years in the Imperial prison, and neither ever recovered from the experience.

A further condition of Francis's release was marriage with the Emperor's sister. The Habsburgs were adroit at weaving Europe in a matrimonial web, and Charles saw the French king's bachelorhood as a golden opportunity to make abundant France part of the family tree. Francis accepted this cross, for he knew that his sons would never be returned if he reneged on the nuptial obligation. Eleanor was thirty-two and drab, unlikely to bear more sons for the king --not that he cared--and was apparently deformed as well. Brantome claimed one of her hand-maidens told him that "when undressed she was seen to have the trunk of a giantess, so long and big was her body, yet going lower, she seemed a dwarf, so short were her legs and thighs."[45] Francis treated her with the requisite deference in public, ignored her the rest of the time, and spent his evenings with the Duchess d'Etampes.

The return of the princes was, naturally enough, negotiated by Louise and Margaret of Austria, Charles's favorite aunt. These women, with assistance from Queen Eleanor, agreed to lessen the severity of the settlement terms, with most of the disfiguring territorial cessions eliminated and the two boys returned to France for a ransom of 2 million gold crowns, a ransom raised from the very lifeblood of France to cover its king's imprudence. While the women came to terms, the two kings could only mutter martial oaths. Charles called Francis a dastard and a scoundrel for not keeping his word regarding the harsh original Treaty of Madrid and proposed that the issue be settled with a personal duel. Francis gladly accepted, and sent an envoy to tell the Emperor that "you have lied in your throat."[46] The "Paix des Dames" was signed in 1529, but Charles and Francis were preparing to go to war. Such were the requirements of honor.

Francis was a legendary roué, an almost ideal courtier, an imprudent general, and an irresponsible ruler. He was also, for a good portion of his fifty-three years, a sick man, despite his outward displays of vigor. The young Francis, swashbuckling and dynamic, fell victim to the era's prevalent diseases; in 1511 and 1512 he was seriously ill with "tertiary fever," and at that time Louise of Savoy wrote of a disease in her eighteen-year-old son's genitals. This quite likely was the first indication of syphilis, a major cause of his ultimate decline and perhaps the cause of his death. Rumors had him similarly ill in 1516 and 1521, and in 1524 the Venetian ambassador confirmed the gossip and reported the king "sick of the French disease."[47]

The visible turning point in the monarch's health came in 1525, when Francis was imprisoned. In the Imperial jail he fell sick with a fever, which suddenly turned for the worse. Three days of unconsciousness followed, and the French king slipped into a coma. Charles's physicians believed that he was dying, and a rumor circulated in France that he was already dead. This went on for weeks. Finally, on the twenty-third day of the fever, an abcess in his skull broke and sent its contents spewing forth from the king's nose. While most unappealing, this signaled the end of danger, as the fever dropped and Francis regained consciousness. The doctors told the king that he was consumptive, and the Emperor feared that he might soon have a dead--and therefore useless --hostage burdening his conscience. Francis laughed at their verdict, and later joked with the Venetian ambassador Giustinian that this misdiagnosis had worked to his advantage, since the apparent infirmity persuaded the Emperor to exchange the king for his sons. Yet the doctors were unusually close to the mark; Francis was indeed a consumptive, and an autopsy revealed that one of his lungs was in shreds.[48]

After his return from captivity, Francis was ill almost

yearly. In 1526 Don Bernardino de Mendoza, the Spanish
ambassador, reported the king "ill with his usual complaint,"
but remarked on the absence of sores on his face. [49] The
"French disease" was a constant and painful companion. In
the hope of effecting a cure, Francis turned to exotic treatments, including "Lignum Vitae," an Indian remedy from the
New World. But this was to no avail. By the mid-1530s
Francis was in an obvious state of decline; he was plagued
with a "rheumatic" pain in his shoulder, fevers, and attacks
of his "usual" complaint. By 1542 ambassadors were refer-
ring regularly to what was variously called "ulcerated bladder," "gathering of the lower parts," or "French disease."
Dental decay further humbled the once-magnificent figure, he
suffered the indignity of having to mouth his words, and his
face grew puffy and pustular. Similarly, his personality
"fluctuated wildly between gaiety and despair."[50] His once
erratic kingship descended to complete neglect, with Francis
not bothering to write down his orders or even conduct daily
business. The annual visitation of his syphilitic abdominal
abscess made him more difficult and suspicious still, besides incapacitating him for months, and the ailment's pain
was matched only by its disgusting appearance; in 1543 a
broken blood vessel turned septic, and ulcers erupted in five
different spots around his groin. Surgeons closed four of the
ruptures, but so diseased was his urinary tract that the final
abscess was left open as a makeshift urethra. [51] Each succeeding year brought a similar episode, and Francis became
restless, short-tempered, and melancholy. The ravages of
disease, not political vicissitudes, transformed the talented
courtier into a pathetic and self-absorbed old man.

Badoer, a Venetian envoy, had once noted that Francis
emperiled his kingdom because "he incurs so much personal
risk." He had warned Francis, he claimed, that "so much
depends on your health."[52] This was the simplest truism,
but whatever actually depended on Francis's fit presence was
doomed to disappointment. Once a playboy-king, Francis
grew to be an invalid-king. In 1547 another abscess broke
out, closed, and sent its infection raging through the weak
sovereign's body. Death was imminent, but Francis recalled
a final spark of mischief and announced to the attending lords
that he could determine his condition by the faces of the
anxious younger generation gathered around his deathbed: if
they smiled, he was dying; if they frowned, his condition
was improving. As Francis could see for himself, the
smiles outnumbered the frowns, and heir-presumptive Henry
was already busy handing out royal patronage. Francis died

in the grip of a consuming fever, but not before warning his successor against excessive submission to women--advice that Henry embraced not a jot. The autopsy done on Francis revealed the sources of his torments. His internal decay was beyond anyone's wildest imagination; inside the once-hearty body were stomach abscesses, shriveled kidneys, "putrefied entrails," a corroded throat, and a shredded lung. [53]

Francis's death left France with an unbalanced successor and an uncertain future, a situation far from the happy promise once offered by the king's three healthy sons. In 1524 the future of the Valois seemed secure, with Francis on the throne and his boys in the royal nursery. Pavia, and Francis's Faustian bargain, changed this comforting picture four years later with severe physical and psychological defects. The dauphin, Francis, left France at the age of eight a perfectly normal little prince and returned a frail and anemic little creature. At the raucous French court, young Francis was conspicuous for his grave, somber, abstemious, and reserved ways, and the story was told that no one had ever heard him laugh. [54] His younger brother Henry was similarly aloof, and their unsympathetic father made no secret of his disappointment in their temperament, telling them in public that the king "does not care for dreamy, sleepy, sullen children." [55] Their distress was far deeper than mere superficial wilfulness, and at the age of eighteen the dauphin simply faded away, with the proximate cause of his death tuberculosis. He had never recovered from his captivity.

With these two steely-eyed sons home from Spain, Francis turned his attention toward his third son, Charles, who had been spared his elder brothers' fate. Charles was truly his father's son in demeanor and inclinations, and the two shared the same frivolousness, abandon, and cleverness. Both were eternal extroverts. While Henry and Francis were solemn and unhappy, Charles was lively and gay--if a bit effeminate. To remedy this the soldier Tavannes (once a page at court) was assigned to toughen up the boy, which he did with admirable success. Soon Charles was a fine courtier, indulging in the huge snowball fights, lavish entertainments, and court pranks, of which one of the current favorites was to place the bodies of hanged criminals in the beds of court damsels. Yet, if Charles was the mirror image of Francis, he also shared his father's lack of good sense; the very qualities that so endeared him to Francis

and the rest of the court proved the cause of his needless
death. While on military maneuvers Charles entered a
plague-ridden house to prove himself unafraid. Shouting "no
son of France has ever died of the plague," he even slashed
at the pillows and bedding and pranced in the feathers, according to horrified companions. The plague, however, made
an exception in his case, and within three days Charles was
dead. 56

All that remained of the once bountiful royal family
were two girls and Henry, an extremely hostile young man.
Henry, unlike the frail and susceptible dauphin, was tough
and resilient, and thus he brooked his physical hardship well.
He even maintained a spark of defiance; when the constable
of Castile asked the princes to forgive him for the hardships
of their captivity, Henry supposedly replied with a barrage
of broken wind. 57 Behind the bad manners Henry possessed
a true streak of sadism and a frightening hatred for his father and favored younger brother. He neither forgot nor forgave. After his return he skulked about and, with the dauphin's death, anxiously awaited his turn on the throne. In
one particularly indiscreet episode, Henry handed out royal
boons at a card game while his feeble father languished in
an upstairs room. This false start, related to him by the
court jester, occasioned Francis's last great outburst of
temper; he arrived at the scene of the game and virtually
tore the room apart. The participants, alas, had fled before
his anguished arrival.

At the age of twenty-eight, Henry prepared to mount
his throne, yet no one really knew much about him. It was
said that he had become Spanish in Spain. His depths were
unfathomable, and only his mistress Diane de Poitiers had
his confidence. The Venetian ambassador Cavalli described
the twenty-eight-year-old Henry as "very robust in constitution, but somewhat melancholy in humor ... of somewhat
mediocre intelligence, slow to react."58 Yet Henry, like
his father, had his physical virtues. Legend claims that he
broad jumped over twenty-five feet, and Dandolo wrote that
"one might believe him all made of muscle."59 A skilled
hunter and gamesman, Henry was undoubtedly "a quicker
spirit and bolder" than his fallen older brother, as the English ambassador reported. 60 But in Henry's aloofness there
was something more alarming, an utter disregard for what
anyone other than Diane thought of him and an unsparing devotion to this ambitious woman.

Henry was his father's exact antithesis, except for one crucial similarity: both men were dominated by women. In Henry's case, only one woman guided him, but Diane de Poitiers had the willpower of any three of Francis I's mistresses. She offered the stilted young man a combination of maternal solicitude and gentle sexual affection, and at the age of seventeen, Henry became utterly hers. Diane, however, was thirty-seven, and her maturity and experience overwhelmed what minimal resolve King Henry, characterized as "born to be governed rather than to govern,"[61] had. Henry bestowed all his affection on his "seneschal," and his gratitude was boundless. Perhaps it was a streak of submissiveness in Henry that rendered him so pliant, or perhaps his malleable character opened up to the novelty of warmth after a childhood of hostility and parental disapproval. Whatever the reason, Diane was laden with privileges and patronage. Henry confiscated the crown jewels from his father's mistress, the Duchess d'Etampes, and gave them to his amour, and Diane handled the large portion of state business to her personal satisfaction. Still more beneficent, Henry arranged for his mistress to receive a fixed percentage of the revenue derived from the sale of offices. Henry denied her nothing. The wrinkled "seneschal" had good reason to be "very haughty and insolent."[62] Henry was pathetic in his dependence; when separated from "her upon whom all my welfare depends," he plaintively confessed, "I cannot live without you."[63] This cloying Oedipal drama was distasteful to some observers, who saw Henry's actions as the height of political folly. The Imperial ambassador wrote that "he continues to yield more and more to the yoke of Silvius [Diane] and has become her subject and slave entirely, a circumstance which his people lament."[64] Worse still, Henry was apparently aware of the dangers of his dependence--for all his failings he was not stupid--and was nonetheless unable or unwilling to take the situation in hand. "It is said," wrote one ambassador, "that the king has intimated that he was conscious of the above mentioned matter; but that he was so deeply involved now and so long since, that he would not know how to withdraw now."[65] What fortitude could be expected from a monarch who was often observed, as Henry was, sitting in the lap of his mistress? The childlike quality of Henry's devotion was certainly touching, if not appropriate. Like a trusting little boy, he wrote, "I did not fear in days gone by to lose the good graces of my father in order to remain near you. I have known only one God and one friend."[66]

Partially obscured by this consuming romance was the

queen, neglected Catherine de Medici. Henry and the seemingly unremarkable Italian princess were married in 1533,
when both were fourteen years of age. Although some felt
the early consummation to be a trifle premature, the Pope
was so pleased at the accomplishment of this mesalliance
between his niece and the French prince that he refused to
wait. To suit his designs he pronounced both parties of
proper age and maturity, and as a final touch the Papal
Prince traveled all the way to France to assure the smooth
conclusion of the nuptials. Once in France he remained, as
he was doubtful of young Prince Henry's virility. For a
month he awaited positive proof of consummation, but, as
the envoy Sacco wrote to Milan in 1533, the prince was doing
his best. Sacco reported that, after putting the couple to
bed personally, King Francis "wished to see them jousting,
and each of them jousted valiantly."[67] Yet the Pope's sus-
picions of inadequate performance were warranted; underneath the thrashing veneer both Henry and Catherine were
genitally malformed. Henry suffered from a condition known
today as hypospadias; a defect in the penis that obstructs the
opening of the urethra, and Catherine had what Brantome
called "a tortuosity of the vaginal canal," and did not reach
puberty for almost a decade after her marriage.[68] Still, the
Pope could not wait forever. He departed after a final word
of advice to his niece: "A clever woman can always have
children,"[69] he told Catherine.

Clever she was, but for ten years Catherine was unable to conceive. "The shopkeeper's daughter," as Diane
fondly, if archly, called her, put all her considerable power
of mind to work. She consulted the famous physician Jean
Fernel, who prescribed myrrh pills, and even stopped riding
mules when it was pointed out to her that such animals were
notably sterile. Gossips spread rumors that the unfortunate
queen turned in desperation to sorcery, a solution that was
hardly past Catherine. But even black magic proved futile,
and finally she threw herself on the mercy of her father-in-
law Francis, weeping and begging forgiveness. For his part,
Henry cared little if at all. His attentions were monopolized
by Diane.

It was no doubt galling to Catherine that Diane's hold
over Henry was so complete, and her realization of the proper role of mistress was so flawless, that "it is often she
who exhorts the king to go and spend the night with the
queen," according to the Venetian ambassador.[70] This
prompting was in fact necessary, for at this stage in her

career Catherine was ignored by virtually everyone. She
had achieved something of a coup with her marriage into the
royal house of France, and as an orphan with no political
leverage, she knew better than to become difficult. It was
her obligation to pay homage to the royal mistress, as much
as she despised her, and she discharged these duties so well
that Diane actually fussed over her when she was ill, afraid
that Catherine's death might lead the king to marry some
new and enticing creature. [71] Yet for all her restraint
Catherine occasionally slipped into the calculated rage for
which she later became so notorious. Her jealousy ranged
from the pathetic (drilling holes in her bedroom floor in
order to observe her husband and Diane in the chamber directly below) to the vicious (asking the young Duke de Nemours to throw corrosive vitriol in her competitor's face).[72]
Without children or her husband's confidence, Catherine was
still queen in name alone. To make matters worse, Henry
had raped a beautiful Piedmontese girl in 1538 and became
a father at last. This was attributable, according to Balzac's
history, to a corrective operation performed on the royal
member. Porcine Catherine was still two years away from
the onset of puberty. Finally, at the age of twenty-four, her
strenuous efforts were rewarded with a veritable outpouring
of children; ten offspring issued from her womb in the next
thirteen years, although their undeniable strangeness served
to confirm Catherine's unnatural road to maternity. This
feat left Henry unmoved, but it provided Catherine a measure
of security. As queen-mother she could insult Diane with
relative impunity; "from time to time at all periods," she
announced in 1558, "whores have managed the business of
kings. "[73] But in France whores would continue to manage
the business of kings, at least while Henry held the scepter.
Catherine remained a wounded appendage, as she wrote her
daughter Marguerite: "Let me serve as a warning not to
trust too much in the love of your husband. "[74]

Outside the sphere of these struggles, larger issues
awaited resolution. Wars proceeded, religious issues took
on new significance, and the economy was burdened by the
court and the campaigns. Yet the royal circle was absorbed
in its own internal struggle. If Diane had at least an ama-
teurish interest in the affairs of state, Henry avoided such issues in favor of sport, good hunting, and his devoted if aged
lover. Like his father, Henry was disinclined to politics and
had, according to an observer, "no fixed purpose, no will
or stable policy of his own. "[75] When he worked it was
merely out of a sense of obligation, but he preferred to let

his friends do it. This naive trust was taken very badly by
astute foreign ambassadors, who mourned that the French
king delivered himself completely into the hands of rapacious
and self-aggrandizing favorites. [76]

To this and other criticism Henry was characteristically indifferent. His feelings were personal and private, and
his reign was tinged with disregard for sensitive issues. In
one facet of government the king chose to act, however ill-
advisedly; both he and Diane believed in the orthodox church,
and together they ordered a policy of intolerance and sup-
pression. Without a full understanding of the situation, Henry
acted unaware of--or oblivious to--the full political consequences of the persecution, a policy that would hang like a
specter over France for the remainder of the sixteenth century. Grimly determined to root out the troublemakers, he
established a special court for the disposition of heretics,
known as "la chambre ardente," and even discussed the possibility of a new inquisition in France. Pope Paul IV, much
to his credit, discouraged the idea. With typical tactless-
ness Henry founded his own avenging arm and plotted the extermination of the Huguenots while one of their sympathizers
stood right at hand. For his restraint this man acquired the
name "William the Silent," and he proved to be a great
thorn to the Catholic cause in the Netherlands. Henry proved
himself more than intolerant, he demonstrated an absence of
human feeling that was chilling. When Diane was incidentally
insulted by a Huguenot tailor, the French king ordered the
man burned on the spot, and remained to watch the festivities.

For all Henry's failings he was nonetheless a legitimate adult monarch, and his mere presence was a stabilizing
force in an era of turmoil. There was, in 1559, every reason to expect that his presence would continue for some time;
at the age of forty, Henry was prematurely grey and rather
aged looking, but he was still in admirable physical condition.
Fittingly enough, a foolish court entertainment shattered this
picture, for in a ritual joust the king forgot to lower his
visor and was pierced through the eye with a broken lance.
Five splinters penetrated to his brain, where they became
infected. His physicians could only bleed and purge him, and
his stubborn constitution was no match for a rampant fever.
A few days later he died, leaving his country in the worst
possible bind. Foreign challenges, a brood of sickly children, a pack of ambitious nobles, and an amazingly clever
widow were left to determine the fate of France.

The tragedy of this death was apparent in both the unsettled climate of religious conflict and, still more ominous, the condition of the royal children themselves. Not a single child was of age to rule, and as a group the offspring of Catherine de Medici showed very little promise of future greatness, particularly the stilted pack of four sons. The eldest of them was only fifteen at the time of Henry II's death, and the rest were, like young Francis II, younger in actual development than chronological years. What seemed an embarrassment of riches--four surviving sons and three daughters--proved a mere embarrassment, as there was not an ounce of royal mettle in any of the seven. Whatever Catherine did, took, avoided, or promised to achieve their births was revenged in full by nature, which sent France a visitation of embodied inadequacy. In this particular circumstance neither the dynasty nor the country were well served by an ample royal family, proving either that it is unwise to cheat infertility or that monarchs should be chosen by virtue of personal capability, which was in fact argued by political theorists towards the end of the Valois' reign. The last of the Valois were arguably a prelude to 1789.

By the time Henry II trotted so carelessly into the lists with his visor raised, the policy of religious persecution had already wrought diehard opposition. Around the hapless new king, Francis II, thronged clever leaders of the great families, who formed factions along religious lines-- more for the advancement of their influence than the salvation of their souls. Although Catherine de Medici was the titular regent, the Guises dominated the immature king through their niece Mary Stewart. According to Queen Elizabeth's ambassador Throckmorton, France had three kings: Francis II, Francis of Guise, and Charles, Cardinal of Lorraine. With Francis II as figurehead, the latter two ruled in tandem, as Charles handled matters of finance and foreign policy and the duke took responsibility for the military. The Venetian ambassador reported that the Guises held secret policy discussions and packed the king's chamber offices with Guise relatives and lackeys. Under this family-gang rule, the persecution was continued, as the Guises were Catholics of the most intolerant stripe.

Other great families resented this Guise hegemony, particularly the Bourbons. They claimed that Francis, fifteen years old, was not of age to rule, nor was he permitted to choose his own advisers. This task, they argued, belonged by right to the first prince of the blood, King Antoine

of Navarre.   Behind Antoine, who was privately mocked as
a dullard, lurked the more menacing Louis, Prince of Condé.
This faction, and particularly Condé himself, supported the
cause of the Huguenots.   The battle lines were drawn.

Such were the politics.   Still more depressing was the
King of France himself: Catherine's firstborn son, her saving triumph after ten years of sterility, was a weak infant
whose condition prompted, as has been noted previously,
court gadflies to condemn the queen for black magic and unhealthy medicines.   Certainly, the dauphin's appearance sub-
stantiated such claims.   The Venetian Dandolo, writing in an
age that lavished praise on even the least-favored royal offspring, pronounced the three-year-old Francis an invalid
"pale and swollen rather than fat."[77]   Dark prophesies were
uttered.   The famed seer Nostradamus told Catherine that
Francis would never see his twentieth year, and that three
of her sons would in turn be king of France.   Desperately
ill at the age of six, Francis grew up a timid mother's boy,
subject to frequent fevers and violent "frenzies."   Whether
this resulted from insanity or the volatile temperament characteristic of consumptives, meek Francis was occasionally
overcome with wild bursts of energy, which he unleashed on
the hunt and other boisterous pursuits.   But underneath it
all Francis was shy and afraid, his mind no more developed
than his pitiable body.

As heir of mighty France, the dauphin had a wife secured for him at an early age.   The charming and frail Mary
Stewart was brought to the French court when she was six
and Francis five, and together they weathered the strains of
the little prince's frequent crises.   By all indications Mary
developed a strong, almost maternal, affection for the puny
creature, which he returned with a warmth he showed no one
else.   Of course Mary was as much in love with her life as
dauphiness as she was with Francis, and when the time came
to solemnize the marriage, fifteen-year-old Francis was
physically incapable of consummation.   For all the apparent
affection between these childhood playmates, Frances was
years behind Mary in sexual development.   The court was
naturally a party to this, and rumor had it that Francis's
genitals were withered and useless.   These reports were in
all probability a comment on a sexual malformation known as
"undescended testicles,"[78] although the ambassador Michiel
was hoodwinked into believing the union physically accomplished.   La Planche, an intimate of Catherine de Medici,
knew otherwise; Francis's "generative organs were constipated and blocked, incapable of functioning."[79]

This was a relatively minor point, for Francis's sexual problems were the least of his physical woes.   His appearance betrayed a fundamentally diseased constitution: "His
breath was fetid; his physical appearance was so alarming,
with red patches on his livid cheeks, that it actually gave
birth to sinister rumors that he had leprosy; from this rumor spread the still more disgusting gossip that Francis
needed to be bathed in the blood of young children, in order
to cure himself. "[80]   The townspeople supposedly hid their
children when the king passed through, and each side in the
religious dispute blamed the other for the onerous malady.
For her part the queen-mother wrote the boy's guardian with
the indelicate instruction that Francis ought to blow his nose
more, thinking this might help. [81]   At the root of all this was
a horrible case of eczema, which to make matters worse was
continually irritated by the tainted discharge from his ear.
This effluvium seeped from a chronic inflammation of the
middle ear, which was itself the result of Francis's constant
childhood respiratory infections--probably tubercular in origin.

This was the unfortunate creature who, at the age of
fifteen and a half, inherited the throne of his fallen father.
Obviously, the inheritance could only be held in trust, as
Francis was recognized by all to be "too young and too un-
well to rule. "[82]   This was apparent even to Francis though
observers noted in him a great deal of self-importance.
When the secretaries presented their business to the new
king immediately following the death of Henry II, Francis
referred them to his mother.   But Catherine, although certainly of the age and inclination to rule, was regent in
name alone.   She was allowed the long-awaited pleasure of
banishing Diane de Poitiers after years of the "seneschal's"
haughty dominance, but Diane's chambers were immediately
occupied by the new power behind the throne: the Guise.
The French wars of religion were less a conflict of doctrine
than a political vacuum into which ambitious nobles were
drawn.   The queen-mother observed that in both factions "religion is a cover which serves merely to mask ill will ...
and yet they have nothing less than religion in their hearts."[83]
Without a strong monarch these ill-intentioned men ran amok,
although even a strong monarch could have done little to
erase the sad record of his predecessors: the crown was 40
million livres in debt, and the effective royal income totalled
only 5 million livres per annum.   This sum was measured
by the interest alone.   The sins of the fathers, genetic, political, and financial, were visited on the sons with a vengeance.   Francis was a reed in the wind, and the breath of

the Guises filled his ear with bigotry. He renewed the death
penalty for all unrepentant Protestants. Many Huguenots fled,
others mobilized for civil war. The Guises took advantage
of their position and arranged to have their enemies assassinated. The brother of one victim, Renaudie, plotted revenge; he and a group of Protestant nobles planned to capture
and depose the Guises at Amboise. But the Cardinal of Lorraine discovered the "Tumult of Amboise" and brought it to
a swift, bloody end. Realizing that the situation was totally
out of hand, Catherine interceded with her pliant son and the
Guises to effect a temporary cessation of hostilities. This
they reluctantly agreed to, and an Assembly of Notables was
called to debate the issue to be followed by a full States-
General. But the Protestant leaders were suspicious, rightfully so, and feared arrest if they attended these deliberations.
Instead, they planned to establish an independent state, and
when the Guises intercepted a courier and learned of this
plan they immediately reverted to their dictatorial stance.
The persecution was renewed once again.

The Guises were perfectly happy with this turn of
events, as it had merely served to confirm their power--
something a conciliation might have diluted. With Francis
as puppet-sovereign, the Guises were virtually unquestionable,
as their edicts carried the stamp of royal authority. Yet,
their new rosebed had a fatal thorn; Francis was clearly not
long for the world. He had been subject all his life to spurts
of fever and even delirium, but in November 1560 his condition took a final turn for the worse. The Venetians lurked
around his bedside and sent home these reports:

> November 20: A sudden attack of cold accompanied
> with some fever, an indisposition to which he is
> subject, and which he is said to have inherited from
> his father and grandfather. It is caused by a cer-
> tain flow of catarrh, which exudes from the right
> ear, and if the discharge be stopped, he suffers
> great pain in the teeth and jaws, with a certain
> inflammation behind the ear like a large nut, which
> increases or decreases according to the greater or
> lesser virulence of the humor. [81]

The "nut" behind the king's ear was, in fact, a diseased
mastoid, and its notable swelling was a barometer of death.
As much as the Guises attempted to suppress news of his
condition, the Venetian nonetheless sensed the urgency of the
king's condition.

November 25:   The king is very weak and feeble,
and that having taken a slight purge this morning
before daybreak he vomitted it a few hours afterwards.   I cannot comprehend what right these physicians had to purge on the 7th, for I know that our
physicians would consider it a great mistake ...
the slightest accident is very hurtful to his Most
Christian Majesty ... during the last few days, although the fever was very slight, he nonetheless
suffered so much that he seemed almost delirious
... he has a very violent pain in the head. [85]

Suriano, who had been effectively shielded from the
king's true condition by the Guises, focused his dire predictions on the political consequences of Francis's death.   This
possibility was frightening, even though the king was no more
than a stooge, because such an event would invite revolt.
"His Majesty's constitution is said to be defective ... were
any catastrophe to take place at the present moment ... a
general revolution might be expected throughout the kingdom."[86]   If this was indeed the case, the event was not far
off, for in late November Francis's diseased mastoid burst.
The infection spread to his brain, he fell into a coma and
died shortly thereafter.   The court greeted this news with
remarkable calm, although Mary Stewart was conspicuous in
her grief.   An autopsy revealed the full extent of Francis's
disease, and according to Suriano, "the body of the late
king has been opened and the whole brain was found diseased,
so that no medical treatment could ever have cured it."[87]

The long-awaited climax of Francis II's assorted ills
did not bring immediate revolution, but rather a new Valois
prince to the French throne.   Francis had been sickly,
pompous, and wholly controlled by the dreaded Guises.
Charles IX, on the other hand, was sickly, mentally unbalanced, and mere putty in the hands of his mother.   Little
had changed with his accession, save the transfer of power
from the Guises--who remained on the scene as leaders of
the most troublesome Catholic faction--to the queen-mother.
Catherine made certain that this child would not escape her
web; she moved into his very chamber and supposedly passed
each night there.   As she later boasted, "After God he
acknowledged no one as he acknowledged me."[88]

Catherine had a great deal of political acumen and a
complete lack of religious dogmatism, as befitted the niece
of a Pope.   Still, Charles was king, and for all his de-

pendence the final word could be his if he chose to so have
it. Although Charles rarely flexed his feeble will, this potential power in his hands did not bode well, for Charles was
no less deformed than Francis, and he was much more deranged. Francis was undoubtedly pathetic, but Charles was
truly warped. Like his brother, Charles reveled in the hunt
despite his diseased constitution, and bursts of frenzied
energy sent him galloping off on horseback. But his passion
for the kill extended far beyond mere sportsmanship; Charles
apparently loved to torture animals, and, if this did not sufficiently expend his rage, he worked off his frustrations as
a blacksmith. These fits were both legendary and frequent,
and they betrayed a definite streak of sadism in the young
king's character. Similar to his brutal exercise habits were
his demented entertainments; he was known to enjoy beating
his companions with stirrup leather and, among many others,
to run around the capital city wearing a mask, creating a
public nuisance. Few European sovereigns took as much
delight in adolescent behavior as Charles. In regard to business, Charles had neither the inclination nor the time. Most
days were given to the hunt, from which he returned exhausted and went directly to bed. [89] Nor was he given the
opportunity to rule; Catherine called him when he was required, but for the most part he was left to his strange
pleasures. What was unique in this regency was its lack of
pretense. As Tavannes noted, "The Queen-Mother, knowing
how entirely she possessed her son, did not care a jot for
his opinions, certain as she was that she could change them
in an instant."[90] Few at court questioned this dominance,
for Charles inspired confidence in no one. This was no service to the institution of monarchy, for it constituted a tacit
admission that a king was unfit to rule, even as an adult.
Charles was deprived, admittedly without much protest from
him, of his hereditary right to rule--a dangerous precedent.
But there were few alternatives. Even in an age of unfit
sovereigns, Charles was conspicuous as a biological and
monarchical aberration. "There is nothing kingly about him, "
sneered the Venetian Suriano, "but the title."[91]

Charles had been a physical puzzle from the very beginning. Even Michiel, an ambassador given to superlatives
in his descriptions of royal offspring, was ambivalent about
Charles when he reported on the king at the age of eleven:
"An admirable child, and in talent, intelligence, affability,
liberality, and courage, everything might be hoped from him
as a king." But, the ambassador cautioned, "He is not very
strong, he eats and drinks very little, and as regards physical

exercise it will be necessary to handle him very carefully."[92] Still worse, there were evidences of lung disease: "He is weak and very short of breath. "   This condition was chronic, and was eventually to cause Charles's death.   The king's appearance was distressing in itself.   Although he was considered to be "handsome of face, " observers looked with disfavor on his feeble neck, bowed shoulders, and spindly legs. A birthmark on his face disfigured his upper lip, and some of his spiteful subjects described him as "le roi morveaux"-- the king with the running nose.   Suriano compared Charles with his dead brother not altogether favorably, and added that "many people think he will not live long because his health is fragile. "[93]

Contrary to all appearances, Charles did have a romantic side, and the only person who shared that part of him was his frumpy Huguenot mistress Marie Touchet.   Whatever her religious heterodoxy, Marie appeared to be genuinely fond of the stilted little king, which made her unique among the royal entourage.   Charles met this plain girl on a trip through the provinces when he was fifteen and she was sixteen, and their relationship continued for the rest of his life. She apparently understood his torments, and patiently withstood his onslaughts.   Ambassadors reported that in his frenzies Charles descended on his mistress with a pathological sexual appetite.   For this compassion Charles wrote her sonnets--"Toucher, aimer, est ma devise. "[94]   Marie had his total devotion, in the sixteenth-century tradition of royal mistresses, and presented the king with a son, Charles, who later became the Grand Prior of France.   King Charles was Marie's, just as his more formidable father and grandfather had belonged totally to their mistresses.   Charles's marriage to Elizabeth of Austria changed nothing; the pious Habsburg princess was part and parcel of a peace treaty and spent most of her nights in prayer.   Charles was pleased with this arrangement.   As he commented when he first saw her picture, "She will not give me a single headache, "[95] and, true to form, she remained in the background.   In three years of marriage, she bore one daughter, Marie Isobel, who died at the age of five.   Marie Touchet did not feel threatened in the least.   "I am not afraid of the Austrian, " she brazenly proclaimed. [96]

At the hunt and in the arms of a devoted mistress Charles passed his time, while Catherine de Medici played one dangerous faction against the other.   The conflicting pressures of the extreme Catholic party--which found expres-

sion in the Guise-led Holy League--and the ever-increasing
ranks of the Huguenots were becoming uncontrollable.
Charles himself was making matters worse with his awed
admiration of certain Protestant leaders, particularly the
Admiral Coligny. By nature Catherine was a "politique"--
hoping to maintain an uneasy truce between the factions--and
she had maintained a precarious religious balance prior to
1572. But fear overwhelmed her courage as the Huguenots
filed into Paris that year for what she had hoped would be
a conciliatory marriage between the Protestant King Henry of
Navarre and her headstrong daughter Marguerite. Catherine
and her favorite son Henry, whom Charles hated for that very
reason, were intimidated by the large assembly of Huguenots,
but they were still more afraid of the Guises. Charles had
suddenly shown an interest in the affairs of state, and was
so taken with Coligny that together they planned a war with
Catholic Spain. This added still another dimension to the
problem, for Catherine knew that if Coligny's influence over
the king continued she would be exiled, and the Huguenots
would be supreme. She also knew that if she did not halt
this development, the Guises would, or would try to, and if
they gained the initiative, her days as ruler of France were
finished. Some drastic action had to be taken, for Charles
was slipping from her grasp; as he resentfully told her after
a conversation with Coligny, the Admiral had warned him
"that all power has gone to pieces in your hands and that
evil for me would come of it. "[97] Catherine decided that the
Huguenot leaders and Coligny especially presented the greatest danger, and she cold-bloodedly arranged to have them
killed.

Meanwhile, the Guises had perpetrated an attack on
Coligny, and the king was promising to revenge the man he
called "mon père. " Charles was cornered by Catherine,
Henry, and their advisers, who encouraged him to order the
death of the Protestant leaders. With rare good sense
Charles demurred, arguing that if the Huguenots were in
fact traitors they ought to be tried publicly. Besides, he
was personally attached to them. Finding the once-pliant
king suddenly stubborn, Catherine applied the persuasion he
was incapable of resisting; she threatened to return to Italy
and leave him to his fate; she told him the Huguenots would
revolt; she told him the Catholics would counter-revolt; she
told him the two of them would be killed; but, most effectively, she simply worked on him incessantly with her co-
conspirators. Under the strain of decision and the inexor-
able arguments, Charles became hysterical. He was never

more than a step away from madness, and his mother's
psychological warfare sent him into a choleric rage. "By
the death of God, since you choose to kill the Admiral, I
consent! But then you must kill all the Huguenots in France,
so that not one shall be left to reproach me.... Kill them
all! Kill them all!" he shouted, mixed with obscenities, as
he fled down the corridors. [98] This was a broader mandate
than anyone had previously envisioned, and it touched off one
of the most senselessly brutal slaughters of the sixteenth
century.

The order to "kill them all" came from a mentally
and physically disturbed individual, as was apparent in his
behavior during the massacre. Once he had been persuaded
to give the order, his zeal exceeded that of the original conspirators. Charles was nothing if not a good hunter, and apparently the prospect of stalking human beings appealed to
his deranged instincts. Although there is some question
about Charles's actual role in the slaughter, contemporaries
insisted that he happily fired on fleeing Huguenots from the
vantage of a Louvre balcony. Sorbin, the king's preacher,
claimed that "the slaughter took place in the sight of the king,
who watched it with great pleasure. " In reference to the slain
Coligny, once the king's hero, Charles supposedly commented:
"The smell of a dead enemy is sweet and delightful, " while
inspecting the Admiral's mutilated corpse. [99] Quite understandably, across Europe Catholic leaders hailed the executions, while Protestants condemned them as dishonorable
slaughter, but the stain of the massacre remained to haunt
Charles. "I know that it is not my son-in-law who governs, "
the Emperor Maximilian wrote, "but that is not enough to
pardon him. "[100] Charles was visited with nightmares and
repented mightily of his evil, yet at other times he gloated
over it. Catherine complained that her son was a lunatic,
and Charles turned on her: "Who but you is the cause of
this? God's blood, you are the cause of it all!"[101]

The weakness of a demented mind had prompted yet
another historical tragedy, to no political benefit: on July
6, 1573, Charles signed the Peace of La Rochelle, which
guaranteed the Huguenots religious liberty.

Through all these events Charles was a sick, perhaps
even an insane, man ever on the verge of death. As one
historian wrote, "The tuberculosis which consumed him had
transformed the charming, pleasant, and lovable boy, who
had been adored by his subjects during a long tour of the

realm, first into an irritable youth, then an irritable man, quick-tempered and capable, like weak people, of the worst forms of violence, and the more sick he grew, the worse became the vices born of his illness."[102] Charles had never enjoyed good health, and as early as 1567 the diplomatic dispatches noted his incapacitating ailments. A "burning ague" caused great alarm in 1571, and by 1574 Cavalli reported that "the king does not appear to take much notice of public affairs, possibly on account of the disease which afflicts him, and not being able to recover wholly from his indisposition, he passes the greater part of his time in bed."[103] The torment of St. Bartholomew's Day sapped what strength the king had left, and in May 1574 Cavalli reported that "a large quantity of blood, instead of issuing by his nose, has flowed down his throat."[104] Toward the end of the month, Charles met his end, too feeble to fight oncoming mortality: "Last night the king's fever gradually increased, accompanied by symptoms of the most violent character, with a violent flow of blood and catarrh, similar to a previous attack, and as the unfortunate king was very weak, he had not the strength to assist himself, and thus two hours after noon today he died."[105] His reign had been a transparent pretext, his life a veritable "danse macabre," and his era a plain warning to the rest of Europe as well as to his own countrymen. Quite simply, a monarchy required a monarch. Suriano understood the gravity of the situation as early as 1562:

> If they [the French] continue to have child kings as long as that it will be too long to wait, because they need a king who has absolute power, is feared by his subjects, respected by neighborly countries, and well thought-of by all, who could carry out some dramatic exploit that would restore the reputation and greatness of the monarchy. [106]

The procession of stunted child-kings left French government impotent, and mighty France slogged in the mire of quarrels and economic neglect.

If there was a lesson to be learned from the reign of Charles IX, that lesson was the St. Bartholomew's Day Massacre, and if there was anyone completely insensible to this lesson, that unfortunate individual was Henry, Duke of Anjou and Charles's successor. This third and favorite son of Catherine de Medici had all the salient traits of his weak brothers with an additional twist of perversion. Euphemistically speaking, Henry III was a fitting conclusion to both the house of Valois and the scions of Catherine de Medici.

As Suriano had stated, France needed a credible monarch, but the monarch they were left with after the death of
Charles IX was yet another feckless Valois princeling, a
veritable icing on the already unpalatable cake.   If Henry of
Anjou was an adult it was only by virtue of his age: twenty-
four.   His internal makeup was that of a spoiled child.
While his brother was nominal sovereign, Henry had been
first a court dandy and then became King of Poland, although
he was in France to spur Charles on to the horrors of St.
Bartholomew's Day in 1572.   His tenure on the Polish throne
was brief, for at the death of Charles in 1574 Catherine welcomed her darling back to France as King Henry III.   At
this most critical time for France--Spain was strong and
threatening, the religious wars continued, the economy lagged
behind the rest of Europe--a most unusual individual returned
to take up the burdens of the monarchy, unusual even for the
singular Valois family.   Henry was the family's greatest
paradox: he was brilliant but lazy, talented but neuropathic,
regal but perverted, lascivious yet pious.   The most promising child of Henry II, Henry III became the most despised
king of his generation.   Such was the enmity he aroused that,
after his murder in 1589, his assassin's mother was hailed in
the streets of Paris and greeted in the churches with the
chant "blessed be the womb that bore thee, and the paps that
gave thee suck."[107]

What had Henry done to win such accolades?   Very
little, but what little he did was an insult to the monarchy.
He supplanted quiet incompetence with flamboyant outrage,
and the ambassador Michiel characterized him as wholly devoted to idleness and voluptuousness.   This was all the more
irritating because Henry was neither a pathetic Francis II
nor a charming Francis I.   In contrast to his withered brothers, Henry was relatively well-formed and attractive, but he
shunned the manly activities even his weak siblings had enjoyed.   Instead, Henry reveled in frivolity: he devoted his
time to breeding small lap-dogs, dressing like the fashionable courtesans, playing "cup and ball," and cutting minia-
tures out of manuscripts.   These strange pleasures were the
daily regimen for the king and his band of dissolute playmates.   The merest dictates of discretion were flouted in
public, as Henry was an exhibitionist of the first rank:

> He wore a gown of pink damask, embroidered with
> pearls.   His enormous sleeves were tied with gold
> and silver threads held in place by trebils of pearls
> and emeralds.   Diamond pendants distended the
> lobes of his ears, and diamonds shone in his hair,

> which like his beard was dyed with violet pow-
> der. [108]

After this bizarre fashion courtiers enhanced their abdomens
with a pillow strategically placed in their doublets and
walked bent forward. [109] Codpieces, ever a gentleman's
ornament, were also celebrated with heretofore unmatched
splendor.

Even these entertainments grew ordinary, and having
plumbed the depths of his imaginative decadence, Henry explored the eroticism latent in religious rituals. Off he went
to his monastery, where he indulged in twenty-hour days filled
with flagellation and veritable orgies of supplication. In the
wake of this new affectation, the queen-mother and her adviser Villeroy feared for the king's health, and the Papal
nuncio asked Sixtus V to order Henry's confessor, one Father Auger, "to see to it that these devotions do not prevent
the king from fulfilling his principal duty."[110]

"Duty" was a concept alien to Henry, and if he was
not performing his unique religious observances, there were
other avenues to ecstasy. Henry's sexual activities remain
something of a puzzle, as his tastes were unpredictably
eclectic. Historians have focused for the most part on his
homosexual predilections, which were freely exercised. But
Henry was also known to have mistresses, of which his first
and favorite was Marie, Princess de Condé. When she died
in 1574, Henry fell into religious hysterics. Unable to function he aborted the southern campaign he had been leading
against the Huguenots and retired to his monastery, where
he beat himself with a "chaplet made of little skulls."[111]
Catherine de Medici had long been parrying and thrusting
with various European courts to arrange a marriage for her
beloved prodigal, but Henry was less easily led than his
brothers, and would have nothing to do with anyone of his
mother's choosing. He allowed Catherine to transact most of
the crown business simply because he had no taste for such
matters, but with more personal issues he would not be
dominated. After the death of Marie, Henry found a young
girl much to his liking on a trip through the provinces; his
choice was Louise de Vaudemont, a cousin to the dreaded
Guises. Catherine was understandably dismayed: the Guises
were powerful and restless, the union had not the slightest
political utility, and finally Louise did not have the constitution "soon to render His Majesty the father of a son, an
event so necessary to the consolidation of the royal author-

ity. "[112]   The fault was undoubtedly as much Henry's as
Louise's.   The ambassador Alberi speculated that the dissi-
pated king's venereal disease had rendered the couple sterile,
and if Louise was truly infertile, another wife could have
been found for him, as had been done with Louis XII and
Henry VIII. [113]   As it was, Henry and Louise produced not a
single conception during fourteen years of marriage, nor was
Henry responsible for any bastard progeny.   Louise quickly
proved to be a passing fancy.   As the Venetian ambassador
reported, Henry "takes but little count of her. "[114]   Like all
Henry's responsibilities she became tiresome shortly after
she became familiar.

What did not bore Henry was amorous intrigue.   As
the Venetian Correro observed, he "delights in the domestic
chase, the palace chase. "[115]   Henry loved to cavort with his
favorites both male or female depending on his mood.   This
was painfully obvious to the Parisians.   A diarist denounced
the fey band:

> These fine minions, with their faces painted, wear
> their hair long, frizzed and refrizzed by careful
> artifice, standing up above their little velvet caps
> like the whores in the brothel quarter.   Their
> frilled ruffs are half a foot wide and when you see
> their heads sticking above the pleats you might
> think it was John the Baptist's head on Salome's
> platter.   They all dress alike in coats of many
> colors and they are sprinkled with violet powder
> and other sweet perfumes. [116]

These debauched youths were satirized in a pamphlet called
"The Isle of the Hermaphrodites" as "The Princes of Sodom. "
But unlike most of the vile calumny that circulated on the
streets of Paris, this comic opera had a ring of truth.
Henry's bed, leeringly slandered as "The Altar of Antinous, "
was all too frequently filled with young boys. [117]   Still, the
king took little notice of his subjects' disrespect, and he
continued to divert himself in the same fashion.   In 1576
the Venetian ambassador Morosini reported that "for the
last few days His Majesty has taken his pleasure by retiring
into a small apartment which has no windows, and where in
order to see, candles must be burnt all day, and to this
apartment His Majesty summons four or five youths of this
city who follow the profession of poets and light literature."[118]
Even the lack of windows and the clandestine candlelight
failed to escape the public eye, which grew more reproachful each day.

What the public saw was the folly of an increasingly ill monarch whose youthful energy had been spent. Some whispered of syphilis, but whatever the direct cause, by 1579 the twenty-eight-year-old king was partly bald, mostly toothless, and had lost a great deal of his famed sexual appetite.[119] In that same year an abscess developed behind his ear much like the one that had killed his brother Francis. Although Henry recovered, the infection left him permanently deaf in the afflicted ear. In 1581 observers noted telltale marks from venereal disease on his face and commented on his bad leg, and in 1582 Henry was visited with attacks of melancholy and pain so severe that the court feared for his sanity, such as it was. These sufferings directly paralleled an upswing in the king's eccentricity and further decreased his ever-limited capacity for serious work. His physicians encouraged him to complete his retirement from public business, as perhaps they knew what the consequences of his interference in volatile state affairs would be. The Venetian ambassador had less regard for the doctors; they had ordered the king to abstain from his duties "a little because of his health, a little because they were sycophants."[120] In pain Henry once again sought comfort in religion, and perhaps at this time he was sincere in his penitence. The ambassador Dandolo was not convinced of the king's devotion, however, and reported to Como that Henry took frequent pilgrimages to sanctuary because he was having an affair with a nun. Nor was the general populace--Henry loved to play before a crowd --inspired by the spectacles the king forced upon them: private indulgences became public demonstrations in May 1583, when Henry and his newly created religious order marched through the streets of Paris with coarse linen sacks over their heads, chanting their litany.[121] The king of mighty France was the laughingstock of the continent.

There was more than mere intolerance behind the open scorn; Henry's minions were violent, debauched, and a horrible drain on the already overextended royal purse. Although all but one of them died before the age of thirty, vast sums of money were given to them as gifts--11 million francs for one's wedding present, twice the usual cost of a judgeship for another. Priuli wrote: "It has been calculated that during these same years His Majesty has given more than four million in gold to just four of these favorites, and only two of them are in good standing with him now."[122] Benificence was bad politics. Politics had, for the most part, escaped Henry, and the tide of events made such lethargy fatal. While the king pranced, Huguenot thinkers had propagated the theory that government was a contract between a ruler and his people not to be violated by either party. To their way of thinking, Henry had flagrantly abused his office and was thus fit to be deposed. Since Henry did not take the initiative against the growing Protestant movement, the Holy League, most notably the "Sixteen" representatives at its head, filled the void. The League called the popular Henry of Guise to come to Paris and take control, and, against the king's prohibition, he did. Paris, filled with staunch Catholics, hailed Guise as its savior, and Henry III finally realized--too late--that he had allowed himself to be caught in the pincer-like grasp of the two factions. Having paid no attention before, he panicked and persuaded his aides to kill the Duke of Guise. Worse still, he perpetrated the woeful dishonor in his own chambers, where he had invited the trusting duke to come for a private conference. With this action Henry had sealed his doom, as Catherine de Medici well knew. "You have ruined the kingdom, " she told him,[123] and twelve days later she died. Instantly, the powerful Catholics demanded Henry's removal and the Pope himself absolved the French people from all duty to their sovereign. Having lost the Catholics, Henry attempted to strike an alliance with the Huguenot Henry of Navarre, but he was a marked man. On the first of August, 1589, a maniacally determined Dominican monk named Jacques Clement slipped into the king's camp and stabbed him in the stomach as he sat on his "chaise percée."[124] It was a fitting end, and Henry was mourned by no one.

Henry was not, unfortunately, the last of the Valois, as three sisters lived to witness the family's fall from the throne. There was also another brother who had never ruled: Francis of Alençon. This "wooly headed, flat nosed, negroid freak" was possibly "the most ill made of the royal children, " which was no small achievement.[125] Still, he was important in European politics: he was a serious suitor to Queen Elizabeth and the titular head of the United Provinces. Like his brothers Francis took these marvelous opportunities and made a complete mockery of them. Elizabeth merely toyed with her "little frog, " and Francis was chased out of the Low Countries by his properly enraged subjects. He hated his older brothers with pathological intensity and was described by the Venetian envoy as "deceitful, evilly disposed, and inordinately ambitious."[126] There were no redeeming qualities to balance the scale; Francis was ugly, stupid, and unscrupulous. Having been chased from the Low Countries, he withered and died at the age of thirty, to the

Chart 5

HENRY OF NAVARRE'S CLAIM TO FRENCH THRONE

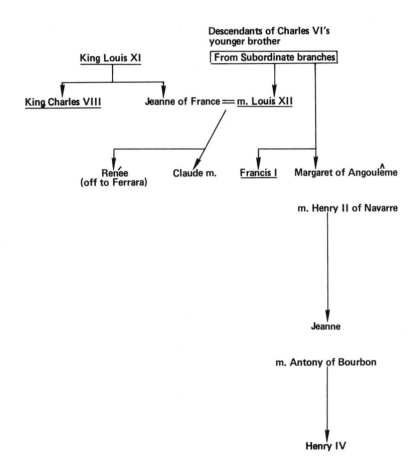

Chart 6

CHARLES EMANUEL'S CLAIM TO FRENCH THRONE

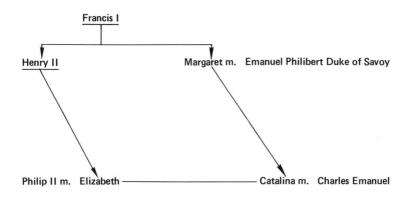

Francis I

Henry II

Margaret m. Emanuel Philibert Duke of Savoy

Philip II m. Elizabeth —————————————— Catalina m. Charles Emanuel

---

relief of just about everyone connected with him.

      The sisters were unusual in their own right. Eliza-
beth, the oldest, was still playing with dolls at fourteen,
when she was sent to be married to Philip II of Spain. At
the age of seventeen, she had yet to menstruate, and after
three grisly miscarriages she died at the age of twenty-three.
Claude was the generally acknowledged runt among the three
surviving sisters. She was hunchbacked and monstrous.
Given to the Duke of Lorraine at the age of eleven, Claude
proved fecund despite her deformities, and nine children
graced the ducal nursery. After this string of births she
died at the age of twenty-seven. Yet by far the most memorable of these women was Marguerite, who rivaled even her
brothers in debauchery. Beautiful, charming, and well
schooled, according to Brantome, she was also clever, bored,
and ambitious. Catherine de Medici called her headstrong
and combative youngest daughter "my curse in the world."127
The queen-mother realized in 1572 that her own dynasty was
crumbling and tied the marital knot between the Valois princess and the likely-looking Henry of Navarre, later Henry IV,
just as Francis I had been brought into rescue the failing

house earlier in the century. This time the ploy went for
naught; Marguerite and Henry hated each other and their marriage was a travesty, with adultery on both sides. Henry
finally divorced her--there were no children--and married
another Medici princess, from which a new line of French
kings descended to replace the spent Valois. Later in life,
after disgracing herself and the crown with her misbehavior
during her marriage to King Henry IV, she claimed to have
been the mistress of both Henry III and Francis of Alençon,
her warped brothers. Few doubted that she was a nympho-
maniac, but this boast stretched all limits of credibility.
Less dubious was her affair with Henry of Guise, her brother Henry's most formidable enemy. When this tryst was
brought to the attention of the volatile Charles IX, the royal
maniac had one of his hair-tearing fits and beat Marguerite
senseless--with the assistance of their mother. Guise was
subtly warned that he would be knifed in the ribs if he attempted to resume the relationship. He wisely left court.

These were the Valois: a collection of miserable,
unhealthy, unstable and self-indulgent individuals who, by the
accident of birth, were the monarchs of sixteenth-century
France. Their opportunities were great, as France was potentially the most powerful country in Europe, but as sovereigns they were beneath the task, so far beneath it that they
mired their house and the monarchy itself in abysmal chaos.
The advent of new blood in the person of Henry of Navarre,
who became Henry IV of France in 1589, prompted a French
resurgence, even though Henry was himself flawed and limited in capacity. Yet his restraint and conscientiousness--
particularly in his early years--were applauded, and the contrast between the new king and his Valois predecessors made
him appear a veritable Solomon. It was a tribute to the
French reverence for the institution of monarchy that such unfit rulers were allowed to hold the scepter for so long.

Chapter Five

THE HABSBURGS: DYNASTY OF DESTINY

"Bella gerunt alli; tu, felix Austria, nube"
(Let others wage war; thou, happy Austria, wed)
                    --Habsburg family motto

The large, amorphous conglomeration of Germanic principalities wedged between dormant France on one side and the
encroaching Turkish frontier on the other might well have
been, as the French philosopher Voltaire later sneered,
neither Holy, nor Roman, nor even an empire, but from
this tangle emerged perhaps the most dynamic family in sixteenth-century western Europe: the Habsburgs of Austria.
Beginning as a flock of unruly nobles, they became the masters of the century's great dynasty, yet history has failed to
document properly the origin and extent of their importance:
a tribute to the biases of English-speaking historians and
Tudor legend, in which plucky little England battles that
bigoted nemesis of the continent, Habsburg Spain. Our fascination with the Anglican tradition, however important to
our culture, nonetheless obscures the actual sixteenth-century
balance of European power. On a more objective scale,
Elizabethan England must be depicted as a gadfly, not as a
great nation; France as a sleeping giant; and the regions we
now call Italy and Germany not at all, for they did not exist
as such. The sixteenth century had its own logic and hier-
archies, most of which bear little relation to the casual
modern student's notions of, among others, Columbus, Henry
VIII, Machiavelli, and Montaigne. Although perhaps we remember such figures best, as prophets of a sort they were
largely without honor in their own time. Henry VIII was
scorned by his continental betters, Machiavelli and Montaigne
were largely ignored by the truly powerful men to whom they

Chart 7

THE HABSBURG FAMILY TREE IN THE 16th CENTURY

(x = died very young or was miscarried)

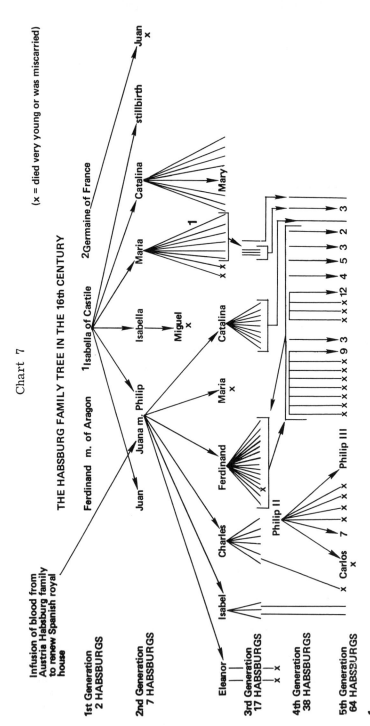

Infusion of blood from
Austria Habsburg family
to renew Spanish royal
house

1st Generation
2 HABSBURGS

2nd Generation
7 HABSBURGS

3rd Generation
17 HABSBURGS

4th Generation
38 HABSBURGS

5th Generation
64 HABSBURGS

Ferdinand m. of Aragon

1Isabella of Castile

2Germaine of France

Eleanor   Isabel   Charles   Juana m. Philip   Isabella   Maria   Catalina   Juan

¹ Two of these individuals, Isabella & John III, produced a number of children listed below their spouses, Charles V & Catalina respectively.

preached, and the great explorer returned from his fourth
and final voyage to the New World in chains like a petty
criminal. Modern chroniclers have listened more sympathetically to these men, but to their sixteenth-century contemporaries the dominant theme of the age was the Habsburg
rise, the Habsburg attempts to maintain the status quo--even
to the point of oppression--and the Habsburg decline in the
face of an expanding world they both opposed and unintention-
ally midwifed. Luther was so nettled by their hegemony that
he termed the Turk invaders a divine visitation of wrath, directed most likely at the Habsburg rulers. The Pope was
also afraid of the Habsburgs and schemed to reduce their
power in the most devious fashion, yet at the same time the
Habsburgs were principal protectors of Christendom. Francis
I of France was so envious of the Habsburgs that he implored
the infidel Ottoman Empire to invade Charles V's lands, allied with these Turks, and hoped that their march across
Europe would decimate the armies of Christendom and humble
his archenemy. In England a Spanish traitor made a very
comfortable living and was invited to the best houses, all
because he told the most scandalous stories--calumny of the
vilest sort--about the Habsburg kings of Spain. Such was
the extent to which the Habsburgs weighed on the minds of
contemporaries. Much of this reaction was undoubtedly
simple jealousy, for of all the countless European potentates
who dreamed of empire, only the Habsburg prince Charles
V, with the encouragement of his minister Cattinara, did not
fantasize beyond his resources.

Let us set the scene. Western Europe in the fifteenth
century was a curious mixture of feudal patrimonies, relatively autonomous city-states, atomistic provinces within a
logical geographic unit (Italy for instance), and discordant
rumblings from worlds beyond: most notably the Ottoman
Empire. A panoply of superstitious and medieval rulers
spent their lives in transit between inconclusive battles,
either in retreat or forward march, and only in the corrupt
Roman Catholic Church did the continent find a coherent linking thread. Religious unity and a sort of political "free
market" characterized the period, just as they would become
the antithesis of the sixteenth-century world. In the fifteenth
century most states were small, competitive, and volatile.
Turmoil was everywhere to be found; Machiavelli bemoaned
the cycle of conquest and palace revolt that beset the Italian
peninsula toward the end of the century; Henry VII of Eng-
land--who garnered his crown by virtue of little more than
good timing and political acumen--absorbed himself completely

with programs to end England's rampant civil strife; the
Hundred Years War debilitated France until 1453, with lin-
gering effects until practically the century's end. "Spain"
was nonexistent: the Iberian peninsula was divided into a
number of regions, including Castile, Aragon, Catalonia,
Navarre, Portugal, and the final stronghold of the Moorish
conquerors, Granada. In addition, civil war smoldered on
the peninsula until 1474, and chaos remained until the 1490s.
Similarly, the map of central Europe not covered by the Ottoman Empire was carved into infinitesimal principalities
linked only by common battlegrounds, long-standing feuds,
and the loose Imperial configuration. Disorganized Europe
virtually quaked before the advancing Turks, whose sys-
tematic march and unified empire were in direct contrast to
the condition of their prey.

From this dangerous confusion came, within a few
decades, the empire of the Habsburgs. And an empire it
truly was. It was not cohesive, but it was coherent. Although it fell short of the monolithic ideal of a Universal
Christian Empire, in historical significance if not in territory
the Habsburg assortment of crowns and patrimonies was arguably the most important western political achievement since
Imperial Rome. By the close of the sixteenth century, the
Habsburg family owned Austria, Tyrol, Styria, Carinthia,
Carniola, all Hungary not in the hands of the Turks, Silesia,
Moravia, Lusatia, Bohemia, Burgundy, and the Low Countries, all outright. Parts of Alsace, Milan, Finale, Piom-
bino, and Naples--including both Sicily and Sardinia--belonged
to them as well. In addition, the Habsburgs were sovereign
in Spain and Portugal, thus in the New World they reigned
over Chile, Peru, Brazil, Mexico, and countless islands.
With great vitality the Habsburgs pursued their ambitious,
quondam medieval course. The Habsburg king Charles V,
most dynamic of all, attempted to win for himself the so-
briquet "la Magne" accorded his French namesake Charlemagne. Emerging from an era of limitations symbolized by
the foreboding Pillars of Hercules in Homer's Odyssey, with
their stern warning "Nec Plus Ultra," Charles adopted "Plus
Ultra" as his devise. Aptly so, for the Habsburgs had both
the vision and the technique to attain their goal: a trans-
European empire woven in a web of relatives, all supported
by the Catholic church.

Such an aggregation of territories stemmed from the
Habsburgs' single-minded devotion to family interests, a
Schopenhauerean will to power, and the practical biological

efficiency that placed them atop their scattered realms and allowed them to remain there. A deliberate pattern of marriages and intermarriages tied the Austrian dukes into royal families across the continent, and a meticulous attention to children, matters of reproduction, and health was their prescient investment in the future of the house. In this way the Habsburgs gained, consolidated, and bound their states. The simple brilliance of this amassment was not, however, matched by a similarly innovative style of rule. Their performance on their myriad thrones was arguably reactionary; for example, their dogmatic insistence on religious orthodoxy, their disregard of regional needs, and an unfortunate taste for pointless and costly wars. Still, their careful plan to root themselves in the shifting loam of continental monarchies was both revolutionary and unique, containing as it did both the potential for growth and the cross-pollinated seeds of incestuous decline, an eventual decay of the family itself on the most basic biological level. The Habsburgs stand as a model, not of military prowess or political astuteness, but of dynastic opportunism.

Such comparisons are in order. In an era of tenuous royal families, the Habsburgs were remarkable for their longevity as well as their breadth of power. The Tudors ruled in England for a little over a century, with a single woman accounting for almost half that time. Still more telling, the Tudors lasted for only two generations on the throne, and peripheral relatives were in short supply as well. The Habsburgs, on the other hand, went through five generations in the sixteenth century alone, and from 1438 until 1808 they reigned over the Holy Roman Empire. In worldly wealth the Austrian dynasty eventually stood heads above all but the French crown. In the 1590s King Philip II of Spain received from Castile, one of his many patrimonies, an income ten times greater than the entire English crown revenue (for that matter, her total revenue was said to be less than Philip's income from his single duchy of Milan). [1] In fact, King Philip's annual yield increased by five times during his reign. The Habsburgs were also fortunate to ride to power in phase with a most felicitous demographic wave: the fourteenth century had been marked by plague and decimation, but between 1460 and 1620 the European population made a great recovery, and may in fact have doubled. [2] In or around 1560 the population surpassed the high mark reached before the onslaught of the Black Death. It was an era of development and expansion.

Still the question remains, whence did this phenomenon arise? At the beginning of the fifteenth century, the Habsburgs were squabbling Austrian noblemen, yet by the close of the sixteenth century they exercised the <u>droit de seigneur</u> across most of western Europe. But until mid-century there were a score of equally powerful families in the Holy Roman Empire alone, the Wittelsbachs for one, all vying for the Imperial crown. Dating back to the "Golden Bull," which had been approved by the great families at the diets of Nuremberg and Metz in 1356, each family was sovereign in its own patrimony, ecclesiastics ruled in a few independent cities, and an elected Emperor supervised the entire confederation, if somewhat loosely. The lay princes, known as "Electors," had the right to pass their lands on to their eldest son, a right that maintained the indivisibility of each principality. Naturally, the princes used the Imperial elections as a springboard for self-aggrandizement, and there was much jealousy and bickering. The Habsburgs had the added disadvantage of discord within their own family. The disputatious clan was leaderless, and they frequently partitioned the family lands, turning a small principality into a collection of even smaller monuments to sibling rivalry. Still, Austria was a natural power in the empire, and simple geographical logic made the early Habsburgs significant almost in spite of themselves. Because of this, their potential competitors forged agreements meant to keep the Habsburgs from the Imperial throne. Propitious marriage provided a means of circumventing these obstacles. They, in effect, married into their laurels. The very first Habsburg to become Emperor, Albert, Duke of Austria, was also the first Habsburg to use effectively his family ties to political advantage. This was more than mere coincidence. By marrying the Emperor Sigismund's daughter, Albert succeeded in 1438 not only to his father-in-law's crowns in Hungary and Bohemia but to the long-withheld Imperial crown as well. The marriage proved a boon, and the lesson was not lost on the family, which would repeat Albert's success with a vengeance over the next two centuries. Albert himself was unprepossessing, as many of his descendants would be, and he died shortly after his accession. But the pattern was set. His cousin Frederick of Styria assumed the burden of the empire in his stead, and for the next four centuries the empire was a Habsburg patrimony. For the next four decades, Frederick governed to mixed reviews. His son Maximilian took the next step; a colorful and complex man, Max best expressed the Habsburg policy of consolidation and expansion. Through his marriage to the heiress of Charles the Bold he inherited all of Burgundy. He also tightened control over his Austrian relatives, and against great resistance he attempted to yoke the Holy Roman Empire, efforts that bore fruit in 1498, when his Imperial Supreme Court was permanently established and a tax was imposed. Never before had an institution been given full jurisdiction in all the principalities. Yet Max was better known as a progenitor of great rulers than as a great ruler himself, with fairly good reason. Some of his schemes simmer with lunacy, such as his plan to abdicate his throne and aspire to canonization, so that his daughter would be compelled to worship him. Whatever his failings, Maximilian I had an unerring knack for propitious marriages. Through his own marriage, those he arranged for his two children, and his well-timed intervention in the lives of his grandchildren, he was truly the architect of the Habsburg rise to European hegemony. He laid the groundwork for an empire the way a new bride gathers together a household--she begins with a trousseau and adds to it wedding gifts and purchases. Under the guidance of Maximilian and his similarly canny sixteenth-century heirs, the Habsburgs accumulated power like a series of wedding gifts. And the best of those gifts came from Spain.

The glory that was to become Spain gave few indications of its imminence in the fifteenth century. As we have noted, the Iberian peninsula was divided into three major, if disorganized, states, which were in turn partitioned into smaller, often uncooperative, provinces. The kingdoms of Portugal, Aragon, and Castile were considered backwaters by the rest of Europe. Safely blocked by the Pyrenees, Spain was absorbed in its internal affairs and played no real part in the power struggles of the rest of the continent, although the Portuguese were already looking toward worlds beyond Europe.

The geographic alignment of the peninsula was awkward; Portugal, on the west coast, dominated the Atlantic and was most notable for its seafaring. Aragon was composed of three fiercely protective provinces--Valencia, Aragon, and Catalonia--that faced the Mediterranean from the east coast and across it the empire Aragon had once controlled. And Castile occupied the arid central region, including most of the peninsula. Neither Portugal nor Aragon was economically vibrant in the fifteenth century. But Castile, with two-thirds of the territory of the peninsula and three-quarters of the population, had enormous potential as a European power. There was wealth in Castile, and still more interesting was a unique combination of circumstances that shaped Castile, dominated Portugal and Aragon, and gave birth to an Iberian state that was to be the Habsburgs sixteenth-century base of power.

First of all, forgetting for a moment the later effects of the Inquisition, Spain was characterized by a heterogeneous society; Jews, Christians, and Moors lived in a spirit of mutual tolerance throughout the peninsula from the Middle Ages until the fifteenth century. Each cultural group developed different sides of the peninsula's multifarious character; the Moors, who had arrived as conquerors in the eighth century and had remained as cultivators, became the backbone of Castilian agriculture. Under their patient care, out of the deserts of Granada orchards and towns blossomed. The Jews, despite occasional persecutions, worked their way into merchant activity, finance, and even the highest circles of government. Many of the Castilian monarchs relied entirely on Jews in matters of finance and also medicine. The Christians had a vitality of a different sort; the warlike, nomadic ideals of the Middle Ages were enshrined in the Spanish nobility, which looked askance at the quiet growth of the multi-religious society. These ideals of chivalry, conquest rather than cultivation, and disdain for merchant activity were not limited to the nobility. They permeated the entire society. As Cervantes's Sancho Panza tells his lord Don Quixote, "I am an old Christian, and to become an Earl that is sufficient." "And more than sufficient," replies the knight. 3 What the Christian nobility added to the mix was a predatory drive toward homogeneity. Since the eighth century they had been wholly consumed with the "reconquista," the struggle to regain their long-lost territory from the Moors. The entire society of Castile was centered on this mission, and as demographic pressure slowly pushed the Moors ever southward, the nobles to whom the crusade was entrusted became increasingly powerful and energetic. Although they comprised less than 2 percent of the population, the aristocracy owned directly or indirectly over 97 percent of the peninsula. 4 The Church was also well endowed with wealth: 6 million ducats was its annual income at a time when one ducat paid the wages of a skilled worker for eight days. 5 Together, the nobility and the Spanish Church would do much to determine the destiny of sixteenth-century Spain.

As the fifteenth century drew to a close, Castile entertained a number of dynamic, convergent threads: the reconquest restored territorial integrity and created a rich, powerful class of aristocrats fit only to wage war: the strengthened Catholic Church supported the zeal of the conquerors and through that zeal became a feasible mechanism of social organization, and while the Christians found their identity in conquests the "alien" cultures helped create Spanish agriculture, commerce, government and finance.

A vacuum of leadership neutralized much of this nascent vitality, for the peninsula had a tradition of ineffectual or unwise kings dating back to the legendary Pedro the Cruel. The elements of a powerful state were present, yet in the face of an entrenched aristocracy, standing monarchical power was limited. Here again a historical juncture presented the individual monarch with a great opportunity virtually to transform his (or her) age. In Spain, a wave had swelled: by the middle of the fifteenth century, it had yet to overtake the entire peninsula, but its energy and momentum clearly gave the promise of a great crest and distance. Its effect would be a question of direction. It remained for the opportunistic monarch to channel the wave's energy, after becoming its master. This was the task before Ferdinand of Aragon and Isabella of Castile, the two remarkable monarchs who engaged most of the peninsula in a common, even holy, mission and thus created the most energetic state in Europe. In a sense they hastened an age, then passed their torch to the Habsburgs as their own family failed to thrive. In doing so, Ferdinand and Isabella embodied all the most admirable, most reprehensible, and, more relevant to our running theme, the most pitiable aspects of Renaissance royalty.

Like their contemporaries Henry VII of England the Louis XII of France, Ferdinand and Isabella (hereafter referred to by the title bestowed on them by Pope Alexander VI: the Catholic Kings) were not "to the monarchy born. " Theirs was the most tortuous and perilous route to the throne, over the obstacles presented by jealous and warped relatives. If outstanding warriors could be endowed with the nobility of the sword, the Catholic Kings were ennobled by the sword of state, through their prowess in statecraft and realpolitik. Isabella had an especially difficult route to power, and only the combination of ineptitude and biological default in her half-brother Henry IV brought the neglected princess out of the shadows. The Trastamara line, which had started less than auspiciously with the bastard sons of Alfonso XI, had come to an abrupt halt with Henry, known to history as "Henry the Impotent. " The best evidence indicated to his contemporaries that he was sterile, if indeed he managed to

summon enough interest in his two wives to bring the issue
to a test. In such matters hope sprung eternal, and there
was a half-hearted attempt to advance the daughter of the
queen as Henry's legitimate heiress. This seems perfectly
reasonable, but the queen was known to be the mistress of
one Dom Beltran de Cueva, Henry was known to be homosexual, and poor Juana was saddled with the humiliating suf-
fix "La Beltraneja." Regardless of Juana's parentage, the
great majority of Castilians aware of the situation doubted
that she was Henry's true daughter, and their scorn made
her a completely unacceptable candidate for the throne. The
succession was uncertain, and Castile fell prey to the same
kind of civil unrest that befell England, Scotland, and France
under similar circumstances. If there was a common pattern across western Europe, civil unrest in the train of an
uncertain succession was certainly a part of that scheme.
Henry IV was himself no comfort to Castilians. He was, at
best, pathetic; fond of young men, weak, and a constant object of ridicule. Among the powerful noble families Henry
commanded no respect, and under his stewardship the monarchical office in Castile was sadly undermined. Perhaps
his biological failings were as damaging to his position as
his political missteps. Foremost among these difficulties
was his inability to sire an heir; a project Henry shared with
his entire court, two different wives, and a bevy of physicians. Their failure was not for lack of invention. Though
no one can be certain, Henry might well have been the first
practitioner of artificial insemination, in this case a crude
business involving numerous and contorted pieces of brass
tubing, the doctors, and the king's male favorites as coax-
ing sirens.

For all this hardship and the reams of calumny elicited, Henry harbored no ill feelings toward his half-sister
Isabella, who appeared likely to be his successor. Political
pressures forced him to reconsider, and as Henry vacillated
between the factions supporting and opposing the heretofore
insignificant princess, life became difficult for the strong-
minded girl. Finally, at a banquet in 1474, Henry was apparently ready to announce Isabella and her husband Ferdinand as his successors, but he was prevented from doing so
by a sudden and mysterious attack. This misfortune was
capped with Henry's death shortly afterwards, his successor
still undetermined. A renewed spurt of rebellion challenged
the unanointed Isabella in her path to the throne, and Castile
was in a pitiable state.

Isabella the Catholic was the eldest child of Juan II
of Castile's second marriage. Juan died four years after
her birth, and her mother--who tottered characteristically on
the edge of madness--had not been quite functional since Isabella's delivery, after which she launched into a "profunda
tristeza"6 and would speak to no one but the king. Under
these circumstances Isabella's education was spotty. Fatherless, with a speechless mother, and safely removed from
the succession, Isabella lingered like an orphan on the fringe;
her parents were unable to look out for her interests, and
her half-brother Henry certainly had no reason to do so.
Mired in his own considerable personal problems, Henry was
persuaded to treat his sibling as a threat to his tenuous sovereignty. It was in his interest to keep Isabella in the background, ill-educated and thoroughly drab. In such straits
she was an unlikely candidate to supplant him. Isabella herself, not given to complaint as an adult, later admitted to
her chronicler Pulgar: "I was brought up in great necessity. "7

As the princess came into her adolescence, Henry
tried persistently, or as persistently as he tried to accomplish anything, to marry Isabella out of his domain. Most
of her suitors were terribly undesirable, including the aged
and corpulent Alfonso V of Portugal--she had sent her chap-
lain off to gather information about them and was not encouraged by his report. 8 Alfonso bore the nickname "El
Africano, " and Isabella was determined to resist him and
the rest of the distasteful assortment. Her strong will more
than matched Henry's weak initiative, and in subtle ways she
proceeded to arrange her own marriage, something that was
just not done at this time in Europe. As apparent heiress
in Castile, her logical choices would appear to have been
Aragon or Portugal. Merged with Castile either state would
have sufficed to begin a peninsular consolidation, but through
biological accident Isabella had a counterpart in Aragon: the
swarthy and small-featured Ferdinand. In 1469 they seemed
to each other an ideal match; both owed their new-found
prominence to the aberrations of elder siblings (Ferdinand's
brother Carlos of Viana was, like Isabella's mother, insane),
both were eighteen, unmarried, and they had complimentary
inheritances on the Iberian peninsula. Thus, with the aid of
Ferdinand's father, who approved heartily his son's marriage
into powerful Castile, the two stole off in 1469, met for the
first time, and married. Ferdinand's father bestowed a title
on his son to enhance his stature and forged the required

Papal dispensation.   The real document was secured shortly after, though pious Isabella felt badly about that part of the elopement.   So the union of the crowns was accomplished, precarious as it seemed at that point.   Henry IV, among a number of jealous others, failed to see the advantage of the illicit marriage, and the couple became fugitives, at least in Castile.   This was more than a formal marriage; from the first the pair were partners, and in the face of adversity --rebellion, royal disfavor, constant travel, lack of money-- they performed admirably in tandem.   From the first they realized the essence of their mission, as they explained curtly in a missive to Henry IV shortly after their clandestine wedding:

> Were it necessary to wait for everyone's accord
> and consent this would be very difficult to obtain
> or else so much time would have passed that in
> these realms great peril would arise because of the
> absence of children to continue the succession. [9]

Circumventing the envious and the failed, Ferdinand and Isabella took it upon themselves to reinvigorate the decayed Trastamara line.   Their very behavior toward each other signaled a return to royal health that was favorably noted by contemporaries; Pulgar wrote the oft-repeated line, "The favorite of the king was the queen; the favorite of the queen was the king."[10]   And Ortiz commented that Ferdinand and Isabella "share a single mind."[11]

Yet the romantic legends of the princely couple who chose each other avoid certain, less harmonious, elements in their union.   Isabella married an eighteen-year-old prince who was already the father of an illegitimate son, and although Ferdinand treated his wife with great courtesy and respect, he continued to wander after marriage.   Isabella, for all her qualities, was not particularly appealing: she had a round face, an irregular nose, and was rather heavy-limbed. Ferdinand fathered five known bastards, not uncommon for robust kings in an unbridled age, but nonetheless a sorrow to the devoted and proud queen.   Still further evidence of her dignity and intelligent restraint, she never allowed her disappointment to become divisive, open bitterness.   She did, however, allow herself the luxury of exiling her husband's paramours once she knew of their existence.

The second major source of disharmony was Isabella's inability to bear a son in their first, politically crucial, years of marriage. The sickly Isabella was born a year after their marriage in 1470, but this august omen was followed by a series of miscarriages over the next eight years. The lack of a son took on added significance after the death of Henry IV in 1474; the Catholic Kings needed a male heir to establish themselves in Castile. Others clamored for the throne. Alfonso of Portugal invaded Castile to advance "La Beltraneja's" claim, the King of France invaded Biscay, and both Ferdinand and Isabella made separate claims to the throne. Modern historians have attributed Isabella's obstetrical failures to her ceaseless travels across Castile to quell rebellion. These political concerns undermined her health, and ironically created more political concerns in the absence of a long-awaited male heir. [12] For all their acumen, the Catholic Kings did not end peninsular war and internal discord until 1478, when they crowned their success and consolidated their gains with the birth of prince Juan. In the next seven years, three more children would follow, providing the crafty Ferdinand with the tools for dynasty building. Like the Habsburgs who would ultimately absorb his dynasty, Ferdinand had a strategy for continental proliferation. As Pulgar wrote to Isabella after the birth of Juan, "If your Highness gives us two or three more daughters, in twenty years' time you will have the pleasure of seeing your children and grandchildren on all the thrones of Europe."[13]

Ferdinand himself was temperamental and easily offended. Like Isabella, he was ignored until his older brother went mad. The prince was raised almost as a barbarian, and at the age of ten, he was sent off to the wars, where he spent most of his youth. Between battles and hunting Ferdinand never changed his quasi-illiterate ways. Perhaps the only auspicious note in his childhood was the alignment of the cosmos at the hour of his birth; the ambassador Mariano reported the heavens to be uncommonly serene as the prince was delivered. [14] Serenity was definitely not characteristic of Ferdinand, however. Despite his overall satisfaction with the Union of the Crowns and with Isabella, he feared that the marriage contract, in which Isabella made it clear that she was to reign in Castile, insulted his manhood, and pouted over incidents in which Isabella revealed something of a masculine character. [15] In one particularly nettling instance, Isabella allowed the Sword of State to be carried before her train while Ferdinand fumed, later claiming that precedent called for the sword to precede his entourage. The Queen of Castile had more political power than Ferdinand, who was King of Aragon but only Isabella's consort in Castile: the two crowns were truly united only in their sovereigns. But what Ferdinand gave away in political power he probably regained in his personal relations with his wife, where he had the undoubted upper hand. Perhaps he used this as a lever, for Talavera admonished the king, urging him to be "far more wholehearted in the love and devotion which you owe to your excellent and very worthy wife."[16]

Regardless of the undercurrents in their marriage and political partnership, Ferdinand and Isabella forged a remarkable achievement. As a modern historian has explained, "They possessed, in well nigh irresistible abundance, native attractions long absent from the Castilian royal house--normalcy, rectitude, bearing, and buoyant health."[17] The stability Ferdinand and Isabella brought to the Iberian peninsula can only be appreciated in comparison with their continental peers. From the time of Ferdinand's accession in Aragon until his death in 1515, Europe crowned and buried four kings of England and France, three kings of Portugal, and two Holy Roman Emperors. The healthy presence of two sane, fertile, adult rulers gave the state the Catholic Kings created from the chaos of Castile and Aragon a great advantage over its global competitors in the late fifteenth century.

The achievements of the Catholic Kings had a common theme: the unification and pacification of the peninsula. To do this, they established a medieval institution known as the Santa Hermandad to police the roads and villages, creating order within Castile. They channeled the energies of the aristocracy toward the final expulsion of the Moors, which was accomplished in 1492, rewarded them copiously with land grants, and financed Columbus in his efforts to find a New World--another outlet for the martial talents of Spain. At the same time they ordered the expulsion or conversion of all non-Christians, a move based on the conscience of Isabella and the calculation of Ferdinand. With these measures, however reprehensible to the modern spirit, they established a unified state, gained a measure of control over the nobility, and infused Spain with a higher purpose. It has been argued, quite convincingly in fact, that with its policy of enforced homogeneity Spain robbed itself of the only native elements that could develop a genuine economic structure. However true this may be, the Catholic Kings achieved the kind of crusading, well ordered state they envisioned, the ideal base for Imperial expansion. Under their guidance Spain became the most dynamic power in Christendom. Perhaps Niccolo Machiavelli, the Florentine statesman and political sage, summed up the achievements of Ferdinand and Isabella best in Chapter XXI of his short handbook on power politics, The Prince:

> Nothing makes a prince so much esteemed as the undertaking of great enterprises and the setting a noble example in his own person. We have a striking example of this in Ferdinand of Aragon, the Present King of Spain. He may be called, as it were, a new prince; for, from being King of a feeble state, he has, by his fame and glory, become the first sovereign of Christendom; and if we examine his actions we shall find them all most grand, and some of them extraordinary. In the beginning of his reign he attacked Granada, and it was this undertaking that was the very foundation of his greatness. At first he carried on this war leisurely and without fear of opposition; for he kept the nobles of Castile occupied with this enterprise, and, their minds being thus engaged by war, they gave no attention to the innovations introduced by the King, who thereby acquired a reputation and an influence over the nobles without their being aware of it. The money of the Church and of the people enabled him to support his armies and by that long war he succeeded in giving a stable foundation to his military establishment, which afterward brought him so much honor. Besides this, to be able to engage in still greater enterprises, he always availed himself of religion as a pretext, and committed a pious cruelty in spoliating and driving the Moors out of his kingdom, which certainly was a most admirable and extraordinary example. Under the same cloak of religion he attacked Africa, and made a descent upon Italy, and finally assailed France. And thus he was always planning great enterprises, which kept the minds of his subjects in a state of suspense and admiration, and occupied with their results. And these different enterprises followed so quickly one upon the other, that he never gave men a chance deliberately to make any attempt against himself. [18]

Machiavelli can be forgiven a few errors; an attempt was indeed made on Ferdinand's life, in 1503, and Isabella was as much a part of the rise, if not more, as Ferdinand, although the Florentine ignored her contribution entirely.

For all this success Ferdinand and Isabella were beset with troubles before the end of the fifteenth century, the
sort of trouble we have noted in so many monarchs. The
essential frailty of their renovated dynasty was their new opponent, a competitor more fearsome than any previous rival.
After 1496 Isabella's health, which had stood the test of so
many trials, began to falter. By September of 1498 she was
extremely ill; for months she was prostrated and lethargic,
unable to consider state business.[19] But the most serious
blows were a series of catastrophes involving her children,
what Spanish historians refer to as her "tres cuchillos de
color": first, the infante Prince Juan died in 1497 after only
six months of marriage. Next, her eldest daughter Isabella,
perhaps her favorite child, died in childbirth in 1498. And
finally in 1500 young Isabella's posthumous child Miguel,
heir to the entire Iberian peninsula because of Prince Juan's
death and his mother's marriage to the King of Portugal, died
at the age of two. In addition, Juan's wife Margaret of Austria miscarried their child shortly after the prince's death.
At the turn of the century, only Juana and two younger daughters remained of all the Trastamara heirs of the Catholic
Kings, and Isabella well knew of the girl's mental instability.
All that she and Ferdinand had accomplished seemed to van-
ish in a rash of child mortalities, and the queen never recovered from the loss. In 1500 she broke down openly and
thereafter spent long hours weeping and brooding. Her religious devotions became alarmingly excessive. Swellings
and ulcers ravaged her legs, she became too weak to walk,
too weak even to write letters by 1503. In that year Pedro
Martyr wrote to Tendilla: "Her whole system is pervaded
by a consuming fever. She loathes food of every kind, and
is tormented with incessant thirst, while the disorder has all
the appearance of terminating in a dropsy."[20] Her heart
failed and her circulation became inadequate: her body
swelled with edema, her limbs ballooned, she had episodic
fits. Medical historians have considered these symptoms,
concluding that diabetes was her basic ailment. But whatever the cause, she was beyond the help of sixteenth-century
medicine, and sought only the comfort of her husband's
presence. This too was denied her during her last hours,
when Ferdinand contracted a fever and was unable to leave
his chamber. By October 7, 1504, all hope was abandoned.
Martyr described the final hours: "We sit sorrowfully in
the palace all day long, trembling awaiting the hour, when
religion and virtue shall quit the earth with her."[21] In her
final testament she asked to be buried next to her husband,
for even after thirty years of occasional clashes she insisted
that they had always lived in "deep love and conformity."[22]

Ferdinand, less conscience-ridden and more sanguine, took his partner's death as an opportunity to consolidate his own power in his dominions--in express disregard of Isabella's will. Ferdinand was, above all, an ambitious man, and his all-too-equal partnership with Isabella had grated on his masculine pride, as we have noted. After Isabella's death he took steps toward the creation of a new peninsular dynasty, in which he was to be undisputed head. To this end he quickly placed himself on the marriage market, in the hope of siring a son and heir to supplant his daughter Juana and her arrogant Burgundian husband Philip "the Handsome." Ferdinand negotiated for the French princess Germaine de Foix, an eighteen-year-old, and married her less than a year after Isabella's death: many found this distastefully soon after the demise of the popular Isabella. In his haste Ferdinand won no bargain; Germaine was "not very pretty, somewhat lame in one leg, given to amusing herself in banquets and fiestas," according to the ambassador Sandoval. [23] Observers duly noted the consummation of the union, but the requisite fruit was not forthcoming; only the sickly Prince Juan, who saw but a few hours light in 1509, issued from the second marriage. And the cunning that Machiavelli found so admirable in Ferdinand won him no accolades in Spain after the death of saintly Isabella. In fact, many Spaniards found his opportunistic assumption of the Castilian regency in Juana's name and his indecently hasty second marriage offensive. He encountered much opposition to his ambitions.

These and other disappointments, including the sorrows so devastating for Isabella, failed to jar Ferdinand's sanguine disposition. His entire career had been marked by a certain insensitivity--he was clearly calculating, while Isabella acted for the most part on the basis of Catholic and Castilian conscience, in that order. Yet this phlegmatic character might have been part of the king's secret for longevity. He merely shrugged off an attempted assassination in 1503 and prosecuted the course of religious persecution without reluctance. In fact, he used the Inquisition both as an instrument of state policy and for personal vendettas. He supervised its every detail, down to the salary paid to doorkeepers at each tribunal, and to cite just one instance, in 1509 used it to pursue a Borgia political enemy. [24] Still more cruel, he allowed his personal physician Ribas Allas to be burned at the stake. Allas was a Jew, as were many of the best Castilian physicians. (What is surprising is that Isabella acquiesced in this matter, as Allas was also her doctor.)

The soldier's lifestyle also rewarded Ferdinand; his temperance at the table and regular exercise took him into his sixties before he encountered serious health problems. But as he attempted to consolidate his position without Isabella, he began to weaken. In 1513, fearful of his fading faculties, he was persuaded to take strange medications to restore his vigor. This treatment backfired, plunging him into maladies previously unknown to him: "Instead of his habitual equanimity and cheerfulness, he became impatient and irascible, and was frequently prey to morbid melancholy."25 Still hoping for a son, Ferdinand allowed his new wife to concoct for him new revitalizing potions. Her choice of ingredients had a certain symbolic, if not medical, logic: hormones from a bull's testicles, for one. Yet the potion only served to make Ferdinand ill.

Heart disease finally ended Ferdinand's peninsular schemes, all of which were frustrated by Castile's unwillingness to accept him as overlord after Isabella's death. Still, the Catholic Kings had accomplished a tremendous amount in tandem; Aragon and Castile were linked, Castile was the closest thing to a workable state in Europe, the New World belonged primarily to Castile, the Moors had finally been expelled, and the crusade for orthodoxy infused all levels of Spanish society with a relatively plastic zeal. How ironic it seems then, that just as these faits became accomplis the entire dynasty virtually sank into the dry Castilian soil. After all they had done to forge powerful sixteenth-century Spain, the Catholic Kings had no one to maintain their achievement. Once again biological catastrophe in the royal line emerged face up, as the wild card in the deck of European development.

In 1485, with the birth of Catherine (later the bride of Henry VIII) the Spanish succession seemed safe, with four healthy daughters and a son. Not twenty years later all appeared lost for the family of the Catholic Kings. Apparently doomed before the revitalization of Ferdinand and Isabella, the Trastamara line resumed its biological decline with their heirs. As was the case with most of the tragedies involving royal offspring, the children of Ferdinand and Isabella were naturally weak, and this inherent frailty was overstrained by the ambitious projects into which they were rushed.

Prince Juan was born in 1478, immediately ending peninsular war and civil discord. After such an auspicious debut, this single son was clearly the Trastamara's hope for

the future.   Yet from his infancy there were signs of trouble.
Even though court observers concentrated only on the silver
lining to this cloud, Juan was a strange creature, and hints
of disease surfaced in his treatment.   The boy was carefully
husbanded, ate only the blandest foods, and according to
Pedro Martyr was treated "like an invalid."[26]   His chief
tutor also described the prince as "often ill."   But to Isabella he was "my angel."   Perhaps she was blind to Juan's
failings, but others were not.   Shielded in his own household,
where he was educated among the sons of Spanish noblemen,
Juan was a conspicuously slow learner.   Although no one
dared voice their suspicion, the prince appeared to be retarded.   Other genetic legacies surfaced in childhood; his deformed lower lip anticipated the famous "Habsburg jaw," and
his voice was strange and squeaky.   In addition, he stuttered.
Court wags spread the rumor that Juan was attached sexually
to his childhood nurse, which was dubious, but there was no
mistaking the boy's abnormally slow development.   One had
only to look at him; he never slept without a night-light and
craved sweets incessantly.

Such a prince was hardly ready for marriage at the
age of eighteen.   Court physicians warned that the boy was
"of precarious health."   In fact, "the young prince had never
been of robust health," they told Isabella. [27]   Yet, by 1496
plans had been made; a suitable princess, Margaret of Austria, had been secured for the prince, with the corresponding
alliance.   Actually, at eighteen Juan was hardly a young
bridegroom, but too much of Ferdinand's plan to encircle
France depended on the union with the Habsburg princess.
The marriage went ahead as planned.   All concerns aside,
Spanish fortunes appeared to be at a high point in 1498.
Negotiations for a general peace--for the first time in years
--were underway, an important alliance had been concluded
that wedged France between Spain, Burgundy, and the Holy
Roman Empire, and the future of the succession seemed assured.   Still, the physicians warned of Juan's frailty and
asked that the honeymoon be postponed until the prince grew
into better health.   But royal marriage was meaningless without demonstrable consummation and cohabitation, and Isabella reportedly answered the doctors with the quasi-biblical
rejoinder, "Those whom God hath joined together, let no man
put asunder."[28]   Was it respect for the institution of matrimony that dulled Isabella's maternal instincts or was it
Ferdinand's ambitions?   Both were undoubtedly taken into
consideration, but Ferdinand's influence over his wife in
such matters is well documented.   Juan, for his part, was

genuinely delighted with the marriage. He found his bride
charming, an opinion confirmed by the rest of Europe.
Everyone seemed pleased, but there were warnings for anyone willing to listen, as Martyr wrote:

> But it is to be feared that these qualities (Mar-
> garet's attractiveness) bring with them the misfor-
> tune and ruin of Spain, because our young prince
> is becoming pallid, consumed with passion. The
> doctors and the King himself beg the queen to inter-
> vene and separate the newlyweds. They ask her to
> seek a respite in the incessant acts of love and
> they warn of the danger that these will incur. Again
> and again they call attention to the paleness of her
> son's face and his fatigued manner, adding that the
> sickness is attacking his marrow and weakening his
> very being. [29]

Later in 1496 Prince Juan died, becoming the legendary
"Principe que Murio de Amor": The Prince Who Died of
Love. One cannot doubt that such avid "copula" may have
drained Juan's strength, but his ultimate demise probably
resulted from the consumption hidden in his genetic heritage.
His death came as a terrible shock across the continent,
especially after he had been celebrated as such a model
prince. The French chronicler Commynes noted that "I
have never heard of so solemn and so universal a mourning
for any prince in Europe. "[30]

If there was any consolation for Isabella in her son's
death it was the pregnancy of Juan's wife Margaret. Perhaps
the princess would deliver a son to take his father's place in
the succession. But as Martyr noted bitterly early in 1497,
"The Imperial Margaret, instead of producing the desired offspring, presented us with a formless mass of meat. "[31]

With Juan dead and his offspring miscarried, the
Catholic Kings' eldest daughter Isabella took on added significance. Their first child, born in 1470, the girl was thin,
pale, strangely serious, excessively religious, and probably
tubercular. Queen Isabella, never lighthearted herself,
dubbed her namesake "madre" ("mother") because of her abnormally sober disposition. Some have taken her lack of
spontaneity and her excessively morbid character to be evidence of neurotic tendencies. If so, her lack of health undoubtedly did much to undermine her attitude. Young Isabella was constantly plagued with pulmonary ailments and

lived the life of a consumptive.   But even frail and melancholy children were assigned a role in dynastic politics; to
her mother's mixture of chagrin and satisfaction about the
alliance gained, the girl was sent to renew Castilian ties
with Portugal in her twentieth year.   Her intended was the
fifteen-year-old heir to the Portuguese throne, Dom Alfonso,
son of John II.   This seeming misalliance apparently turned
to warm regard, only to be thwarted eight months later by
Alfonso's untimely death in a hunting accident.   While out
riding the prince was swept off his horse by a protruding
tree branch and he never regained consciousness.   Isabella's
moroseness was further entrenched, and she made it known
to her parents that she would not remarry.   The sovereigns
were suitably impressed by her grief to let the issue pass
unchallenged. 32   Her behavior was certainly somber; she reportedly slept in wool and lived the life of a nun.   With dry
understatement a contemporary reported that "she is more
given to tears than singing. "33   For all her undoubted misery, one cannot be certain whether these prostrations stemmed
from the death of Alfonso or the natural inclinations of the
princess.   Her family was noted for its melancholia.

Melancholy aside, Isabella's Portuguese marriage had
served a useful function.   It had severed these Castilian
neighbors from the cause of Isabella's nettling rival "La
Beltraneja. "   Yet the alliance was endangered after Alfonso's
death.   Oblivious to such concerns Isabella lived for eight
years in retirement, spurning offers of marriage.   Her most
persistent suitor was the uncle of her late husband, Manuel
"the Fortunate, " an extremely vain man prone to private
magnificence. 34   What Manuel lacked in personal charm and
achievement he compensated for, to some extent, with his
virility; Manuel the Prolific fathered twenty-two legitimate
heirs after claiming the throne from his relatively fruitless
brother, according to the Portuguese observer Cabrera de
Cordoba.   His suit was encouraged by Ferdinand and Isabella, who savored the prospect of a unified peninsula.   The
eldest son of a marriage between mournful Isabella and
potent Manuel stood to inherit Portugal, Aragon, and Castile
and had claims to smaller territories.   Isabella finally
yielded to their persuasion, although not before stipulating
her conditions.   First, she demanded an austere wedding, to
which she apparently wore black; she was then in mourning
for her brother Prince Juan.   Isabella was also, like her
mother, a devout Catholic, and before she finally agreed to
espouse Manuel, she insisted that he join his Spanish neighbors in the crusade for religious homogeneity.   In practical

terms, this meant that Portuguese Jews who failed to adopt
Christianity were forced to leave, and an Inquisition similar
to the fearful Spanish tribunals was given license to root out
"heresy." With this marriage Castile allied itself almost
inextricably with Portugal, and, still more interesting, even
exported its own basis of social organization.

Within months of the wedding in 1498, Isabella became pregnant. The succession problem of the Catholic
Kings appeared to be solved. Isabella herself would not suffice, as the Cortes of Aragon had indicated when she came
north to be proclaimed heiress to her father's domains. Invoking the age-old ban on female succession, they refused to
accept her. Yet, through some obscure legal provision, her
son was perfectly acceptable to the Cortes. Everything
awaited the result of her pregnancy, as she well knew.
Tragically, Isabella's constitution was no stronger than her
brother Juan's had been. Later in 1498 the sickly twenty-
eight-year-old princess summoned forth an almost Herculean
effort and delivered her son Miguel, heir in Castile, Aragon,
and Portugal. The protracted strain of this difficult birth
overcame Isabella's resistance, and she died almost immediately after the ordeal. Sad, dutiful Isabella had accomplished
her dynastic mission. Now all hope centered on the frail
baby prince. This too was unfounded, for Miguel lived only
two years. After his death in 1500, with Queen Isabella's
health failing as well, the fate of the peninsular monarchies
seemed no more secure than it had been in 1474.

After Isabella in the Castilian-Aragonese succession
came Juana, Maria, and finally Catherine. Maria was non-
descript and by all accounts the most normal of the royal
brood, and historians have characterized her as the happiest
as well. What her own feelings were regarding her life can
only be speculated, but hers was certainly a successful career from a diplomatic perspective. Raised at court along
with her brothers and sisters, Maria had none of Juana's
talent, Juan's charm, or even Isabella's stubborness. A
recessive chin marred her appearance, which none of the
contemporary chroniclers bothered to exalt. And as the
third daughter she attracted little notice anyway. Yet even
neglected princesses had a role to play; Maria's was given
to her at the age of eighteen, when she was sent to Portugal
to salvage that crucial alliance after her sister Isabella's
death. Manual "the Fortunate," once her brother-in-law,
became her husband, and like the dutiful princess she was
Maria bore the Portuguese King ten children during their

seventeen-year union. Eight of the ten lived to adulthood, providing Portugal with a full generation of heirs. The delivery of her final child, Prince Antonio, ended the bland queen's life in 1517. Her youngest sister, Catherine, might well have wished for the same, common fate: death in childbed with a male heir. Sent off to England as a part of Ferdinand's strategy of encirclement, Catherine was illtreated by the Tudors and through no fault of her own became embroiled in controversy. She had been sent to marry Prince Arthur, but Arthur died shortly after their nuptials. Many doubted that the marriage had been consummated, and Catherine herself denied that conjugal relations had taken place. There was evidence, however circumstantial, to the contrary, and for years after Arthur's death, the English were at a loss about what to do with the stranded princess. Despite her misery Ferdinand refused to bring her back to Spain, preferring to negotiate a match with Arthur's brother Henry. This was accomplished in 1510, the same year Henry became king. As the first of Henry VIII's six wives, Catherine's sad story is all too familiar. Prematurely aged and unable to deliver a son, she was scorned by her husband and too far from Spain to be aided by her dwindling family. Her plight was her dilemma alone until her nephew, Charles V of Spain, refused to allow the Pope to divorce her from Henry VIII at Henry's request.

The mixed careers of the two youngest daughters notwithstanding, it was Juana who stood to inherit the crowns of the Catholic Kings after the death of sister Isabella and her son Miguel. This was a sobering prospect that pleased neither Ferdinand nor his queen. Yet Juana was perhaps the most attractive, most lively member of the royal family. Although gadflies pointed to her dark complexion, strangely formed left eye, long nose, and curious forehead, most regarded Juana as a slim and pretty brunette. Nor did she lack intelligence. In 1495 she was lauded as "very clever for her age and sex at writing."[35] She was musical and often performed before the assembled court. Yet even as a child she was subject to strange and arbitrary moods and sought seclusion. Her health belied her mental disturbance, however, as she was far more robust than her brothers and sisters.

In 1496, when the Trastamara fortunes appeared secure, Juana had been married to the Habsburg prince Philip "the Handsome" simultaneously to her brother Juan's union with Philip's sister Margaret. The Emperor Maximilian

deployed his two children prudently, for there could be no
better match from a dynastic standpoint than dynamic Spain.
And with this pair of marriages, Maximilian had tied his
house to their fortunes, almost as though he knew that the
inherent fragility of the Trastamaras would present the Habsburgs with an unparalleled windfall. Such pragmatism aside,
the love Juana nurtured for Prince Philip is in itself one of
history's strangest stories. According to Martyr, who observed the scene, Juana was "perdidamenta enamorada" almost from the moment she set eyes on her husband to be. [36]
The profligate Philip was hardly the proper consort for an
unstable woman such as Juana. He was an insatiable sexual
athlete, with a particular yen for deflowering virgins, and
he grew bored of his conquests almost as soon as his yearn-
ing had been sated. Poor Juana was no exception to this
rule. In addition to his other failings, Philip was dull of
mind, a vain braggart, undisciplined, and spoiled. He had
the attention span of a ten-year-old, but against better counsel he insisted on dabbling in politics, a field in which he
succeeded only in antagonizing virtually everyone forced to
deal with him, including his father-in-law. Ferdinand was
so put out by this Burgundian buffoon that he remarried partly to produce an heir to subvert Philip's chances at the
thrones of Castile and Aragon, kingdoms that he stood to inherit through his wife. Apparently, Juana either perceived
something worthwhile behind her husband's almost effeminate
features or was satisfied with the delicate features themselves, for she manifested a passion that was pathological
in its intensity. Philip himself was lusty, and the first
meeting with his seventeen-year-old betrothed was apparently
a memorable occasion. Legend has it that Philip greeted his
bride with a searing glance, commanded the nearest cleric
to solemnize their union on the spot, abbreviated the ceremony, and finally carried his young mate up the winding
stairs to the nearest bedchamber, where they indulged their
mutual haste and hunger to the astonishment of onlookers. [37]

All was not to be so inspired as this instant honeymoon, however. In a more rational light, Philip was not
even handsome, with his bad teeth and a ruined knee. Some
of his personality problems no doubt stemmed from his uneven childhood, during which he was passed back and forth
between Burgundy and his father Maximilian's base in Austria. In the shuffle the prince was never educated properly;
in fact, he was never even instructed in the traditional language of the Habsburgs: German. In addition he was raised
in a more licentious atmosphere, for the court of the Nether-

lands had a much less rigorous code of sexual ethics than its more austere Spanish counterpart. Juana and her attendants were initially scandalized by the goings on, but Philip circumvented her distaste by dismissing her Spanish retinue, thus ending their Spanish influence on the girl. In these early years Philip established complete dominance over his bride, a control with repercussions both personal and political. Yet, Juana did not complain. Even if politically neglected and disarmed, the disturbed princess was satisfied romantically, and was only too willing to forget all for her lover. However rewarding their romance, Philip soon returned to his errant ways. Rumors had it that he was again on the prowl only months after his nuptials. Here Juana made her stand. Political privileges meant nothing to her, but infidelity spurred her to violent action. Unlike her long-suffering mother, Juana was unable to restrain her jealousy. In one particularly grim episode, the raving princess attacked a beautiful blond paramour in full view of the assembled court. She scratched the poor girl's face, pulled her hair, and ordered that her blond locks be shorn. Philip reacted to the outbursts with indifference, for he had a powerful lever against his frantic wife: his sexual attentions. Juana craved sex, and when she did not acquiesce to Philip's wishes, as she once did by refusing to dismiss a suite of Moorish slaves, he simply refused to sleep with her. Once, after Philip returned from a hunting trip with a sore leg and locked himself in his chambers, Juana spent the night pounding, scratching at the door, and screaming to be let in. This ardor grew tiresome for Philip, and he took refuge in frequent hunting trips to avoid her incessant demands.

This brusqueness drove Juana further into madness. Her fits became legend, including the wild evening she chased members of the Council around her chambers with a hot poker in hand. In her consuming jealousy she withdrew into her own inner world. "She lived away from all women of the world, except for a laundress, who ... washed her clothes in her presence. And in such a state she existed and curbed her passion before her husband, attending to her needs and waiting on herself like a poor slave," wrote an anonymous Flemish witness. [38] As Fuensilada reported back to the anxious Ferdinand in November 1504, "Things had reached such a bad state between the prince and the princess that unless the Lord miraculously rescued her from the world of fantasy in which she lives and gives him another disposition, it would be impossible for them ever to be in agreement." [39]

Were Philip and Juana merely troubled aristocrats with marital problems, their difficulties, however bizarre, would hardly seem worthy of much attention. But they were not. After 1504 Juana was Queen of Castile, and stood to rule one of Europe's most powerful states. Philip had already inherited Burgundy, and the stewardship of the Holy Roman Empire awaited him after his father Maximilian I's death. This was a frightening prospect. The most immediate problem was Juana. After Isabella's death Ferdinand met with Philip, whom he disliked no end, and agreed that since Juana "was not able or did not wish to rule," they would guide Castile in her stead. [40] Philip went so far as to proclaim himself King of Castile, like Ferdinand directly defying Isabella's will. This was a sad day for Castile; Philip was the first foreign king since the founding of the monarchy eight centuries earlier, and he was a fool in addition. Among other unfortunate episodes, he allowed a Spanish fleet to virtually freeze to death in Iceland. But the nobles welcomed him to Spain in 1506, preferring him to Ferdinand and his schemes. Three months later Philip suddenly took ill, his tongue swelled and blocked his throat, he sank into a coma, and finally died a ghastly death, with his pregnant wife hunched miserably over his smallpox-ridden corpse.

Despite this tormented relationship's warped course, in a practical sense the marriage accomplished much of its original purpose. Reproduction was truly the royal acid test, and relatives on both sides of the family gloried in the couple's biological success. An envoy sent to assess the princess's health in 1498 wrote that he found Juana "beautiful and fat and pregnant."[41] The great matrimonial diplomat Maximilian himself was so taken with the children that he boasted, in the face of so much contrary evidence, that "God was a very good matchmaker when he gave such a woman to such a husband, and such a husband to such a woman."[42] For all her temper storm, Juana had produced an indisputably fine string of children, beginning in the very first years of her marriage. The births of Eleanor in 1498 and then Charles in 1500 sparked great celebrations across the Low Countries. Robust Juana went through her deliveries effortlessly, "without pain or trouble," and some claimed that she actually sang during labor. [43] Her timing was occasionally a bit off though; her labor pains for Charles came about so suddenly that she was unable to reach her chambers, so the greatest prince of the sixteenth century was ushered into the world in the Renaissance equivalent of a bathroom, located off a corridor leading from the great ballroom in the palace at Ghent.   Three more daughters and a son followed Eleanor and Charles in rapid succession.   Most significantly, all of these children lived to adulthood: an almost unparalleled record of six healthy royal offspring born in fewer than ten years of marriage.   This brood was Juana's contribution to the rise of the Habsburgs, for it was these six children who ultimately wrapped the continent in a Habsburg web.   The marriage of Philip and Juana, tumultuous and short-lived as it was, was really the making of the family.   Their eldest son, through his four grandparents, stood heir to: Aragon, from Juana's father Ferdinand; Castile, from Juana's mother Isabella; Austria and quite likely the title Holy Roman Emperor, from Philip's father Maximilian; and the Low Countries, from Philip's mother Mary of Burgundy.

Paradoxically, or so it would seem, the years of Juana's dynastic achievement were also years of increasing instability and declining health.   After Philip returned to Burgundy in 1502, Juana was observed wailing, weeping, or distractedly staring off into space. [44]   Martyr speculated that "perhaps her spirits would improve once her labor pains begin, that is if she should have a happy delivery and should not die due to the disorder of her mind."[45]   But the delivery of her second son Ferdinand, named for his maternal grandfather, did not lift her spirits.   In fact she immediately gave the boy to a wet nurse and set off for Flanders in pursuit of her prodigal Philip.   Once there, she slept badly, ate little or nothing at all, and spoke to no one, according to doctors Soto and Julian.   By 1503 it was whispered in court circles that Juana was becoming consumptive, as her older brother and sister had been.   Reports claimed that since her return to Flanders she had not left her room.   It remained for the peasants who watched her occasional outbursts and strange solitude to coin her nickname: "Juana la Loca" they dubbed her, or Joanna the Insane.   Queen Isabella came to realize her daughter's condition, and wrote the following missive to her son-in-law:

> I beg the prince, my son ... to write to Monsieur Melu or Madame Aloin giving them full authority, that is from the moment the princess leaves us until she reaches his side, to curb her and restrain her from doing the things that her passion can lead her to do, and to keep her from doing anything that will bring danger or dishonor to her person. [46]

But dishonored she was, especially so after the death of Philip in 1506. She had his body exhumed from the monastery of Miraflores and embarked on a strange journey with most of her small children in tow. Everywhere they went observers noted the bizarre procession, and as one onlooker dryly related, "The body did not have the aroma of perfume."[47] Needless to say, this behavior was a great embarrassment to Juana's royal relatives. Reports stressed the gravity of the situation; in 1508 the Bishop of Malaga wrote Ferdinand the Catholic:

> Since then [the last time Ferdinand had seen her] she has not changed her shift, nor, as I believe, has she touched or washed her face. They say that she sleeps on the ground as before. They also report that she urinates very frequently, in a manner never before seen in another person.[48]

She apparently ate from the floor as well. Upon hearing this and other relations, Ferdinand had his daughter moved to the less visible castle of Tordesillas, where she lived the rest of her surprisingly numerous days out of the public view. But there were incidents; in 1518 the captive queen injured a woman after heaving an earthenware tub at her head.[49]

For over thirty years Juana remained at Tordesillas, locked in her own mania. For the purposes of Europe, she had died with her husband in 1506, yet she was still nominal Queen of Castile, and when the provincial oligarchs known as the Communeros rose in revolt in 1520 they talked of restoring her to the throne. Because of Juana's occasional moments of lucidity, the rumor had arisen that she was merely a political prisoner. Unfortunately for the Communeros this was not the case, and after they took Tordesillas and made their case before her, all they could elicit was a benign nod. This episode soon passed, and the queen settled back into darkness. Finally, in 1553 Juana's strong constitution succumbed to an onslaught of infection, bed sores, and ulcers. That she lived to be seventy-six is in itself remarkable, but still more remarkable is the fact that she died of wounds she received after being scalded in a bath, not of geriatric infirmity.

After Philip's death in 1506, the Habsburgs had been in a difficult position; true, the young children stood to inherit much of Europe, but they were not of an age to take on that responsibility. In the meantime there were realms to govern. Ferdinand of Aragon, regent in his mad daughter's name, filled the void in Spain until his death in 1515. After that time the regency fell to Queen Isabella's spiritual adviser, confessor, Inquisitor General, and Archbishop of Toledo: Francisco Ximenez de Cisneros. His was purely a custodial regency. In the north the Emperor Maximilian retained control in the name of his grandson Charles. Maximilian had effectively saved the dynasty during the early years of the century. He rescued the small children from mad Juana and had them brought to Burgundy, where they were nurtured, protected, and educated under the guidance of Margaret of Austria, the unfortunate widow of the Spanish infante Juan. With the single exception of Ferdinand, who was taken by his grandfather Ferdinand to Spain to serve as something of a surety for the future, the children were kept together in a warm royal family environment unique to the Habsburgs. The care lavished on these children cannot be over-emphasized; Charles, for example, was required in Castile--the strongest of his inheritances--as early as 1506, yet he was kept a relatively normal aristocratic youngster in Burgundy until he turned seventeen, "aged in the cask" so to speak.

The children were undoubtedly an extraordinary group. As the eldest son Charles was the most visible, and would become the family's head, but his brothers and sisters were remarkable in their own right. The four sisters became extremely dutiful servants of the family interest across the continent: Eleanor in Portugal and France, Isabella in Denmark, Maria in the long-coveted lands of Bohemia, and Catalina in Portugal. Eleanor was perhaps the least auspicious of the women. Although she was Charles's favorite, she was quite unattractive, with a deformed lip and an odd shape. She was tall, sallow, and long-faced, and one of her ladies at the French court later told the voyeuristic Brantome that "when undressed she was seen to have the trunk of a giantess, yet going lower, she seemed a dwarf, so short were her thighs and legs (see p. 102)."[50] At the age of twenty-one, this unappealing princess was betrothed to the prolific Manual "the Fortunate" of Portugal, who had outlived two previous brides, both of whom were Eleanor's aunts. For all his good fortune and longevity, Manuel himself was aging rapidly, and in 1521, two years after the marriage, he died. He left, not surprisingly, two children with Eleanor, although neither inherited their father's good luck: Carlos died in infancy, and Maria would ultimately be rejected in marriage by Philip

II of Spain. Dubbed "La Abandonada" after this misfortune, she died a spinster at the age of fifty-six.

After Manuel's death Eleanor hastened back to Spain, leaving Maria behind. The Eleanor who returned to Spain was placid, middle-aged in appearance if not in years, and colorless. Yet even this poor princess was not spared from the vile calumny that followed royalty across Europe; there had been rumors that she was pregnant by her stepson John III, and the ambassador Sanuto reported that she planned to marry the boy--which proved only that even the sage Venetians were wrong on occasion. [51] Those who saw her were shocked. Dantiscus, who had seen her ten years before, noted in 1526 that she had become almost hideous. She was now fat, heavy featured, and dotted with angry red patches "as if she had elephantiasis."[52] But for all these flaws, she was still available in 1526, and her Imperial brother Charles had plans for her. In that year King Francis I of France had been taken prisoner at the battle of Pavia in Italy. Francis was a widower, and Charles saw a golden opportunity to enmesh giant France, the empire's most dangerous enemy, in the family net. What he was unable to subdue in battle, Charles attempted to conquer through marriage. Francis did have sons, but strange calamities befell heirs (in fact two of the French king's three sons died very young) and extending the family matrix was seen as beneficial diplomacy all the same. Perhaps the only flaw in this plan was Eleanor herself. Through no fault of her own, she was the most unsuitable match imaginable for the voluptuary King of France. Francis was forced to espouse Eleanor as a condition of his release from the Imperial prison, but once in the safety of his own borders he treated his new bride with "an indifference verging on contempt."[53] The marriage was purely for public consumption; Francis continued his hedonistic ways, and Eleanor retreated into a religious retirement. There were, quite understandably, no children. In 1558 Eleanor died of the combination of fever and asthma. She was sixty and had outlived Francis by a full decade.

If this ambitious attempt bore little fruit, either dynastic or diplomatic, it was nonetheless indicative of the family's policy. Few corners of Europe were left uncourted. Eleanor's younger sister Isabella was sent to Denmark, the betrothed of King Christian II. At the time the marriage was negotiated, in 1515, Christian reigned over the Union of Calmar, which since the end of the fourteenth century had included both Denmark and Sweden. Yet unbeknownst to the

Habsburgs, they sent the fourteen-year-old Isabella to "a wedded life of indescribable unhappiness."[54] Christian was older (thirty-four) and had a rash and aggressive temperament that was to prove his political undoing. The first of Isabella's many sorrows was the little innkeeper's daughter known as "dat Duweken" (or the "little dove") who lived in the royal household as Christian's mistress. Worse still, the little dove had a hawk-like mother who became Christian's veritable and venerable mentor. Isabella complained vehemently to her brother, but Charles paid no heed to her complaints and continued to support Christian politically until 1523, when the melancholy Dane earned the distinction of being the only European sovereign to be deposed officially (Henry III of France was assassinated) in the sixteenth century. His policy of brutal repression in Sweden, which culminated in the outrageous "Stockholm Bath of Blood," had incited a powerful backlash led by the first of the remarkable Vasa family, Gustavus I. The Habsburg's hoary patriarch Maximilian finally brought Charles's attention to the matter, and urged him to assist his sister: "The displeasing and shameful life which our brother and son-in-law the King of Denmark leads with a concubine, to the great sorrow and displeasure of our daughter and your sister is blamed by all her relatives."[55]

Maximilian presumably referred to Isabella's failing health. In 1526 she died at the age of twenty-five, while her dethroned husband languished in the prison of Sonderborg with only a Norwegian dwarf for company.[56] She left three children, all of whom were taken to be raised by the Habsburgs in Austria. The Emperor was particularly fond of the son, Prince Hans, and was prepared to reclaim the family lands and place the boy on his father's ill-used throne. Unfortunately, Hans died at the age of fourteen. His two sisters, Christina and Dorothea, were married into smaller patrimonies as they came of age, serving the family in Milan and the Holy Roman Empire respectively.

If the marriage of Christian and Isabella provided only small benefits to the Habsburgs thanks to Christian's ineptitude, it was not because of a flaw in the family's strategy. The Danish king's actions could hardly have been forseen. Isabella's two younger sisters had better luck with their similarly engineered marriages. The third sister, Maria, was betrothed as an infant to the baby prince of Bohemia, just as her brother was promised to the prince's sister. This "double alliance" was a unique feature of Habsburg diplomacy. A

single marriage could easily go awry, but two marriages--
especially when they encompassed both scions of another
dynasty--provided a lasting bond. Such a bond had, after
all, brought Spain to the Habsburgs. Maria was herself no
prize; she, too, had a deformed lower lip, and contemporaries considered her tastes rather masculine: "She is a
Virgo; she is never so well as when she is riding on horseback, and hunting all night long."57

Maximilian had long cast his covetous glance over
Bohemia, and the two marriages to Bohemia's heirs were his
special project. His dreams were realized all too quickly;
Maria was married at the age of sixteen to the fifteen-year-
old Lewis, and before she had time to settle into adulthood,
her husband was killed at the battle of Mohacs. Poor Lewis
did not even have the glory of a death at the hands of his
Islamic enemy; instead, his horse stumbled while the king
fled from the victorious Turks, throwing armor-laden Lewis
into a stream, where he drowned. But Lewis had been no
stranger to embarrassment. While he lived his wife had
been forced to purchase his wardrobe from her own funds,
such was his poverty, and the Venetian ambassador reported
that "sometimes there is nothing to cook in the kitchens, and
the court sent out a servant to borrow fourteen ducats."58
Through this altogether ignominious episode, Bohemia passed
to the heirs of Maria's brother Ferdinand and his Jagellon
wife, Anne of Bohemia, as Maria and Lewis had no children
in their five-year marriage. Bohemia safely in the family
fold, Maria had no desire to spin--or have spun for her--the
matrimonial roulette wheel again. There were other positions to which her talents could be applied. The family arbiter Charles was impressed with his sister's "judgment and
energy" and appointed her regent in the troublesome Netherlands. 59 Yet she would not accept this signal honor until
the Emperor promised that she would not be forced into another marriage. She saw all too clearly the plight of her
sister Eleanor with King Francis. At the age of twenty-five,
she assumed the regency in the Low Countries, where she
proved herself capable in the face of stiff regionalist opposition. But her almost masculine strength was barely equal
to the task, and her health began to fail in her late thirties.
Dutiful, loyal to a fault, she held on until the age of fifty-
three, when she finally succumbed to a heart ailment. Contemporaries found it significant that her death followed her
beloved brother Charles's demise by only five days: she
joined him in death as she had served him, and the Habsburg family, so well in life.

Catalina was the youngest daughter, reputedly the most beautiful, and unfortunately was the last to be liberated from her mother's gloomy prison. Attempts were made to part the two, but Juana became so hysterical that the child was returned to calm her. Back at the castle the child's only pleasure, or so the story goes, was in tossing coins out her window to the urchins below so she could watch their games. It remained for Charles V to remedy the pathetic situation, and he instituted changes in his sister's regimen at Tordesillas. Treatment befitting a princess was arranged, and finally in 1524 a marriage was negotiated with the Portuguese heir John III. This was all in the family, so to speak. John was the son of Maria, mad Juana's sister. The marriage of the two cousins produced nine children, and served to renew the peninsular alliance between Spain and Portugal. Each generation a scion of the main Habsburg line would remarry into the Portuguese house, a policy that bore fruit after Catalina's children died young, leaving the crown to the Habsburg prince Philip II of Spain. The entire Iberian peninsula was united, if only through the three main states' common sovereign.

This was the matrix of Habsburg marriages; not always successful, but ever ambitious. Through sons and daughters the family proliferated across western Europe. With the next generation the Habsburgs would intermarry further in a remarkable--if genetically disastrous (see Charts 10 and 12, pp. 245 & 276)--attempt to consolidate the pioneering ventures of Charles and his siblings. But before we consider the great Emperor Charles, the boy who filled Maximilian's place as both Emperor and family architect, we must consider his brother Ferdinand. This prince, although obscured in his own time and on the pages of history books by his peripatetic brother, forged and maintained a vibrant family empire within the Holy Roman Empire, an empire that would remain even after the pan-European gains of Charles proved impossible to cement.

Unlike his brothers and sisters, Ferdinand was spirited off to Spain by his grandfather Ferdinand of Aragon, where he became very popular. As such he grew up a wholly different sort of person; while his brothers and sisters were quiet, even saturnine, he was cheerful, outgoing, and pleasure-loving. Charles did not meet his brother until he journeyed to Spain in 1517 to claim his crowns. By previous agreement Ferdinand was to retire gracefully to Austria after Charles's arrival in order to prevent a faction from

forming around him, as was quite possible with the popular
native prince.   There were other reasons to fear the infante,
foremost among these was his own quality: he compared
favorably with his older brother, who was reserved and awkward.   One of Charles's Flemish counselors himself remarked
that "Ferdinand was so nice and full of great nature, he
comported himself so modestly and openly with the king, his
brother. "[60]   In addition, Ferdinand was more attractive than
the hook-jawed Charles, although he too suffered from this
family defect.   On the darker side, Ferdinand could be trucu-
lent and had a temper like "a powder keg that could explode
at any minute. "[61]   This side of the prince was not in evidence during their pleasant first meeting, but soon afterwards
Ferdinand chafed under his brother's dominance.   Ferdinand
had his own ambitions, some of which conflicted with his
Imperial brother's wishes.   These quarrels remained within
the family and were often mediated by their sisters, but the
two brothers were never close.   Yet they worked nonetheless
toward a common end: Habsburg domination of western
Europe.

As a consolation Charles gave his brother title to the
family lands in Austria in 1522.   Ferdinand added to these
by winning the free elections in Bohemia and Hungary.   Of
course, this owed much if not everything to Ferdinand's marriage to the native princess Anne Jagellon.   Their marriage
was one of the great matrimonial success stories of sixteenth-
century western Europe.   They were betrothed when each
was thirteen years of age, and were married in 1521.   This
union was more than felicitous, it was a model for the rest
of Europe (see Bishop Grindal's famous sermon in eulogy of
the prince in Chapter Eight).   Ferdinand's fidelity in particular was the talk of European courtiers.   Apparently, he saved
his energies for his wife, whom he proudly boasted was
"after God my greatest and dearest treasure. "[62]   Fifteen of
their offspring graced the royal nursery, of whom all but
three lived to adulthood.   On this score the Spanish Habsburgs were no match for their Austrian cousins, and this
proved a constant source of enmity between them.   Anne's
fecundity was almost an embarrassment of riches, although
it finally claimed her life.   Still, for a princess to die in
childbed at the incredible age of forty-four with her fifteenth
healthy infant delivered from the deathbed was hardly tragic.

Ferdinand held this success over his brother's head
and made no secret of his disdain for Charles's philandering.
When criticized about the expense incurred for his wife's

ubiquitous presence on his trips, he replied rather sancti-
moniously that "it is better to spend money on one's lawful
wife than on whoring. "63   These outbursts of frustration
were no doubt prompted by Ferdinand's belief that he, to use
a figure of speech, was homesteading on the plains while
Charles found fame and fortune prospecting for gold in the
mountains.   Others attributed them to mental instability, a
charge that would seem frivolous were it not for the family's
legacy of lunacy--from Carlos of Viana, to Isabella the Catholic's mother, to Juana "The Insane. "   The ambassador
Suriano wondered what to believe, as he wrote in 1556 of
another envoy's query: "He told me that he had advices
from Brussels that the Catholic King was informed that the
King of the Romans (by 1556 Ferdinand had succeeded Charles
as Holy Roman Emperor) had shown some signs of mental
aberration, inquiring of me whether I had heard anything of
it. "64

Ferdinand and Charles had their most vehement dispute over the future of the Holy Roman Empire; each wanted
it to pass to his son.   The debate on this point became so
fierce that they finally refused to speak to one another, and
Charles had to summon their sister Mary to act as an inter-
mediary.   This particular battle went to Ferdinand, who
claimed the title himself after Charles abdicated in 1556 and
it remained in his family thereafter, although for the most
part they followed the lead of Philip II--Charles's heir--for
the rest of the century.   Charles blamed their discord on his
brother's advisers, with their "evil and ugly words. "65   He
urged Ferdinand to ignore them, but later from his retreat
at the monastery of Yuste, Charles complained that Ferdinand was the real demon seed.   He accused his brother of
embarking on schemes Ferdinand knew he would be unable to
complete and lamented that he failed just when he was needed
the most. 66   To their credit, these disputes were always
kept sufficiently within the family.   To the rest of Europe,
they presented a united front.   At the time of his death in
1564, the sixty-one-year-old Ferdinand had entrenched his
family in central Europe.   Quite understandably, this became the family fortress, while Charles and Philip occupied
themselves with more ambitious projects, such as the exploration and subjugation of the New World, the creation of a
Christian empire across Europe, and the pacification of England, the Netherlands, and the Italian peninsula.   Without
family members to rule in place of the true sovereign in his
multiple domains, such far-reaching schemes and indeed the
Habsburg imprimatur on the continent would have been

chimerical. The Habsburgs achieved their hegemony as a family.

Yet there was one who stood out: Charles, arguably Europe's greatest emperor since Charlemagne, or perhaps even Caesar. Yet for all his accumulated glory, both inherited and achieved, Charles was a dichotomous historical figure. As a ruler he advanced the arts of diplomacy and bureaucracy, yet his character and ideals were almost medieval. He labored in vain to save Catholicism from the Lutheran schism, yet he did much to make the Church subordinate to the state. In 1523 the Spanish ambassador wrote to Charles triumphantly, claiming that "this Pope is entirely your Majesty's creature--so great is your Majesty's power that even stones become obedient children."[67] Still more ironic was the fact that Pope Clement VII allied himself with Spain's traditional enemy France in order to save himself from the leading Defender of the Faith. Charles was also a tireless perambulator, yet a series of ailments made it impossible for him to travel during a number of crises. He was a family man who had no peer among major European monarchs, yet he was separated from his wife and children for much of his adult life, so much so that his son Philip knew Charles more as a legend than a father. Charles both reflected the contradictions of his transitional, pre-nation-state era and stood above it as what the nineteenth-century philosopher Hegel called a "World Historical Individual." But even the great Emperor was subject to many of the weaknesses we have noted previously in other rulers. What marked Charles was his ability to rise above them through good organization and self-discipline.

As a youth Charles gave little indication of his promise; he was an odd-looking creature with a high forehead, prominent cheekbones, bent nose, and hooked jaw. These facial aberrations were the least of the young Flemish prince's problems. His tumultuous genetic heritage had left him with epilepsy, a predilection toward severe melancholy, and worst of all, crippling gout. The ambassador Sandoval referred to the future Emperor as a normal child with normal interests, but others claimed that Charles had a "tender and delicate" constitution.[68] His stamina was suspect as well; when traveling he was forced to stop and rest every two or three leagues, and doctors were uncertain whether he would have the strength to survive childhood.

Much to his credit Charles's will was stronger than

his physique. To compensate for his frailty he adopted a
stoic attitude, and to remedy his weakness he took to hard
exercise, notably riding. The results of this self-control
were encouraging as Charles grew into manhood. Contemporary chroniclers dwelled less on the prince's limitations and
focused instead on the man he had become: strong and self-
possessed. His skill in horsemanship and jousting drew
great praise. As Charles came into his adolescence, tutor
Adrian of Utrecht was able to write truly to Marguerite of
Austria--the widow of the Spanish Prince Juan who raised
Charles and his sisters--of his changes: "Monsieur my
nephew and mesdames my nieces are in good health and disposition. "69

    Yet there were infirmities beyond the control of a
strong will, even for Charles. The most disturbing of these
was a series of epileptic fits that struck him in his late
teens. In 1518, after a game of tennis, Charles fell prey
to an attack that lasted for several hours. Observers noted
that the prince took on the pallor of a dead man. Two
months later the episode was repeated, and in 1519 an even
more frightening fit overtook the newly crowned King of Aragon and Castile, leaving the French ambassador suitably impressed: "El rey Carlos, que oia misa, cayo en tierra
cuando estaba do rodillas y se desplomo durante dos horas,
temiendoso que estuviera muerto, sin recombrarse y con la
cara toda vuelta. "70 The effects of fevers were not to be
denied either, as Vital noted in 1517: "Le bon prince ne
prenoit en rien plaisir. "71

    Hand in hand with Charles's precocious willpower
came a natural severity of temperament. Even in his youth
the prince was no boy. In fact, there was something strangely morbid in his character. Yet Charles was not another
Edward VI: a stilted little manikin, even a manqué. Some
observers found Charles lacking in youthful charm. Pedro
Martyr for one claimed that the heir to his beloved Isabella
the Catholic's throne had the mannerisms of an old man at
the age of sixteen. 72 Cardinal Contarini termed him a
"melancholic, "73 and Santa Cruz described him as a "lonely
figure, not prone to laughter. "74 But Charles _was_ prone to
duties of state. His bouts with depression were overmatched
by his will to power. By all accounts, he found genuine
satisfaction in the chores of rule, for he had a love of government coupled with a strong sense of mission. As Alean-
der reported to Pope Leo X in 1520, "This prince seems to
me well endowed with ... prudence beyond his years, and

to have much more at the back of his head than he carries
on his face. "[75] Whether this was a full compliment or merely an admission that the recently elected Emperor was not
as dull as his homely features suggested can only be surmised. To other skeptics Charles would soon prove prudence
his byword, sanguinity his shell, and the family his touch-
stone. Although his empire came to him largely through a
series of biological accidents: the death of Prince Juan, the
death of little Miguel, Princess Isabella's death in childbirth,
his mother's insanity, among others Charles felt responsible
for its proper governance, and even its enlargement.

Still, for all his enthusiasm Charles had a great deal
to learn about politics in those early years. Surrounded by
his Burgundian advisers, Charles came to Spain in 1517 in a
wave of arrogance, or so it seemed to the Spaniards. The
regent Cisneros, aged as he was, journeyed to meet the
prince and his party, only to be snubbed. The Burgundians
had been convinced that the old Archbishop was a bigot and
an unpopular dotard, and they avoided him and his proffered
advice. The old man died shortly afterwards. More un-
forgivable than this cruelty was Charles's inability to speak
the language of his new vassals. The prospective King of
Spain knew no Spanish, just as the future Holy Roman Emperor knew no German. In time he would master these and
other dialects, but as a youth Charles was Burgundian to the
core, something his Spanish subjects found odious.

Charles exacerbated this cultural chasm by a brusque
approach toward the cornerstone of his empire. He was
clearly anxious to carve a niche, not in a single domain,
but in all of history, and with his native predilections he
focused his ambitions on central and northern Europe. In
this pursuit he was driven to an extreme, and each snag in
his scheduled dynastic assembly line evoked in him gloomy
prognostications; he feared above all that he would fall short
of greatness. Temporarily short of resources in 1524, he
despaired before a triumphant battle on the Italian peninsula
raised his spirits: "I cannot but see and feel that time is
passing, and I with it [he was then twenty-four], and yet I
would not like to go without performing some great action to
serve as a monument to my name. "[76] The key to this monument, or so he believed, was the Imperial title. This traditional Habsburg sinecure fell vacant after the death of Maximilian in 1519, and Charles devoted himself entirely to its
pursuit. "It is, " he wrote to his old tutor Adrian of Utrecht,
whom he left as regent in Spain, "so great and sublime an
honor as to outshine all other worldly titles. "[77]

This insatiable craving for new titles was hasty to the point of being a serious political flaw. Spain was Charles's strongest inheritance, and there was much groundwork to be laid after his arrival. He was, after all, a foreign prince with a stable of suspicious foreign counselors, and Spain had been bereft of a true monarch since the death of Isabella in 1504. During the thirteen-year interregnum, a number of potentially divisive problems had arisen, most notably a rebelliousness in some of the outlying towns. When Charles assembled the Castilian Cortes (a representative assembly) in 1518, it presented him with eighty-eight specific demands, all respectfully phrased but an insistent message to the new ruler all the same. But in his callow youth, Charles moved through Castile and Aragon like Odysseus journeying from one test to another. He spent but four months at Valladolid, in Castile, although Castile was the domain from which he was to draw his greatest revenues. It had voted him a large servicio (subsidy) of 600, 000 ducats and was irked by his flight. In Aragon he passed most of 1519, but it too looked askance at his departure for Germany early in 1520. Still worse, he left just as an inchoate revolt of the towns (a movement known as the Communeros) broke out and did not return for three full years. Just as Spain needed leadership, Charles was nowhere to be summoned. This would be characteristic of his reign in so many states, for despite his peripatetic movements across Europe, he was always an absentee ruler. States accustomed to a native sovereign complained that Charles was insufficiently sensitive to their problems, demanded more of his attention, and were not placated in the least by their role in the empire. So Charles was forced to develop a political balancing act, which in his youth he was insufficiently dextrous to align.

But even these early difficulties held the seed of ingenuity, necessitated innovation, and forged a number of new techniques. More than any of his contemporaries, Charles was forced to rely on his counselors, and in each of his domains the Councils of State were staffed with able and well-educated men. These men processed and digested every issue for the unstudied and impatient Charles, so that he "need not break his own head over it, " as they wrote. [78] More and more the bureaucrats assumed everyday state functions, while the monarch himself was freed to rove about and bless each state with his personal presence. Men of the caliber of Chievres, Sauvage, Granvelle, Tavera, and Mendoza applied their considerable talents to Imperial business. Charles gave them a good deal of leeway; recognizing quality, he advanced and rewarded it. The most influential of

all was Charles's Piedmontese chancellor, Mercurino Gattinara. He became the Emperor's partner in global schemes,
formulating in detail the universalist plans so enticing to
Charles. The influence of these professional statesmen--as
opposed to the aristocrats or cronies who conducted business
for other European monarchs[79]--has been considered in detail, [80] but their value extended beyond mere good advice.
They acted as shields to deflect dissatisfaction; they took the
unpopular measures and became the targets of vituperation.
Perhaps the Emperor took this lesson from Machiavelli, for
it is clearly stated in The Prince. Charles himself remained
largely unscathed, and when he abdicated and toured his
realms for the final time he was greeted with great affection
everywhere he went, even in the troubled Low Countries.
That invention of seventeenth-century chroniclers, the Spanish
"Black Legend," later made Charles appear a bigoted monster,
if not quite so villainous as his son Philip. But during his
lifetime Charles inspired admiration and even love among his
subjects, even though they often despaired of his presence.

Charles had mixed results as a politician, yet the
foundation of his success was not really political. Charles
was a dynast, and a dynast of the "old school" so to speak;
he began with his family, extended as it was, and attempted
to impose it upon western Europe. In this Charles found his
forte. No sixteenth-century ruler had more respect for his
family, and none benefited more from family allegiances, a
good wife, and a well-disciplined kin. The Habsburgs were
still very much like Austrian Burghers. Their rise was recent and owed much if not all to marriage. Thus, the family members, and Charles in particular, had a unique regard
for the institution. While their European peers dallied, the
Habsburgs made marriage a part, indeed a central part, of
their mission in life, for which they were well rewarded.

In 1526 the assembled Cortes strongly urged Charles
to marry and provide a regent for the kingdoms of Castile
and Aragon. A peninsular consort seemed the only solution,
and as luck would have it a twenty-three-year-old Portuguese
princess was available. Isabella was the Emperor's cousin,
acceptable to the restive Spaniards, and a good match for
Charles into the bargain. Portraits reveal her to be a frail
and lovely woman, and if we are suspicious of sixteenth-
century portraiture, as well we might be, we have contemporary accounts that confirm these impressions. In addition,
Isabella was described as dignified to the point of coldness,
a reserve that both attracted Charles and compelled his great

respect. Theirs was not a relationship of fleeting passion, but rather a firm bond of mutual regard. Charles spoke and acted with the utmost courtesy toward his wife, and, still more telling of his admiration, entrusted her with much. Until her death she was the sole regent in Castile during his frequent jaunts and had complete responsibility for the upbringing of their children. This task she handled with a loving severity unique to Habsburg families. Charles saw his progeny only infrequently and took those opportunities to show his love. He had a tendency to indulge them, but the Empress put the proverbial fear of God into their lives.

Despite their serious natures Charles and Isabella shared a warmth that their formality belied. As the Portuguese ambassador wrote after their wedding, "When the bride and groom are together, though everybody may be present, they have eyes only for each other."[81] Charles himself wrote his brother Ferdinand to inform him that "I have entered upon the estate of marriage, which pleases me well."[82] This was good news indeed from the characteristically undemonstrative Emperor, and still better news was to follow: within months of the nuptials, the Empress was pregnant.

This felicitous picture was dimmed somewhat by Charles's frequent absences. Perhaps his greatest difficulty was not the Turks, Luther, or France, but the plethora of competing claims on his time and attentions. Dutiful as he was, his responsibilities were almost too many and too widely scattered to be reconciled to his subjects' satisfaction or even to his. Although Charles genuinely loved his family, the needs of his states superseded their claim on his time. His odyssey included nine visits to Germany, six to Spain, seven to Italy, four to France, two to England, and two to Africa. He made eleven sea voyages. All in all, he was out of Castile for over five years during the thirteen years he was married to Isabella. These absences notwithstanding, Charles managed to sire six children, but only three survived their infancy. The first two, Philip and Maria, were healthy infants, but later three successive sons died in their first year. These were tragic occurrences by themselves, but their effect on the Empress was still more damaging. Isabella was never a robust woman, and each of her pregnancies undermined her health. During the painful and protracted labor for Philip in 1527, she demanded that all the curtains be drawn around her face so that the many observers, including Charles and assorted grandees, would not see her grim-

Charles V

ace. She told one of her attendants that she would rather die
than scream, another instance of Habsburg fortitude and de-
corum. [83]

Such restraint merely stalled an inevitable denouement,
for Isabella suffered much from the weight of her duties as
regent, the absence of her husband, and crippling arthritis.
Her attacks of arthritis began in 1530, the year she gave
birth to the infante Ferdinand, who died shortly thereafter.
This marked the beginning of the end, as in 1533 the Empress's life hung by a thread on two separate occasions.
Yet the final onslaught did not come until 1539, when she
delivered a stillborn son. The birth was fraught with complications, the most unfortunate being Isabella's inability to
bring forth her child unaided. The easy births of strong
women did not occasion much medical intervention, which
left the mother with at least a chance to survive. But like
so many royal deliveries, Isabella's difficult labor encouraged court charlatans to kibbitz in their horribly unsanitary fashion, and the result was the dreaded puerperal fever, a
malady no doubt responsible for many if not most of the
deaths in childbed. Sick as she was Isabella apparently
feared the doctors more than her ailments: a "relazione"
stated that: "her great shyness about uncovering her body
and her lack of confidence in the science of those discredited
physicians were more than her attachment to life. "[84] Unfortunately, her fears were well founded, and her life came
to a painful end at the age of thirty-six. Charles would not
marry again, although as one might expect, he kept his grief
to himself.

Throughout their married life Charles had been a
model of temperance. Melanchthon, the Protestant intellectual, enthused over Charles's private life despite their dia-
metrically opposed stances on the religious debate: Charles,
he said, "was a model of continence and temperance. "[85]
Yet, the Emperor was certainly no angel, and was subject
to the same temptations that lured many of his contemporaries from their duties. His confessor Loaysa had to warn
him repeatedly against his indulgence in "sexuality and
carnal pleasure. "[86] But even in this weakness, his compul-
sion and his sense of order triumphed. Charles was not
averse to an occasional romance, but he never involved himself on an emotional level with his mistresses. Love was
not a court game, but a helix of obligations; on the other
hand, a king constantly on the move had certain physical
needs--or so the indulgent sixteenth century explained it.

These needs were discharged by Charles with Prussian self-control. Let us not forget that adulterous love affairs dominated Charles's contemporaries Henry VIII and Francis I for a number of years. Charles distinguished himself by treating his paramours as mere physical comforts, never to interfere with duty. His first known liaison, outside of the Flemish fleshpots he frequented as a young prince, was a young Flemish woman named Jeanne van der Gheenst, who achieved immortality of a sort with the birth of the Emperor's illegitimate daughter Margaret, later to become the famous Margaret of Parma. Margaret showed talent as regent in the Netherlands, but her mother was quickly forgotten. The same convenient amnesia applied to Barbara Blomberg, an eighteen-year-old bourgeois who caught the Emperor's eye in 1546. Her legacy was the proud and dashing Don John, who later became the Spanish hero at the decisive Battle of Lepanto against the Turks. Don John was clearly his father's child, for his mother was a hoyden. In one particularly unpleasant conversation, she attempted to humble her son with the revelation that he could just as easily have been the son of a common soldier who had enjoyed her favor at the time of her liaison with the king of Spain. Barbara also attempted to create trouble for Charles, demanding money and raising a loud fuss over what she considered shabby treatment. Charles ignored her. But he took care of his bastards, who were arguably more talented than his legitimate children. Perhaps the only distressing facet of these adventures was the ailment that Charles suffered after his dalliance with Barbara, a well-kept secret that prompted treatment with the gujac wood then fashionable among European physicians. This exotic medicine was found only in the New World, and was used principally for the relief of venereal disease. Whether Charles actually had this common malady is indefinite but not unlikely. What we do know is that it did not become a major problem and never interfered with his strenuous lifestyle.

But if sex was just a part of the Imperial routine, epicurean delights were Charles's favorite and most troublesome diversion. He was insatiable, and the foods he loved best were those most disagreeable to his digestion. As Miguet noted, "Mais encore il se plaisait à faire usage des ailments, qui é'taint la plus contraires a sa santé. "[87] Loaysa, the confessor who warned Charles against carnal delights, was equally concerned with the Emperor's eating habits:

Je la supplie de ne point manger des mets qui

nuisent a sa santé: personne n'ignore que votre
estomac est ennemi du poisson; pour l'amour de
Dieu, considerea que votre vie appartient a tous
aussi bien qu'a vous. [88]

But Charles had no intention of restricting himself to those
foods that were good for him.   On any given day his waking
fare might include capons with milk, sugar, and spices.   He
would then take Communion (he received special permission
from the Pope to eat before Communion--he was unable to
wait) and return to bed.   Rising, he would snack on a variety of meats.   After Vespers came another snack, followed
by a final meal before bed.   Even these "snacks" were larger
by far than modern meals.   Neither was Charles discriminat-
ing about his treats; he was a blatant gourmand, with a yen
for such spicy and unusual foods as sardine omelets, Estre-
madura sausages, eel pies, and pickled partridges. [89]

This and other bad habits had a cumulative effect on
the Emperor's health.   Charles, as we noted earlier, was
not inherently strong, although he did enjoy a spell of ro-
bustness from his late twenties until his middle thirties.
The strong will that helped him to overcome his childhood
feebleness could just as easily turn into destructive stubbornness, which often prompted him to disregard his health and
exacerbate latent ailments.   His disdain for hygiene was almost barbarian, and he persisted in the activities that had
the most deleterious effect on his constitution.   For example,
in 1532 he injured a leg in a riding accident.   The injury
was not serious in itself, but "the following morning when we,
the doctors, came to see him at the usual time, we found
his leg red with weals where he had scratched it. "[90]   Nor
was this the end of the problem; with continued abuse the
wound grew so painful that Charles reportedly considered
amputation.   The ministrations of the physicians, who apparently consulted with the Emperor each day, were of little
help, as we might expect.

The worst of Charles's ailments was his gout, something his grandfather and other relatives had suffered with
to no end save death.   Charles added to this genetic predilection by his culinary misbehavior and his constant travels.
As early as 1528 mention was made in the diplomatic dispatches of this curse, and for the rest of his life, gout would
attack him at almost regular intervals.   These "attacks"
were not merely moments of discomfort: Charles experienced
those each day of his adult life.   Instead, they were month-

long (or longer) onslaughts of total incapacity. Eleven such
attacks were recorded, many of them strangely coincident
with important military campaigns or political unrest. By the
1540s Charles was extremely ill, and his increased aware-
ness of death evidenced his fears about the future. In 1543,
after recurrent attacks of the gout, Charles wrote a detailed
political testament for his son Philip, hinting of his own proximity to death. His entire right side, particularly his foot,
neck, and hand, had been totally paralyzed for over ten weeks
earlier in the year. Charles was a defeated man. His temper was never mild, and became explosive under the strain
of physical discomfort. During this time he challenged the
French king to single combat. But all was not finished yet,
for in 1546 Charles took a cure for his gout that met with
some success, and his spirits were raised enormously.

Gout was only one of Charles's infirmities. He was
subject to chest ailments, as so many of his predecessors
and cousins had been. This was noted as early as 1530,
when one of his counselors advised him that "your chest is
sometimes heard farther off than your tongue."91 Hemor-
rhoids also troubled him for years, particularly so because
of his uncleanliness. These embarrassing irritations became
a more serious problem in 1550, when the usual blood flow
burgeoned into a dramatic torrent. To compound this peril,
Charles's doctors prescribed frequent bleedings, which
further depleted his blood supply. Symptoms of diabetes also
began to appear at this time--some modern medical historians maintain that his insatiable appetite was triggered by this
hormonal imbalance--and his limbs began to swell. Again
the ritual treatment of strange woods and herbs from the
New World and purges every eighth day was applied with no
success, until in 1552 a Neapolitan medicine apparently
brought some relief. By and large these moments of comfort were few and far between. The rigor of the Emperor's
life could be seen in his fingers. By 1556 they had become
so swollen that he was unable to untie the strings on official
documents, much less write the letters themselves, as he
had often done in his youth. This decline did not catch
Charles unaware. In 1548 he felt the imminence of death
at the important Augsburg Diet, and roused himself from his
feverish delirium to compose the famous letter to Philip in
which he detailed the responsibilities of kingship. For the
next nine years, Charles was a semi-invalid, and his infirmity was no secret to the courts of Europe. The ambassador Baersdorp believed the once-magnificent Emperor had
at least one foot in the grave as early as 1549: "L'oeil

abbattu, la bouche paste, le visaige plus d'homme mort que vif, " he wrote. 92

    Recognizing the problems posed by his weakness, Charles took characteristically decisive action; he abdicated his thrones in order to smooth the transition of power and relieve himself of the duties of rule, to which he was no longer able to attend. Beginning in 1555 he toured his various domains, Philip in tow, and received his well-deserved adulation. In Brabant a number of the assembled luminaries of the seventeen provinces of the Low Countries wept as the Emperor explained his reasons for stepping down:

> This is the fourth time that I am setting out hence for Spain.... Nothing that I have ever experienced has given me so much pain ... as that which I feel in parting from you today without leaving behind me that peace and quiet which I so much desired .... But I am no longer able to attend to my affairs without great bodily fatigue and consequent detriment to the state.... The cares which so great a responsibility involves, the extreme dejection which it causes, my health already ruined-- all these leave me no longer the vigor necessary for governing.... In my present condition I should have to render a serious account to God and man if I did not lay aside authority.... My son, King Philip, is of an age sufficiently advanced to be able to govern you, and he will be, I hope, a good prince to all my beloved subjects. 93

Such was the remarkably prudent final salutation of a most remarkable prince. Whatever sins Charles had amassed with his ambitious schemes and religious persecution were forgiven him. Disappointed in life, despite his signal achievement of perhaps the ultimate dynastic empire, Charles was allowed a gracious retirement.

    Charles left for his final resting place at the monastery of Yuste--designed to his specifications--in September 1556. He would remain there for the rest of his life, never again to see Philip. At his retreat he continued to be gluttonous and infirm. By the summer of 1558, he had become so weak that a cold plunged him into his final spiral. After three weeks of intense suffering--delirium, fits of controllable shivering, fever (speculated to be of a malarial nature), and unquenchable thirst--Charles finally died. His life reflected a genuine desire to "plus ultra," as his aptly coined devise enjoined, but he was limited by his all-too-human failings and a body that finally would "nec plus ultra." With his passing, the true dynastic dream ended, and his successors struggled merely to halt the erosion of the family empire into national units with social, political, and religious ideas of their own.

Charles left only one son to succeed him, which under the circumstances was probably advantageous; the Habsburgs did not lack for sons, and in fact the bonanza of the Austrian branch exceeded the territories available for them to govern. Charles was forced to pass to his brother Ferdinand the title to the Holy Roman Empire, as much as he wished to keep his achievement whole for his son Philip, in order to keep the peace within the family. Yet Charles did not plan his lack of heirs. Rather he sired four sons. But two of the three born alive died in their infancy, apparently of the epilepsy that had so distressed their father in his early years.[94] This misfortune was at least partially offset by the promise of Charles's two daughters, Maria and Juana. Charles took his brother Ferdinand's dictum about daughters no less seriously than his prolific sibling, and both girls were put to good use. Maria was sent to Austria to marry Maximilian II, son of Ferdinand and future Holy Roman Emperor, and Juana married her cousin Juan, prince of Brazil, the son of her aunt Catalina and John III of Portugal. In this manner the main line of the Habsburg family renewed its biological ties with its two subordinate branches. These unions were only moderately felicitous, but both produced boons of a sort for the family as a whole. Maria was unhappy for most of her married life with Maximilian, but she bore him sixteen children and assured the future of the Austrian Habsburgs. Juana was known as an extremely cold woman, although she apparently warmed to Juan sufficiently to sap his limited strength with "matrimonial excesses."[95] He died in the first year of their marriage, leaving her pregnant with Sebastian-- the final hope of the Portuguese crown, as Juan's six uncles and four brothers proved infertile, unfit, or ecclesiastically oriented. One, more interestingly, became a historian, and for this and his fruitless marriage he was criticized as ineffectual. This left Juana with a ponderous responsibility, which she curiously avoided. Sebastian was born in 1554, but his mother proved her coldness and abandoned him three months later to return to Spain, where she entered a convent. After this the only mention she attracted was a brief bit of gossip about her carryings on with her spiritual adviser,

St. Francis Borja. [96]   Yet even this travesty worked to her
family's advantage; after Sebastian died in battle, the Portuguese crown fell into the hands of Philip II of Spain, his
cousin, and the consolidation of the Iberian peninsula was
finally completed.

The yoke of the empire fell squarely on the stooped
shoulders of the eldest son Philip.   The yeoman's work done
by Philip II's sisters was no more than what was expected
of Habsburg daughters, just as his own obligations were
merely his paternal inheritance.   Let us consider just a few
of these duties: as King of Spain Philip ruled the strongest
--and most restless--power in Christendom; as ruler in the
Netherlands, he presided over an expanding commercial society hostile to his demands both religious and financial; as
leading defender of the Church, he faced powerful challenges
from both the Protestants and the menacing denizens of the
Ottoman Empire; as continental master he was subject to the
sniping sabotage of island Britannica; as the magnate of the
New World, he had the encroachment and piracy of other
European powers to consider; and in addition to these, he had
hundreds of smaller political cares, all of which were laboriously delineated in his pained scrawl across the pages of
thousands of state documents.   To make an exceedingly long
story short, let us begin by saying that Philip had his problems: physical, mental, and political.   He was a reflective
and sensitive man, and these difficulties weighed much more
heavily on him than they had on his more taciturn father,
whose ease and mastery Philip tried desperately to equal.

As a child Philip was sickly and malformed.   Besides
the characteristic jaw the boy had an oversized upper lip and
a useless nose, which left him unable to smell or breathe
properly.   He was often ill.   At the age of four, he was
seriously indisposed with grippe, and as a nine-year-old, he
was described as debilitated and flaccid.   Probably most
embarrassing were the boy's intestinal difficulties, the beginning of a lifelong problem with diarrhea.   This was seen
as a sign of unmanly anxiety, and prompted many disdainful
comments, such as the following report from the secretary
to the Duke of Tuscany: "Ser propia de las liebres, conejos,
y otros animales timidos, "[97] he wrote.

Philip was acutely aware of his flaws, which made
him all the more retiring.   After the extroverted father the
son was puzzling and even disappointing.   It was not for the
lack of trying on Philip's part, for he attempted to compen-

sate for his inadequacy by indulging in the athletic contests
so dear to Charles. But it was apparent to all that the
prince was no athlete. At the jousts of Augsburg in 1550,
the French ambassador jeeringly reported that "the Spanish
prince was the worst of all."[98] This kind of criticism,
coupled with his frequent and embarrassing maladies, no
doubt molded his dignified, aloof, cautious, and fastidious
character. He was close to no one, and, as the Venetian
ambassador commented, "solitude is his greatest pleasure."[99]
He was an exaggeration of his forebears: phlegmatic in appearance and of a melancholy disposition. He was concerned
with his health to the point of hypochondria.

Other facets of the future "Rey Prudente's" childhood
could be seen in the man he became. His upbringing had a
strongly repressive tone. His father, as we have said, was
a virtual stranger, and Philip regarded him with a respect
verging on worship. His mother, on the other hand, was
stern and punitive, although only out of her belief that such
an approach was the proper way to raise children. It was
not uncommon for her to beat the boy with her own hands,
and on at least one occasion, she punished him so severely
that a number of her attendant ladies sobbed at what they
termed "such cruelty."[100] To digress a moment, can there
be any question why Francis I of France, whose mother was
ever his slave, became charming, open, and irresponsible,
while Philip was repressed, secretive, and diligent to the
point of obsession? Which was the better training for a prospective monarch? The Habsburgs were not usually so harsh
toward their progeny, and one suspects that Philip's reticence
resulted more from his own nature than his mother's brutality. Still, the fact remains that the Habsburgs produced an
unequaled string of dutiful and prudent princes.

But what worked so well for many Habsburg children
was oppressive for Philip; in fact, everything was oppressive
for Philip. As the eldest son of Charles V, his responsibilities were unimaginable. Perhaps their sheer magnitude
overwhelmed him, for he was slow to develop. At the age
of seven, he could neither read nor write. When Charles
learned of this, he rebuked the boy's tutor Siliceo for leniency. Philip would never be the man Charles expected him
to be, but he would have to do nonetheless. His education
in statecraft came at the feet of Europe's masters, and few
monarchs devoted as much attention to their successors as
Charles. Philip was taught and then thrust into the fire at
the age of sixteen, when he was appointed regent in Castile

while Charles journeyed elsewhere. More foresighted than most rulers, Charles was determined to cheat his impending mortality of a confusing interregnum. To this noble end Charles took the timid prince in hand--after he had acquired experience as regent--and paraded across Europe to his many inheritances. This occurred in the 1540s, so that Philip's future subjects would get a glimpse of their next prince. These visits only enhanced Philip's awe toward his father and confirmed his feeling of inadequacy. As King of Spain Charles had been a peripatetic prince of all Europe. His son would take refuge in Spain and rule the more cosmopolitan of his inheritances from a distance. The epitome of a dutiful son, Philip found Charles's schemes confusing and was flustered even by the careful directives Charles left for him. Unable to duplicate his father, he would have to find his own way.

The young prince's marriage to his Portuguese cousin Maria Manuela was conducted under the careful, even oppressive, scrutiny of Charles and his advisers, and here the overbearing Emperor set the tone of his son's relations with women. Both bride and groom were in their fifteenth year at the time of their wedding in 1542, and from the start there were problems. Philip was something of a reluctant bridegroom to begin with, and Charles only made matters worse with his reams of advice. The Emperor had never forgotten that his own path to so many crowns had been cleared by the death of Prince Juan, who reportedly perished from over-strenuous lovemaking. This impression was only confirmed by the death of Prince Juan of Brazil, husband to Philip's sister, in the first year of marriage, again supposedly the result of mortal passion. With this in mind Charles took pains with his only son's sex life. After receiving assurances that Philip approached marriage a virgin, he gave the following instructions:

> When you are with your wife ... be careful not to overstrain yourself at the beginning, so that you could receive physical damage, because besides the fact that it [sex] may be damaging both for the growth of the body and for its strength, it often induces such weakness that it prevents the siring of children and may even kill you, as it killed Prince Juan, by whose death I came to inherit these kingdoms. [101]

Sex, Charles explained to his rather squeamish son, was not for pleasure but for the procreation of children.

Excessive gallantry was not required, and, as if matters were not already clear, Charles plotted a strategy for his heir.

> The remedy is to keep away from her [his wife] as much as you can. And so I beg you and advise you strongly that, as soon as you have consummated the marriage, you should leave her on some pretext, and do not go back to her too quickly or too often; and when you do go back, let it be only for a short time. 102

Unfortunately for the adolescent Philip, who was faced with the doubly difficult task of establishing his manhood while obeying paternal sanctions, Charles meddled still further. The Duke of Gandia was appointed unofficial chaperone, with instructions "to keep her [Maria] away from the prince except for the times which his health and life can stand. "103 One is tempted to lambaste the Emperor for his interference, but that would mean having it both ways: his enforced caution probably presented less of a threat to Philip's well-being than the unreal sexual expectations imposed on princes at other courts.

Still, it hardly comes as a surprise to discover that Philip and Maria had an exceptionally cold relationship. The die had been cast, and Philip would never be fully at ease with women, nor would he display much of an appetite, although there were the usual allegations about mistresses. A devout Catholic and a good son, Philip learned his lessons well. Women remained an enigma to him. Although contemporaries found this abstinence rather odd, it certainly was no political liability. Quite the contrary, few monarchs were more controlled or businesslike. This exemplary discipline allowed the "Prudent King" to make his necessary political marriages with grace and tact, including a most distasteful union with the aged Mary I of England. Inhibited he undoubtedly was, but even Freud, who in the nineteenth century pioneered the psychoanalytic approach, acknowledged that such inhibition forms the backbone of a civilization. And despite Protestant badinage, Philip was a civilized man. He sought order above all, and in that respect he was an ideal successor to Charles in the disordered empire.

From the very beginning Philip was forced to ignore what must have been his natural inclinations. Maria was not very attractive, as Charles had admitted when he arranged the marriage. She was fat rather than slim, he said, but, as if to offer some small consolation, he claimed that she had been even heavier as a young girl. [104] He also noted that she was of a type likely to have children, which to him more than compensated for her lack of charm. Philip's opinion was not recorded, nor was it taken into account at the time. He did, however, find his father's advice about avoiding his wife fairly easy to follow, and in a notable turn-about Charles was forced to rebuke the prince for his cold-ness toward Maria while she was pregnant with Don Carlos in 1544. If Philip found her trying, an end was in sight; during Don Carlos's delivery the physicians manhandled her. In an age of brutal childbirths, hers was exceptional, and while she fell ill with the dreaded puerperal fever, her doc-tors engaged in mutual recriminations over her prostrated physique.

It is quite likely that Philip felt nothing at Maria's passing except pity for her and relief for himself. In the most curious episode of their union, he had become ill im-mediately after their wedding with the "sarna, " a skin problem that resembled mange. Was this a product of repressed dis-taste or the Emperor's injunction internalized to a ridiculous extent? In any event, Philip was not anxious to marry again. Charles, still very much alive and paternal in 1545 if not as vital as before, had other plans, however. Mary, the bottom-heavy Queen of England, a fellow defender of the faith, and a spinster, had thrown herself on the Emperor's good judg-ment, asking him to resolve for her the question of her mar-riage. With Philip conveniently single in 1553, this was a matter Charles was very happy to dispose. He suggested his son, and Mary veritably blushed at the thought of such a young husband. She was thirty-eight and looked older, Philip was but twenty-seven and still labored in his father's shadow. In truth, Mary looked as though she had lived each of her thirty-eight years trembling with mortal fear, which of course she had. This development occurred just as Philip was car-rying on for the first time in his life with the ladies, or so it was reported. He did as he was told and left for England in 1554 to face his bride. He had no illusions about his mis-sion. As his friend Ruy Gomez wrote, "The King [before he sailed Charles made him a king principally to enhance his stature in England] realized fully that this marriage was made for no fleshly consideration, but in order to cure the dis-orders of this country and preserve the Low Countries. "[105] (See Chapter Two for further details of the marriage.)

It was indubitably a fine opportunity: England faced the only side of France the Habsburgs did not already border; the revolts in the Low Countries could be supplied from England if the English monarchs willed it so (Elizabeth later did just that); and England had been lost to Catholicism since Henry VIII's divorce shattered the Church in 1533. Charles was overjoyed--as much so as his gout permitted--at the possibilities; Mary coquettishly awaited her dashing Spaniard; and Philip, glum yet gallant, made the best of the situation. But shortly after his arrival, he realized that the situation was hopeless on all counts. Mary was apparently unable to bear children, her subjects resented Philip and his Spanish attendants, and without a child the Habsburgs stood to gain nothing. Clearly, as Mary's consort Philip would never rule England, nor would his claim to the throne in the event of her death be taken seriously. There seemed no cause to linger in the midst of so much antipathy, yet the lovelorn queen complicated matters with her dogged devotion. Her pleading added a plaintive note to a generally pathetic escapade, but Philip had little sympathy. He managed to spend only fifteen months in England during the four nominal years of their union. When it was obvious to all that Mary would never have a child, Philip left for good in 1558. Bitter and broken, Mary died soon afterward.

Up to this point Philip had occupied himself mainly with dynastic business, and the real political crises awaited him. But in 1558 there was still an unresolved dynastic issue that took precedence: a proper heir. The king was now 31, and his single heir was the strange Prince Don Carlos, who had already proven himself a trial. This his childhood nurses could attest: four of them had lost nipples to his sharp, seemingly malicious teeth. As Carlos's behavior grew more frightening, Philip placed himself on the marriage market once again, but at this time there were few available princesses of suitable rank. Only Elizabeth Valois had the proper pedigree, and she had just turned fourteen years of age. The recently negotiated Peace of Cateau-Cambresis made her available, even desirable, as tangible proof of the new accord between France and Spain, traditional enemies. Age had proved no barrier to other dynasties, as we have seen in England, Scotland, and France. But the Habsburgs were more careful, and the consummation of marriage was usually delayed until both parties reached the age of seventeen. Elizabeth was brought to Spain nonetheless, but only to await her coming of age, even though an alternative heir was becoming increasingly important with each of Don Carlos's mad moments. Sadly enough, even as she came of age, Elizabeth was exceptionally underdeveloped for a seventeen year old. Her menses did not begin until her sixteenth year, and she was still playing with dolls on the eve of her marriage. Philip was now thirty-three, and his patience was short with his child-bride. He warmed to her in time, but time was precious. Elizabeth was not ready for childbed, immature and constitutionally frail as she was. Ready or not, her pregnancies came quickly after marriage, and in the first five years of their actual union she endured five deliveries. Only two daughters survived, and one can imagine the agony she went through. Miscarriages terminated her other pregnancies (for gruesome details see Chapter Six) and finally ended her life, as her filthy-handed physicians brought forth a premature daughter in 1568 and killed the queen in the process. For the first time Philip grieved genuinely over the death of his wife. But still the succession problem loomed large, even larger in 1568 because of Don Carlos's descent into his personal hell. All who saw him could certify his insanity, and Philip was forced to wrestle with his own ambivalent feelings toward his son. He finally concluded that it was necessary to imprison the prince before his wild schemes drew blood. Carlos died in jail after a bizarre hunger strike.

From France came the offer of Elizabeth's sister Marguerite in 1570, but the Valois daughters were reputed to be barren. Still worse, Marguerite (see Chapter Four) had supposedly lost her virginity to the Duke of Guise, and more vicious gossip suggested that she had incestuous relations with her effete brothers, a claim she herself would later trumpet. With such bleak prospects and his own reticence, Philip was in no particular hurry, but duty overrode his personal reluctance. As he wrote,

> I very much desire to remain as I am; however, having the succession problem which I have, and ... with the obligation we princes have in this respect to our Kingdoms, I cannot avoid complying with and satisfying the suggestions which have begun to be made to me on this point. [106]

Once again Philip prepared to marry a close relative --incest with a vengeance. This third time his mate was to be a full-grown niece, twenty-one-year-old Anne of Austria, daughter of Philip's cousin Maximilian II. Like the good Habsburg she was, Anne quickly began to make inroads into the succession problem. In the first five years of marriage, she bore three sons. None, however, lived past the age of seven. Finally, after eight years of disappointment, she produced Philip, the rather dim-witted answer to the dilemma. Of her seven births only he would live to adulthood--at least physical adulthood, for there were some who doubted that his mind ever reached that plateau. And if Ceres, the goddess of increase, was equivocally kind to the royal couple, then Venus, the goddess of love, was downright hostile. Anne's relative fertility did not forge marital accord, for she was basically incompatible with her surroundings, including her husband. While she was warm and open, Philip "suffers from the same malady as his father; that is, suspicion," wrote the Venetian ambassador Donato in 1574. [107] The queen was anathema at the somber Castilian court, which made her miserable. The French ambassador commiserated with her, and reported that she "hardly ever leaves her apartment, so that her court resembles a convent of nuns."[108]

Philip was obviously indifferent to his queen, and courtiers gossiped about their conjugal unhappiness. But whatever their true feelings were, duty proved stronger than distaste, and they soon settled into a functioning, if not companionable, relationship. A household officer wrote thankfully of their apparent harmony: "They sleep together every night and there is no trace of the things which kept them apart, thanks to God and to the queen. . . . I do not know if they make love often or not, since neither of them talks much."[109] Philip and Anne maintained an extremely formal demeanor, and the daily visit paid by the king to the queen became a part of the king's routine, but he pursued his other activities alone. Anne was thirty-one when she began her final pregnancy, a stillbirth that weakened her sufficiently to invite a respiratory ailment, "catarro." She died a few days afterwards, the third of Philip's queens to perish shortly after childbirth.

The problems of marriage and his paucity of fit heirs weighed heavily on Philip, but they were hardly his sole concerns. The Habsburgs had proved that an empire could be won with opportunistic marriages, large families, and obedient children. But could such an empire be maintained? More precisely, was the family dynastic state a viable political institution? As Philip faced the second half of the sixteenth century, there were more and more voices across Europe veritably shouting that it was not.

Briefly, Habsburg Europe became a misaligned amalgam; the Low Countries and Spain were incompatible (as Charles realized late in life), and northern resentment had long been simmering under what the people considered to be unjust taxation: tithes taken to finance Habsburg wars for Italian plunder. Charles had managed to quiet this excitement with periodic visits, but Philip was more of a homebody. After 1559 he was never more to the Netherlands than a foreign overlord. About this time a number of unpopular measures were taken; the Church organization in the Low Countries was "reformed," leaving fewer sinecures for native aristocrats; more Spaniards were placed in high offices; despised Cardinal Granvelle administered the government; and the people in general were nervous about the possibility of the dreaded Inquisition spreading to their religiously casual provinces. Protestantism was still confined to a few small "cells," but these cells were attracting important people whose influence was disproportionate to their number. And even the Catholics were not attuned to the more severe Spanish attitudes. When the issue came right into their pockets, they formed rank to express dissatisfaction with their countries' role in the empire. At first, this was done formally, but the sovereigns continued to bleed native resources, and in 1566 the boiling point was reached. In that year the nobles combined with the Protestants to stage the contrived "popular uprising" known as the "iconoclastic fury," which sent dupes into the churches on statue-smashing sprees. Philip was never tolerant about such matters, particularly when they involved the beleagured Church, and his reaction to this minor uprising was pure panic. He dispatched the Duke of Alva to the scene with an army of 30,000 men. This brought temporary order, but the Spanish king was too poor to support such a garrison, and in 1568 the funds for the army ran out. Alva was forced to impose a tax on the people of the Netherlands to pay for their own army of occupation. Needless to say, this provoked a genuine popular revolt. For eighty years Habsburg rulers would pour money and men into this yawning abyss with no success. In modern terms, the Netherlands became Spain's Vietnam. Philip was supposed to go to the Low Countries in 1568 to placate his subjects; in fact, Alva counted on this visit to bring order. Yet, Philip did not go, and the revolt raged on. Here in clear chiaroscuro we see the interface of sixteenth-century politics, personalities, and biology; the dynastic multi-state depended on a roving ruler to reassure the subjects of each realm that they did indeed have their own monarch. Charles carried this somewhat quixotic arrangement off. Philip, however, was awkward, anxious, and above all Spanish. He did not fool anyone into believing him the true King of the Low Countries. He was a foreign prince. Even if Philip had been suited for the role, at the crucial moment he was enmeshed in his immediate problems: his dynasty lacked an heir (Don Carlos died in 1568), and he himself had just experienced his painful attack of gout. He was miserable, exhausted, preoccupied, and the Low Countries were probably the farthest thing from his thoughts. No king could be everywhere, but that was what his realms required in 1568. For Philip, the more urgent problem seemed his inability to accomplish anything, even in one place.

Philip had only to look across a map to be reminded of his other curses: a checkerboard confusion in the Holy Roman Empire, where the established principle of "cuius regio eius religio" dictated that each prince determined the religion of his principality; eastward, the Turks--still a threat until the climactic sea battle of Lepanto in 1572-- who diverted forces and funds from continental chores; to the north, England, which was becoming more adventurous under Elizabeth and sought to check the power of Spain with sniping raids and aid to the rebels in the Netherlands; directly above the Pyrenees, France, which was beginning to show signs of life toward the end of the century--a bad sign for the empire because of the sleeping giant's natural blessings and its strategic position.

If Philip was further inclined toward gloom, which he was, there was the economy to consider, or rather the lack thereof. The merchant Netherlands were as good as lost; the most productive elements of Spanish society had been expelled for religious reasons; the various realms of the empire had been taxed past their ability to pay (a Castilian peasant gave almost half his income to the crown); and still the monarchy was perennially broke. Given the demands of the empire, expenses were not likely to decline, and New World silver could only pay for so much.

As the century drew to a close, Philip was fully aware of these problems, and his eyes reflected the strain of so many nights spent pouring over countless sheets of bureaucratic correspondence. In the final analysis there was little he could do, and he resigned himself to God: a limited man with unlimited responsibilities. His limitations were particularly sad because of the man his father was, and in

his losing battle to maintain the viability of the empire,
Philip probably tortured himself with that thought. We see
hints of this in something as mundane as his bowel habits;
accused of being a nervous rabbit, his diarrhea was well
noted, but alternately he would suffer with extreme constipa-
tion, just as the similarly obsessed Luther's state of mind
could almost be read by the condition of his large bowel. [110]
Physicians tried emetics, clysters, even turpentine, but no
purge seemed to work. These difficulties made the king
finicky about his personal habits, and each fortnight he would
try a new chamber pot.

The years after 1580 were not good ones for Philip.
His letters to his personal secretary Vaquez during the period from 1572 to 1591 were full of "mutual commiseration
over fevers, migraines, and gout."[111] Cloistered in his
monastic palace of the Escorial, he worked in solitude, which
he preferred. But at the same time he was depressed, found
it difficult to walk, and was often prevented from attending
to the business of state. In 1587 he became so ill that his
two top aides were forced to administer his responsibilities,
and with the great enterprise against England (better known as
the Armada to English schoolchildren) only a year away, there
was much to be done. In this unsatisfactory state of infirmity, Philip passed into the 1590s. A stamp became his sig-
nature, a pioneering variant of a wheelchair served to move
him about, a strange hoist helped him in and out of bed.
Observers marveled that a human being in such a state could
survive for so long. Such a stubborn hold on life required
a wrenching separation. In 1598 Philip fell ill with a combination of gout, fever, and a blood infection. His entire body
broke out in hideous boils, and he was unable to move this
mass of sores for fifty-three days. We are told he suffered
greatly. [112] The worst of his torments, according to his valet
Lhermite, was the filthy final course of his illness:

> He was forced to be incontinent, which, without a
> doubt, was for him one of the worst torments imag-
> inable, seeing that he himself was one of the clean-
> est, neatest and most fastidious of men the world
> has ever seen [from his valet no less] ... the evil
> smells which emanated from the said sores was
> another source of torment and certainly not the
> least, on account of his great fastidiousness and
> cleanliness. [113]

Across Europe there were many other, less celebrated

Habsburgs. But these family members were no less important to the dynasty than Philip or Maximilian. The lesser-
known sons and daughters were the shock troops of the Habsburg march across the continent. Few were the European
corners they did not reach, from Naples to Norway, England
to Hungary. Let us note a few of them, in no particular
order or rank of importance. The fifteen children of Ferdinand, Charles V's brother, were not exactly a sterling brood,
but many of them had interesting careers. Maximilian II,
who succeeded his father as Holy Roman Emperor, was gay,
pleasure loving, and a bit wild in his ways. He was also
extremely bright, mastering seven languages during his prodigal youth. As an Emperor he was enigmatic; he found his
sober Spanish cousins distasteful and was sympathetic to the
Lutheran religious dissenters. Still, he kept his feelings
under wraps, and when it came time for his marriage to the
plain, heavy-jawed daughter of Charles V, Maria, he obe-
diently assented, although he showed a bit of defiance with
his debauchery prior to the wedding. Unlike his Spanish
cousins Maximilian tended only his own fences. More precisely, he tended only his younger brothers, for their father
had arrived at a novel solution to the problem of multiple
sons. In the "Hausordnung" of 1554, Ferdinand stipulated
that the family lands should be divided equally among his
three sons, with Maximilian as overlord of the entire parcel. Maria he kept pregnant and melancholy with sixteen
children. She carried the spirit of Spain within her and urged
her husband to enforce religious orthodoxy among his people.
Max preferred to think the matter over with his cherished
band of intellectuals and rant at the Spanish. He was by all
accounts a popular and far-sighted ruler, a patron of the
arts and scholarship.

The other two sons of Ferdinand were worthy in their
own right. Young Ferdinand was charming and handsome,
although for some odd reason he was called "the old one."
He shared the family love for the arts and had a mania for
collecting things, clocks in particular. Ferdinand also had
the nerve to do the unthinkable; he married a commoner, a
wealthy daughter of a banking family named Philipa. This
impulsive act did not strip him of his lands, but it incurred
the wrath of the rest of his family. He and his wife spent
the rest of their life in retirement in Tyrol, his patrimony,
until her death. The youngest son, Charles, married his
sister's daughter, Maria of Bavaria. They lived a quiet life
on their family lands, but their son Ferdinand (a regrettably
common name in the family) would one day accede to the Im-

perial crown after Maximilian's numerous sons were unable
to produce an heir. With Habsburgs everywhere, it seemed
that an heir was always available within the family.

Some of the daughters of Emperor Ferdinand (Charles
V's brother) were espoused to secondary dynasties in territorial competition with the Habsburgs. Isabel went to Sigismund Augusto, King of Poland; Anne wed Albert III of Bavaria; Mary became the wife of the Duke of Juliers and
Cleves; Catalina married the Duke of Mantua, and later,
after the death of her eldest sister Isabel, she wed Sigismund
Augusto. Eleanor also married into the Gonzaga family of
Mantua, and her husband became duke after the death of his
older brother. Of their children, one married into the Medici family and another married into the Este of Ferrara;
Barbara also married into the Este family. The last daughter, Joanna, surpassed them all in the end. As the wife of
Francis de Medici, she gave birth to Marie de Medici, who
would marry Henry IV of France and give birth to Louis XIII.

Other children of other Habsburgs found their way into useful alliances. The two daughters of Isabella, the unfortunate wife of Danish King Christian II, were married at
various times to Sforza of Milan, a Count Palatine, and a
Duke of Lorraine. In Portugal marriages were often arranged with native noble families as well as to Habsburgs in
Austria and Spain--both Charles V and Philip II married
Portuguese princesses who were their first cousins. Of
those who married elsewhere, Beatrice went to Savoy as the
bride of the duke, and their union produced the reknowned
Emanuel Philibert, "the Ironhead." The children of Manuel
"the Fortunate" and his Spanish wife Maria died young for the
most part, but their fourth son Dom Eduardo produced two
significant daughters: Maria became the Duchess of Parma
and perpetuated the Farnese line with her sons Odoardo and
Ranuccio. And Catalina became Duchess of Braganza. Her
male heirs ultimately succeeded to the Portuguese crown
after the Spanish King Philip IV was finally deposed in that
part of his patrimony in 1640.

But of all these dutiful Habsburg progeny, none provided more service to the dynasty than Emanuel Philibert.
Vigorous and energetic, the Duke of Savoy was a noted war-
rior and a particular thorn in the side of the French. He
was instrumental in the Spanish advances leading up to the
Peace of Cateau-Cambresis in 1559, and as a reward for his
efforts--as well as to demonstrate the new Franco-Hispanic

alliance in a tangible fashion--he was to be given the hand of
Marguerite Valois, a princess who had spent too many years
on the vine. She was the daughter of a French king, but she
was thirty-six nonetheless. Emanuel considered her less a
prize than a punishment, and threatened to marry Elizabeth
Tudor instead. But such petulance soon passed, and the good
soldier Emanuel did as he was urged. He even went through
the motions with zest, causing the Venetian ambassador to
exclaim "The Duke is either the most amorous of men or an
inimitable actor."[114] Three years later Marguerite gave
birth to Charles of Savoy, the Pope certified it as a miracle,
and Emanuel eased up on his dutiful fidelity. His wanderings
were discreet, however, and were perhaps muted by the painful gout with which he suffered.

There is a postscript to the story of the sixteenth-
century Habsburgs, and it is antithetical to the story of rise
and expansion. It is a tale of biological and genetic decay,
and it began before the end of a century of Habsburg domination. Inbreeding began to erode the fine qualities of prudence,
dignity, restraint, and discipline that had marked Maximilian,
Charles, even Philip II. Instead, in their places, a deranged
and unfit generation of princes came to the fore. There had
been hints of hereditary madness from the very beginning,
as both Ferdinand the Catholic and his wife Isabella had a
family history of insanity, their daughter Juana was unquestionably demented, and there were hints of the malady in the
Austrian Habsburgs as well before they married into the decayed Spanish dynasty. But these tendencies surfaced in
monolithic fashion toward the end of the sixteenth century.
The heirs of all three family branches--Don Carlos, Sebastian, and Rudolf--were insane. All three lines ended with
strange punctuations, so to speak.

To begin with the most blatant case, Don Carlos of
Spain was twisted in almost every conceivable respect. Even
as a child he appeared strange, and his humanist teacher
Honorato Juan told Philip II that he believed his pupil mad.[115]
As a young man Carlos was known to indulge in acts of sense-
less and whimsical violence; he attacked honored grandees at
court, tried to throw his treasurer Juan de Lobón through a
window, and drew a dagger against his father's chancellor
Espinosa, among other incidents.[116] Everyone feared him;
he had no fear. From the more timorous he fashioned his
cruel entertainments, the most chilling being his sexual perversions. His favorite, it was said, involved the flagellation
of young girls.[117] In calmer moments he confined his sadism

to the torture of animals.   Philip II was finally obliged to
imprison his son and heir, and the Spain-hating wags of the
continent had a field day.   Legends of "habeas corpus"--or
wrongful imprisonment--flourished, and those who were eager
to root these "Black Legend" stories in the minds of others
claimed that the poor prince had committed no crime save
his blood relation to the despicable Philip.   Philip justified
his controversial action in the following letter to Pope Pius
V in 1568, a rationale that seems quite reasonable in the
light of modern scholarship regarding Don Carlos:

> But since for my sins, it has been God's will that
> the prince should have such great and numerous de-
> fects, partly mental, partly due to his physical
> condition, utterly lacking as he is in the qualities
> necessary for ruling, I saw the grave risks which
> would arise were he to be given the succession and
> the obvious dangers which would accrue; and there-
> fore, after long and careful consideration and hav-
> ing tried every alternative in vain, it was clear
> that there was little or no prospect of his condition
> improving in time to prevent the evils which could
> reasonably be forseen.   In short, my decision was
> necessary. [118]

Don Carlos raged in captivity, and the crown had to allot
seven gentlemen and eight Spanish and German sharpshooters
to restrain him. [119]   His death was as bizarre as his life
had been; long known for gluttony, he subjected his frail body
to a hunger strike, followed this with huge meals, and finally consumed massive quantities of ice. [120]

Sebastian of Portugal was less obvious, hiding his
mania behind the facade of celebrated martial courage.   But
he was no less crazed.   The crown had fallen to him on his
fourteenth birthday, and almost from that moment he was
obsessed with the idea of battle against the Moors in north
Africa.   He applauded the Saint Bartholomew's Massacre,
that cowardly act of Charles IX of France, and egged his
own commanders on to such fury.   Taunting his governor of
Tangier with imprecations that his sexual desire exceeded his
desire for military glory, the young king of Portugal managed
to incite the poor man into a quixotic charge on the enemy.
When the quondam governor was found, over a hundred holes
were noted in his corpse. [121]

Perhaps Sebastian was merely jealous of the sub-

Rudolf II, Holy Roman Emperor
(Note the famed "Habsburg Jaw")

ordinate's sex drive, for it was rumored that Sebastian was
impotent. The king did nothing to allay these fears; he made
only the faintest-hearted attempts to secure himself a bride
and his people an heir. Instead, he dashed off to Africa,
after unsuccessfully attempting to enlist other European sovereigns in his holy cause. He advanced to the Alcazar, where
his flawed generalship proved fatal. Without a thought for
strategic considerations, he charged blindly and almost singly
into the fray, and when one fight quieted, he galloped wildly
across the field to find other similarly desperate actions.
Contemporaries lionized his valor; modern analysts would
probably term it a death wish. The battle was lost, and he
was cut down on the field despite the fact that he began the
day with a distinct advantage over his adversary, Abd-el-
Malek. Unable to face the prospect of sexual failure, consumed with an impossible crusade, "we may be sure that he
gloried in the spilling of his royal blood."[122]

Rudolf's was a more subtle malaise. As a fragile little boy, remarkably sensitive to light, noise, or any other
disturbance, he had revealed a melancholy, even mystical
nature. Later, when he had become Holy Roman Emperor,
he indulged this side of his character, studying occultism,
consulting astrologers, and engaging in experiments. He
considered himself quite the alchemist, and had special labs
built for this age-old pursuit. These affairs he kept secret
from everyone save his cherished band of intellectuals and
laboratory assistants. Even his wife, a commoner named
Catherine da Strada, was kept in the dark. Of course, the
dark was where Rudolf lived. His younger brother Matthias
referred to him as a man lost in the stars. 123 Rudolf did
little to counter this perception and hid behind a strange five-
pointed silver star, which he thought to have supernatural
powers. His attention to state business was lax, and his
depressions were legendary. At one point he himself thought
that he was bewitched by the devil--a common sixteenth-
century explanation for insanity. Perhaps he took some comfort in the erotic paintings he had commissioned of the noted
portraitist von Aachen, but whatever pleasures he derived in
the contemplation of these works was short lived. And his
inner demons could not always be appeased with erotica and
amulets. Despair drove him to violence. In his middle
years Rudolf tried to slit the throat of Rumpf, one of his
advisers. Failing at that, he turned the flailing rapier on
himself, and only the timely reaction of his valet saved him.
Finally, in a burst of lunatic energy he broke free once
more, smashed a window, and raised a shard of glass to his
jugular. But the dutiful valet once again pried the makeshift
dagger from Rudolf's grasp, slicing his own fingers in the
process. After this Rudolf subsided. It would seem only
fair for the epigram "no man is a hero to his valet, " even
if he was not.

Age only deepened Rudolf's mad ways, although he
kept out of sight in his beloved laboratories; almost too much
so, claimed the four archdukes, who became convinced enough
of the Emperor's fecklessness to send him the following suggestions: "Because of his majesty's indisposition, it is necessary to name a successor and to entrust the government of
Hungary to one of his majesty's brothers or cousins. " Matthias was urged upon his reclusive Imperial brother. 124 It
is important to stress that although Matthias had long been
ambitious in this regard, the other archdukes were only persuaded to adopt this course after years of Rudolf's bootless-

ness.   In the end they felt it necessary to journey to Prague
in order to press their suit on Rudolf in person.   With characteristic indecision Rudolf fretted, called together his astrologers, and found the timing of their visit to be cosmically
unpropitious.   To humor him they waited on the outskirts of
the city for several days.   But neither alchemy nor the stars
could save Rudolf from his disposition.   His state of mental
imbalance proved fatal, just as it did with Carlos and Sebastian, just as it did for the Habsburg dynasty as an entity
after the golden sixteenth century.   For these unsuitable,
even demented, rulers the Habsburgs have become one of
history's whipping boys: the cause of everything from the
Inquisition to the decline of Spain.

But this slide into insanity could not take the "golden
age" away from the Habsburgs.   To coin a phrase, the
Habsburgs were undoubtedly the dynasty of destiny in sixteenth-
century western Europe, rising as they did in fifty years'
time from obscure Austrian insignificance to the mastership
of western Europe.   They dominated what historians refer to
as the Early Modern Period, or the late Renaissance, as
most have termed it in the past.   The territorial conquests
of the Habsburgs during this era were the result, as we
have shown, of planned matrimonial alliances and the frailty
of competing dynasties.   While other royal families withered
on the vine for the lack of suitable progeny, the Habsburgs
spread their kindred tentacles over new lands.   Their strategy: to intermarry with their competitors, hence becoming
heirs presumptive in the event of a break in the other house's
male line, an all-too-common occurrence in the sixteenth
century.   This plan relied on a strong sense of family loyalty among the far-flung Habsburg kin.   This loyalty was both
natural--family ties were far stronger than "national" consciousness in the sixteenth century--and cultivated; the Habsburgs orchestrated marriages of cousin to cousin each generation, linking inextricably the Portuguese Habsburg heirs
with the Austrian Habsburg heirs, to name but one example,
in a web of filial obligations.   Only among the Habsburgs, it
was said, could one prince be brother-in-law, son-in-law,
and cousin to another.

The foundation of this success was simple enough:
the Habsburgs were the only major dynasty with children to
spare.   For each of their diplomatic coups, there always
seemed to be satisfactory young offspring to offer in marriage.   In fact, toward the end of the sixteenth century,
Habsburg progeny were being squandered on the Church for

lack of suitable marriage partners, while competing dynasties were precariously close to extinction, and the royal blood of Europe was anemic. With their surplus of children, the Habsburgs reproduced themselves into the empire abdicated by their child-poor continental rivals. The most magnificent of the Habsburgs, Charles V, succeeded to the thrones of Castile, Aragon, Burgundy, the Netherlands, Milan, and others solely through his fortuitous genealogy and the misfortune of others, not his Machiavellian virtú.

Charles's multiple inheritances were strictly a coincidence of birthrights, but all the same, his good fortune was no accident. The Habsburgs planned their conquests with an astute sense of timing and a great deal of foresight. To cite an aforementioned example, the Austrian patriarch arranged to marry both a grandson and a granddaughter into the dwindling Jagellon family of Bohemia and Hungary in a double marriage alliance--the most successful variety of Habsburg marital diplomacy. When the Jagellon King Lewis II died at the battle of Mohacs, leaving no heirs, his vast lands passed to the Habsburgs through the descendants of grandson Ferdinand and his Jagellon wife Anne. By contrast, when the Valois King Francis I of France dispatched his sister-in-law Renée (a more full-blooded Valois than Francis himself) to a marriage in Ferrara she was thereafter forgotten, and France accrued no real benefit from the alliance. Renée's children remained in Ferrara, served only the interests of the Este family, and even allied with the Habsburgs later in the century. Such fragmentation of the royal family negated the original purpose of many Valois, Stewart, and Tudor marriages, as the various branches of the family became distinct and even openly rivalrous, serving their own interests instead of their ruling cousin's. The Habsburgs, however, forestalled this kind of entropy by marrying into correlate families each generation. Although this was decidedly unhealthy from a biological standpoint (see Chart 8), it served to maintain interfamily ties and reinforced the concept of an extended family across Europe. There were tensions nonetheless; Charles V and his brother Ferdinand were often at odds over their conflicting ambitions. Still, perhaps to soothe these ruffled feelings, Ferdinand's son Maximilian II married Charles's daughter Maria, and Charles's son Philip II made Maximilian II's daughter Anne his fourth wife. Whatever their disagreements, the tie that binds bound more stringently among the Habsburgs than in other houses. While royal children were being destroyed by the Tudors and wasted by the prodigal Valois, the Habsburgs employed their progeny systematically in the service of the dynasty.

The Habsburgs were quantitatively superior to their rivals from a biological standpoint, although not by the margin that might be expected. The average lifespan--at birth--for Habsburg males was well into the twenties, and even reached thirty-six in the third generation: the highest figure attained by royal families in sixteenth-century western Europe. Habsburg women lived still longer, and Habsburg children, unlike their Tudor and Stewart counterparts, did not disappear in childhood. Nor were these children married at unreasonable ages. They were thus shielded from the dangers of early childbirth for the most part. Their unions were not exceptionally long in duration, nor were they unusually fertile; Habsburg parents averaged about one surviving son per marriage. But more telling was the fact that a great majority of their children grew up, married, and had children of their own, all of whom the family gladly encompassed. Each Habsburg who reproduced averaged about four or five live births during the course of his or her life, and well over 50 percent of these live births went on to reproduce themselves. Most important, about 40 percent of the male live births lived to reproduce. And each Habsburg male who reproduced was himself responsible for over six live births on the average. Fewer than 20 percent of Habsburg marriages were barren. Therefore, with each relative contributing to the family effort, Habsburg fortunes were not dependent on the massive fertility of a small group, which the conditions of sixteenth-century life rendered improbable if not impossible. Steady and unspectacular, the Habsburgs prospered as a dynasty because they had enough depth as a family--and a commitment to the family from all its members--to cover occasional breakdowns. The Austrians seemed to have a biological Midas's touch; there was no credible male Spanish heir when the Austrian Philip the Handsome married the Spanish princess Juana, daughter of Isabella the Catholic. Yet after this infusion of Habsburg blood, in the next two generations there were respectively eight and seven plausible male heirs available.

But of course not everything went so smoothly for the Habsburgs, and at the close of the sixteenth century, even their biological superiority deserted them, leaving a pack of disturbed princes to dissipate the empire. And from the beginning of the sixteenth century, they were less able in their financial, military, and political maneuvers than in the advancement of their family. There were the disastrous wars in the Netherlands and the inconclusive attacks on England to atone for. Charles V trebled Spanish taxes over the course of his reign to finance his grandiose schemes, although this increase was not far in excess of the real economic growth during the period. Money was something the Habsburg rulers used as it came into their hands, without thinking of what economic conditions were necessary to insure long-term prosperity and growth. On the heels of this prodigality came severe crises: toward the end of Philip II's reign, the interest alone on the juros and asientos (equivalent to bonds) he had issued consumed two thirds of his huge revenues. His eventual bankruptcy, along with that of his commander in the Netherlands, the Duke Alva, ruined the mighty Fugger bankers, who had been dragooned into making them staggering loans. This fiscal mismanagement, and the inflationary influx of New World silver, sent Europe into a flux. By 1600, for example, all German currencies were in a tumult. In addition, the religious discord sown by the Reformation still discomfited authorities both civil and religious, and long-standing rebellions continued to simmer. These were but some of the difficulties that faced the Habsburgs, part of the fungus that ate away at the tendrils of their family tree. In many ways their main problem was the result of success itself; the family empire proved too big to manage, even for a ruler as forceful as Charles V. For all their dynastic guile, even the Habsburgs could not impose the harmony of a universal Christian empire on the dynamically discordant sixteenth century. Still, they were uniquely clever in their attempts, and whatever coherence can be identified in the sixteenth century was in large part a product of those far-reaching attempts.

Part II

SEASONS IN THE KING'S HOUSE

Chapter Six

BIRTH

"A Figlio d'Inganno non manca mai la figlioanza"
(A clever woman can always have children)
> --Pope Clement VII to his niece
> Catherine de Medici on the eve
> of her marriage to Prince Hen-
> ry of France, 1533

"In this country," wrote the Imperial ambassador Simon Renard from England, "the queen's lying-in is the foundation of
everything." He may be excused his hyperbole; the importance of what transpired in royal "accouchements" across
Europe could hardly be exaggerated. Here was the real future of each dynasty, even the present. Renard believed that
the birth of a male heir to the throne could end civil strife,
which it did in Spain and--though only briefly--in Scotland.
The ambassador counted on this blessed event as a cure for
English unrest in the 1550s. "One of the queen's physicians
has told me that she is very probably with child," he reported. "If that is true everything will calm down and go
smoothly here."[1] The rumor itself was a temporary panacea,
and Renard wasted no time confirming the good news. "I
have already started a rumor for the purpose of keeping the
malcontents within bounds."[2] Renard's focus on obstetrical
affairs was echoed by many of his diplomatic contemporaries,
who knew the importance of continuity in the royal house.
Four decades earlier the Venetian envoy Guistinian placed
news of Queen Catherine's impending delivery at the head of
his dispatch, with the following hope: "Within a month, or
rather more, this most serene is expecting her delivery,
which is looked forward to with great anxiety by the whole
realm. God grant she may give birth to a son, so that hav-

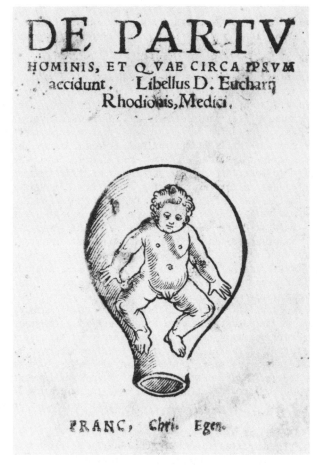

DE PARTV
HOMINIS, ET QVAE CIRCA IPSVM
accidunt. Libellus D. Eucharij
Rhodionis, Medici.

FRANC, Chri. Egen.

Title page of the Latin edition of Roesslin's
The Birth of Mankind, 1532

ing an heir male, the king if necessary may not be hindered
embarking in any great undertaking soever."[3]

At the base of this concern was the succession, always a critical issue. Without an assured male line, the
sixteenth-century dynasty was faced with impending chaos and
popular discontent, as the ambassador Michiel noted in 1557
in his précis regarding a decaying royal family: "On this
topic it merely remains for me to add that in like manner
as the danger about the succession would be very great by

reason of the disturbances and riots which might take place both at home and abroad were it [the choice of a successor] delayed until the queen's death, or if the decision were protracted. "4 Chaos enveloped an uncertain succession, and this common prospect--feared across Europe--cast a pall of anxiety over each pregnancy in the royal house. To fail in childbed was to fail as sovereign; Elizabeth I never rested easy because of her childlessness. She feared everyone around her, especially her relatives, and in the most benign actions she saw treason and malice. Bereft of an heir, unfortunate monarchs faced sedition and tumult. The French attempted to forestall such a pattern with their failures; each widowed queen of a childless king was placed in seclusion for six weeks, ostensibly to discover whether there would be a posthumous child. There never was, nor was there adequate reason to think there would be. Yet this play was a sage custom nonetheless; during the waiting period divisive confusion was held at bay, nothing was done hastily, and a successor could finally be confirmed with at least a modicum of order and ceremonial reverence. The results of this tactic were promising. In the span of a hundred years the crown passed to three different branches of the royal family, yet during this time there was no true succession crisis. Still, such cleverness was only a ruse. The ideal of government-- and the proof of the health of state--was continuity, and each king was judged on his progeny as much as his own performance. Edgy nobles with revolt ever on their lips indicted the depopulated royal family. For self-preservation as well as for the future of the house, a monarch depended on his family.

But the sixteenth century was not a felicitous era for royal families, as the age of the Renaissance dynasty was also an age of staggering infant mortality and obstetrical difficulty. Arrogant kings were not exempt from humble problems. The sixteenth-century ideal of hereditary monarchy required that each king reproduce a healthy male successor; the actual course of European dynasties in the early modern period hardly followed this simple ideal. Two of the four major dynasties perished entirely because of failure to reproduce, and the two that survived lingered on the brink of extinction at various points in the sixteenth century for the same reason. 5 The historical canard "accident of birth" was in fact no accident at all. Certain royal families--the Habsburgs in particular--proved capable of maintaining their biological balance while others either destroyed themselves or allowed themselves to be destroyed by the brutally difficult

conditions of life. Sheer biological survival opened the door
to dynastic success in an age where survival was a virtue and
not a fact. Charles V, the talented heir of a reinvigorated
house, became overlord of most of western Europe because
of the collapse of other dynasties, a coup effected almost
wholly through a deliberate marriage strategy and an unparalleled surplus of princes. The Habsburgs' ability to
capitalize on the failures of their competitors stands as a
testimony to their acumen and a lesson in sixteenth-century
dynasty building.

For all their political cares, birth was the essential
bottleneck facing the sixteenth-century royal families. Conceptions in royal houses were frequent and in most cases
regular, but the production of healthy heirs was a different
matter. The only truly sterile adult monarch in this period
was the last of the Valois: Henry III, whose venereal disease, homosexual inclinations, and genetic legacy rendered
him hopelessly infertile. Other monarchs kept their spouses
pregnant, yet failed to leave an heir. Henry VIII's first two
marriages yielded fourteen recorded conceptions, but only
two daughters survived. The wife of King John III of Portugal gave birth nine times, but only one of her children lived
to the age of twenty. These two cases were not atypical; the
great majority of royal births resulted either in miscarriage
or infant death. [6] A significant toll was collected from the
prospective mothers as well. Over half the Habsburg queens
themselves died in childbed, and other dynasties experienced
a similar rate of attrition. Thus, the true limitation on the
size of royal families was not their lack of conceptions, but
their inability to bring these conceptions to a successful term
completion. There was, as Shakespeare noted, "many a slip
'twixt the cup and the lip. "

Every culture uses ceremony to highlight important
events, and the ritual that surrounded royal childbirth left
no doubt in the observer's mind as to the magnitude of the
occasion. Tapestries detailing the illustrious history of the
family covered the walls of the elaborate "lying-in" chamber
where Tudor queens awaited their delivery, attended by a
gaggle of functionaries. The expectant mother wore certain
robes of historic import and followed a prescribed symbolic
regimen. [7] Nothing was spared to produce the appropriate
tone. The Girdle of Our Lady--one of the most efficacious
relics in Christendom--was loaned to Mary Stewart by the
Abbot of Westminster on the eve of her delivery, and Elizabeth York used a similar talisman. French queens tradition-

Caesarian delivery, from Mercurio's
La Commare o' Raccolitrice, first published in 1596

ally gave birth outdoors, under an oak tree. If we may believe some of the many spectators, it was a grand spectacle.
But despite the careful routine, the time-honored methods,
and the elaborate facades, royal childbirth was truly a grim
procedure, and the result was in no way enhanced by the
pageantry.

The spectacle, designed to herald the birth of a future ruler in an appropriately grand fashion, built the expectations of king and kin to a fever pitch. The queen was of course acutely aware that her fate was both politically and physically attached to her umbilical cord. Pregnancy was at once an opportunity and a nightmare. To the mother of a healthy male heir went the spoils. Jane Seymour, mother of Edward VI, became Henry VIII's best loved wife as a result, and King Hal requested that he be buried next to her even though he spent less than a year with her in life. But that did not mean that her safety was considered as she agonized during the reported forty-eight hours of labor. [9] Her son was delivered by caesarean section, although her doctors knew this procedure meant an almost certain death for the mother. Even in the dark-age medicine practiced by sixteenth-century physicians, such deliveries were not recommended, at least with a live mother. But a queen presented a special case, for her own importance was dwarfed by the child inside her, who, as the ambassadors claimed, could assure both the immediate and long-term future of the dynasty. Although harrowing, a death in childbed was at the very least honorable. Nothing was more ignominious and wretched than a barren queen. The child was always the first priority. Inability to produce a male heir was more than sufficient reason to divorce a queen in the sixteenth century: Catherine of Aragon and Claude of France were dishonored for their failure, and Catherine de Medici, Marie de Guise, Anne Boleyn, and Elizabeth Valois all found themselves on the verge of the same fate. On the other hand, those who succeeded in their dynastic mission were lauded, even to the point of sainthood. When the thirty-nine-year-old Marguerite Valois bore her husband, the Duke of Savoy, a healthy male heir, the Pope himself issued a congratulatory message to the aged duchess remarking on her miraculous delivery, a miracle only slightly more credible than the Immaculate Conception: "Elizabeth peperit et filius orationis est riste puer. "[10]

Only a male would do, as daughters were discounted by all but the astute Habsburgs. In the context of the sixteenth century, there were satisfactory reasons for this bias; it was claimed that most domains would not accept a female as overlord, and, owing to the notions of medieval philosophers, the birth of daughters cast a shadow over the king's prowess. According to the theologian St. Thomas Aquinas:

As regards the individual nature woman is defective

> and misbegotten, for the active force, the male
> seed, tends toward the production of a perfect like-
> ness in the masculine sex, while the production of
> a woman comes from a defect in the active force
> or from some material indisposition. [11]

Contemporaries greeted the birth of daughters with disdain,
the birth of sons with fanfare. Although Giustinian was ever
eager to speculate on the details of the English queens' pregnancies, he was positively nonchalant after the birth of a
daughter:

> Today, also ... Queen Catherine brought forth a
> daughter. I shall go pay due congratulations in the
> name of your highness; and had it been a son, I
> should have already done so, as in that case, it
> would not have been fit to delay the compliment. [12]

After so many communiqués about the most minute details,
the final result elicited only this postscript to the Venetian's
report. Others were similarly disappointed. At the birth of
Anne of Denmark, future bride of James I of England, her
father Frederick II reportedly burst into his wife's chambers
to upbraid her for her failure. [13] And another Venetian described the gloom of another court: "Nothing worthy of your
serenity's knowledge has chanced since mine of yesterday,"
he reported, "save the most serene Queen was this night delivered of a daughter, which to the few who are as yet ac-
quainted with the circumstances, has proved vexatious, for
never had this entire kingdom ever so anxiously desired anything as it did a prince. "[14]

This pressure had a markedly detrimental effect on the
pregnancies of many queens. Mary Stewart's miscarriages
were partly the product of extreme anxiety, [15] Anne Boleyn
claimed that worry over Henry VIII's hunting accident had occasioned her mishaps, and Catherine de Medici was so desperate after ten barren years that she refused to ride mules
because popular wisdom decreed that these unfortunate animals transmitted their infertility to riders. [16] Perhaps it
was not mere accident that the easiest deliveries among royal
princesses in the sixteenth century occurred with a woman
too immersed in her own world to feel external pressures:
Juana "la Loca" gave birth effortlessly, "without pain or
trouble. "[17]

With the exception of Juana, the actual birth experience

of queens was inevitably traumatic, often unsuccessful from
both a physical and political perspective, and not infrequently
fatal for both mother and child. Catherine de Medici was a
relatively hearty specimen, but her inability to conceive in
the first ten years of her marriage jeopardized her position
as queen. A combination of strange remedies, including the
myrrh pills prescribed for Catherine by the famous physician
Jean Fernel and an operation on her husband's penis, apparently cured the royal couple's reproductive difficulties. But
when it came time to deliver, Catherine must have longed for
the halcyon days of sterility. Her last birth, a set of twins,
was the worst, as "Victoire remained dead in her belly for
a full six hours and one of her legs had to be broken to
save the said lady. "[18]

The entire realm of England rejoiced at the long-
awaited arrival of Prince Edward in 1537, but rumors circulated to the effect that Queen Jane had been brutalized during
the delivery. Her child had supposedly been "torn from her
womb" at the doctor's command. [19] Jane fell ill with the
dreaded puerperal fever shortly after the savage delivery and
died twelve days later. The grim pattern rarely varied
across Europe. Each of the Empress Isabella's successive
deliveries brought complications, until a badly handled stillbirth ended her life. After her extremely unsanitary delivery in an already weakened condition, she too fell victim to
the dreaded puerperal fever. Isabella's contemporary, Margaret Tudor, was unable to raise herself from the bed in
order to dress herself for three months after her seventh
delivery. [21] Margaret's granddaughter, Mary Stewart, was
an extremely large woman, but her size did nothing to ease
her "long, painful, and difficult" labor for James VI. [22] Her
pain was such that the Countess of Atholl tried to transfer
it to a surrogate through the medium of witchcraft. The
poor wench assigned to the task moaned along with Mary but
alas did not succeed in alleviating her distress. [23] Mary was
unable to walk for five days after the birth of James and
within two months suffered a severe attack of her mysterious
disease. She vomited over sixty times, convulsed unconsciously, and was considered on the verge of death. "All
her limbs were contracted, her face distorted, her eyes
closed, her mouth fast, her feet and arms stiff and cold. "[24]
The experience of her first birth was terror enough for the
highly strung queen. Shortly thereafter she ceased sexual
relations with her husband and was unable to carry her two
subsequent pregnancies--the result of virtual rape--to term.
Mary's aunt Margaret Drummond also had an early, pro-

longed labor "while in flight in a very uncomfortable place. "
She suffered greatly with a pain in her right leg, and was
unable to raise herself from the bed for three weeks after
her delivery. "It would pity any man's heart to hear her
shrieks and cries, " wrote Sir Christopher Garneys, one of
her companions. [25] It was a familiar story, and the result
of these ordeals was often as tragic as the process itself.
Prince Juan of Spain, the fond hope of Ferdinand and Isabella, died prematurely, but left a ray of hope with his
young wife, who was pregnant. This glimmer soon vanished,
as Pedro Martyr wrote to the Archbishop of Braga, describ-
ing what must have been a gruesome scene: "The Imperial
Margaret, instead of producing the desired offspring, presented us with a formless mass of meat. "[26] With this
tragedy, the Spanish male line was extinct.

Even success had its price. Louis XIV supervised
personally the delivery day of his daughter-in-law, Princess
Victoire. While she grasped the bars of the special childbed
that had also been used by her predecessor Marie de Medici
and Anne of Austria, ambassadors and foreign princes thronged
about the contraption engaging in the normal routine of court.
It was August and the heat was stifling, so oppressive that
the king, in a fit of magnanimity, reassured the fading princess that he would be pleased even if the child was a girl.
He was greatly affected by her torments. For over thirty
hours the pains continued, until finally, just as the onlookers
began to lose hope for mother and child, the Duc de Bour-
gogne was born. The crowd was ecstatic, as was Louis, and
their attention shifted immediately to the infant prince. But
Victoire's torments were only beginning; her doctor had a
live sheep skinned in the chamber and wrapped the new mother in the dripping garment. There in her sealed room Victoire remained, at the height of the summer heat wave, for
nine full days. [27]

The most harrowing description of sixteenth-century
royal childbirth was provided by the physicians and ambassadors who surrounded the frail young Queen of Spain, Elizabeth Valois, in the final months of her life. Because of the
great Habsburg empire's lack of an heir by the end of 1568,
Elizabeth's travails took on paramount significance.

The queen's most felicitous childbed experience itself
had been a gruesome ordeal, as reported by three of her
physicians. Throughout her pregnancy in 1567, she had been
subject to the sort of maladies we normally associate with

gestation: nausea, fever, fainting. But Elizabeth's symptoms had a more menacing tone; on August 5 the doctors reported that "she tried to vomit but was unable to do so."[28] And on August 7 she vomited a combination of phlegm and food that appeared strange. On August 9 they described her regurgitation of "bilious, phlegmy, and gelatinous vomit."[29] On the 10th she abstained from all good but was nonetheless beset with powerful paroxysms of nausea, fever, and great pain in the "vicinity of her pubes."[30] This sequence ended happily later that night when Elizabeth "gave light" to a little girl.

Yet the queen continued to feel ill long after the birth. In truth she had never quite recovered from a miscarriage she had suffered in August 1564. Her Italian physician Vincente Montguyon described that ordeal, just as he did the more successful occurrences of 1567. Montguyon recounted the court's benign neglect of Elizabeth's distress, thinking it to be a natural accompaniment to her obvious pregnancy. Montguyon chided them for not calling in the doctors, and noted that the queen was truly feverish when finally the physicians were summoned. To remedy this they decided to bleed her over Montguyon's objections. They took seven ounces from her right arm. Shortly thereafter Elizabeth began to bleed from the nose, prompting the Italian to wax reproachful. But she was bled again, this time from her left arm. Understandably, she grew weaker. On the seventh day of this confused regimen, Elizabeth began to have abdominal pain. And at midnight "she delivered a piece of meat of the color and texture of the liver of a chicken, with a bit of blood and the sort of humors that leak out of women on similar occasions."[31] Two days later, Elizabeth "gave birth to a large chunk of meat, greasy and resembling a sheep's heart, and covered with a subtle skin with a bit of grease attached."[32] With this painless, bloodless expulsion Elizabeth's fever continued, and a great controversy arose among the assorted doctors. The Spanish physicians wanted to bleed her again; Montguyon suggested a rhubarb purge instead. They settled on another bleeding, this time from Elizabeth's right foot. It was necessary, they claimed, to eliminate the bad humors that had not been expelled with the second phase of the miscarriage. Weak to begin with, Elizabeth was transported to the threshold of death by these ministrations. Finally, as she was about to receive extreme unction, the more moderate Italian was allowed to assume command, and as he modestly related her life was thus saved.

Elizabeth had long been a problem. She had not

menstruated until the age of sixteen, and she was of a weak
constitution. Spanish statesmen across the continent were
apprized of the queen's gynecological status almost daily,
such was the moment of her longed-for pregnancies to the
empire. Perhaps it was this pressure that prompted Elizabeth to hold back her menses after her success of 1567,
simulating pregnancy and damaging her reproductive system.
Finally, in 1568 the combined effects of her previous ordeals,
burdensome obligations to the state, and current pregnancy
simply overwhelmed her, as the Secretary Zayas reported to
the Duke of Alba, then leading the Spanish forces in the
Netherlands:

> One month after the queen our lady gave birth to
> the infanta Dona Catalina she gave us to understand
> that she was pregnant again (without having cause
> for it), because each month her menstrual flow
> diminished. Having this persuasion she made great
> efforts to detail it. Later, after five months, she
> had certain signs and believed herself clearly preg-
> nant, having filled herself with the bad blood and
> ruinous humors she had detained. Because of this,
> bad administration and her great frailty--which be-
> came all the more pronounced--other fearsome weak-
> nesses came to plague her. Such as: her pulse
> was sometimes faint; she had difficulty breathing to
> the point of choking to death; her head would swell.
> After these mishaps occurred it was believed that
> she had never been worse, but in truth she had al-
> ways had bad color, been frail, and had gaunt skin.
> The doctors considered these incidents life threaten-
> ing and they told this to the king. If she did not
> take better care of her self her life was in grave
> danger. The king was persuaded of this, and the
> queen was put to work on the matter. But she was
> the enemy of doctors and medicine and she hid many
> things, which they knew less of than the maids.
> The queen kept getting weaker, growing always more
> frail and of bad color. A strong pain occurred in
> her kidney, and it was strongly suspected to be
> stones, because it spread to her bladder. Her
> right leg became numb, where before it had hurt,
> and she vomited much and urinated frequently with
> heat, leaving much red kidney stones in her urine.
> This illness was soothed with some conventional
> remedies. Then, on the 22nd of September, a
> small fever developed, but malicious and of bad

quality, and she began to have blackish-red diarrhea, which lasted four days. The diarrhea stopping, the pain in the same kidney came to her as
before. The illness was clamorous; the vomiting
continued, thick and phlegmy, and after the rage
and melancholy came continuous fainting fits and
swellings in a manner that made her head dizzy.
This lasted until Thursday the 1st of October.
Then the fever increased and all the symptoms
were augmented and her forces weakened. The
pain in her kidney was manifestly soothed, however.
All these things continued to grow until Sunday the
3rd of October at 4:00 in the morning, when the
queen took the holy sacrament that already the day
before, having confessed, she was unable to receive because of her vomiting. At 7:00 they gave
her extreme unction, the queen having asked for it
devotedly. At 10:30, things having gone from bad
to worse, came the miscarriage of a girl child that
was alive when she left the womb and received the
water of Holy Baptism. She was believed to be
five months or a bit less. Afterwards, unable to
deliver the afterbirth, the queen gave her soul to
our Lord, like a Christian, and with great and wise
judgement, as though she was not ill; and very
quietly, as though she was falling into a very deep
sleep. 33

There were reasons why royal childbirth was so gruesome and disappointing. The rigors of reproduction are
hazardous even for the most fit women, and sixteenth-century
queens were almost invariably weak and constitutionally diseased. Mary Stewart was apparently wracked by porphyria,
as was her grandmother Margaret Tudor. Anne Boleyn had
a number of congenital deformities. Isabella of Portugal was
arthritic, and Catherine of Aragon wrote her father early in
her marriage to Henry that "I have had so much pain and
annoyance that I have lost my health in a great measure; so
that for two months I have had severe tertian fevers and this
will be the cause that I shall soon die. "34

Perhaps the most unnecessary cause of misfortune in
the royal childbed was inept medical intervention. Virtually
all difficult pregnancies were guaranteed to result in tragedy
because court physicians interfered in these cases. With
filthy hands--the forceps was not used until the seventeenth
century--these ignoramuses plunged into the womb, and

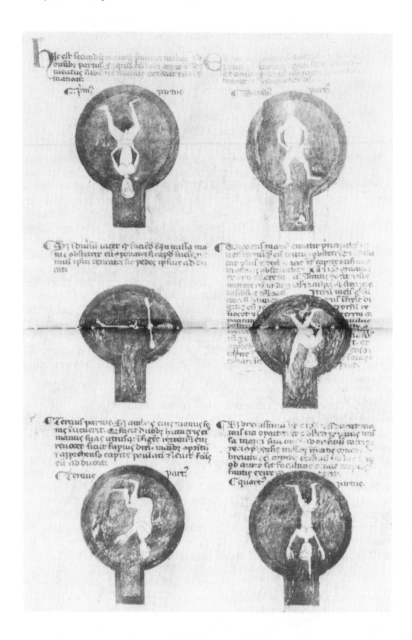

Roesslin's illustrations of fetal positions

puerperal fever almost inevitably followed them in. This in-
fection, not the strain of birth itself, caused the death of
Elizabeth York, Empress Isabella, Queen Maria of Portugal,
Maria Manuela of Spain, Jan Seymour, Anne of Austria,
Queen Isabella of Portugal, and a host of other princesses.

Medical thought regarding gynecology and obstetrics
was not one of the notable advances of the Renaissance. The
sixteenth century was not wholly unaware of the delicate process of childbirth, and surprisingly there were insights into
the relation between mental state and physical health in the
era's dominant text: the Rosengarten of Eucharius Roesslin.
In The Birth of Mankynde, Thomas Raynalde's English trans-
lation of Roesslin, there were the standard errors, including
the depiction of fetuses with full sets of teeth, hair and without umbilical cords (see facing page), but there was also an
occasional trenchant observation in between the unsubstantiated
musings. A miscarriage "may happen ... by some sudden
anger, fear, dread, sorrow, some sudden and unlooked for
love."35 This was precisely the rationalization many queens
used for their misfortunes, with some justification, no doubt.
But few readers focused on this pearl, and the influential
text was more a work of superstition than a treatise on medicine. Mixed with the reasonable ideas were medical bon
mots, such as the following method for disclosing whether the
husband or the wife was at fault in cases of marital barrenness: to paraphrase a long and complicated procedure, one
set of wheat corns, barley corns, and beans was to be
steeped in a man's and another in the woman's urine, and
both were then to be potted. For eight to ten days the man
and the woman were to water their "pot" with their urine,
and the pot that grew best was said to belong to the fertile
party. One can only wonder whether those who adopted this
method administered proper nutrients to their plants sur-
reptitiously, but such a diagnostic technique can hardly have
fostered marital concord. Raynalde himself admitted the un-
reliability of this method. "Trust not this far-fetched experiment," he warned.36 Of greater certainty was a technique in which an odiferous substance was inserted into the
woman's vagina. If the scent ascended from her generative
organs to her nose, Raynalde explained, the fault could not
be hers. If the woman was unable to detect the odor, then
she was the culprit. If these grievously unfair methods can
be taken as any indication of Renaissance thought, we can
see why the majority of barren marriages were blamed on
the wife. Proud kings were especially quick to lay the burden of their childlessness on their queens, as in the cases of
Ferdinand of Aragon and Henry VIII.

At the sixteenth-century royal court, medicine was practiced on its highest level, such as it was: one of the physicians attending Philip II of Spain was Ludovico Mercado, who wrote the most important sixteenth-century treatise on women's diseases; the noted Swiss doctor Mayerne attended James I of England; Jean Fernel prescribed for Catherine de Medici; and Ambroise Paré ministered to Henry III of France, among other famous sixteenth-century doctor-patient combinations. But even these most "enlightened" physicians labored in largely fruitless vineyards. Paré made advances in surgery, but believed nonetheless that, for example, monsters were born of sexual unions between man and beast, and that pregnancies could last eleven months. He also copied many of Roesslin's mistaken anatomical illustrations. [37]

It was not until the work of the Austrian obstetrician Semmelweis in the mid-nineteenth century that doctors began to understand what killed women in childbirth: infection. Even then, Semmelweis was frustrated in his attempts to enforce hygenic standards in his own hospital. Sixteenth-century physicians knew nothing about infection, and thus were powerless to treat their worst enemy. Instead, they administered bleedings and rhubarb purges, hardly the thing to pick up a languishing new mother. Occasionally their treatments became truly ridiculous. Martin Luther's favorite story along these lines involved an Austrian Empress engaged in a difficult labor. Her physicians decided that fear alone would speed the delivery, so they arranged to have twenty-two felons brought into the queen's chamber to be whipped in her sight. Two men died, yet the labor continued its agonizing pace. [38] Doctors were actually the worst enemy a pregnant queen had. Mary Manuela's old Portuguese doctor had disagreed on the course of the Spanish queen's treatment with the Spanish court physicians, and protocol dictated--since Maria was a Portuguese princess--that his suggestions be followed. Such was their combined ignorance that the unfortunate queen died before any of them realized that her life was in danger. After this blunder was uncovered, the sage Portuguese fled Castile on a mule, fearing the reprisals of his colleagues. [39] There were some clever doctors, although few of them cared to linger in the sycophantic atmosphere of court, where a mistake or a loose phrase could cost them their life. Lewis II of Bohemia, although born premature, had a fine doctor, and was saved by the novel use of warm animal carcasses as incubators.

With medicine at such a loss to treat even simple

complaints, superstition reigned even among those who commanded the best care the age could provide. In common wisdom birth defects were attributed to divine displeasure, and those who had bad thoughts during conception were thought to be punished with "monstrous births."[40] Anything but the blandest sexual acts were also supposed to produce misshapen children, or so claimed the prevalent doctrine of preformation, which stated that each embryo was formed completely at the moment of conception.

Other examples of tragedy in the royal lying-in chamber abound, and the lesson for the sixteenth-century dynasts was that a healthy succession could not be founded on a handful of conceptions. To survive the vicissitudes of childbirth, the royal family had to produce a number of conceptions in a number of princesses. Only constant reproduction insured survival, and only the Habsburgs were able to muster the numerical forces necessary to beat the bleak odds.

Chapter Seven

CHILDHOOD AND ADOLESCENCE

"The child is the father of the man"
                                    --Wordsworth

For those few survivors who crawled out of the sixteenth-
century royal nursery into the harsh dynastic limelight, childhood was an unreasonably pressure-laden and traumatic phase
of life.

Each adult member of the house of Habsburg produced
an average of approximately four live births, and approximately half of those live births lived to reproduce themselves.
These were the most fecund dynasts. [1] Only a third of the
Tudor births in the sixteenth century survived through infancy.
As these statistics demonstrate, children were undoubtedly a
precious commodity for the ruling houses of western Europe,
but this did not prevent the monarchs and their advisers
from subjecting royal progeny--both consciously and acci-
dentally--to rigors that further decimated their ranks.
Farmed out to wet nurses and hostile aristocrats, educated
to the point of suffocation, isolated from other children, denied the spontaneity of youthful pursuits, burdened with unceasing and often unhelpful preparations for the monarchical
office, young princes bent like saplings before the unhealthy
strain of their training.   It was perhaps no accident that
some of the most successful sixteenth-century monarchs--
Henry VII and the Catholic Kings of Spain are good examples
--were not accorded a royal childhood because of their apparent insignificance at birth.   The Scottish poet David Lyndsay's epigram, "Unhappy is the age which has o'er young a
King"[2] might well be turned around to fit the perspective of
the royal heir: unhappy is the young king who had over him
the burdens of an entire age.

216

James I and VI of England and Scotland, age seven

Almost from birth the royal child found contrived misery awaiting. One can imagine the discomfort occasioned by Mary Tudor's infant swaddling "of stiff silk and damask covering her from chin to toes."[3] The infant Arabella Stuart's arms were held down to her sides and her "legs straightened and wrapped tightly together."[4] With this stiff binding, dermatitis was common among royal infants, and many grew up with weak arms and legs as well. Anne of Denmark did not walk until the age of ten, and James VI crawled until the age of six.[5] Nor were these children properly cared for, despite the scrupulous window dressing: "Often the child lay in its own excrement for days."[6]

There were of course notable exceptions to the unfortunate pattern, and it is certainly significant that many of the truly talented figures of the sixteenth century were among the exceptions. Henry VII was shifted from country estate to country estate, but he led a healthy outdoor life as a child and was in the hands of good tutors. He grew into an extremely prudent and balanced prince. Francis I was hardly balanced or prudent, but he was celebrated by Castiglione as the epitome of a Renaissance courtier.[7] His genuine magnificence was as unusual as his upbringing. Never was a royal child so spoiled, loved, and protected. Francis's mother insisted on raising the boy herself, and she fiercely shielded him from external demands. He was grounded in the classics by fine tutors at Blois, and he ultimately emerged into the arena of court as the most captivating, and most self-indulgent, man of his generation.[8] Charles V, separated from his lunatic mother and her eerie court, was placed in the capable hands of Adrian of Utrecht. Adrian, who would later succeed to the Papal throne, was an outstanding humanist educator. Charles was also the beneficiary of a well-ordered home life, superintended by his aunt Margaret, whom he adored.[9] The rather weak young man was wisely sheltered until he reached the age of nineteen. While his scattered empire awaited the royal touch, Charles was allowed a protected and sanguine youth. It was time well spent.

The great majority of royal children found their youth much less gentle and constructive. In the family itself these sensitive, anxious youngsters found repression, indifference, and even hatred. Parents were taught to be stern towards their progeny, and royal parents were further removed from their children by layers of court functionaries and the emotional distance created by the standard practices of sixteenth-

century child-rearing. The children were taught obedience
above all:

> Dread the curse of parents thine
> It is a heavy thing.

wrote the poet Hugh Rhodes during the reign of Henry VIII.[10]
The malediction of parents was in fact thought to have supernatural powers. The care of royal parents was itself a heavy
thing, a stifling thing, to be certain. After the death of his
brother Prince Arthur, the future Henry VIII was isolated
and sequestered; he could only go out with selected keepers,
and even then his trips were limited to a specially enclosed
area. For all his reputed gusto, young Henry was intimidated by the entire scenario, feared his father, and never
spoke in public.[11] Royal parents often showed a peculiar
indifference toward their children. Princess Juana of Portugal was married at eighteen, widowed at nineteen with a
small son. She left her child voluntarily and summarily after
his third month of life, entered a convent, and never saw him
again.

If royal children almost always trembled before their
parents, they quite often snarled among themselves. In the
competitive environment of court, where the eldest son was
revered worlds above his siblings, natural rivalry often developed into life-long, pathological hatred. To name but a
few examples: Francis Alençon despised, and plotted against,
his elder brothers Charles IX and Henry III of France; Henry
II of France hated his more charming younger brother Charles;
Edward VI was openly hostile to his sister Mary and only
slightly less reproachful toward Elizabeth. These sores fes-
tered for years, and were doubtless grist for the mill of
later political rivalries and insurgencies. Still, parents
aroused the greatest enmity. Marguerite of Navarre reacted
violently to her upbringing, and was in almost perpetual revolt against her mother, Catherine de Medici. There was
quite obviously nothing the young girl would not do to embarrass her mother. "She is crazy," Marguerite jeered.[12]
This battle originated in her childhood, which, as Marguerite
described it, was a constant attempt to avoid Catherine's
wrath. She claimed to have shuddered at the very sight of
her mother. "I did not dare to speak to her, but when she
looked at me I trembled with the fear of having done something to displease her."[13] When adulthood freed her to se-
duce her brothers, tryst with the family's greatest enemy,
and shame her husband, Marguerite took her revenge. Cath-

erine was rewarded with a daughter she herself described as the bane of her existence. "I see that God has left me this creature for the punishment of my sins through the affliction she gives me. She is my curse in the world."[14]

Royal parents were only rarely beloved of their children, but the fault for their children's wrath was not all theirs. Others shared in a royal child's upbringing, and so from a cold family the offspring passed into the harsh hands of guardians, most of whom were dominated by the severe sixteenth-century notions of proper child care and education. As the philosopher Erasmus, himself a tutor to royal offspring, wrote: "Of what consequence is it to have begot a son for the throne, unless you educate him for this role."[15] This education began almost in infancy, and was grounded in the belief that "there is no beast so wild, so terrible, that the skill and endurance of his trainer will not tame him," as Erasmus postulated in his widely read guidebook on The Education of a Christian Prince. Such was the hub of the sixteenth-century attitude toward the well-born child. As veritable babes these princes learned control and discipline; in Roesslin's Rosengarten the sixteenth century's leading pediatrician and obstetrician advocated stringent and early toilet training. In this he exceeded modern standards by years, with the stated end to produce the all-important control in even the smallest children. His method could hardly have been pleasant for the children. Roesslin directed his many readers to:

> make a suppository of honey, sodden till it be hard and mass, and let the suppository be the length of your little finger, and the bigness of two wet strayes bound together, then dip it into oil and convey it into the child's fondament.[16]

Modern psychohistorians have linked, at least tentatively, this approach to the melancholia so prevalent in Tudor England, a melancholia that was clearly a part of the character of each sixteenth-century English monarch.

The severity of sixteenth-century child-rearing was prompted by the belief that children were, in essence, evil, just as all men and women were fallen creatures. "Much folly and lewdness" was "couched in a child's heart," wrote a contemporary authority, and if this "was not purged, it will burst forth into foul enormities."[17] Mothers and tutors were urged to administer discipline freely: "The more she loveth him, the sharper she beateth him ... and all is for love. "[18] Children were expected to act as miniature adults --an impossible demand, as we know today. And royal children were held most specifically to the highest standards of conduct, including sobriety and attention to duty. There were regulations concerning almost everything, and all were to be kept in mind under penalty of humiliation and even beatings. Erasmus wrote a detailed catechism for virtually all situations, including the proper way for a prince to blow his nose; if he must hawk phlegm and spit on the ground, he must then tread over it with the sole of his shoe. [19] Under constant observation, princes were lectured on the import of their simplest gesture. Harmless facial expressions were categorized as signs of character; ebullient laughter or even untoward smiling were taken as evidence of either deceit or madness; licking of the lips was said to indicate folly; biting the underlip was taken as a portent of bad intent. [20] There was much to remember, and many to fault the royal child if he or she failed to act in an exemplary fashion.

These children responded in many ways to such treatment. Some, like the future Emperor Maximilian I, turned inward. According to Johannes Cuspinianus, who spent some time in the Emperor's service, Max was bafflingly backward as a child. He was apparently speechless until the age of nine, and it was feared that he would grow up a mute, to the great lamentations of his mother. [21] Jane Grey was said to be a prodigy, but her only thanks for her tutor came in the form of screeching invective. The man, Harding by name, had abandoned his Protestantism on the accession of Mary I. Steadfast seventeen-year-old Jane, awaiting her execution in the Tower of London for her unwitting part in the Protestant revolt against Mary, rebuked him so severely that one wonders whether her outburst was the catharsis of a lifetime's resentment. Harding, she said:

> who seemed sometime to be the lively member of Christ, but now the deformed imp of the devil; sometime the beautiful temple of God, but now the stinking and filthy kennel of Satan; sometime the unspotted spouse of Christ, but now the unshamefaced paramour of anti-Christ. ... When I consider these things I cannot but ... cry out upon thee, thou white-livered milksop ... sink of sin ... child of perdition ... seed of Satan[22]

James I of England had received a standard princely

education and was certainly aware of etiquette. But according to the Frenchman Fontenay, he chose instead to act in a crude manner, almost as if he wished to flout his training. "In speaking and eating, in his dress and in his sports, in his conversation in the presence of women, his manners are crude and uncivil and display a lack of proper instruction."23 One can certainly sympathize with his delayed rebellion.

The classic example of a royal child destroyed by his upbringing was Edward VI of England. At the age of six, the child was placed in the hands of cold and disciplinarian tutors, who drilled his emotions and human feelings away. By the catachetical standards of the day, Edward VI was a supremely well-educated little boy. Father Henry had his overgrown ego massaged with sickeningly obsequious missives from his six-year-old son--in Latin--and smiled happily at the prince's progress. 24 Henry had no real contact with the boy outside state occasions. Few monarchs personally supervised their progeny, although the English king set impossible standards for Edward based on prevalent notions of princely education. Edward was frequently beaten for not living up to these rigid guidelines, but for the most part he was a model pupil. This was unfortunate, for his very success in the program prescribed for him made Edward an almost inhuman creature. He reportedly laughed only once in his life and was truly "a precocious and fatuous little boy mouthing the stilted language of his elders devoid of compassion and obsessed with his own deficiencies."25 When he died, three months short of his sixteenth birthday, it was questionable whether the diseased and disheartened little king retained any desire to live at all.

Edward's half-sister Mary was born virtually with her head in a noose. Although her father temporarily masked his disappointment over the arrival of a daughter instead of the longed-for son and heir, the storm clouds loomed on the horizon. 26 Subsequent failures brought Mary's mother repudiation; Henry claimed their marriage had been sinful from the start, and after years as an English princess, Mary became an unwanted bastard. Her dishonor was public and brutal: she was forced to testify in court that her parents' marriage had been "incestuous and unlawful in the eyes of God and man."27 In fact, Mary's childhood was so terrible, and so universally observed to be terrible, that in 1533 an eccentric named Mary Baynton traveled the English countryside claiming to be Princess Mary "put forth in the broad world to shift for her living."28 Shortly after her courtroom trauma, Mary began to suffer from the psychologically triggered gynecological problems--notably amenorrhea, the absence of the menstrual flow--that posed a chronic threat to her well-being. 29 This ailment, and Mary's concurrent retreat into her Catholicism, became highly significant politically when Mary succeeded to the throne in 1553. Her sister Elizabeth had an equally humiliating experience. As a young girl she was forced to walk down a long corridor toward her father Henry VIII on her knees. When at last she reached the bloated and pitiless sovereign, she begged his pardon under the sullen gazes of the court party. The purpose of the exercise was to stem Elizabeth's willful nature.30 This it did not do. Rather it confirmed her distrust and intransigence, and later in life the Virgin Queen, as if to prove her own attained mastership, subjected Lord Essex's sister to the same punishment. Willful as ever, Elizabeth spent her entire life guarding against, and subjecting others to, the humiliations fostered by her dishonored youth. This misery was not confined to the British Isles; in Spain, Princess Isabella was so dour as a child that her mother called her "madre" in jest. 31 Not all parents had a sense of humor, however. Lady Jane Grey described the fury unleashed by her mother and father when the recital of her lessons was less than letter perfect:

> I am so sharply taunted, so cruelly threatened,
> yea presently sometimes with pinches, nips, and
> bobs, and ways, which I will not name, for the
> honor I bear them, so without measure misordered
> that I think myself in hell. 32

The bitter lessons of childhood were not forgotten or forgiven --if in fact such forgiveness of the forces that shape human character is possible.

A great deal of emphasis was placed on the physical condition of the royal child, although little was done in the royal nursery to develop good health and vigor. Each child entered the marriage market almost in infancy, and the bargaining invariably depended on certain physical attributes, particularly evidence of proper sexual function. Henry VII invited ambassadors to peep in on the naked eighteen-month-old Prince Arthur, and these envoys were suitably impressed with what they termed his "qualities quite remarkable. "33 What remarkable qualities an eighteen-month-old infant might possess escapes the modern imagination, but the display of royal babies to foreign ambassadors was a common occurrence, and formal inspections of Mary Stewart, Catherine of

Aragon, and the infant children on Francis I attracted much attention in the diplomatic dispatches. [34]

Monarchs went to great lengths to prove their heirs suitable marriage material in all respects. To cite a notable example from the seventeenth century, Louis XIII was sexually molested as a fifteen-month-old infant in the hope that he would confirm his virility before court observers. The dauphin's physician Heoard wrote:

> The dauphin goes after Mlle Mercier, who screams because M. de Montglat hit her on the buttocks with his hand, the dauphin screamed too. She fled to the bedside; M. de Montglat followed her and wanted to smack her rear. She cried out very loudly; the dauphin hears it, takes to screaming loudly too, enjoys this, and shakes his feet and his whole body with joy.... They make his women come; he makes them dance, plays with little Marguerite, kisses her, embraces her, throws her down, casts himself on her with quivering body and grinding teeth.... He strives to hit her on the buttock with a birch rod. [35]

Although debauchery passed like an heirloom down the French royal line, this account probably tells us more about the carnival atmosphere of the court than about the actual carnal inclinations of the infant Louis. What is remarkable is the apparent attempt to prove the kinglike masculinity of the little boy. Heoard admitted that the dauphin was provoked. "The Marquise often puts her hand under his jacket." [36] One may wonder if these strange experiments contributed to Louis's later impotence and assorted perversions. The psychological implications of such childhood experiences are obvious, and this pattern was not restricted to France. The very same sort of pressure stood behind frail Prince Arthur's morning-after boast of sexual conquest: "I have spent the night in Spain." [37] In fact, his marriage to Catherine of Aragon was quite likely still unconsummated. Reacting to similar circumstances, the adolescent Mary Stewart manifested symptoms of pregnancy, although her husband, sickly Francis II, died before reaching puberty. [38] Mary's body simply reacted to the unreal expectations of those who surrounded her. The sexual development of sixteenth-century royal children occurred in a fish bowl, and many of them later manifested predictably perverted notions of the crucial business of reproduction.

The family whose issue fared worst in the sixteenth century was undoubtedly the Stewarts. Each child stood almost as an island, since only one royal Stewart offspring survived in each generation. [39] These infants had the additional burden of minority succession; they were all without parents to shield them from the vicissitudes of politics, and the politics of Stewart Scotland were a maelstrom. As a result, the Stewart princes were raised under horribly insecure conditions. James V was taken from his tutors and encouraged to debauch himself, while James VI was raised in an extremely hostile household where he was beaten frequently and taunted with the failings of his mother. [40]

Habsburg children probably had the best childhood lot among their dynastic peers. There were usually a number of them, and the brothers and sisters formed a supportive group. After the Emperor Maximilian rescued Juana's children from their mother's mournful court, Charles and his sisters were sent off to a peaceful existence in Burgundy while brother Ferdinand was sent to Spain and raised as old grandfather Ferdinand's personal favorite. The family allegiance so peculiar to the Habsburgs was no doubt nurtured in these family groups: European royalty's closest approximation to the nuclear family. All Habsburg children were educated carefully, and had parents or kind surrogates who monitored their progress. Charles V, although absent from Spain much of the time, still found occasion to consider his son Philip's curriculum with the boy's tutor Siliceo, and to rebuke the poor instructor for his apparent leniency. [41] Similarly, Ferdinand of Austria's letters to his prodigal son Maximilian II have none of the chill formality found in comparable Tudor documents; instead, they are the very soul of paternal concern. [42] And Max turned out to be quite an interesting and long-lived monarch. Although often spirited to the point of wildness, Habsburg princes--even the somber family of Charles V--enjoyed their training, at least by comparison with their competitors. This worked to their pedagogical advantage as well; Maximilian II mastered seven languages, if only to facilitate his excesses across the continent, and his fellows were also talented. Philip II was himself a noted family man, and his letters to his two daughters, whom he loved more than anything, were touchingly human. [43] The unique family arrangement of the Habsburgs was the cornerstone of their success; Habsburg children were dutiful and obedient, and Habsburg parents were genuinely concerned with their issue. All labored steadily in the family vineyard. By contrast, the Stewart King James IV effected the murder of

his father, and the Valois King Francis I sexually proposi-
tioned his sister. [44] The concept of "family" lacked the
Habsburg vitality in these dynasties. Although royal childhood was a difficult experience, it was perhaps less difficult
for the progeny of the sixteenth century's most successful
royal family.

Chapter Eight

MARRIAGE

"Let no man say that marriages are made in heaven.
The Gods are not so unjust."
> --Marguerite Valois,
> wife of King Henry IV of France

"But what does the state get out of all this? If the mutual
alliances of princes would give peace to the world, I should
wish each of them to have six hundred wives."
> --Desiderius Erasmus,
> The Education of a Christian
> Prince

The marriages of royalty were not designed to satisfy the
individuals involved. Their purpose was to secure the future
of the dynasty, and this might be done in two different ways:
the production of healthy heirs, and the formation of useful
alliances. In fact, as Erasmus noted, these marriages often
failed to fulfill their stated purpose, besides bringing added
misery into the lives of the haphazardly matched couples. As
for children, almost 40 percent of Tudor marriages proved
barren, and even the notably prolific Habsburgs were childless in almost 20 percent of their unions. [1] And in terms of
political advantage, few of the hopeful alliances formed
through marriages between houses bore even diplomatic fruit.
For the most part it was a sad and disappointing business.
Yet so important was marriage to sixteenth-century diplomacy
that even those sovereigns whose age or continental position
placed them in low esteem on the marriage market maintained
a facade of eligibility. To keep her flame burning, for reasons both political and personal, Elizabeth I of England was
careful to feed speculation regarding her nuptial plans, even

though she had no intention of marrying.   As the Spaniard
de Quadra recounted in 1563, "She was extremely angry with
them [the Lords, for proposing that she name a successor]
and told them that the marks they saw on her face were not
wrinkles but pits of smallpox, and although she might be old
God could send her children as He did to St. Elizabeth. "[2]

What was so enticing about these matrimonial alliances
was their seemingly unlimited promise of material gain, a
possibility that dwarfed any thoughts of personal compatibility.
We are told that Manuel "the Fortunate" of Portugal, upon
hearing of his wife's death, "was very sad, and very grieved
by the loss of such a wife and so great a dominion as he had
lost, " according to his contemporary Garcia de Resende. [3]
His wife was Isabella of Spain, and through her Manuel believed himself a potential successor to the Catholic Kings of
Spain.   If this was but wishful thinking, certainly their son
Miguel would be a fit candidate.   As Resende noted, Manuel's
grief for Isabella was actually disappointment at the severance
of his tie to Castile.   Isabella herself could never be the
prize Castile was.   This sort of calculation worked both ways;
the Catholic Kings had equally material reasons to mourn the
passing of their daughter.   To win her hand the Portuguese
king had been persuaded to expel the Jews from his domains,
a victory for the religious policy of Queen Isabella of Spain.
The Catholic Kings could count on good relations with their
son-in-law.   Also, the infant son Princess Isabella had given
her life to deliver was heir to the entire Iberian peninsula,
a logical furtherance of the Catholic Kings' attempts to consolidate the peninsula.   For both Manuel and his Spanish
cousins, the alliance had offered tangible benefits.   Other
alliances were less balanced in benefits, notably the union
of Princess Mary Stewart of Scotland and the French dauphin
Francis.   Mary gained only personal comfort, prestige, and
an escape from the bloody fray that enveloped her barbaric
native land.   In return, the French convinced the happily ex-
patriated young girl to sign a series of documents that, had
they been honored by the Scots, would have made Scotland a
mere French appendage.

There were many marriages a sovereign could not afford to refuse.   James V of Scotland would gladly have married his mistress, but his financial woes left him no choice
but to seek a foreign dowry.   And Henry IV of France was
so indebted to the bankers of Florence that when they offered
to cancel his debts--on the condition that he wed Marie de
Medici--he assented, although like James he had a precontract

with one of his mistresses. But this, too, had a cost for Henry, as the spurned Henriette turned to that favorite pastime of the French court: treacherous intrigue. In her bitterness she became a spy for Philip IV of Spain while still serving as faithless Henry's mistress.

Propelled by the need for money, land, and political security, the whole process of royal matrimony became a game of impersonal barter. With cold ambition the standard, personal considerations were neglected almost to an absurd degree. Eccentricities could be rationalized, flaws glossed, sickness ignored--at least from diplomatic distance. Juana of Spain, known to be insane, was nonetheless a proven progenitor--she had six healthy children--and was courted by many marriageable rulers. "The English seem little to mind her insanity, especially since he has assured them that her derangement of mind would not prevent her from bearing children," wrote de Puebla to Ferdinand of Spain. 4 This pragmatism was unseemly, even distasteful. Philip II of Spain had endured a most depressing liaison with Queen Mary I of England in which he had avoided her as much as was possible politically. When she died, with him at a safe distance on the Continent, he immediately offered to marry her sister and successor Elizabeth, with no intention of treating her any more kindly than he had treated poor wretched Mary. He would spend little time with her, wrote one of his confidants, "whether he left her pregnant or not."5 Still less decent was the advice of the Portuguese ambassador Barrossos in 1521, after the death of King Manuel. The new king, John III, was scheduled to wed Catalina, the younger sister of Manuel's widow Eleanor of Austria. Catalina was some distance away, Barrossos argued, and, rather than pay for her lengthy journey, it seemed to him expedient to espouse John to Eleanor, who was already present at court. It was a case of a bird in hand, and to the Portuguese these Habsburg princesses were apparently interchangeable. 6

Less decent and still more deadly were the Tudors, who were so convinced of the power of marriage alliances that they made it a crime of the highest severity for anyone of English royal blood to marry without crown permission, and such license was only rarely forthcoming. The English sovereigns used this power to destroy, not to build their dynasty. Fearful that consolidating marriages among their lesser relatives would pose a challenge to their own questionable genealogical right to the English throne, Henry VIII and Elizabeth I virtually eliminated their kin by denying them

Chart 8

INBREEDING IN THE HOUSE OF HABSBURG

Ferdinand m.▭Isabella

1st Generation

Juan m.——Margaret
of Austria

Joanna m.——Philip the
Handsome

Isabella m.ⅣⅣAlfonso
ⅣⅣManuel
of Portugal

Maria m.ⅢⅢManuel

Catherine m.

Arthur; Henry VIII of
England

2nd Generation

Charles V m.▭Isabella of
Portugal

Ferdinand m.——Anne of
Bohemia & Hungary

Eleanor of Austria m.ⅣⅣManuel; Francis I
of France

Isabel m.

Christian II of Denmark

Maria m.——Lewis II of Bohemia & Hungary

Catalina m.▭John III of Portugal

Dom Fernando m.

Dona Guiomo
(from obscure noble
family)

Dom Eduardo m.ⅣⅣIsabel of Braganza

Beatrice m.

Charles of Savoy

3rd Generation

Philip II m.▭Maria Manuela
▭Mary Tudor
Elizabeth Valois
▭Anne of Austria

Joanna m.▭Juan Prince of Brazil
Maximilian II m.▭Maria
Ferdinand m.   Philipa (commoner)

Charles m.▭Maria of Bavaria

Isabel m.

Sigismund, King of Poland

Anne m.   Albert III, Duke of Bavaria

Mary m.

Guillermo, Duke of
Juliers & Cleves

Catalina m.——Francis, Duke of Mantua
- - -Sigismund, King of Poland

Gleanor m. ——Guillermo, Duke of
Mantua

Barbera m.   Alonso, Duke of Ferrara

Joanna m.

Francisco de Medicis,
Duke of Florence

Christine m.   Francesco Steraa,
Duke of Milan

Dorothea m.

Frederick, Count Palatine

Maria m.ⅣⅣAlessandro, Duke of Parma

Catalina m.ⅣⅣJohn, Duke of Braganza

Emanuel Philibert, Duke of Savoy m. Marguerite Valois

LEGEND

ⅣⅣⅣ relatives

▭▭▭ close relatives

—————— double marriage alliance

– – – – remarriage within family to save alliance

the right to marry, thus choking off their reproduction (see charts 2, p. 38, and 8, p. 230). When a relative defied royal edict, married, and had children, the sovereigns intervened and annulled the union. The children of these ill-fated matches became bastards in the eyes of the law, and several unrepentant relatives were actually executed by the crown. Lord Hertford escaped with a mere £15,000 fine for "seducing a virgin of the royal blood"[7] when he attempted to marry a peripheral princess, but when close relatives Arabella Stuart and William Seymour married secretly in 1610 both were clapped into the Tower. James I claimed that "she hath eaten of the forbidden tree," lending his personal pronouncement a typical biblical solemnity.[8] And when Katherine Grey and Edward Seymour wed secretly and "went into naked bed, in a manner both together," and, as they later admitted, "had carnal copulation," Elizabeth I punished both severely. Katherine in particular was "in the queen's great displeasure, who could not well abide the sight of her," wrote the English ambassador in Madrid.[9] There was a note of jealousy in the spinster queen's rage, and Elizabeth's sanctimoniousness was undoubtedly the product of intense fear and distrust of marriage itself, certainly understandable given the nature of royal marriage and the experiences of her childhood. But her father's preaching on the subject was pure hypocrisy; of his sister Margaret, who was living out of wedlock with Henry Stewart, he wrote: "She hath made herself a shame and disgrace to all of her family ... it is impossible for anyone to lead a more shameful life."[10] With characteristic solipsism Henry found his own disgraceful behavior in and out of marriage justifiable. Such chest-beating notwithstanding, both in their own unfortunate unions and in the marriages they feared of their relatives, marriage was an exceedingly sore subject for the rulers of sixteenth-century England.

With this and other evidence on which to stake their case, some fairly detached contemporaries doubted the efficacy of political marriages. Erasmus expounded on these unions in his well-known treatise The Education of a Christian Prince, in which he professed bafflement at the entire structure of dynastic marriages. With a cool logic that apparently escaped him in his opinions on child-rearing, he argued that:

> the marriage of Princes is really a private matter
> of their own. It is called the greatest of human
> affairs so that we too often have recurrence of what

> happened to the Greeks and to the Trojans because
> of Helen. But if you please to make a choice be-
> coming a prince, your wife should be selected for
> her integrity, modesty and wisdom and [she should
> be] one who would be an obedient wife to a good
> prince and would bear him children worthy of both
> of their parents and of the state. 11

Erasmus noted both political and personal failings in the accepted pattern of princely marriage:

> In a word, by alliances of this sort the sway of
> princes is perhaps increased, but the affairs of their
> people are weakened and shattered. A good prince
> does not consider his own affairs prosperous unless
> he looks out for the welfare of the state. I shall
> not talk about heartless effect [the result of these
> alliances] on the girls themselves, who are some-
> times sent away to remote places to [marry] men
> who have no similarity of language, appearance,
> character, or habits, just as if they were being
> abandoned to exile. They would be happier if they
> could live among their own people, even though with
> less pompous display. Although I am aware that
> this custom is too long accepted for one to hope to
> be able to uproot it, yet I thought it best to give
> my advice in case things should turn out beyond my
> hopes. 12

He was of course correct about the entrenched marital habits
of European royalty, and in addition he was unable to understand the princely perspective on such unions. Even his examples could be turned against his argument: "What was
gained," he queried, "a few years ago by the alliance of
King James [IV] of Scotland [to Margaret Tudor], since he
invaded England with his hostile forces?" Using Erasmus's
previous argument, Margaret was indeed a sort of Tudor
Helen: an English sympathizer and perhaps even an operative
in James's camp. This was undoubtedly of some use to
Henry VIII. There was also the possible benefit of expanding English suzerainty to include Scotland in the event James
died without male heirs, something Henry VIII desired very
much. But from the Scottish perspective, England could well
be theirs through Margaret in the case of a break in the
male Tudor line. And this in fact came to be in 1603, when
James IV's great-grandson James VI became James I of England, a fine reward indeed for the long harassed Scottish

royalty.   His accession to the English throne was a direct
result of the alliance Erasmus selected to illustrate his
point about the bootlessness of such marriages.   With such
carrots as incentive, sixteenth-century monarchs hardly
minded the length of the stick.

The parries and thrusts regarding marriageable
princes and princesses were, for better or for worse, the
basic substance of sixteenth-century diplomacy.   As the
Archbishop of Capua wrote to Charles V, "In time of war
the English made use of their princesses as they did of an
owl, as a decoy for alluring smaller birds. "[13]   And Charles
himself noted that "the best way to hold your kingdom together is to make use of your children. "[14]   The treaty of
Cateau-Cambresis was sealed with no less than three royal
nuptials, and a main condition of the settlement dictated by
the victorious Charles V to Francis I in 1526 was the wedding of the French king to the Emperor's sister Eleanor. [15]
Even though sixteenth-century rulers rightly visualized great
benefits from these alliances, such unions were generally
fleeting, as the notion that countries could be inextricably
linked merely by an exchange of vows between self-styled
feudal overlords was a medieval illusion.   With an occasional
spectacular exception, Erasmus's analysis proved trenchant.
England's only meaningful sixteenth-century matrimonial alliance was with Castile; Philip II and Catherine of Aragon
were the only foreign consorts of English sovereigns during
this period.   Yet despite these two marriages, England and
Spain were mortal enemies for much of the latter half of the
century.   Although the dynasts themselves concentrated on
the occasional success and regarded these marital alliances
as essential to their position in the European hierarchy,
these alliances were in fact quite frequently superficial, unhappy, and ultimately destructive.

Even the marriages that proved felicitous despite the
humiliating obstacles often brought tragedy.   Juan of Castile,
heir to the thrones of Aragon and Castile, was married at
the age of nineteen to a Habsburg princess and died six
months later from the strains of excessive "copula, "[16] although he had been delighted, obviously, with his bride.   Juan
was of a ripe age when he married, weak though he was.
Few of his peers were as mature, at least chronologically.
Catherine de Medici was barely fourteen when she traveled
to France for her wedding.   There the young girl became
the principal actress in a tawdry bedroom farce-cum-
consummation observed by a Pope, a king, and the assem-

bled luminaries of court. That this spectacle took place in
a bed said to have cost over half the princess's dowry was
hardly redemptive, probably still more discomfiting. [17] Margaret Tudor was thirteen in the year of her journey to Scotland, where by the grace of a Papal dispensation for "con-
sanguinity, affinity, and non-age"[18] she was wedded to debauched James IV. Such instances were quite usual in royal
circles. And lesser lights followed the lead of their princes;
Charles Brandon, husband of Mary Tudor, married his underaged ward Catherine Willoughby after Mary's death, and St.
Augustine, in his <u>Confessions,</u> admitted that he had wished
to marry a ten-year-old girl. "I liked her, and was prepared to wait."[19] His patience would not be put to a test
here; Roman and Canon law set the age of binding marriage
at fourteen for boys and twelve for girls.

What these tender youths faced first in royal marriage
was a ghastly ritual: the scrutiny to which their early relations were subject. Such matters were the province of the
entire court, perhaps the entire realm, even the continent.
Each had representatives present. Without proper consummation both the marriage and the alliance were void. Into
a lion's den the bewildered children were cast, with elaborate
ceremony to further inform them of the import of their performance. Eighteen-year-old Mary Tudor was taken from her
wedding festivities by attendants, unclothed, and then rerobed
in special garb before being taken to her decrepit fifty-two-
year-old husband Louix XII of France. The bedroom chamber itself was a virtual Roman coliseum; voyeurs peered
through cracks in the door, there was a crowd at each window, and still more inventive onlookers gathered around the
holes they drilled in floors, walls, and ceilings. [20] "Each
cry, each complaint of the bride, would provoke on the part
of the audience a rain of bravos in honor of the husband."[21]
The ladies were no less curious than the men in this regard,
according to the poet Clement Marot, a participant in the
wedding of Renée of France to the Duke of Ferrara. He
wrote of the spectacle in his <u>Chans Nuptial:</u>

> You who still sup, come, leave the laden table;
> The less you eat, the better you will dance.
> Up, almoners, you Graces of old fable
> The husband says it is time now to advance.
> He's tired of day; he longs to hurl a lance.
> Then dance! dance! dance often and yet more,
> Till the time comes to listen at the door
> While he makes the assault without a light.

Our appetites are gone; then to the chore:
Oh, dangerous is that very happy night. [22]

Dangerous indeed, but happy it usually was not.   Castilian
law required the presence of notaries at the royal bedside on
wedding night, and other countries subjected their dynastic
progeny to similarly oppressive scrutiny. [23]   After both Francis I and the Pope watched fourteen-year-old Henry II and
Catherine de Medici consummate their nuptials, the ambassador Sacco wrote to Milan that "Francis wished to watch
them jousting, and each of them jousted valiantly. "[24]   This
effort was all the more valiant for Henry's stoic disregard of
his deformed organ, his broken lance.   The joust could hardly have been pleasant.   Since marriages were not legally
binding until they had been consummated, the intimate relations of kings and their spouses became public domain.   As
with all royal acts, there was much protocol to observe and
many traditional injunctions to be obeyed.   Habsburg princes
were constantly warned against overindulgence, and the English had a similarly dark view of "carnal marriages. "   Cecil wrote that "carnal marriages begin happily and end in
tragedy. "[25]   No details of the marital relationship could be
concealed.   The very sheets of the nuptial bed were often
paraded for public inspection, and woe unto the prince who
had left them unspotted.   Sovereigns were constantly reminded by these and other indignities that marriage and legitimate procreation were state business, not personal pleasure.   The Duke of Wittenberg might happily sit astride his
wife booted and spurred, but his more regal peers found their
marital relations a chore. [26]   For those who failed in the
sight of these gossipy observers, shame blotted their career.
Brantome claimed to have seen Francis II of France "fail
a number of times" with his Scottish bride Mary Stewart. [27]
The court clucked over the boy's reputed deformities, and
rumors of his frailty spread across Europe.   Sebastian of
Portugal, fearing perhaps a similar dishonor, refused to
marry at all, neatly avoiding the issue but effectively terminating his dynasty.   According to a contemporary chronicle, the young king feared impotence: "He wishes also to
marry in order to have an heir, but the doctors fear that he
will be unfit for generation. "[28]   Perhaps to assuage doubts
about his manhood, Sebastian was the fiercest of warriors.
He sought battle madly and gloried in bloodshed, even his
own.   He died at age twenty-four.   Because of his disinclination to reproduce, Portugal fell to the Spanish Habsburgs.

The issue of consummation was equally traumatic for

the women, especially if their sexual past gave them secrets
to conceal. While theirs was the passive role, their husbands and the assembled throngs--to put the matter bluntly--
expected blood on the wedding night as proof of chastity. Although we now know this test to be fallacious, dishonored indeed was the sixteenth-century princess who was proved im-
pure on her wedding night. Catherine Howard was executed
by husband Henry VIII for her extramarital affairs, and an
English statute forbade "unchaste women" to marry the king
on penalty of death. This penalty also applied to royal wives
who attempted to conceal their previous misadvantures. [29]
Yet we are told that many women of royal blood engaged in
premarital activities, and apparently few were detected.
Perhaps the answer to this apparent mystery can be traced
to the variety of folk remedies known to the sixteenth century.
Brantome described one such crude method for regaining virginity:

> It is necessary to have blood suckers and put them
> to do the work of nature, to draw and suck the
> blood, which blood suckers, in sucking, leave and
> engender small ampules and fistulas full of blood,
> in so likely a fashion that the gallant husband, who
> comes to assail them on the wedding night, breaks
> these ampules from which the blood gushes out, he
> and she both being all bloody, which is a great joy,
> to one and to the other, and thus the "honor of the
> citadel is saved. "[30]

Brantome, though his chronicle dealt with the sixteenth-
century French court, did not indicate just which princesses
had recourse to this method. But this was only one of many
such techniques, though probably the least appealing. To
cite another, the sixteenth-century physician Caspar Wolff
recommended the application of parsnip juice one hour before
initial coition to tighten the orifice and impede penetration. [31]

Some royal couples found connubial bliss despite the
haphazard means by which they were thrown together. Charles
V loved his Isabella dearly, and Henry VII felt the same way
about Elizabeth York. But the sterling marriage of the century was the union of the Habsburg Prince Ferdinand with
Anne of Bohemia. Although this couple was betrothed when
both were thirteen years of age, the match ripened well in
the lively and gay Austrian court. Anne ultimately brought
fifteen children into the world, and Ferdinand's fidelity was
the wonder of Europe. The English cleric Grindal held the

Austrian prince as an example to all men. "He was a chaste prince, a prince that did truly and (as they say) precisely keep his wedlock--a notable virtue in any man, but more notable in a prince, specially in this loose and licentious age. "32 Ferdinand's monogamy was a rare virtue among princes, and Grindal continued his sermon by explaining how this unique prince had been rewarded.

> And Behold, I beseech you, how wonderfully God blessed him for his chaste observation of matrimony, for where other princes, living heretofore incontinently, have been plagued of God with sterility and want of royal issue of their bodies, and so the direct line of succession hath been cut off after them, God hath given to this prince plenty of honorable children, both sons and daughters, but also, according to the verse of the psalm, caused him to see filios filiorum, his children's children, to a very great number. 33

Grindal's critique equated marital fidelity with fecundity and noted the failures of other more self-indulgent European sovereigns in this respect, a failure of which the monarchs themselves were painfully aware. James IV tried to absolve his wanton behavior with frequent visits to the shrine of St. Ninian, often stopping to refresh himself with a mistress en route. 34 But since few princes found their marriages personally satisfying and the opportunity for debauchery was unlimited, the royal male usually relaxed with his paramours and ignored his wife. Henry II's cherished Diane de Poitiers actually had to lead him off to spend the night with his wife on occasion, in order to provide for the succession. 35 With marriage a chore of kings, the status quo at royal courts often favored the mistress; as previously noted, Diane was so secure that she actually grieved deeply when her lover's wife lay deathly ill, afraid that if Catherine de Medici died Henry might marry an attractive young princess and lose interest in his "seneschal. "36

The less compatible royal marriages were the general rule. The aforementioned Marguerite Valois was espoused to the heir-presumptive, Henry of Navarre, in a purported attempt to ease religious tensions and also to bring the dynamic Henry into the decaying French royal family, just as Louis XII and Francis I had married Valois princesses as part of their incorporation into the French royal house. But in the case of Marguerite, the enmity between husband and wife prevented this graft from taking root. Their marriage produced colorful, ribald lore from its very inception. Marguerite was known to have a mind of her own, which she put to use primarily to find new ways to embarrass her mother with messy affairs. She wanted no part of Henry and had to be forced to the altar. Even before this auspicious beginning, Charles IX knew exactly what he was giving his Huguenot enemy: a wanton girl and a false peace. The occasion of their wedding brought all the important Huguenot leaders to Paris, uneasily to be sure, and on the worst possible advice, Charles took the opportunity to massacre the troublesome heretics. The day after this massacre, which took place on St. Bartholomew's Day, the blood-drunk Charles exulted over his sister's role in the slaughter. "Teh! but my Margot has a gentle c...! By the blood of God! I do not think there is another like it anywhere in the world; it has taken all my Huguenot rebels like a bird call."[37]

If Marguerite had no conscious part in this atrocity, she quickly earned her own stripes in the wars of religion. Henry had married her only of necessity and had no desire to enter the Augean stables of her milieu. To be sure he had his own frequent diversions, but his wife he left to her own devices. The contemporary writer l'Estoile explained that "he had taken back [after one of her misadventures] his wife in a manner of acquittal, and for the command which his Majesty had laid upon him; it was never possible to persuade him to sleep with her, even for one night, and to caress her with fine words and a good face, at which the mother [Catherine de Medici] and the daughter were greatly enraged."[38] However much exaggeration went into the creation of Marguerite's reputation, which included the seduction of two of her brothers and numerous courtiers, it was certainly common knowledge that she misbehaved. Even her beloved brothers found her habits annoying. After she left the city of Agen, to which she had been ordered after disgracing herself in public, her brother Henry III angrily told his court that "the cadets of Gascony are not able to defile the Queen of Navarre enough, and she has left them to seek the muleteers and braziers of Auvergne."[39] Divorce came to Henry IV's mind shortly after he became king, when there was no longer the political need to maintain the pretense of their marriage. He reportedly discussed divorce and remarriage to his mistress Gabrielle d'Estrées with his adviser Sancy who, to his everlasting discredit, was said to have told the king that "whore for whore, he would prefer the daughter of Henry II to the daughter of Madame d'Estrées,

who had died in a brothel. "[40] Of Henry IV this story can
be believed, for he was devoted to his ministers above his
women--although he spent more time with the latter than the
former.

The eventual divorce trial provided further opportunity
for the sharp-tongued couple to lambast each other. When
asked by the Cardinal Joyeuse whether they had consummated
their union, Henry supposedly replied: "We were very young
on the day of our wedding, and each of us was so lecherous
that it was impossible for us to refrain. "[41] If this sounds
slightly suspicious, Marguerite's supposed rejoinder can be
told with more certainty. Henry, she announced to the tribunal, had noxious armpits and malodorous feet. This was
confirmed by another of Henry's intimates, Henriette d'En-
tragues, who apparently said of him that "it was a good thing
that he was king, for otherwise no one would be able to endure him, and that he stunk like a carrion. "[42] Army offi-
cers further corroborated this final assertion. The wanton
Marguerite also testified that, "to my profound regret, conjugal affections did not exist between us during the seven
months which preceded my husband's flight in 1575; although
we occupied the same couch, we never spoke to one another. "[43] In the royal bed the king and queen supposedly
clawed and cuffed each other like animals and were conspicuously barren. [44] A divorce was arranged, and the illusion
of a continuous French royal house was shattered.

Yet this ill-matched pair was by no means atypical.
It was with good reason that Queen Christina of Sweden wrote
in her memoirs: "More courage is required for marriage
than for war. "[45] There was more than a kernel of truth to
the waggish comments about Francis I of France and his un-
appreciated wife Claude. When Francis died, twenty-three
years after careworn Claude, they were laid to rest on a
marble slab at St. Denis. It was said that the slab was the
only bed they had ever shared. [46] Margaret, the daughter of
Charles V, hated her Farnese husband with ample reason.
Doubtless, she would have begrudged him a place in her tomb
as well. As the Emperor's faithful servant Mendoza reported, "I understand that Duke Ottavio will try to come
straight over here without detaining himself in Piacenza.
Madama [Margaret] knows about the [syphilitic] boils that he
has, and she cries about it every day. They say that a
symptom of this disease is the enjoyment of giving it to one's
partner. Your Majesty may please advise what should be
done. "[47] Mendoza had earlier encouraged the youngsters

toward intimacy, now he was faced with diehard frigidity. As Charles's brother Ferdinand was told, "Madama holds him off as long as she can. They say she has done so ever since the Duke came from there [Ferdinand's court] with the ailment. They also say that he still has something of it in his throat, and there are malicious people who believe that His Holiness [the Pope disliked Margaret] would not be very sad if he gave it to his wife. "48 Other instances of discord stemmed from less visceral quarrels. Renée of France complained frequently of her husband Hercules de Este's niggardliness, and he held even more serious transgressions against her; she first became a Calvinist, and then she persuaded her son Alfonso to steal off to the French court, much to the chagrin of Hercules and his cohort Charles V. Nor did their discord end there. Hercules ultimately believed that his wife and son were trying to poison him, and in 1557 he imprisoned them both. 49 Renée's nephew, King Henry II of France, sided with Hercules, and advised him to "deal with her as he saw fit. "50 The untender nephew did not, however, prevent her from returning to France in 1560 after her husband's death--not, at least apparently, by her hand.

These were, in truth, extreme cases, but even less spectacular rifts contained more than a hint of menace. Henry VIII's idea of a lover's warning was to obtain a warrant for the arrest of his wife Katherine Parr, who had been a bit too impertinent in conversation, on charges of heresy, an offense for which convicted transgressors were burned, and place it on her night table. 51 Her response was unrecorded. Interestingly enough, this sixth marriage was regarded as Henry's calmest. With such precedents, the reluctance of the highly intelligent Jane Grey in regard to marriage appears natural. It took a whipping to change her mind immediately before the solemnization of her nuptials with Guilford Dudley, an ill-fated union that culminated with her execution. 52

The legendary King Hal of England was not alone in his conjugal misery, but the import of his rash acts moving in and out of marriage had a profound effect on Europe. In a sense, his marital history was a comedy of errors, but those involved found it anything but amusing. In the first act the brave and determined Catherine of Aragon fell victim to her obstetrical failure and Henry's fragile sense of virility, and the English Reformation had begun. Divorce was not unheard of in the sixteenth century; in the village of Clayworth twenty-one of the seventy-two husbands married more than once, and three were wed three times. Not all of these remarriages were due to the death of previous wives either. [53] And there were other ways to dissolve a marriage legitimately; if a king would consent to three amatory sessions in the presence of midwives, and his wife remained undeflowered after this observation, the marriage could be annulled. [54] But no king would so dishonor himself, and for anxious Henry divorce seemed the only solution (technically he claimed that his marriage had never been valid because of Catherine's equivocal relations with his brother Arthur during their brief marriage). Their divorce, an unpopular move in England and a direct slap to the powerful Emperor (Catherine happened to be his aunt), created a new set of political difficulties. The break with the Catholic Church isolated England, made Henry's only child a bastard (and therefore poison on the continental marriage market[55]), and sowed dissension on the island itself. Talented and devoted crown servants, of whom the most conspicuous was Sir Thomas More, found their consciences wrenched by the "King's Great Matter." This trauma might have been justifiable if Henry's subsequent marriages had yielded a fit son. But at the start of the second act Henry had been captivated by decidedly unmaternal Anne Boleyn, daughter of a London merchant, and Anne had ambitiously fended off his advances until the infatuated monarch promised to marry her. [56] Henry ignored the injunction of the Habsburgs: "princes do not marry for love," and made the same mistake four times. [57] Sensitive, troubled, sexually ambivalent, and often ill, Henry was never long away from the marriage market. These complicated wranglings consumed much time, made everyone concerned miserable, diminished English prestige and credibility abroad (Francis I dubbed his rival "the lady killer," and princesses were reluctant to marry in England after the decapitation of not one but two queens), [58] and split the public into hostile camps.

The Tudors' Scottish cousins also blundered their way through a series of imprudent marriages. James IV's anglophile wife Margaret Tudor, as we have noted, secretly plotted against her husband. Their son James V followed his inclination and engaged in a love-match with the frail Madeline Valois against the wishes of his council, whose members warned him that Madeline was unlikely to produce heirs; she in fact died forty days after reaching Scotland, and negotiations had to be resumed once again. Valuable time and effort had been wasted, and James still lacked an heir. He ultimately sired only an heiress. Mary Stewart also indulged her whims, marrying her abrasive and dangerous cousin

Chart 9

TUDOR DESCENDANTS OF HENRY VII
Marital Obstructions

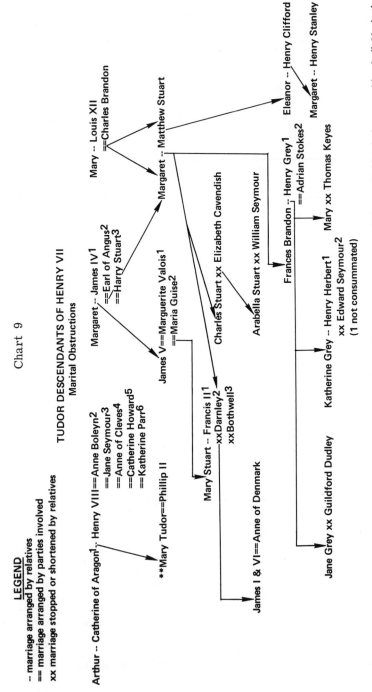

Arthur -- Catherine of Aragon[1]; Henry VIII==Anne Boleyn[2]
                                          ==Jane Seymour[3]
                                          ==Anne of Cleves[4]
                                          ==Catherine Howard[5]
                                          ==Katherine Parr[6]

Margaret -- James IV[1]
            ==Earl of Angus[2]
            ==Harry Stuart[3]

Mary -- Louis XII
        ==Charles Brandon

Margaret -- Matthew Stuart

Eleanor -- Henry Clifford

Margaret -- Henry Stanley

James V==Marguerite Valois[1]
        ==Maria Guise[2]

Charles Stuart xx Elizabeth Cavendish

Arabella Stuart xx William Seymour

Frances Brandon -- Henry Grey[1]
                   ==Adrian Stokes[2]

Mary xx Thomas Keyes

**Mary Tudor==Phillip II

Mary Stuart -- Francis II[1]
               xxDarnley[2]
               xxBothwell[3]

Katherine Grey -- Henry Herbert[1]
                  xx Edward Seymour[2]
                  (1 not consummated)

James I & VI==Anne of Denmark

Jane Grey xx Guildford Dudley

**After viewing Henry VIII's exploits his children had little interest in marriage.

"The near in blood, the nearer bloody." Macbeth

Darnley. Initially drawn to this vain character, the match
soon made her miserable, and threw yet another bone of contention to her unruly cousins. Mary's third marriage, to
Darnley's accused murderer, torched a public outcry. 59 That
Mary had little control over her destiny was apparent to all,
and her downfall and imprisonment swiftly followed this act
of desperation. Her son James VI married quite well; Anne
of Denmark was of hearty stock and capably secured the succession. But his relatively naive wife was incapable of deal-
ing with her husband's unusual sexual desires. The couple's
difficulties were public knowledge, and the majority sided with
the queen. "It stands very hard between the King and the
Queen," wrote an observer in 1595. 60

The remarkable Ferdinand of Austria's career epito-
mized the possible gain to be derived from political marriages
under ideal conditions. Not only did he produce fine children
--"an angel's choir," enthused the Papal legate Alexander61--
but he also obtained the coveted territory of Hungary for the
Habsburg family. The Emperor Maximilian I had arranged
Ferdinand's marriage for that very reason, and after the
death of Lewis II at the battle of Mohacs the crown of Hungary passed to the heir of Ferdinand and his wife Anne. The
succession was amply insured, the family lands increased
dramatically, and Ferdinand became respected across Europe
merely by making his marriage work properly. Ironically,
his sole achievement came as a family man. As a prince
he was difficult and uninspired. He quarreled with his brother, the Emperor Charles, entertained grandiose notions of
power, and gloated over his moral superiority.

Most royal marriages were unhappy, all were awkward and contrived in origin, and many served no real purpose, political or personal. Only the Habsburgs used a deliberate and comprehensive marriage strategy to accomplish
their political ends. Each generation of Habsburg princes
and princesses were sent across the continent to form alliances, many of which proved extremely valuable to the house.
The marriage of Philip of Austria to Juana of Castile founded
the sixteenth-century Habsburg dynasty, as the house had previously been only one of a number of central European ruling
families. This alliance also profited Ferdinand the Catholic,
as he forged a ring around dangerous France. 62 The marriage of Ferdinand of Austria to Anne Jagellon brought Bohemia into the Habsburg fold, and successive marriages with
Portugal eventually placed the Portuguese crown on Philip II's
head. Other dynasties made significant foreign marriages,

but only the Habsburgs worked to maintain their family affili-
ations, and Habsburg princes were quite often dutiful spouses.
At very least they were instructed to be such. As the Emperor Charles V told his son Philip, "Since you have not, I
am sure, had relations with any women other than your wife,
do not commit any further wickedness after your marriage
because ... apart from the discomfort and ills which may ensure from it between you and her, it will destroy the effect
of keeping you away from her. "63 Along with this prudent
continence, every generation correlate branches of the family
were married back into the main line (see Chart 10, p. 245).
The Habsburgs reinforced every alliance they made, often marrying both a son and a daughter to the siblings of another
house. Forgetting for a moment the biological implications
of such inbreeding, the Habsburgs forged a remarkable political achievement by keeping their conquests "in the family, " so to speak. As a modern historian explains, this
created an intricate web of family ties. Writing of the later
lunatic Habsburg, Carlos II:

> A man's ancestors in the third, fourth and
> fifth generations comprise eight, sixteen and thirty-
> two relationships respectively. Thus Carlos's par-
> ents, like everyone else, each had fifty-six such
> relationships in their family trees, or one hundred
> and twelve between them.
> These one hundred and twelve relationships in
> their care were shared between only thirty-eight
> individuals.
> Of Carlos's mother's fifty-six ancestors, forty-
> eight were also ancestors of his father.
> Of the thirty-two women in the fifth generation,
> that is the sixteen of one parent and sixteen of the
> other, twelve were descendants of the mad Isabella,
> mother of Isabella the Catholic.
> In the two family trees the name of Juana la
> Loca occurs eight times, the names of her two
> sons nineteen times. Seven out of the eight great-
> grandparents of Carlos II descended from Juana la
> Loca. 64

With these double marriage alliances--exclusively a Habsburg
maneuver--there was a much better chance of keeping the extended family concept operative. The long-term effectiveness
of royal marriage depended on its issue, and two couples
were far more likely to be successful in this respect than
one. The family patriarchs actually evolved a doctrine to

Chart 10

INTERMARRIAGE IN THE LINEAGE OF SPANISH PRINCES

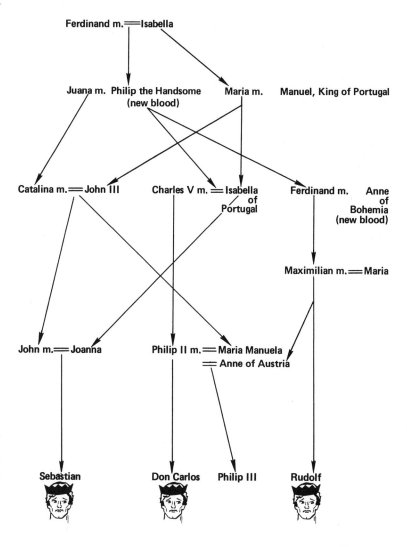

Ferdinand m.══Isabella

Juana m. Philip the Handsome   Maria m.   Manuel, King of Portugal
(new blood)

Catalina m.══John III   Charles V m.══Isabella   Ferdinand m.   Anne
of   of
Portugal   Bohemia
(new blood)

Maximilian m.══Maria

John m.══Joanna   Philip II m.══Maria Manuela
══Anne of Austria

Sebastian   Don Carlos   Philip III   Rudolf

 Insane

guide their actions.   Ferdinand of Austria theorized that
"princes must welcome daughters even more gratefully than
sons, for sons may tear apart the family state, while daughters bring helpful friendships and in-laws. "[65]   This eminently pragmatic marriage strategy paid generous dividends to
every Habsburg generation in the form of marriageable children.   By the end of the sixteenth century, there were sixty-
four full-blooded Habsburgs, while only six Tudors survived
the Tudor penchant for dynastic self-extinction. [66]   And two
of these Tudor curiosities had been bastardized by Elizabeth
while another was imprisoned and driven mad by James I.
The Habsburgs prized their relatives, realizing the need for
trustworthy partners in the far-flung dynasty.   With their
emphasis on duty, they for the most part avoided the destructive conjugal wrangling of their peers.   Whether they were
"happier" as a result can only be surmised, for duty is not
delight, and the Habsburgs were of a characteristically melancholy temperament.   For them questions of happiness were
irrelevant; questions of power were crucial.   Such was the
attitude necessary for those who wished to benefit from the
roulette wheel of dynastic marriage.   And largely through
their marriages the minor house of Habsburg rose to become
the unchallenged sixteenth-century master of the family empire.

Chapter Nine

SEX

"Satiety engenders disgust"

--Montaigne, Essays

One does not have to read a preoccupation with sex into the lives of sixteenth-century royalty. It was most certainly there, and it was also of great significance. The monarchs themselves were inordinately interested in the subject, and those around them fairly reveled in it, as the prevalent modes of humor and the high level of romantic intrigue would seem to indicate. The sexuality of important princes, of whom some were avid, some were timid, some were perverse, and some were dutiful, existed in a sort of "contrapposto" to the doings of the court. All of this was observed in the most prurient manner. Well it should have, for sex was subtly connected with virtually every other phase of royal life: health, mental outlook, family interests, and affairs of state. Reproductive acts--or unsuccessful and distorted reproductive acts--were a central determinant of dynastic success. A disciplined approach to sex benefited the Habsburgs greatly. But the Valois, whose sensuality ran rampant without pragmatic sanction, were uniformly destroyed by their sexual aberrations; the family history was a downward spiral from Francis I's venereal disease to Henry III's undiscriminating promiscuity.

If the various houses had different approaches, there were certain common experiences. For almost all princes education in sexual matters began early and confusedly. In this they were not alone, for tender youths of other stations were perhaps equally familiar with libidinal adventures. Such episodes were acknowledged with complete indelicacy. Mon-

247

taigne boasted of his youthful passions, accomplished "long
before the age of choice and knowledge," and was blunt in
his assessment of the interlude's aftermath: "Hence goatish
odors and a quick growth of hair, and an early beard that
astonished my mother," he crowed, echoing Martial.[1] This
last strange thought was only part of the entire cornucopia
of bizarre sexual attitudes that came to princes along with
their early initiations, the result of superstitious misinforma-
tion and the precepts of medieval thinkers. These notions
did not prevent experimentation, but they did create guilt and
shame; Maximilian I believed that venereal diseases were
sent by God as a divine punishment for the luxurious, voluptuous spirit that had sapped the crusading zeal of Europe.[2]
If there was such a spirit at work in sixteenth-century courts,
it restricted its activities to extramarital affairs. Legitimate
spouses were purely functional, with the production of children as the all-encompassing purpose of each royal union.
"Princes do not marry for love, they take wives only to beget children," wrote Ferdinand of Austria, who certainly
knew whereof he spoke regarding children.[3] Within this
framework passion was discouraged. Although their marriages were likely to be tepid at best, monarchs were further
obstructed in their legitimate relations by Church dicta. According to canon law carnal enjoyment was no less sinful in
marriage than in adultery, and the marital relations of
princes were monitored with great care by prelates and wags
alike.

On the other hand, a modicum of privacy could be had
with illicit amours, and royal males had a tantalizing menu
of alternatives. Mistresses were easy to find, of their own
choosing, and could be jettisoned on a whim. Their allure
was less a comment on their own qualities, which were often
quite unremarkable, than a statement of the untenable arrangement of royal marriages. Henry VIII, for example,
mistakenly believed that he would retain the pleasure of his
relationship with Anne Boleyn even after it had been shifted
from the illicit to the legitimate level. Happy with Anne as
his chaste mistress, he was miserable soon after she became
his wife, and their union entered into the realm of pressures
and expectations so burdensome as to cause immediate fric-
tion. The comfort of extramarital exploits might well be forgiven the monarchs of the sixteenth century as a few moments of beauty in a generally bland and even crude life;
some of the Renaissance's greatest charm can be found in the
rituals of chivalric love. This grand posturing in imitation
of the Morte d'Arthur lent an atmosphere of gentility to the

underlying baseness of the court, and European sovereigns
reveled in the panoply of mock-courtship and combat.   Henry
VIII, Francis I, Henry II, James IV, and Ferdinand the
Catholic all prided themselves on their chivalry, and the
royal mistresses were a necessary adjunct of this pursuit.
Only they could animate the "forbidden love" so crucial to
romance and gallantry.   The entire allegory of the elaborate
court life directed the king toward his paramour of the moment and away from his queen.

Back in his own bower, not to be mistaken for Pope's
"Bower of Bliss," the monarch was entreated to use the conjugal bed "more for the desire of children than bodily lust"
for perfectly good reasons. 4   If kings allowed themselves
more exciting, less sober relations with their wives they
could expect to sire children of ill health, even "monstrous
births. "   So warned the doctors and midwives of the period. 5
With this in mind, Henry VIII became convinced of Anne
Boleyn's wickedness after she brought forth one such por-
tentiously deformed miscarriage.   And James IV of Scotland
increased the frequency of his expiatory pilgrimages after his
queen delivered a number of stillborn males.   Monarchs inevitably philandered, had bad thoughts, and produced weak
strings of children.   To the medieval mind, the causal sequence in this pattern was unavoidable and troubling.   These
antiquated notions of sex, marriage, and childbirth held the
field, at least formally, until the eighteenth century, when
Musitanus wrote: "Passionate coitus is to be avoided, for it
is unfruitful. "   He added, to elaborate his argument, that
Spanish women were uniquely passionate.   He pointed to their
"Phrygian dance" during intercourse as a cause of their
sterility. 6   These well-known doctrines were impressed on
passionate princes, who were then haunted in the conjugal
bed by the specter of ill-formed children.

Such doctrines were at least partly responsible for a
marked ambivalence toward sex in many royal figures.   Even
reknowned rogues had moments of indecision.   Despite his
tirade against the voluptuous spirit, Maximilian I fathered
eight acknowledged bastards and three legitimate children.
Yet when he was urged to marry a third time, he answered
that the mere thought of a naked woman made him ill. 7
Henry VIII would never have admitted such a sentiment, but
he was nonetheless prudish, sensitive, and easily disenchanted
with his women.   The evidence would suggest that he found
intimacy painful; despite six marriages, only four of his
wives received his conjugal attentions, and each of them re-

ceived this boon only for a limited period. When they tired or offended him, as three of them did, he was clever enough to use the sexual misconceptions of his day to be rid of them. With Catherine of Aragon he cited Leviticus as evidence that marriage with his brother's widow was sexually improper. He pointed to their relative barrenness as confirmation of this. With Anne Boleyn, who gossipped about the king's reluctant and ineffectual carnal character, he invoked witchcraft; she had seduced him, according to the rumor he spread, through the use of spells. [8] To contemporaries this rationalization had the ring of truth.

Part of the reason princely relations were so traumatic, both in and out of the matrimonial bed, was the equivocal position of women in the retinue, indeed in life itself. In the lore of chivalry, they were no less than goddesses, but in the world of court they were often no more than harpies. Their appearance and behavior were rarely worthy of the legendary heroine Isolde, and the reality of the situation compelled Montaigne to point out: "Both kings and philosophers defecate, and so do the ladies."[9] If in truth these women were no more than creatures of their era, there were still ideals that dictated their conduct. For the most part they were treated as special creations in the ballet of chivalric love, as inferior beings in the actual workings of court. Above all, the sixteenth-century noblewoman was supposed to be chaste. The indiscretions of princes could be winked at, but according to the Tudor idea of female virginity, "break ice in one place and it cracks the more."[10] The lapses of queens were all the more reprehensible. At Anne Boleyn's trial it was alleged that her miscarriages were the result of infidelities. For this and other alleged crimes she was condemned to death.[11] And when a witness testified that Henry VIII's fifth queen Catherine Howard and her paramour "would kiss and hang by their bellies together as they were two sparrows" she was quickly assigned the same fate as her predecessor.[12] Yet it has been speculated that it was her aura of experience that attracted Henry in the first place, and her adventures before their marriage could easily have been discovered with the slightest bit of checking. That he was blind to such evidence testifies to Henry's confused reaction to her allure.[13] Such confusion was common: Henry II of France's sexual attraction to maternal Diana de Poitiers, twenty years his senior, for instance.

It is not surprising that women, even princesses, of the sixteenth century found themselves unable to match the

standards set for them. Some, like Marguerite Valois, re-
belled openly. Similarly, Henry IV of France's daughter
Henriette Maria had so many liaisons before the age of seventeen that her confessor advised her to take Mary Magdelene
for a model and England (she was married at seventeen to
Charles I of England) as a penance. [14] Margaret Tudor let
her lust be her guide in her actions following the death of
her husband James IV of Scotland, and several English princesses made not-so-secret trysts with their forbidden lovers
(see Chart 2, p. 38). Elizabeth, who made a career of pre-
venting such behavior in those around her, deceived many
with her austere appearance. But the Spanish ambassador
was not hoodwinked by her facade: "She is possessed with a
hundred thousand devils," he wrote, "yet she pretends to me
that she would like to be a nun, live in a cell, and tend her
beads from morning till night."[15] The devils to which he referred were her numerous paramours, who proved that kings
were not alone in their prodigality with kittenish mistresses;
Elizabeth personally made the fortunes of many of her gentlemen. Through her, Leicester became one of the richest lords in
England, Sydney received vast land tracts in America, Raleigh acquired 40,000 acres in Ireland, and Hatton rose from
obscurity to become Lord Chancellor. Nor was the Virgin
Queen above the taint of scandal. She and her current favorite Leicester were at Windsor in 1560 when Leicester's
estranged wife Amy Robsart "fell" down a flight of stairs at
their home and died of a broken neck. Many, including the
Spanish ambassador, believed the queen and her constant companion responsible for this suspiciously convenient accident.

At the French court the expression "putain comme une
princesse," or "whorish as a princess," gained currency, and
in fact became part of the idiom. [16] It was also said that
noblewomen were more foulmouthed than common wenches.
Courts across Europe were undoubtedly populated with a
healthy share of female bawds, and far from the ideal of
gracious, proper, and virtuous damsels was the actual assortment of upwardly mobile young women and languid aristocrats who surrounded males of royal blood. In a literary
"mock-combat" devised by the chronicler Brantome, the "doctors of love" award the ladies of the French court first prize
for their amatory skills, but in their decision they graciously
observe that the competition was fierce: "There are whores
everywhere and cuckholds everywhere, and chastity does not
inhibit one region more than another."[17] This was sometimes a delight, sometimes a plague for the princes. It was
always a distraction. The sexual wrangling of court often

interfered with business, created disharmony, disease, and became work itself.

The sine qua non of a truly strong sixteenth-century monarch was fit heirs, and a satisfactory sexual relationship with the royal spouse was the only way to accomplish this crucial end. Since a monarch's public image was determined in part by the size of his family, an absence of children in the royal nursery cast aspersions on the king's virility. The self-image of early modern rulers also depended in good measure both on their conjugal performance and their kingly appetite in other affairs. The royal retinue was the king's reflecting pool, and the entire court was privy to details of the king's intimate affairs. These details often provided the most unflattering reflections, as an almost astonishing balance of royal dalliances tended towards the gross and the absurd. One of Henry IV of France's youthful romances was with a woman laughingly dubbed "La Baveresse" (the slobberer), "so named because she sweated so."[18] Less for penance than for pleasure, Henry III of France formed a sado-masochistic religious order. "There were some," according to the diarist L'Estoile, "even among the mignions, according to what is said, who lashed themselves in this procession, and whose poor backs were seen to be all red from the blows which they gave themselves."[19] As a corollary to their frequent orgies, these public spectacles failed to satisfy the deranged king, and for further pleasure he had his friends whipped in the privacy of his chamber. In this pastime he was joined by his contemporary Don Carlos of Spain, who liked to have women beaten while he watched.[20] By contrast, the fairly routine lechery of Scotland's James V hardly seems worthy of the poet Lyndsay's vehement reproach:

> For Lyke and Boisterous bull, ye rin and ride
> Royatouslie lyke and rude Rubeatour,
> Ay Fukkand lyke ane furious Fournicatour.[21]

For any court observers who cared to witness, kings proved themselves easily tempted, often by unconventional lures.

Yet to joke about such matters was dangerous, for the kings themselves took their manhood seriously. Both Henry VIII and Philip II jailed men merely for impugning their virility in conversation. And for all the falsified charges of treason and witchcraft, the event that really triggered Anne Boleyn's execution was her indiscreet revelation to her brother and other wags of Henry's clumsy and frustratingly brief performances in the royal bed.[22]

Sexual matters were quite understandably a royal pre-occupation, in light of their enormous disruptive potential. Yet they were also a source of humor. Since sixteenth-century wits laughed at lepers and howled at the most abysmal conditions of life--Boccaccio and Rabelais were only two such black humorists--it is not surprising to find that sex was also lampooned in the same sort of gallows style, even though many monarchs were quite touchy about the subject. In the frankly libidinous world of court, stories about famous persons were repeated with relish. When James I's chief justice Edward Coke (pronounced "Cook") took to wife the widow of Sir William Hatton, she "was with child when he married her. Laying his hand on her belly (when he came to bed), and finding a child to stir, 'what, ' said he, 'flesh in the pot?' 'Yea, ' quoth she, 'or else I would not have married a Coke,'" or so the tale runs. 23 The Virgin Queen of England herself had a ribald wit; the story is told of her clever riposte to the young groom of her privy chamber, Thomas Gorges, who appeared at court with his right leg bedecked in finery. When asked by the queen why his left leg was not likewise adorned, Gorges replied that a misstep on the dance floor had resulted in his right leg being tangled with those of the beautiful Marchioness of Northampton, and thus honored. The queen laughed and told Gorges that perhaps someday he would succeed in having both legs so honored. Her drollery vanished, however, when the pair married without her consent, and as a result of this second misstep Gorges found himself between cell walls instead of his wife's legs. 24

On the other side of this coin, speculation and crass jokes about princesses and princes were just as ubiquitous, if less open. Elizabeth was as much a target as a taunter. The writer Ben Jonson told intimates that the queen "had a membrane on her which made her incapable of man, though for her delight she tried many.... A French surgeon undertook to cut it, yet fear stayed her. "25 But no European entourage matched the ribaldry of the French court. Early in the sixteenth century, the French courtesans grew jealous of their paladins' unceasing expeditions to Italy--apparently for both war and frolic. They charged the poet Marot to write a satiric rejoinder to the "Courtiers of France Being Then in Italy" and their Italian demoiselles. In his mock debate Marot compared both camps point by anatomical point, and had his rhetorical ladies conclude:

> To judge the case
> By the law

> We'll drop our skirts
> And win with awe;
> Without debate,
> For pleasure's state
> a finer sight you never saw. [26]

The epistle ended with a plea for the return of pleasure-loving Francis I, a request he was probably only too happy to grant.

Such was the backdrop against which many princes of the Renaissance performed. This was not an ideal situation, although it was undoubtedly colorful and interesting. Ideally, a sovereign would have been a family man on the order of Ferdinand of Austria. Monarchs of this sort earned great respect: Henry VII, Charles V, and Emanuel Philibert of Savoy were lauded for their relatively upstanding conduct, were blessed with suitable progeny, and avoided the labyrinth of dangers associated with unchecked philandering. Nothing practical was to be gained through indulgence, and everything, including life itself, might be lost. Still, sixteenth-century monarchs and their relatives were for the most part unable to restrain themselves, despite the obvious hazards. "Was there ever a court more like a brothel than this?" rhetorically asked the Florentine ambassador to the court of Francis I. [27] In the case of the French king, royal licentiousness was not confined to a mere mistress or two, it was frequently the business of the day. The Venetian ambassador Contarini described Francis's routine as follows: "He rises at 11:00, hears mass, dines, spends two or three hours with his mother, then goes whoring or hunting, and finally wanders here and there throughout the night, so one can never have an audience with him by day." [28] Even royal mistresses occasionally indulged in illicit affairs, and only clever planning staved off disaster. One day Francis arrived at his mistress's apartment unexpectedly, "Bonnivet was in his shirt, and had barely time to dive into the fireplace.... Francis was blithely unaware. He made love to Françoise and then ... freely made water into the fireplace." [29] According to Brantome and Sauval, Henry II had a similar misadventure. He arrived to visit his mistress just as she was otherwise engaged with the Marechal de Brissac. Brissac hid in a panic under the bed as Henry sauntered in to take his customary place with Diane. Then, complaining of hunger, Henry arose, and the trembling Diane brought him a box of sweetmeats. This he tossed immediately under the bed, saying to his rival: "Take them, Brissac! Everybody must live!" A pretty story, even if apocryphal. [30]

In most respects Henry II deliberately avoided his father's footsteps, but his sexual inclinations were problematical in their own right. As a fourteen-year-old boy, he had been captivated by thirty-four-year-old Diane de Poitiers, a combination of mother and lover. Her hold on the king was complete. As previously noted, she had to lead him off to spend an occasional night with the queen for the succession's sake. Henry was on occasion to be found sitting on Diane's lap, which must have amused Catherine de Medici as she viewed the proceedings through a specially constructed hole in the floor between her room and Diane's. [31] In these early years Henry was highly insecure. The young prince suffered from hypospadias: his urethra did not exit properly from his penis. This deformity was a source of great amusement to court ladies. [32] Diane, ever solicitous and maternal, restored his confidence, and an operation cured the defect.

Henry's sons were warped creatures in their own right, with little interest in sex and all the characteristics of androgynes. Francis II's testicles refused to descend from his pelvis, and as a result he was reputedly prepubescent at the age of eighteen. [33] Charles IX was a mother's boy, and Henry III's tastes were inclined toward the bizarre. Out on the town in drag between orgies and public spectacles, Henry and his minions--dubbed by Parisians "the princes of Sodom" --experimented constantly in excess and sought new bodies for Henry's bed, leeringly slandered as "the altar of Antinous." [34]

Henry III was replaced on the throne by his Huguenot cousin Henry IV, known to be a leader of courage and intelligence. This Henry was a much less decadent figure, hardened as he was by his struggle with the Valois and the Guises. He was aware of the political chasm that awaited the overly indulgent monarch. As he wrote his brilliant minister Sully:

> The Scriptures do not absolutely forbid having any sins or defects, inasmuch as such infirmities are attached to the impetuosity and quickness of human nature, but they do require that we shall not be dominated by them, nor permit them to reign over our wills, which is a thing which I have studied being able to do no better. And you know, from many things which have passed concerning my mistresses (those passions which all the world regards as the most puissant in my case), whether I have

> not often maintained your opinions against their
> fantasies even to the point of telling them when they
> became too importunate, that I should prefer to lose
> ten mistresses like them to losing one servant like
> you, who are necessary to me in all honorable and
> useful things. 35

For all his good intentions, Henry could never make
continence and sobriety more than theoretical virtues.   Valued
Sully himself mourned that his liege was so easily swayed by
what the minister called "this pimpery and these female
wiles."36   Unhappy in marriage, a victim of gonorrhea, Henry replied to such criticisms with the explanation that as a
good soldier he was entitled to some recreation.   These diversions had none of the languid perversity of his predecessors, yet they were certainly beyond prudence.   If idle sensuality had been a part of the Valois' daily routine, for Henry
such pleasures became a chivalric quest.   As he wrote to his
mistress "La Bell Corisande, " his blood was indisputably
steaming: "I devour your hands ... and kiss your feet a
million times ... it would be a desolate spot indeed where
we two would be bored together."37   If this passion strikes
us as disarming, contemporaries viewed some of his quests
with less amusement.   Perhaps the most controversial episode revolved around the king's obsession with Charlotte de
Montmorency.   He was fifty-six, she was sixteen, but he was
determined to have her.   As a first step he arranged to have
her married to the Prince de Condé.   Henry's mistress Henriette reportedly found these machinations amusing.   "Are
you not wicked, " she teased him, "to want to bed with the
wife of your son?   For you well know that you have told me
that he [the prince] was your offspring."38   Like many royal
peccadillos this was only rumored and alleged by contemporaries, but the absolute veracity of the story in this case
is less important to us than its popular acceptance as fact
and the consequences of this acceptance.   Gossip about this
misadventure helped to spark Catholic unrest and quite likely
put the notion of assassination into the unbalanced mind of
Francois Ravaillac.   Henry died at the fanatic's hands in
1610.

The perversions and lechery of the Valois were unmatched and did much to effect their downfall.   The family
depopulated itself by the end of the sixteenth century, and
the tolerance of the public faded as each generation exceeded
its predecessor in decadence.   But other dynasties followed
roughly the same pattern, particularly the Stewarts.   James

V "spared neither man's wife nor maiden, "[39] and roamed the countryside in disguise to rouse fresh game. And after the poet Lyndsay watched him take a scullery maid in a puddle of ale, he penned a scathing rebuke. "Would God the lady that lovit you best / Had seen you there swetting like twa swine. "[40] James VI's cavortings with his male favorites disgusted his subjects and baffled his queen. Osborne wrote, "The love the King showed was as amorously conveyed as if he had mistaken their sex and thought them ladies; which I have seen Somerset and Buckingham labor to resemble in the effeminateness of their dressings ... the King's kissing them after so lascivious a mode in public ... prompted many to inquire some things done in the tiring house. "[41]

The open decadence of Scottish kings was probably only fitting. The poet Pittiscottie admitted that his native land was "but the arse of the world" in the rest of Europe's estimation. [42] But even the disciplined Habsburgs committed their share of indiscretions. Philip the Handsome was noted for his unholy interest in virgins, and was apparently a sexual athlete of no small achievement. [43] Maximilian II was another Austrian rogue. In his teens he dallied with one of his mother's ladies, the Countess Anna of East Friesland, and sired a daughter. While making a reluctant journey to meet and wed his Habsburg cousin Maria, Max stopped in Mittenwald long enough to "capture several women. "[44] His father dashed off an admonishing letter to the prodigal:

> Maximilian! I hear with great sorrow that you are not behaving yourself at the Emperor's court. ... From what I hear you are drinking great quantities of strong wine and have shown signs of drunkenness and it appears that whenever you were free you have been most often drunk.
> I am afraid that after my death you may become dissolute and shameless. I warn you that you must avoid lewdness![45]

Maximilian's behavior would have won him laurels at the French or Scottish courts. But the Habsburgs realized the dangers immoderation posed for the dynasty and trained their children to lead disciplined lives. For them a stoic discipline was protection against fleshly pitfalls. Charles V took an almost inordinate interest in his son Philip's affairs, and inculcated the boy with the family's spirit of moderation. In a letter, Charles wrote:

> When you are with your wife ... be careful and do
> not overstrain yourself at the beginning, so that you
> could receive physical damage, because besides the
> fact that it [sex] may be damaging both for the
> growth of the body and for its strength, it often in-
> duces such weakness that it prevents the siring of
> children and may even kill you, as it killed Prince
> Juan, by whose death I came to inherit these king-
> doms. 46

Overbearing Charles might have been, but the Habsburgs certainly were not harmed by their sexual habits.   They neither
feared sex, as the Tudors did, nor reveled in it, as the
Stewarts and Valois did.   Recognizing the hazards of car-
nality, the Habsburgs were determined not to be undone by
it.   To this end Charles advised Philip that sex was exclu-
sively for the production of children, and that to avoid death
and disgrace:

> The remedy is to keep away from her as much as
> you can.   And so I beg you and advise you strongly
> that, as soon as you have consummated the mar-
> riage, you should leave her on some pretext, and
> not go back to see her too quickly or too often; and
> when you do go back, let it be only for a short
> time. 47

At the austere Spanish court, sex was not the open preoccupation it was at other western European courts.   The Habsburgs prized their health and vigor, and the lesson of Juan,
"the prince who died of love" was never forgotten, especially
by Charles V.   This constant theme of moderation and self-
preservation, hand in hand with their deliberate marriage
policy, was perhaps the unique characteristic of the sixteenth-
century Habsburgs. 48

But discipline was not disinclination, and even Habsburg princes could fall victim to infatuation.   Ferdinand,
Maximilian II's brother, cast aside his birthright to wed a
commoner.   His beautiful wife was the heiress of a well-to-
do banking family, but their morganatic children were nonetheless unrecognized by the crown, and were thus unable to
inherit their father's lands.   Maximilian II was especially
peeved after Ferdinand deserted on the battlefield and returned home to his wife.   Max claimed that this inconceivable
act of bad faith was caused by some letters sent by "der
loser brekin." "Afterwards he had no rest either by day or

by night, only fell into a fit of melancholy, even into a fever ... so off he goes.... I wish the bitch were stuck in a sack and no one knew where ... God forgive me. "[49]

Charles V was by all accounts a relatively cold individual, but he was nonetheless unable to deny his physical needs while on his constant journeys. The Emperor fathered three known bastards, two of whom went on to have remarkable careers. But Charles's romantic pursuits were much like another of his favorite pastimes: an interest in clockwork. Brantome noted that "whenever he slept with a beautiful woman (for he enjoyed love, and too much for his gout) he would not leave until he had had had her three times. "[50] Apparently no more, no less. His reknowned gluttony aside, Charles was the epitome of Prussian self-discipline.

There was clearly no general lack of sexual desire within the royal families of the sixteenth century, but that desire was often wasted from a dynastic perspective. The attentions showered on mistresses, favorites, and serving wenches were distractions, having no constructive purpose. Sexual irregularity not only induced infertility and self-doubt, it also promoted jealousy and factions, along with discord in the family itself. Favorites gained undue access to power with strangleholds on lovesick sovereigns, distorting the chain of command and demonstrating for all to see the king's lack of self-control. And despite the veneer of tacit acceptance, philandering was a source of much unhappiness in the royal household. Jealousy raged no less hot in royal blood. Catherine de Medici attempted to persuade the young Duc de Nemours to throw vitriol in the face of her husband's mistress, and even the devoted Isabella the Catholic exiled her husband's inamoratas as soon as she discovered their identity. [51]

Worse still, such indulgences might yield dividends in disease above and beyond their effect on family relationships, mental well-being, and court dynamics. A contemporary proverb stated that "an old man in love hugs death, "[52] and this was certainly borne out in the deaths of Louis XII of France and Ferdinand of Aragon. But even young princes could be stricken with sex-related ailments that would shorten their lives and terrorize their days. Casual trysts with women of questionable standards left both parties open to infection. Perhaps there were even those who wished to punish wanton princes with venereal disease; at the French court the rumor was circulated that Francis I had contracted the "pox"

from his beautiful mistress "La Ferronière." She had, in
turn, been infected by her insanely jealous husband, who had
"sought this infection in a bad house in order to infect both
of them [the king and his unfaithful wife]."[53] Such malevolence was hardly necessary. Venereal disease was as common as the flux at most royal courts, and the malady ruined
many a promising prince. What they contracted was not our
eradicable equivalent. It was a horrible, virulent, disfiguring, and chronic malady. As the poet Baif wrote in his
Passetemps:

> For having haunted the Bordeaux,
> Your features with the chancres go,
> And nothing's left of nose or face
> But two small nostrils in their place. [54]

This was no exaggeration. The considerable individual sufferings of princes were echoed by widespread outbreaks,
testaments to the inconceivably macabre nature of the disease. In 1498 Paris was beset with victims, a circumstance
many attributed to the army recently returned from Italy.
The unafflicted, including the nobles gathered to pay homage
to the new king, Louis XII, were horrified by the profusion
of hideous sufferers. To rid themselves of this visitation
they passed a law that forbade the victims to enter city limits on penalty of death. Whether this penalty held any fear
for the syphilitics is debatable. A chronicler described them,
with their

> ulcers which might have been taken for glands, to
> judge by their size and color, from which issued a
> villainous and infected mud which almost made the
> heart stop beating; their faces were greenish black
> and otherwise so covered with wounds, with scars
> and pustules, that nothing more hideous could pos-
> sibly have been seen. [55]

Even in an age accustomed to physical wretchedness these
creatures drove the Parisians almost to a frenzy of revulsion.
Yet this was the same venereal disease that many kings and
queens endured for much of their lives. Francis I was the
most gallant courtier in France until his abdomen began to
rot with virulent syphilis. On one occasion his ulcerated
bladder broke out in three places. Surgeons closed all but
one of the ulcers; the remaining issue was left open as a
replacement for his decayed urinary tract. [56] Such gruesome
sickness was more terrifying than we can imagine, but the
rulers of western Europe knew these horrors all too well.

Even with such dangers the company of one's chosen
mistress was no doubt more pleasant than the formal and
pressure-laden visits to the queen's chambers.   Charles V
and Maximilian II did not allow their pleasure to interfere
with business.   On the other hand, the French kings after
Francis I virtually avoided their wives.   Henry II reluctantly
spent enough time with Catherine de Medici to keep her pregnant, but Charles IX and Henry III did not even bother to keep
up appearances.   "She will not give me one bit of trouble, "
Charles pronounced happily when he first saw the portrait of
his prospective bride. [57]

The sexual problems of Tudor sovereigns were even
more complex.   Henry VIII had an ambivalent attitude toward
women and a strange desire for incestuous relationships and
sexual rivals. [58]   He was most tantalized by the women who
had been pursued--and perhaps won--by other courtiers; Anne
Boleyn and Catherine Howard.   But this very source of attraction eventually triggered Henry's vindictive jealousy.   When
his sexual betrayal came to light, Henry had both these women
executed.   In the wake of his pathological pattern, Henry's
successors thwarted their sexual instincts.   Mary Tudor suffered from amenorrhea, an absence of the menstrual flow. [59]
The pathetic princess was deathly afraid of men after her
tumultuous childhood, and married at the age of thirty-eight
only to satisfy the urgent requests of her advisers.   As
Renard noted, "She claims that never has she felt that which
is called love. "[60]   She also confided to the Imperial ambassador that she had resolved to remain celibate.   Her sister
Elizabeth, on the other hand, "enjoyed being made love to
with an abnormal avidity that was the result of a deranged instinct, "[61] and beginning in her fourteenth year had a series
of sexual affairs.   Young men were her favorite pleasure
throughout her long life, but she had a pathological aversion
to marriage, and the best evidence indicates that she ended
her affairs just short of copulation.   She was afraid of making a man her lord and master, and told the French ambassador de Foix that whenever she thought of marriage she felt
as though "someone were tearing her heart from her bosom. "[62]   Although a few of the lesser descendants of Henry
VII enjoyed stable family relationships, his direct successors
were crippled by their mental torments.   Distorted notions
of sex colored the Tudors' conception of their dynastic mission.

The sexual aberrations of King Henry IV of Castile
were a sterling example of the impossible interface between
political requirements and the personal inclinations of sixteenth-

century monarchs. His country was bereft of an heir, and Henry's tastes ran to young men, but in desperation the royal physicians devised a novel treatment: "a tube was fashioned of solid gold, and the precious object was thrust into Juana. Then someone masturbated Henry; it was hoped to trickle semen through the tube. But the experiment failed to work: what little they at last wrenched out of Henry proved so thin and watery as not to be worth the bother."[63]

There were often other barriers separating king and queen. As couples were matched with no regard for personal compatability, language and cultural differences made early relations all the more strained. Another problem was the extreme ugliness, even deformity, of the marriageable progeny of sixteenth-century royal families. The portraits we have do not tell the true story, painted as they were to the satisfaction of the royal subject. To cite a few examples of the general unattractiveness of these people: Louis XII's first wife Jeanne "was as lacking as the sorriest cripple in the kingdom,"[64] James I slobbered and was weak-legged, Charles V and his descendants had deformed jaws, and Eleanor of Austria had grotesquely stumpy legs. She had also, by the age of twenty-eight, grown corpulent, heavy of feature, and had angry red patches on her face "as if she had elephantiasis," wrote the envoy Dantiscus.[65] She was not a fit wife for Francis I. Even Philip "the Handsome" had rotten teeth and a ruined knee. Henry "the Impotent" was less appealing; he had a profile so concave that his chronicler claimed his face looked as though a large piece had been removed from it.[66] Manuel of Portugal was reputed to have arms so long that his fingers rested at the level of his knees.[67] Anne of Cleves was so horsey that she was called "The Flanders Mare," and her husband Henry VIII was not much better looking by the time he married her. "The king was so fat that such a man has never been seen, three of the biggest men that could be found could get inside his doublet."[68]

Others were more severely deformed. One of Queen Elizabeth's principal objections to the Duke of Alençon, one of her suitors, was his pox-puffed nose. Henry II of France's penis did not have a proper exit for his urethra, Anne Boleyn had rudimentary sixth fingers--her rival Catherine of Aragon, herself described as "rather ugly than otherwise" even as a young woman,[69] used to force the young girl to play cards in order to showcase the defect--and axillary nipples that gossips took as evidence of witchcraft. Toward

the end of his life, Louis XII had a scrofulous condition
that caused him to shed large patches of skin, and he was
forced to trade jewels for kisses from his young bride. [70]
The English Princess Mary Grey was a dwarf called "Crunch-
back Mary" by unkind courtiers. [71] And Henry, Lord Darnley, had won Mary Stewart's affections despite what intimates
described as his horrible breath--the result of his syphilis. [72]

Perhaps the unkindest cut of all was a verse of contemporary doggerel about Queen Mary of England who, though
described by Francis I as "more dowdy than queenly," was
actually regarded as more attractive than many of her queenly contemporaries.

> Better the milkmaid in her russet gown
> than Queen Mary without her crown. [73]

With all this ugliness cluttering the courts of Europe we can
understand why Henry VIII was so wary of unseen princesses
that, when it came time for his fourth try at matrimony,
"he proposed that a bevy of ladies from France should be
gathered at Calais for him to make his choice. "[74]

On top of natural, exculpable flaws, the princesses of
Europe defiled themselves further with the most scarifying
cosmetics.   The very ingredients of these paints were harmful; "fucus," a red paint, was actually mercuric sulfide.
This ate into flesh and left trenches if used heavily, which
it often was.   "Cerusa," a whitening agent, was still more
toxic, being white lead.   Heavy use of this substance, quite
popular in an era that held pallor in the highest regard, mum-
mified the skin, turned hair white, and caused intestinal
problems.   Many a young woman's early death was at least
partly attributable to lead poisoning.   Perhaps the allure
these women gained through such paints had its uses, as the
standards of beauty required painstaking artifice: "The bosom
was considered particularly enhanced if the veins were painted
in blue. "[75] But all the same such practices were often satirized.   Marguerite of Navarre was described on her way to
Communion with "her face plastered and covered with rouge,
with a great uncovered throat which more properly resembled
a behind than a bosom. "[76] Even at that Marguerite was said
to be a beauty, and had many admirers.

This alone might have sent European princes out into
the countryside in imitation of Diogenes, looking for an honest woman--to corrupt.   But in truth, the plethora of cir-

cumstances we have noted conspired to drive the sexual activity, traumatic and unusual as it often was, of many sixteenth-century royal figures out of the marital arena and into dark, dangerous places. The consequences of this pattern: unhappy marriages, broken alliances, disease, distraction, and guilt, among others, were yet further proof of the unhealthy strain of monarchical existence, and the difficulties involved in a political system predicated on the biological stability of a given family.

Chapter Ten

HEALTH

"So much depends on your health"
> --Venetian ambassador Badoer
> to Francis I of France

Let us begin with a reasonable premise: those who suffer
with considerable physical discomfort are often absorbed in
their pain and can even be subject to major alterations in
personality. Their actions can be rash and ill-considered,
and in their malaise they can vent their rage in anger, suspicion, and even malevolence toward those around them. In
other words, if one could choose the qualities of an absolute
ruler, stable health might head the list.

Given this premise, it is of great moment that the
sixteenth century was an age of rampant sickness and disease.
And the royal families of Europe found their scepters offered
no protection against the devastation of illness. So much depended on the stamina and ability of the sovereign, yet most
of these individuals spent a considerable portion of their time
indisposed. These sick people were often angry people, and
their actions were sometimes as unhealthy as they, tinged
with vengefulness and imprudence. For instance, Charles IX
was a promising prince, but his galloping consumption "transformed the charming, pleasant, and lovable boy, who had been
adored by his subjects during a long tour of the realm, first
into an irritable youth, then an irritable man, quick-tempered
and capable, like all weak people, of the worst forms of violence, and the more sick he grew, the worse became the
vices born of his illness."[1] The frenzied fits gradually
eroded Charles's limited self-control, and he was thus easily
manipulated. He ordered the dreadful St. Bartholomew's Day

Massacre during one of these lapses, after Catherine de
Medici and Henry d'Anjou overcame his weak resistance.
The utter malfeasance of this act appalled contemporaries
even in an age dominated by cruel events and unbalanced
rulers.   The English statesman Walsingham wrote to Queen
Elizabeth's beloved Leicester that "of all these tragedies this
last [St. Bartholomew's] is the most astonishing and extraordinary.   To go in person to watch the execution of one of
his subjects and one of his oldest subjects is a most rare
and uncommon instance among Christians." In truth, it was
not the Massacre that was uncommon; it was the fact that
Charles watched with such relish.   Walsingham added that
"God will not allow a prince of such a temper to remain for
long over his people. "[2]   God in fact allowed Charles only two
more years, during which his insanity changed from rage to
terror.   But almost as if to prove His mysterious ways,
Charles's successor was of much the same ilk.   During both
reigns France was virtually at the mercy of a tormented individual's will.   The connection between royal and state health
was reciprocal and obvious.   Sometimes the linkage was embarrassingly evident, as it was with Henry IV of France, who
was stricken with diarrhea as a battle neared.   It was a vicious circle; either the internal diseases of the monarchs
were imposed on events--as was the case with dying James
V of Scotland at the tragic battle of Solway Moss--or events
took their toll on the monarch, or both.

The effective governance of large countries required
a great deal of personal attention, an impossible demand on
the unhealthy and self-absorbed sovereigns of the sixteenth
century.   Their tumultuous well-being sparked a great deal
of political unrest.   The empire of Charles V was fused only
by his position as head of state in a number of dominions.
Each country required his presence, which necessitated constant travel.   While he was able to roam, order was maintained.   After the Emperor's gout made such travel impossible, nascent discontent surfaced in open defiance.   This
was a familiar pattern across the continent.   And who was
to suppress the ever-present confluence of divisive forces?
Even monarchs reknowned for their strength had an Achilles
heel.   Catherine de Medici was a paradigm of survival, yet
the Spanish ambassador wrote that "she always seems to me
like one who has come out of a bad illness. "[3]   Her son-in-
law and enemy Henry of Navarre, later Henry IV of France,
was known as a strong soldier, but his venereal disease
made it impossible for him to eliminate his urine, [4] a most
debilitating turn of events.   Such a severe illness in the

A watercolor depiction of an operation,
from Caspar Stromayr, Practica Copiosa, 1559

royal palace triggered chaotic forces, as Louis XII discovered. The Venetian ambassador Quirini reported to the
Signory that "King Lewis, on recovering from this last severe illness, besides discovering that a secret negociation
[sic] had been going on between Spain and France, had also
become aware that, had he died, his wife and daughter would
have been in trouble, because all the princes in France were

Chart 11

PORPHYRIA IN THE HOUSE OF STEWART

	Evidence from contemporary reports
Margaret Tudor (marries James IV)	erratic behavior, undescribed "attacks," melancholy, breakdowns, lameness in her leg, inability to write properly
James V	erratic behavior, melancholy, insomnia, "hysteria," "attacks," nervous collapses, strange and premature death
Mary Queen of Scots	"attacks," stomach problems, "hysteria," lameness, inability to write properly, melancholy, insomnia, constant pain in side
James VI & I	"attacks," stomach problems (which he told his physician he had inherited from his mother), lameness, melancholy, pain in side, insomnia, fragile skin, discolored urine

The evidence is also good for Margaret Tudor's descendants by Angus; Margaret Douglas and Arabella Stuart both exhibited classic symptoms. The disease must then have entered the Stewart house with Margaret Tudor, since her descendants by two different husbands manifested the disease.

"Attacks" refers to the onset of sudden and violent illness followed by notably quick recovery. Mary Stewart recovered so quickly from her attacks that some contemporaries believed she was feigning them to gain sympathy or achieve her political ends. These brief episodes are characteristic of the porphyrias.

---

intriguing against them; and therefore he perceived that his only remedy was to marry his daughter to the dauphin."[5]
An invalid king offered an invitation to anarchy.

How ironic it was that in western Europe monarchs were believed to possess great curative powers. Tudor sovereigns up to the reign of Elizabeth I "touched" regularly for scrofula, epilepsy, and associated diseases. [6] This ability was taken as critical proof of the legitimacy of kings, and Elizabeth's "touch" was said to be evidence that the Pope's Bull of Excommunication regarding her family had failed. French kings also made a practice of "the touch." Apparently, this gift did not apply to its possessor, because in royal households frequent illness was the rule, not the exception. That supposed pillar of strength, Elizabeth I, was actually one of history's great invalids. It was a rare year when she was not seriously ill. [7] At the age of fourteen, she concluded her traumatic affair with Admiral Seymour, and for the next few years she suffered with migraines and pain in her eyes. Most importantly, her monthly periods were few and far between, a problem noted with great interest in diplomatic dispatches. The Spanish found this condition of the highest moment and bribed a washerwoman to keep track of Elizabeth's menstrual flow. Yet luck seemed to be with the princess. Paradoxically, only a deathly illness saved her from a presumably tragic fate during Wyatt's Rebellion in 1554. As mentioned in Chapter Two, Queen Mary I ordered her to London, worried that the young girl would become the standard-bearer for the Protestant forces. But as Mary's physicians were forced to concede, Elizabeth was on the verge of death and could not be moved. In succeeding years chest problems, an ulcerated leg, smallpox, rheumatism, "nerve storms," and digestive disorders alternately incapacitated Queen Bess. An observer noted in 1560 that "she looked like she lately came out of childbed,"[8] which of course she had not and never would. Two years later she had a fierce attack of smallpox. A German physician named Burcot was summoned, and he had the queen wrapped in blankets, with one of her hands submerged in a bottle of "comfortable potion." Elizabeth recovered from the onslaught, but her nurse Lady Sydney was so disfigured by the disease that "she retired from court to a life of seclusion."[9] By 1584 another source lamented that England had "a Queen of no great good health or robustious and strong constitution."[10] The myth of the independent and haughty queen was entrenched in the public mind, but in the words of one historian, "throughout her life she had moments of collapse in which some man took charge of her and told her what she must do."[11]

Epidemic diseases posed a constant threat to royal

health. Particularly common was the "sweat," which visited England periodically between 1485 and 1551 and then disappeared mysteriously. The Tudor sovereigns lived in mortal fear of the disease. Henry VIII professed great love for his mistress Anne Boleyn, but when the first feverish signs of the illness appeared in his beloved he fled, "keeping on the move for several weeks, dosing himself with numerous medicaments, hearing three masses, and confessing daily."[12] This caution was warranted, if not gallant. Others were less prudent. Recall the dashing Prince Charles of France (Chapter Four), the younger brother of Henry II and a celebrated courtier in his own right, who sought to prove his bravado by rushing into a plague-ridden house crying "no son of France has ever died of the plague."[13] The plague made an exception in his case.

Such communicable diseases thrived in close, unclean environments. These were simply everywhere. Sixteenth-century royalty certainly did not live in the Garden of Eden either figuratively or literally. And if the health of the monarchs and their families was not up to par, there was no serpent to blame, except perhaps their own lifestyle, if such a base existence could rightly be said to have a style. As Montaigne wrote in his essay On Physiognomy: "No man ever knows how to stop at the limit of his needs; of pleasure; riches, and the power he grasps more than he can hold; his greed is incapable of moderation."[14] Nowhere was this more apt than at court, but entire cultures in western European domains were marked by practices and conditions utterly foreign to our more delicate sensibilities. Cruelty was a feature of the society as a whole, and virtually everyone partook from the common cup of brutality. Of course, monarchs and their relatives were in a position to administer much of this violence, while the lower classes suffered the brunt of the punishments, the pestilences, and the constant insufficiencies of life. But even kings felt the lash of such misfortunes, and the tone of the age reflected these base forces. Human life was held in low regard, and it was a bad time to commit--or be suspected of committing--a crime. Under Henry VIII of England, poisoners were boiled alive; in Salzburg a convicted perjurer "shall have his tongue torn out by the neck"; and for lesser offenses miscreants across Europe --both male and female--might be scourged, lose a hand, foot, ear, nose, one or both eyes, or be branded with a hot iron.[15]

Kings were understandably most concerned with those

who plotted against them, and the criminals accused of trans-
gressing against royalty were hit with the full range of tortures invented by the Renaissance imagination. Under torture
a companion to Francis, the eldest son of King Francis I of
France, named Montecucculi was made to confess to the
dauphin's murder, though all evidence absolved him of guilt
in the boy's death, which was truly the result of well-steeped
frailties. Still, the alleged murderer's punishment was a
lesson to all who might entertain thoughts of deposition or
regicide; his four limbs were tied to four teams of horses,
which were then driven in four different directions. But before this finale, the townspeople were allowed to vent their
anger on the poor innocent Italian. They "cut his remains
into little morsels, hacked off his nose, tore out his eyes,
broke his jaws, trained his head in the mud, and 'made him
die a thousand times before his death.'"[16]

In more felicitous hours people gravitated toward
gross, unhealthy practices of their own choice and invention.
Common wisdom decreed it. A Danish barber-surgeon advised his clients: "It is very good for persons to drink
themselves intoxicated once a month, for the excellent reasons that it frees their strength, furthers sound sleep, eases
the passing of water, increases perspiration, and stimulates
general well-being."[17] Few were so continent as to restrict
their binges to once a month. The denizens of the Holy Roman Empire were notably obsessed with eating and drinking.
A circus performer amazed his German onlookers with the
prodigious consumption of a pound of cheese, thirty eggs,
and a loaf of bread all in one sitting. Unfortunately, the
Gargantuan did not live to enjoy his fame. He died after the
meal. Less conspicuous epicureans lingered over their
tables for seven hours, weddings provided occasion for unlimited swinishness, and one prince closed his letters with
the injunction "valete et inebriamini," or "be well and get
drunk."[18] Christian II of Saxony did just that, and died at
the age of twenty-seven, a victim of alcoholism. With the
pervasiveness of this disease, a temperance society was
formed, but its first president died of drink.[19] It took little
insight for contemporaries to realize that such debauchery
was shortening the life span of many well-to-do Germans,
including many of their princes. While those too poor to buy
food starved, the upper classes ate and drank themselves to
death. It was a paradoxical era.

Given the sort of life these people lived, we can hardly vilify them for taking what enjoyments they could, even if

those revels ultimately killed them.   Interestingly, the same
miseries that drove them to the table for so many excesses
drove a number to Luther, himself a great eater and drinker.
As ironic as this may seem, Luther's angry God conformed
to what people knew of the world.   A temporary escape into
gluttony only postponed their fear, and the horrors were certain to return--perhaps as indigestion.   Luther's God was a
deity eminently capable of punishment and terror.   The
"nasty, brutish, and short, " character of sixteenth-century
life was of great moment to the changing religious sentiments:
a shift from warm comfort to believable vengeance.

That the lower and middle classes in Germany lived
such lives is not surprising; perhaps the living conditions of
royalty at the purportedly gracious courts of Europe are.
Life at court was itself cruel, callous, debauched, and dirty.
And for all the showy finery, monarchs were not above the
most immediate, visceral level of existence.   The court
amused itself with vicious gossip, repartee, and the mockery
of human curiosities.   Deformities were fodder for jokes,
and dwarfs were kept as good-luck charms; they were thought
to have special powers.   Such creatures were ubiquitous as
jesters or servants.   If mockery of the cruel conditions of
life proved insufficient to distract them from their own fear,
monarchs could shut the most pressing external affairs out of
their insular microcosm.   Court was almost a world apart,
and little impeded its rituals; on the day after the grim St.
Bartholomew's Day Massacre of 1572 Catherine de Medici
held an elaborate ballet, the French court's favorite entertainment, in the gardens of the Tuileries.   Royalty required
display, and on public occasions most sixteenth-century monarchs summoned the full measure of their dignity, important
as it was to implant the image of sovereignty in the minds of
the people.   But in the special milieu of court kings and
queens were free to behave as they chose, which often meant
the celebration of the bawdy, the vulgar, and the perverse,
tastes current in the society as a whole.   Their activities
and comments were often anything but regal.   Elizabeth I
slugged or hugged courtiers as her whim dictated, tickled
the back of her paramour Dudley's neck as he knelt to receive
his earldom, and spat wherever she pleased. [20]   According to
Ben Jonson, when "the earl of Oxford, making his low obei-
sance to Queen Elizabeth, happened to let a fart, at which he
was so ashamed and abashed that he went to travel, seven
years.   On his return the queen welcomed him home, and
said, 'my lord, I had forgot the fart. ' "[21]   Perhaps this tale
was an invention, for Jonson was not above such things.   But

still, its apparent credibility for English readers tells us
much about the tone of the court, a very low tone at that.
Stories of crass behavior on the throne abounded. Elizabeth's successor James I was far more foulmouthed than she,
and did not restrict his badinage to court; he stood up in
church to disabuse a preacher in scatological terms: "I
give not a turd for your preaching, " the king concluded.
With such sovereigns to set the fashion, many courtiers attempted to outdo each other in corruption. The greatest
lords and ladies of many European domains engaged in
coarse and dangerous amusements, as Castiglione's messer
Federico detailed in The Book of The Courtier:

> Sometimes, thinking to be witty and droll, they say
> the dirtiest and most indecent things, in the pres-
> ence of ladies and often to the ladies themselves;
> and the more they see them blush, the more they
> think themselves good courtiers, and they go right
> on laughing and priding themselves on having the
> fine virtue they think they have. Yet they do these
> many stupidities for no other reason than that they
> wish to be thought jolly good fellows: this being the
> one name that seems to them worthy of praise, and
> in which they take more pride than any other; and
> to acquire if they engage in the crudest and most
> shameful improprieties in the world. They often
> push one another downstairs, deal each other blows
> with sticks and bricks, throw fistfuls of dust in one
> another's eyes, cause their horses to roll one on
> the other in ditches or downhill; then at table they
> throw soups, gravies, jellies, and every kind of
> thing in one another's face: and then they laugh.
> And the one who knows how to do the most things
> of this kind deems himself the best courtier and the
> more gallant, and thinks to have won great glory.

Those who declined to participate were jeered as
prigs. These entertainments were not the supercharged
adolescent antics of college fraternities, but rather the diversions of the most important nobles of the realm. Some
of their pleasures defied delicate explanation, as messer
Federico continued:

> But I can tell you worse: there are some who vie
> among themselves and lay wager as to who can eat
> and drink the most vile and nauseating things; and
> they concoct things so abhorrent to human sense

that it is impossible to mention them without the greatest disgust. [22]

Vile and nauseating entrees were often standard fare at royal tables, so we can imagine just how vile the menu referred to by Federico must have been. Still, such cuisine failed to suppress court appetites, and with dirty hands the entire party dug heartily and regularly into the heaps of spoiled meat at table. Forks would not grace even royal tables in the sixteenth century. The size of royal entourages, such as Francis I's, which was said to include 15,000 people, and their constant perambulations to escape pestilence and their own accumulated mess made supply and storage an almost impossible task. Henry VIII's reduced traveling court consumed daily "six oxen, eight calves, forty sheep, twelve pigs, thirty six capons, ninety six good capon, seven swans, twenty storks, thirty four pheasants, one hundred and ninety two partridges and the same number of cocks, fifty six herons, eighty four pullets, seven hundred twenty larks, two hundred forty pigeons, twenty four peacocks, one hundred ninety four plovers and teals."[23] And according to a Spaniard, the Elizabethan court consumed more beer in a given summer "than the river would hold at Valladolid."[24] Court eating habits were patently unhealthy; the food was of poor quality, often spoiled, and monarchs overate. As a result, Henry IV of France and Philip II of Spain suffered with diarrhea, Charles V had awful gout, and Henry VIII was tormented with indigestion, as were many of his peers. One poet who had observed the royal table wrote in The Regimen of Salerno:

A kinge that cannot rule him in his diet
Will hardly rule his realm in peace and quiet. [25]

For a male debaucher, the choice was between bad food and wilted women, the both of which could maim or even kill. But the pleasures of the table did not advertise quite so much as the courtesans. Montaigne commented that "our ladies (dainty-nice though they may be) are many times seen to go open breasted as far as the navel."[26] Fine costumes were a court essential, and at the French court a gallant considered himself destitute if he lacked twenty-five different and costly garments. But beneath the elaborate dresses and breeches was the specter of uncleanliness. Few monarchs bathed regularly--or more frequently than once a week--and much of the material used in royal apparel could not be washed; silk, velvet, ermine simply accumulated dirt and perspiration, and were renewed with cloaking scents. [27]   Although this was a dilemma shared by all, some monarchs were nonetheless filthier than their noble servants.   Juana of Spain neither washed nor changed clothes.   But she was insane.   Henry IV of France had no such excuse, yet according to one of his aides he "stank like a corpse. "[28]

Devoted court swains, kings and princes included, overlooked these anti-aphrodisiacs, just as they grew accustomed to the veneer of toxic cosmetics.   The Spanish humanist Vives depicted the unfortunate sight of a woman whose paint had melted "by the occasion of sweat or heat, " and complained of the danger posed "both by the reason of ceruse and quicksilver" used as ingredients in makeup. [29]

The stage for all these dowdy doings was no more gracious than the courtesans whose faces melted and dripped. Like the rest of the leitmotiv, castles and palaces were dank and dirty.   The sixteenth-century court changed its locale regularly, and for a reason; with the size of the retinue, their habits, and the crude facilities--from cooking to sanitation--a particular castle became uninhabitable after a surprisingly short time.   Even in the most sumptuous castles, sanitation was hardly worthy of the name.   Those who occupied old castles located their latrines in large projections "on the face of walls, their effluvia discharged into deepwalled pits, moats, or streams near the walls. "[30]   These "jakes, " as they were sometimes called in England, usually had two seats for simultaneous use and lap robes for warmth on cold days.   Less hardy souls continued to use chamber pots and simply tossed their contents out the nearest window. A minor problem in the country, in the city this was an enormously foul practice.   Whichever method was followed, the Renaissance castle was permeated with bestial odors. Plants were brought into living quarters at this time more for the need of scent to disguise these smells than of the esthetic appeal of greenery.   But it was not only the housing that stank; even some of the surroundings were defiled.   By the first part of the seventeenth century, the Thames River was so foul that James I of England threatened to move his court to Windsor to escape its noxious vapors.

The very lifestyle of sixteenth-century royalty had disease, dissolution, and overwhelming vulgarity as central elements.   It was for the most part an unhealthy, visceral, and solipsistic existence.   The court itself was in all likelihood a breeding ground for disease.   It was characterized by large

Chart 12

INSANITY IN THE ROYAL FAMILIES OF SPAIN AND PORTUGAL

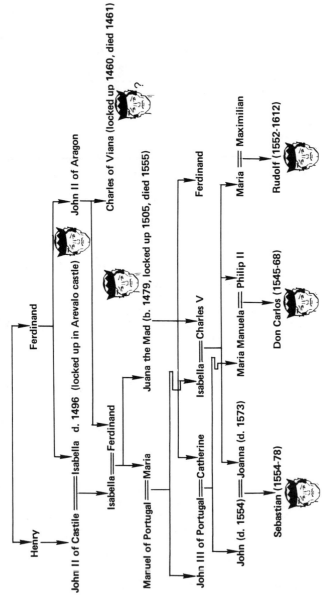

groups of people gathered together without proper sanitation; gluttony and drunken revelry; excess in sexual pleasures; the wearing pressures of intrigue and dynastic duty; and a gaggle of physicians to compound even the smallest problem.

There was also mental health to consider, itself a bleak horizon for sixteenth-century royalty. To cite one afflicted monarch, Maximilian I was a noted dynastic politician, but he was still subject to ridiculous delusions about his sanctity. "I am sending tomorrow to Rome, " he wrote his daughter Margaret, "to find a way for the Pope to make me his partner, so that, after his death, I can be sure of the Papacy and of becoming a priest and later a saint. You will then have to worship me when I am dead, which will be delightful. "[31] Others, including Queen Juana of Spain, Don Carlos of Spain, Sebastian of Portugal, Rudolf of Austria, and Charles IX of France, were still less balanced.

The most heartbreaking ailments in the royal house were those of promising young heirs. Although the withering of a middle-aged monarch could be accepted as a natural phase of the royal cycle--"le roi est mort! Vive le roi!"-- the untimely demise of a young prince was a tragic sign of God's disfavor. Prince Juan of Asturias, heir to the crowns of Castile and Aragon, was a sickly child who never slept without a night-light. [32] The boy's tutor Pedro Martyr grumbled that Juan was treated "like an invalid. "[33] Although the prince had a deformed lower lip, stuttered badly, and was rumored to be mentally retarded, he was nonetheless the darling of the royal circle. But at the age of nineteen, only six months after his marriage, he fell ill with a fever and passed away. Given the frail prince's physical condition, this could hardly have come as a complete surprise. Yet the court of Ferdinand and Isabella was devastated. Commynes reported that "I have never heard of so solemn and so universal a mourning for any prince in Europe. "[34] In Spain 1497 was otherwise a banner year, but Juan's death was interpreted as a bad omen, and it broke the spirit of pious Isabella. Young Francis II, son of Henry II, was another unfortunate and greatly mourned prince. Francis's body was barely functional, as ailments with the symptoms of otitis, adenoidal infection, tuberculosis, and a defect in his reproductive organs (LaPlanche claimed that "his generative organs were constipated and blocked, incapable of functioning"[35]) combined to make him a lifelong invalid. Francis was also terribly ugly, with viscuous discharge and eczematous patches covering his skin. [36] Like most sixteenth-

century consumptives, Francis had bursts of frightening energy, and during these frenzies the prince's mental instability
was painfully obvious. Yet this pathetic creature was still
a legitimate male heir, and his final release from a tortured
life triggered a great sense of loss and a feeling of unease
in the house of Valois. Even more unhappy was the long
sickness and eventual death of Francis's contemporary Edward VI. The stiff little prince had always been sickly, and
a harsh youth stripped him of what small vigor he originally
possessed. But he was the only male Tudor standing before
the heirs of a foreign dynasty (the Stewarts) in the line of
succession. Edward was personally inclined toward bigotry
and was something of a puppet in the hands of his self-
aggrandizing protectors. [37] He was also chronically ill
throughout his entire life. Still, his impending death was
nonetheless viewed as a great tragedy, particularly so because a Catholic princess stood to succeed him. In this
case, as in the cases of Juan of Spain, Sebastian of Portugal,
and Don Carlos of Spain, the death of a royal heir occasioned
inconvenience, unrest, and a sense of impending disaster for
the sixteenth-century dynasty.

The general physical condition of most royal family
members was characteristically fragile, but the mistaken
ministrations of court physicians only served to exaggerate
inherent weaknesses and genetic predispositions. With these
preconditions, the main health problem for sixteenth-century
royalty was one of both excess and access: too much food,
drink, sex, and particularly too much bad medical care was
available to them.

It was probably wiser to avoid the convoluted treatments of court doctors, as the Empress Isabella intuitively
realized, than be subject to their blind experimentation.
The medical profession was composed of an unstandardized
lot of charlatans, mystics, and the incurious devotees of an-
tiquity. Medical education was not a prerequisite for practice,
and the schools themselves were mired in error. One visitor
was appalled at the academic debate he witnessed in a Spanish medical school; the academics and students occupied
themselves with a long discussion on the fate of people who
lost fingers. [38] The little they learned could freely be put to
use, as whatever licensing committees then in existence were
more concerned with the religious orthodoxy of doctors and
midwives than their competence. [39] One such body, the Royal
College of Physicians in London, was established in 1518 to
license and sanction genuine doctors. By 1589 the college

had only thirty-eight members. [40] Even this group, the standard-bearer of medical science in England, persisted in almost unquestioned adherence to the notions of Galen and other age-old, non-empirical oracles. Under this onus it seems less than ironic that a young English physician, John Geynes, was forced to make a public retraction of his previously expressed opinion that Galen was fallible before he was allowed into the Royal College. [41] Such was the open spirit of inquiry that animated sixteenth-century medicine. Since the Royal College represented the supposedly legitimate practitioners, Queen Mary I gave the president of this august body the power to incarcerate "quacks." He might just as well have jailed his own members for the sake of justice. Although they did not defraud deliberately, "legitimate" physicians were almost as far from the truth about the human body and its maladies as the charlatans.

With this vacuum of sound theory and practice, many colorful characters gained great prominence. As Galenic medicine, the accepted teaching of the academics, was shown repeatedly to be inadequate, mavericks regaled both common and crown patients with new approaches. One of the most famous of these sixteenth-century revisionists was Philippus Aureolus Theophrastus Bombast von Hohenheim (1493-1541), better known by his Latin pseudonym Paracelsus. An eccentric and a braggart, Paracelsus simply turned Galen on his head, denying virtually all the tenets of Galenic medicine. This was a step in the right direction, although Paracelsus could hardly have known, for his theories themselves were no more the product of empirical observation than Galen's had been. Truly empirical medicine was centuries away, but with his gems of insight, Paracelsus won a large following, filling lecture halls and influencing his contemporaries across Europe. He had a number of notable patients, including Erasmus. Still, Paracelsus was more showman than shaman. And although he broke free of the pervasive doctrines, he had nothing comprehensive with which to replace them. For all his fleeting acclaim, he remained an outsider and even an outcast. To fortify his considerable nerve, he never lectured unless he was half-drunk, and never attended a patient unless he was wholly inebriated, according to his secretary Oporin. [42]

Beside such renegades were the men of the stars who called themselves "students of physic and astrology." Critics called these astrologer-physicians "piss prophets" because of their study of a patient's urine to the exclusion of the pa-

tient. [43] Yet virtually every court had its resident astrologer.
In England Henry VII had the Italian William Parron, Henry
VIII had Nicholas Kratzer (and also prevented his bishops
from censoring the art), and Edward VI had an entire treatise on the subject dedicated to him in 1550. The boy's tutor Cheke was even more of a devotee. The astrologer Je-
rome Cardan predicted that Edward would live to the age of
fifty-five at the very least, a prediction that pleased his
patron. When Edward died at fifteen, Cardan published his
tables pertaining to the king with an apologia entitled "What
I Thought Afterwards on the Subject. " In this paper he
claimed that his mistake resulted from shirking extra calcu-
lations that would have taken over a hundred hours. He also
professed relief that he had not been forced to predict the
death of a sitting king, a forecast that would have been unpleasant, if not suicidal. [44]

Most diagnoses were based on superstition, old saws,
and a subjective appraisal of the patient's "personality type. "
Montaigne wrote: "They [doctors] describe our maladies as
a town crier does a lost horse or dog of this color, this
height, and with this shape of ear--but show him the animal,
and he will not recognize it at all. "[45] What these physicians
did recognize was urine and its changes in coloration. The
inspection of a patient's urine by true physicians was known
as "water casting, " and was for many years the principal
occupation of the medical profession. The urine-flask became their aegis. [46] This technique was combined with crude
estimations of the balance of four "humors, " or fluids in the
body. An excess of one of these humors or an imbalance
among them inevitably produced symptomatic behavior. Henry IV of France's personal physician André du Laurens had
this to say about the sanguine temperament, caused by an
excess of blood:

> The sanguine persons are borne for to be sociable
> and lovers of company: they are as it were always
> in love, they love to laugh and be pleasant ... and
> yet such folk are not the fittest for great exploits,
> nor yet for high and hard attempts, because they
> be impatient, and cannot be long in doing about one
> thing, being for the most part drawn away, either
> by their senses, or else by their delights, whereto
> they are naturally addicted. [47]

Whether Laurens referred consciously to the past few generations of French kings for this description, Henry III and

Francis I in particular, cannot be ascertained, but his typol-
ogy is curiously true to French royal history. And Laurens
himself was a royal physician in the service of an undeniably
"sanguine" king. Royal medicine was no more than an off-
hand assessment of humoral balance, and if their subjective
efforts can tell us much about monarchical personalities they
told the monarchs precious little about what ailed them.

Needless to say, this group of water casters and their
unconventional rivals inspired little confidence. "In the realm
of medicine," wrote Montaigne, "experience is at home on its
own dunghill, where reason gives place to it entirely."[48]
Thomas Hobbes thought he "would rather have the advice or
take physic from an experienced old woman that had been
at many sick people's bedsides, than from the learnedst but
inexperienced physician."[49] Francis Bacon concurred. "Em-
pirics and old women," he wrote, were "more happy many
times in their cures than learned physicians."[50] As for
surgeons, whom the more socially acceptable physicians categorized with barbers and other lowly species of men, the
public rightly feared their craft: mostly amputations, trepanning, cutting for stone, and incising abscesses. In the common parlance a seventeenth-century treatise on surgery,
Severall Chirurgicall Treatises (1676), was known as "Wise-
man's Book of Martyrs."[51] Other voices were still more
vehement. Secretary Lodowick claimed that doctors of
physic were "the greatest cheats ... in the world. If there
was never a doctor of physic in the world, people would live
longer and in better health."[52] Even physicians vilified the
medical meddling of the sixteenth century. The great English physician of the seventeenth century, Sir Thomas Sydenham, thought that it would have been better for humanity if
the art of physic had not been invented. He also speculated
that many poor men and women owed their lives to their inability to pay for doctors.[53]

The men of medicine themselves regarded their profession in different terms; physicians, the most respectable
group, thought of themselves as seers, not healers, and their
true mission was the interpretation of divine signals. Often,
the message boded ill for the nervous sovereigns. Royal
patients were not merely indisposed, they were punished by
an act of God, which made their ailments all the more disconcerting.[54] Surgeons, on the other hand, were craftsmen
whose approach was keyed to efficacious amputations and re-
movals. While their loftier contemporaries contemplated the
natural signs, surgeons bled and purged their patients. Al-

though perhaps the surgeons were less pompous than the
physicians, they were nonetheless uneducated bunglers, like
their counterparts. At least part of their ignorance stemmed
from their limited knowledge of the human body--which was
understandable; the Church prohibited the dissection of corpses
for educational purposes. If the physicians could only gauge
the state of their royal patients in reference to chimerical
humors and irrelevant typologies, the surgeons were limited
to only the vaguest idea of what they were cutting for, and
what to do with it when they found it. If disease was truly
a sign of divine wrath, the real visitation was not always the
malady; it was just as frequently to be found in the cure.

Monarchs often were ambivalent toward their doctors.
James I of England, opinionated in all things, thought that
all academic medicine was mere conjecture, and was therefore useless. Isabella the Catholic, Queen of Spain, refused
to let her doctors treat her painful fistula, and her husband
Ferdinand was actually dosed into a variety of ailments previously unknown to him. The Catholic Kings had good reason
to distrust doctors, but their physicians had equally good
reasons for distrusting the sovereigns. Having burned their
Jewish physician at the stake and expelled the Moors from
Spain, the Catholic Kings were left to the sort of old Christian incompetence Cervantes satirized in Don Quixote. But
even those monarchs who were kind to their healers received
harmful medical care. Charles IX of France saved the surgeon Paré from the carnage of the St. Bartholomew's Day
Massacre in 1572, but for the next few years Charles was
beyond medical help. Mary I of England was a patron of
the Royal College of Physicians, yet her doctors were unable
to alleviate her suffering. In fact, they only worsened her
condition with bleedings and purges, for Mary's main problem
seemed to be psychological: the desperate need for love and
affection. Even when physicians effected a cure the miracle
was often attributed to more credible agents. The surgeon
Vesalius was called to attend the stricken Spanish Prince Don
Carlos after the crazed heir had fallen down a flight of stone
stairs in pursuit of a serving wench. By trepanning his skull
Vesalius brought the comatose prince back to life, such as it
was for the troubled young man. But ironically and sadly for
the talented Vesalius, the prince's miraculous recovery was
attributed by most observers to the century-old remains of
a holy Franciscan friar that had been put into Carlos's bed.
Philip II immediately petitioned the Pope for the canonization
of the friar.

There were moments of ingenuity. Since they dealt primarily with appearances, sixteenth-century physicians could on occasion be quite resourceful with psychological illnesses. A French doctor had a patient who believed himself possessed by the devil. He took a surgeon and a priest to the man's home, along with a live bat in a sack. The priest offered a prayer, the surgeon made a small incision, and the doctor released the bat from the bag. "Behold there the devil is gone," he cried, and the man believed himself cured. 55 But more violent forms of madness were thought to involve true demonic possession. James I of England himself wrote a treatise on the subject, Daemonologie, that advanced this thesis. The method of treating such "devils" was anything but inventive. It was brutal and horrifying. Some victims were termed witches or warlocks and were burned. Mere melancholy, on the other hand, was thought to result from a humoral imbalance, and was treated with the usual purges and bleedings. Yet as in the case of the French doctor and his medicinal bat, occasionally the mentally ill were handled with imagination. Henry IV's physician related a most ingenious solution to one patient's strange delusions:

> The pleasantest dotage that ever I read, was of one Sienois a Gentleman who had resulved with himself not to pisse, but to dye rather, and that because he imagined, that when he first pissed, all his towne would be drowned. The Phisitions shewing him, that all his bodie, and ten thousand more such as his, were not able to containe so much as might drowne the least house in the towne, could not change his minde from this foolish imagination. In the end they seeing his obstinacie, and in what danger he put his life, found out a pleasant invention. They caused the next house to be set on fire, & all the bells in the town to ring, they perswaded servants to crie, to the fire, to the fire, & therewithall send of those of the best account in the town, to crave helpe, and shew the Gentleman that there is but one way to save the towne, and that it was, that he should piss quicklie and quench the fire. Then this sillie melancholike man which abstained from pissing for feare of loosing his towne, taking it for graunted that it was now in great hazard, pissed and emptied his bladder of all that was in it, and was himselfe by that means preserved. 56

Such cleverness was rare, and most medical treatment was the antithesis of the above-noted flexibility. Doctors fit patients into limited typologies and pursued a standard course. These courses were often inappropriate, had side-effects, and could even be intrinsically dangerous. In Elizabethan England shingles and burns were treated with a juice of house-leek and cream, mild "madmen" and those with paralysis were given a syrup of the conserve of cowslips or "palsy worts, " and scurvy called for a salad of fresh cuckoo flower heads. [57] Some respected physicians across Europe prescribed dried toads in a bag, to be worn as a necklace, to bait the trap to catch and disarm evil humors in plague sites. [58] And for those unfortunates who contracted syphilis, the ounce of pleasure could hardly have compensated for the untold misery in their pound of cure. Mercury, a common prescription, was often "violently destructive, dissolving even the solid parts, and rendering the teeth black and loose. " Diarrhea, nausea, and fetid breath were noted side-effects of the drug. The doctors explained the incidence of such discomfort as evidence of the cure's power. Corpses were seen with the mercury still clinging to bones. It was powerful indeed, but it was no real cure. A London handbill of the period put the matter plainly: "A night with Venus, " it advertised, "and a month with Mercury. "[59]

Some medical remedies were themselves more damaging than their targeted complaint. A sixteenth-century medical text prescribed the following treatment for gout: "Roast a fat old goose and stuff with chopped kittens, lard, incense, wax and flour of rye. This must all be eaten, and the drippings applied to the painful joints. "[60] If this proved ineffective a "warm and bleeding pigeon might be applied to the soles of the sufferer's feet. "[61] Conventional wisdom dictated that a significant loss of blood called for more bleeding to restore the balance of the humors, as in the case of Elizabeth Valois. Often, royal patients were so depleted by this treatment that they succumbed merely for lack of strength during an otherwise minor illness. Henry II, although severely wounded in the head at a tournament in 1559, appeared to rally, but he was immediately purged and bled twelve ounces. [62] He died a few days later. Queens weak from strains of childbirth were also subjected to this enervating program. Elizabeth Valois's miscarriage in 1564 was apparently initiated by the successive bleedings she endured in the final stages of her pregnancy.

Many a royal death was hastened by the actions of

physicians, whose actions and remedies were characteristically harsh and too frequently applied. In a single year Louis XIII of France was given two hundred and fifteen enemas, bled forty-seven times, and had two hundred and twelve drugs poured down his throat. [63] For those with a black sense of humor, medicine must have been amusing when it wasn't brutal. Montaigne told of certain special treatments made available only to prestigious patients:

> ... the left foot of a tortoise, the urine of a lizard, an elephant's dung, a mole's liver, blood drawn from the right wing of a white pigeon, and, for those of us, who have the stone ... the pulverized droppings of a rat. [64]

But whatever one's sense of humor, the death of king Edward VI of England was indisputably grim. Edward was constitutionally frail, but the directionless efforts of his doctors administered the final blow.

> Being ignorant, too, as these officials acknowledged themselves to be, they, of course, hesitated to act, except at random, and then without any admitted principle. This seems to have been their policy. After certain experiments, which did no good ... and had done more harm than good, they confessed themselves beaten by the disease and its complications. [65]

Other avenues were then explored. Edward's nominal "protectors" particularly wanted the sick king to appear alert, as a front for their schemes.

> Some persons induced the council to allow a notable female empiric to treat the king's complaint. This woman--apparently a disciple of the more ignorant nativity casters and conjurers, and a comfortable "gospeller" to boot--eagerly undertook the work, and administered in turn various herbs, potions, and powders to the prostrate and debilitated youth, but all in vain. Greater sickness supervened, together with paroxysms of pain, fainting fits, and extreme prostration.... He could retain nothing whether in the form of fluid or substance. [66]

The drugs administered by this charlatan stimulated the dying prince, but they ultimately deprived him of his hair, large patches of skin, and his fingers and toes. This poison, not his underlying consumption, was the proximate cause of Edward's death.

The infirmities and torments occasioned by disease and doctors had a notable impact on both the personalities of ruling family members and the course of events in sixteenth-century western Europe. Charles V's absence during the siege of Metz--he was suffering from his yearly siege of gout--was a crucial factor in the loss of this important battle. 67 The insanity of Don Carlos and the precarious health of Elizabeth Valois prevented Philip II from joining Alva for the pacification of the Low Countries, as the king felt his most urgent need was to produce a fit heir. The poor health of Mary Stewart weakened her judgment as well as her body, and prevented her from rising above the destructive and petty intrigues so characteristic of her unfortunate inheritance. Kings and queens were only people, sickly and unhappy people at that, yet they were expected to be the state. Inbred defects, constitutional weaknesses, psychological derangement, and excessive lifestyle imperiled the very survival of the dynasty, which was of course the first concern of sixteenth-century rulers. Full attention to the business of state was a veritable luxury left for periods of relative health, the fortuitous moments of dynastic stability.

Chapter Eleven

DEATH

"Hotspur: Doomsday is near. Die all, die merrily"
                    --Shakespeare, <u>King Henry IV</u>,
                    part 1. IV, i, 134.

The frailty of royal life could be seen in the bargain a clever
Frenchman struck with his king, Louis XI; he promised to
teach the king's mule to speak within a year if the king pardoned his crime, for which he was to be executed.   Louis,
a curious sort, accepted the offer.   According to the con-
vict's sage reasoning, within a year the following things could
happen: Louis might die, the ass might die, he might die,
or least plausibly, the ass would talk. 1   Perhaps such flights
of fancy distracted monarchs from the long shadow of inchoate
mortality.   But sixteenth-century monarchs realized that no
laurels awaited them at life's end.   They could look forward
only to a long and painful decline leading to a grim death.
An act of violence would end the life of Henry III, James IV,
and Mary Stewart, among others.   But the natural deaths of
their contemporaries were probably far more fearsome.   The
chronically poor health of these people served as a constant
reminder of impending mortality, and aging kings frequently
turned inward, hoping to find comfort and strength for the inevitable last struggle.   Even the most disciplined and vigorous monarch of the period, Charles V, became almost hysterical as his decaying faculties signaled the proximity of
death.   He retired to the monastery of Yuste, thus becoming
the only sixteenth-century monarch to willingly abdicate, and
adopted an attitude of "immoderate penance, anguished fear,
and a consuming necrophilia. "2   The once-magnificent Emperor "scourged himself til he bled, sang hymns the night
through, wept uncontrollably, and awoke the Jeronomite monks

lest they miss a single second of their vigil for his soul. 3
For the crowning touch Charles allegedly settled into a coffin
and watched his own burial ceremony. 4   The Netherlands,
the Turks, and the French had never damaged the Emperor's
composure, but the prospect of death was more than he could
stand.

The Emperor Maximilian I rivaled his grandson's
preoccupation with death.   Like Charles, in his last years
he made detailed plans for the care of his body after he surrendered the ghost; he was to be shaved and depilated, his
teeth were to be extracted, ground into powder, and burned,
and above all he was to be clad in a pair of pants for de-
cency's sake. 5   While these funeral thoughts were being
formulated, Max was known to travel with his coffin in tow,
and was even heard conversing with it late at night.   There
were those who whispered that he slept in it as well. 6   In
light of the ends that awaited most sixteenth-century monarchs, this was hardly an over-reaction.   The essential
events of life: birth, reproduction, and death, were inexpressibly cruel for the royal families of western Europe.

Few monarchs died quickly, and the protracted struggle against infirmity became a consuming obsession.   Declining kings were kings in name only.   The last seventeen
years of Henry VIII's life were a season of torment.   His
belly expanded to fifty-four inches and the royal medical bills
increased by a factor of seven in only four months. 7   Henry's
pain must have incited him to violence, as the expense of
rhubarb increased notably on the treasury rolls.   Rhubarb
was used primarily to neutralize a choleric disposition.   When
at last Henry lay prostrate on his deathbed, his energy spent
in anger, around him swirled a carnival.   A flock of doctors
consulted their urine flasks, cathartic prescriptions, and as-
trological charts while courtiers milled about to a background
of flute music.   Rose oil and ambergris were employed to
hide the stench of the rotting monarch. 8

Henry's rival Francis I died a similarly gruesome
death.   Syphilis had rotted holes in his abdomen, and these
abscesses grew infected.   He died in a raging fever.   An
autopsy on his corpse revealed shriveled kidneys, putrefied
entrails, a corroded throat, and a shredded lung in addition
to his horribly decayed stomach. 9   Juana "la Loca" was
scalded in a medicinal bath.   Because she was confined to
her filthy bed, boils and ulcers broke out on her buttocks
and legs.   A black suppuration on her left buttock was cau-

Maximilian I, deathbed portrait

terized, but the pain was insufferable, and Juana refused to
be treated again. The infections became gangrenous and
Juana vomited incessantly. With her last burst of energy she

lifted herself up and beat her breast, shrieking, "Christ cru-
cified help me, " and then fell back lifeless. [10] Juana's husband Philip had preceded her in a similarly dreadful death.
After falling prey to an undetermined pox, Philip could not
swallow, bled profusely, had diarrhea, and ran a high fever.
The Castilian regent, Archbishop Ximinez de Cisneros, called
in his favorite physician, a Dr. Yanguas, but the court party
was so appalled by his opinion that they called him a witch
doctor and he left in a huff. [11] Meanwhile, a burning sweat
had possessed Philip. Black and red spots erupted on his
skin, his tongue bloated and stuck to the roof of his mouth,
and he sank into a mortal coma.

Francis II's guardians tried to suppress news of his
final ailment. Their power was predicated on his live, al-
beit virtually comatose, presence, but the grim reaper's
scythe was obviously hanging over the boy. The Venetian
ambassador reported that "the King is very weak and feeble,
and that having taken a slight purge this morning before daybreak, he vomited it a few hours afterwards. I cannot comprehend what right these physicians had to purge him on the
7th [purges were usually administered in seven-day cycles],
for I know that our physicians would consider it a great mistake ... during the last few days, although the fever was
very light, he nevertheless suffered so much that he seemed
almost delirious. "[12] A large lump had formed behind the
prince's ear, apparently the manifestation of a severe mastoid
infection. Physicians sought to relieve the unbearable pressure by piercing the lump, but this ultimately created a fatal
abscess in the brain. Suriano, another Venetian, was present
at the autopsy. "The body of the late King has been opened,
and the whole brain was found diseased, so that no medical
treatment could have cured it. "[13]

Causes of death varied. Maximilian I was said to
have hastened his own end with a gluttonous meal of melons,
Don Carlos of Spain went on a suicidal ice-eating binge after
days of fasting, and according to Brantome's simple epitaph,
Francis I died "of the pox, which he had. "[14] But at the end
there was a gruesome sameness to the deathbeds of sixteenth-
century monarchs. To paraphrase a modern epigram, they
lived fast and died young, but they failed to leave a good-
looking corpse. A letter from a Church official suggested
that Edward VI of England was poisoned, so horrible was his
end. "The skin peeled off in flakes. " He looked like a leper,
fingers rotted, scaly eruptions all over his body. Rumor had
it that he was buried secretly--he was so ugly that another

corpse had to be substituted for his in public. [15] Ferdinand the Catholic of Spain was hearty in life, but so decrepit in death that his jaw fell off as he was being prepared for burial. And according to the embalmer's report, his daughter, the discarded English queen Catherine of Aragon, had a heart that--besides being broken by Henry VIII--"was quite black and hideous to look at. He washed it, but it did not change color; then he cut it open and the inside was the same. Moreover, a black round body stuck to the outside of the heart. "[16]

The final hours of these tattered figures were a court spectacle, even a civic observance. When the Queen of Spain, Elizabeth Valois, died in 1568, the city of Madrid's leading intellectual, Lopez de Hoyos, was ordered to compose funeral allegories and a book on the entire episode. Prominent among those involved in the work was a young and struggling writer named Miguel de Cervantes. [17] Yet for all this literary and courtly panoply, this final "progress" lacked any of that grace that surrounded kings and queens in their public role. In fact, most of these scenes stripped the king of all regal dignity and reduced him to simple pathos. Francis II's youngest brother took his elder sibling's name after Francis II died in 1560. But there was no one left to carry on the illustrious name after the youngest Francis died "of a hemorrhage accompanied by a slow fever--which had shrunken him up little by little until he was all dried up and emaciated, " according to the contemporary L' Estoile. [18] Deformed little Francis slowly withered before the eyes of his retinue, but others were subjected to greater indignities. James I of England and Philip II of Spain were incontinent during the last stage of their lives, as was the unfortunate Queen Juana of Spain, whose soiled bedsheets caused her open bedsores to fester. The finicky Philip found this condition especially horrifying. According to his valet Lhermite, this was "for him one of the greatest tortures imaginable, seeing that he himself was one of the cleanest, neatest, and most fastidious of men the world has ever seen ... he could not tolerate a single mark on the floors or walls of his rooms ... the evil smell which emanated from the said sores was another source of torment, and certainly not the least, on account of his great fastidiousness and cleanliness. "[19] Haughty Elizabeth Tudor was also a sad sight in her final days. She would not eat, refused to change clothes for days, and could only sit on a stool bolstered with cushions. She kept one finger inside her mouth, and stared glazedly at the floor. [20] A far cry from the glory of 1588.

Deathbed of Henry II of France, 1559

Although their own approaching deaths preoccupied the autumnal thoughts of monarchs and their relatives, ironically the deaths of others often passed unnoticed, even when those deaths were cruel, terrifying, and at the command of the sovereign. Philip II took his entire court to a celebration of his return to Spain in 1559. The entertainment for this festival was an <u>auto da fe</u>, a public punishment of heretics by the Inquisition. Thirteen condemned heretics had been saved especially for the occasion and were added to the pyre while the young monarch watched, sanguine and unmoved. [21] He recorded the event without comment in his diary.

The approach of death weighed equally on the mind and the body of the sixteenth-century sovereign. Many of these tormented souls could think of almost nothing else. Mortal illnesses were rarely merciful or short in duration, and while they progressed the state lacked an effective ruler. This vacuum of power might last for an extended period. Three years before the death of Philip II, the Venetian ambassador claimed that the royal physicians regarded the king as "so withered and feeble that it was almost impossible that a human being in such a state should live for long."[22] Decrepit monarchs held the reins of state, but the actual control of power fell to someone else. As various factions struggled to fill the void, the net result was a balance of forces in which no one held power long enough to govern effectively. This almost unavoidable phase of the ruling family cycle was one of the principal disadvantages of the early modern monarchy as a form of government. This chaos, abetted by the autumnal monarch's preoccupation with approaching death, induced a period of hibernation in the aged king's country: external inaction masking internal restructuring. It was a period of self-absorption few countries could afford.

Chapter Twelve

AFTERWORD

"Authority forgets a dying King"
                              --Tennyson

I think the king is but a man, as I am:
the violet smells to him as it doth to me;
the element shows to him as it doth to me;
all his senses have but human conditions. His
ceremonies laid by, in his nakedness he appears
but a man.
                    --Shakespeare, Henry VI

This book has focused on the most basic elements of monarchical existence, what I have termed the "royal facts of
life. " Surely, these were the most fundamental issues in
the lives of kings, queens, and their families, issues ranging
from marital discord to obstetrical tragedy to faltering health.
Given the case studies of the four major royal houses, these
were not only basic--they were some of the most important
problems faced by the rulers of sixteenth-century western
Europe.   The monarchs themselves noted the broad significance of such factors in letters and through their actions.
Yet there is a temptation for the modern reader to find a
consideration of such private struggles somewhat "ahistorical";
past generations have savored loving and detailed accounts of
royalty's panoply, but surely a few monarchs do not make an
age, and perhaps such figures have been overstressed. More
to the point at hand, sixteenth-century monarchs lived in an
age that was generally cruel and unpleasant. Why pay special attention, it might reasonably be asked, to their distress? A commendable current school of historical scholarship seeks to reach down from the lofty echelons of the aris-

tocracy into the lives of common men and women, whose history is now thought by some to be a broader index of meaningful societal change. If Henry VIII of England suffered, many would say, so did the unrecorded multitudes heretofore neglected by scholars with an elitist bias. Perhaps this bias stems at least partly from the wealth of material available to students of the great. The documentation of royal lives is of course ample and relatively easy to use, but has it been overused? Are the mundane affairs of kings and queens worth pursuing when there are so many unsorted lives to be pieced together?

I believe there is still much to illuminate in the history of sixteenth-century western European royalty. Although much has been written on the subject, the backdrop against which these figures operated has possibly been given short shrift. The early modern period was an age of great monarchical license, a license that became almost impossible in later, more limited, monarchies. In truth, this license was limited by tenuous royal finances. Still, sixteenth-century rulers, when they were of an age and a capacity to rule, wielded enormous power, sometimes foresightedly and responsibly, sometimes despotically. To what end they used their scepters was all too often a function of their "humor," or state of mind. Shakespeare wrote in the age of Elizabeth I and James I, and in <u>King John</u> he considered the import of royal whim.

> It is the curse of kings to be attended
> By slaves that take their humors for a warrant
> To break within the bloody house of life,
> And on the winking of authority
> To understand a law, to know the meaning
> Of dangerous majesty, when, perchance, it frowns
> More upon humor than advised respect.
> (IV, ii, 207-14)

Did majesty "frown more upon humor than advised respect"? In many sixteenth-century examples, the sovereign's humor reigned supreme, and the humor of kings preoccupied with unhappy marriages, ambitious mistresses, unfit heirs, poor health, pain, and the ever-present specter of death was understandably volatile.

The immediate, pressing problems of monarchs and their families are obviously of intrinsic interest as a study of monarchical life in the sixteenth century, a very limited

social history. But there is still greater significance in the
effect these malaises had on public developments. The linkage is not so simple as the trite "for want of a nail the shoe
was lost" approach to causation, and the reader can rest assured that I do not intend to attribute the Lutheran revolt
against the Catholic Church, say, to some sickly heir's head
cold or the momentary fancy of an indisposed sovereign.
Nonetheless, there were many junctures during the period at
which "royal facts" figured predominantly in European genesis.
There are a number of important events and even historical
trends that can be better understood through a consideration
of the seemingly mundane issues of monarchical life. The
men and women who left a shaky imprimatur on the pages of
Renaissance history were not always cool, rational masters
of realpolitik, not Metternichs or even Gattinaras. They
were frightened, limited creatures always on the verge of
personal and political extinction. Their approach to life was
notably superstitious; their approach to rule was for the most
part uneven, personal, and idiosyncratic. Yet they lived in
an age that, as Shakespeare's King John noted, made much
of even the merest whims of its sovereigns. One epithet
must be denied; biology is not necessarily destiny. But perhaps this can be replaced with a more cautious notion; at
the intersection of politics and biology, history was virtually
bound to collide with tragedy.

Of course, some monarchs were in no position to impose themselves or their whims on their patrimonies. But
these families, of which the most obvious example is the
sixteenth-century Stewarts of Scotland, were limited by their
biological instability just as much as by their political opponents. In fact, the inability to place fit adult monarchs on
the throne frequently figured in consuming disputatiousness,
in Scotland and elsewhere. In other cases the biological
weakness of royal families did not preclude the careers of
strong individual monarchs but rather emerged at unpropitious
times, in the midst of critical events, and prompted moments
of collapse or vulnerability to bad political effect.

An obvious intersection of politics and royal biology
occurred in France in 1572, when Charles IX and (or) the
Catholic faction (depending on which account is assumed) attempted to extinguish the fire of the Huguenot challenge with
mass assassinations. There are many theories about the
St. Bartholomew's Day Massacre, but certain things are not
disputed; since the death of Henry II in 1559 France had
lacked an effective monarch, and the success, in fact the

very existence, of the Protestants owed much to the wretchedness of royal leadership. Although Henry II himself had been
inclined to persecute heretics, he had been able to suppress
the Protestant factions. After his unfortunate and premature
demise, followed by the investiture of the first of his pathetic
sons, nascent discontent surfaced in open rebellion. France
plunged into what Montaigne described as "an unnatural war!
Other wars act outwardly; this one acts inwardly also, gnaw-
ing and destroying itself with its own poison. It is of so
malign and destructive a nature that it ruins itself together
with everything else, and in its frenzy tears itself limb
from limb. " The erratic alternation of action and inaction on the part of the French kings after Henry II did
much to increase this conflict. Weak and easily swayed,
Francis II and then Charles IX succeeded their father and
the result was a hydra-like course that created only confusion and proved to all the crown's inability to control its subjects. Waves of tolerance and persecution ebbed and raged,
depending on which faction was in temporary ascendancy.
Francis II survived only a year on the throne and was putty
in the hands of the Guise family; his brother and successor
Charles himself left matters of state to others. Yet certain
heinous acts required the stamp of royal authority. The
Massacre was such an occasion. The king was personally
attached to one of the Huguenot leaders and was apparently
reluctant to order the carnage, according to certain observers.
In truth, there were often those who attempted to incite sovereigns to unwise actions. Strong monarchs resisted such
sirens of death. Charles could not. Perhaps he was eager
to kill the Protestants all along, as others have speculated.
In either case, his behavior during and after the Massacre
was the manifestation of a warped personality. Charles was
indubitably a sick boy, a weak king, and in part through his
failings, France was locked into a seething chaos. At that
crucial juncture in 1572, Charles's physical and mental problems were of the greatest political moment.

The importance of royal facts was not limited to pathetic saplings. Henry VIII of England was no weakling, and
in most of his actions there was a core of calculation. His
break with Rome, however, revealed a king in the grasp of
forces--personal and biological as well as political--that were
beyond his control. His decision prompted a wrenching
separation from the Church, a traumatic period for the king
and his family, indeed for England as a country. For what
was such unhappiness unleashed? Henry was tired of his
careworn wife, who was older than he, and lacked a male

heir. Catherine had suffered tragedy after tragedy in child-bed; the king considered this a bad omen, and it brought to mind his earlier objections to the union. In truth, he had been somewhat leery of espousing his brother's widow from the very beginning, but as a young man he suppressed such thoughts. Later, as a restless and aging figure with a short temper and nagging ailments, Henry was more inclined to be rash. After their marriage tree finally proved blighted beyond a doubt, the issue of his union returned to the king's thoughts, and he found biblical justification for his desire to be rid of Catherine. By all accounts, Henry truly believed in the righteousness of his case for divorce. But on the simplest level the break with Rome was necessitated by the king's distaste for his aged wife, his lack of a legitimate son, and his fragile sense of virility, which called for him to have many sons in proportion to his stature as a man. In addition, Henry was very much taken with another woman, Anne Boleyn, and wished to make her his queen. These desires had less to do with the king's appraisal of England's needs than his personal inclinations. Insulated by his characteristic solipsism, he followed his desires with apparent insensitivity to their many ramifications. Although all England probably wished to see the birth of a male heir, it was largely to suit his own needs that Henry split his inheritance into hostile camps, isolated himself from the Catholic world, and perhaps still more disconcerting, cast his subjects into the abyss of religious limbo. Although this separation might ultimately have worked to England's advantage in many respects, at the time it was simply a tragic schism.

To cite a specific incident in which a biological problem all but overshadowed crucial political issues, let us make note of King Philip II of Spain's dilemma in 1568. The Ottoman Empire was once again reaching its tentacles toward the West, but still more critical to the Habsburgs was the revolt in the Netherlands. This northern corner of the family empire had been disaffected since the abdication of Charles V in 1556 and had proved unresponsive to Philip's long-distance directives, particularly those regarding religious orthodoxy and taxation, the both of which the seventeen provinces wanted no part of. After a series of embarrassing incidents, some involving Protestant demonstrations, Philip dispatched the Duke of Alva to the scene with 30,000 men. This wave of terror quashed the open defiance, but the characteristically over-extended Spanish crown was unable to support the large garrison, and a tax was imposed on the Low Countries to be used to pay for its own army of occupation. This was not

taken well, and a new wave of still more powerful discontent
broke.   Philip's father had quieted such unrest with personal
visits, and had often earned the olive branch merely through
his presence.   The Habsburg Empire was just that: a collection of states linked only by their common ruler, the Habsburg family.   Each state resented the multiple demands on
its prince, and sought to monopolize his attentions.   This
sort of possessiveness required a delicate balancing act, but
Philip was more the reticent homebody by nature and had not
been in the Netherlands since 1559.   The plan for the pacification of the Low Countries in 1568 called for Philip to
meet Alva and lend the all-important royal touch to his neglected inheritance.   But Philip was totally occupied with
matters closer to home, veritably his home.   Specifically,
Philip had reached a crisis point with his single son and heir
Don Carlos, who was becoming more petulant each day.   He
was also plotting against the crown in such an obvious manner that he was more of an embarrassment than a threat.
Within the year he would be dead in the prison to which
Philip had felt compelled to restrict him.   The king's first
concern was his lack of an heir.   In 1568 his queen, Elizabeth Valois, was pregnant again and in precarious health,
and the king decided that the tangled state of his family affairs took precedence over the Netherlands.   Philip remained
in Spain, the revolt blossomed, and with it perhaps a turning
point in the Habsburg global empire had been reached.   Because of Philip's reticent nature, and even more importantly
because of his family problems, the "royal touch" so necessary for the maintenance of the empire of Charles V was
sorely lacking in his son's reign.

There was perhaps a pathological note to many monarchical tragedies in the sixteenth century.   Take the case
of Sebastian of Portugal, who died on the battlefield and
passed his inheritance to the Spaniard Philip II.   As mentioned in Chapter Five, his seemingly martial demise had apparent roots in the young king's unbalanced mental state.
Sebastian reportedly despaired of his ability to sire children
and manifested a marked blood lust, perhaps to compensate
for what he perceived as his manly inadequacy.   His death
came not in a heroic war of defense or even in a logical
war of conquest.   Instead, he lit off to Africa on a quixotic
crusade with an undersized, under-supplied expeditionary
force.   Once there, he raced frantically off into the desert
in pursuit of his Moslem quarry, rushed into an unwise battle, and led suicidal charges across the field again and again
until he was finally cut down.   Whether the hotheaded young

king was motivated by a death wish or maniacally exaggerated
bravado is debatable, but whichever his imbalance, the end
result was tragic in view of his Portuguese subjects, who
were not amenable to the prospect of Spanish rule.

The untimely death of many European princes shifted
the balance of power across the continent, elevated one dynasty to prominence and created great confusion for the rest.
The dynasty that profited most from the demise of other
princes was of course the Habsburgs. The cornerstone of
their empire, Spain, came to them after three deaths: those
of the infante Juan, his sister Isabella, and Isabella's son
Miguel, all of which occurred within five years. Yet for
every dynasty that benefited from such misfortune that were
many that collapsed. The Stewarts, although they managed
to avoid extinction, were crippled throughout the sixteenth
century by the deaths of their infant princes and youthful
kings. This created an unfortunate rate of turnover, as it
were, on the throne, which meant that for most of the sixteenth century, Scotland was "ruled" by child monarchs. The
timing of a king's demise was in some sense fortuitous, but
when the monarch died at an unpropitious time, confusion
reigned. The untimely death of Henry II, for example, paved
the way to open religious war in France, as did the death of
Edward VI in England to a lesser degree.

Of the more dramatic examples of biological impact
on political development perhaps the career of Juana of Spain
is most gripping. As previously noted, she was wildly insane, and before her enforced retirement to the castle of
Tordesillas, she proved her unfitness for rule by a whole
series of manic acts. Her problems had both an immediate
and long-range import for her native land and her family;
after the death of her mother, she was Queen of Spain, a
frightening prospect, and after her husband's death, she had
no one to temper her except her aging father. Fortunately,
she was kept from the public, and there was no attempt,
save the abortive revolt of the Communeros in 1520, to make
her more than nominal ruler. The Spanish monarchy and
the house of Habsburg recovered from this temporary hiatus.
What neither escaped was Juana's legacy of madness. Mental problems had passed down both sides of her family, and
although her children seemed well enough adjusted, there
were echoes of insanity in her grandchildren and genuine
hallmarks of lunacy in three of her great-grandsons, who
happened to be the most important princes of that generation
of Habsburgs. There were, of course, many economic,

social, and political reasons for the decline of the Habsburg empire. But the unfitness of important Habsburg princes cannot be dismissed as a factor in the slide. Even Philip III, who did not share the obvious defects of his three cousins, seemed to lack the mental capacity of his ruling forebears.

Not all of the "royal facts" manifested themselves in such a vivid manner. And often the effects of ill health, marital failure, distorted sexuality, harsh childhoods, excessive lifestyles, gruesome deaths, and so on were not connected in an obvious fashion to events and broad issues. It must also be said that some of the monarchs of the sixteenth century transcended the brutal rigors of their existence to demonstrate remarkable talents; Elizabeth I, sick as she was, still animated one of England's most memorable reigns. Charles V was perhaps the most dynamic figure of his era, and Francis I proved a charismatic, if prodigal, ruler whose subjects appreciated his personal qualities and ignored his natural languor. Could this be the same king who, rumor had it, ordered the execution of a man in a moment of indisposition and awoke the next morning unaware of what he had done? Certainly, and even if personal problems were not immediately visible in the pattern of events they were still the central determinant of the monarch's state of mind. The sort of life lived by these all-important individuals provided a backdrop for their actions in the larger sphere. And that backdrop was virtually guaranteed to create anxiety and even volatility. Elizabeth I was uneasy on the throne, historians have posited, because she feared challenges to her sovereignty from her own people, particularly her relatives (see Chart 2, p. 38). This fear had a modicum of validity because of Elizabeth's politically costly hostility toward marriage, which prevented her from providing England with an heir and sparked uncertainty about the succession, an uncertainty the queen perceived as a threat to her own position. Similarly, her eventual successor, James I, was raised in an environment of constant confrontation. He learned to manage this situation with a haughty and tough demeanor that made him appear arrogant and crude to his English subjects. Loving only his male paramours, James was impervious to the enmity he aroused in his windfall state. To move ahead a reign, these sins of the father might well have been visited on James's son, Charles I, in 1640. Monarchs were not voluntary martyrs, although each had his or her cross to bear, and suffering left an indelible impression on their temperaments and characters. In the confused, expanding political world of the sixteenth century, the principal actors were these confused, limited individuals.

Having noted many monarchical problems, there were still certain advantages to monarchy as a form of government in the age of the Renaissance. The king was a believable entity, his body became the symbolic vessel of state, and the web of vassalage that surrounded him created a many-tiered social structure with an understandable pattern of social obligation. With the growth of European economies, exploration to worlds beyond Europe, religious dissent, and other developments, many people became dissatisfied with their spot in the hierarchy, and this would pose the greatest challenge to the static order presupposed by the monarchies, most of which still operated on vaguely medieval premises. But the kings themselves proved inadequate, on a cumulative basis, to build and maintain the kind of ideal monarchy depicted in chivalric stories and works on political theory. Perhaps the rulers of the sixteenth century fantasized about such kings: strong, revered, long-lived, sure, prudent, and wise. But the circumstances of actual reigns, personal and political, rendered the simple blueprint obsolete. And perhaps the most insurmountable of these obstacles was the sheer personal instability of the rulers and their families. Simple survival on the throne was an accomplishment, not a commonplace occurrence, and even those who survived were never far from the edge. With a sick, underaged, weak, or blatantly imprudent sovereign, the European monarchies became ineffectual or destructive. Such vulnerable monarchies were all too frequently rewarded with revolt; chaotic self-aggrandizement by the unharnessed nobility, foreign invasion, and general mayhem.

At bottom, history is the study of human beings in juxtaposition with each other, with natural forces, with their societal constructs. Sixteenth-century royalty was a mere agglomeration of men and women frightened by the uncertainties of the age, the tenuous nature of their power and health, and the lurking presence of those who opposed them. Highlighting their weaknesses and limitations does not reduce them, I hope, but rather adds another dimension to their historical characters. An understanding of the myriad problems they faced, the difficulties of mere survival, can only increase our admiration for their occasional triumphs: Charles V's empire, Elizabeth's defense of England, Ferdinand and Isabella's Union of the Crowns and their creation of a powerful state in Castile, among others. The royal facts of life were cruel and consuming limitations on the quality of life and had the effect of restricting monarchical effectiveness. Others suffered, some more, some less, no doubt. But in no group of contemporaries was that suffering more significant for the society as a whole than the torments of monarchs and their families. Certainly, kings and queens were among the dominant figures of the sixteenth century, and the royal facts of life, the difficulties they faced in the simple progression from birth to death, were just as certainly among their most pressing concerns.

ENDNOTES

___

Introduction

1. L. Stone. The Crisis of the Aristocracy, 1558-1641, p. 167-68. Oxford, 1965.

2. R. Mols. Population in Europe, p. 69. In C. Cipolla, editor. The Fontana Economic History of Europe. Fontana, 1972.

3. Ibid., p. 72.

4. Calendar of State Papers--Venetian. Vol. VI, 882.

5. H. F. M. Prescott. A Spanish Tudor, p. 395. Columbia University Press, 1940.

The Tudors

1. Peter Saccio. Shakespeare's English Kings, p. 180. Oxford, 1977.

2. N. Williams. Henry VII, p. 21. Weidenfeld and Nicolson, 1967.

3. C. Morris. The Tudors, p. 54. Fontana, 1972.

4. C. Williams. England Under the Early Tudors, p. 64. Longmans, 1925.

5. Antonia Fraser. Lives of the Kings and Queens of England, p. 144. First Contact, 1977. Originally published by Weidenfeld and Nicolson, 1975.

6. Gladys Tempersly. Henry VII, p. 390. Constable, 1914.

7. J. Gairdner. Henry VII, p. 44. Macmillan, 1899.

8. N. L. Harvey. Elizabeth of York. Macmillan, 1973.

9. H. W. Chapman. The Sisters of Henry VIII, p. 160. Cape, 1969.

10. Gairdner, p. 92.

11. Ibid.

12. Harvey, p. 191.

13. G. Mattingly. Catherine of Aragon, p. 256. Vintage Books, 1960. Originally published by Little, Brown, 1941.

14. J. Gairdner. Memorials of Henry VII, p. 223. Rolls Series, 1858.

15. C. A. Sneyd. A Relation of the Island of England, p. 42-43. Camden Society, 1847.

16. Morris, p. 71.

17. L. B. Smith. Henry VIII: The Mask of Royalty, p. 106. Panther Books, 1973. Originally published by Jonathan Cape, 1971.

18. Ibid., p. 192.

19. J. J. Scarisbrick. Henry VIII, p. 486. Eyre and Spotswood, 1968.

20. Neville Williams. Henry VIII and His Court, p. 156 and p. 246. Macmillan, 1971.

21. A. F. Pollard. The Reign of Henry VII from Contemporary Sources, p. 317. Longmans, 1913.

22. Ibid., p. 261.

23. Calendar of State Papers-Venetian. Volume V, 1230.

24. Ibid.

25. Scarisbrick, p. 9.

26. Ove Brinch. "The Medical Problems of Henry VIII" in Centaurus, voL V (1958) p. 341.

27. Smith, p. 127.

28. Francis Hackett. The Personal History of Henry VIII, p. 174. Modern Library, 1949.

29. A. S. Currie. "Notes on the Obstetrical Histories of Catherine of Aragon and Anne Boleyn." In Transactions of the Edinburgh Obstetrical Society, v. VIII (1887-88).

30. Smith, p. 55.

31. A. F. Pollard. Henry VIII, p. 191. Longmans-Green, 1930.

32. Mattingly, p. 234.

33. Hackett, p. 335.

34. M. L. Bruce. Anne Boleyn, p. 201. Coward-McCann, 1972.

35. N. B. Morrison. The Private Life of Henry VIII, p. 79. Vanguard, 1964.

36. Bruce, p. 252.

37. Brinch, p. 344.

38. Smith, p. 56.

39. Pollard, Henry VIII, p. 347.

40. Bruce, p. 274.

41. H. W. Chapman. The Last Tudor King, p. 30. Cape, 1958.

42. Brinch, p. 346.

43. L. B. Smith. Catherine Howard, A Tudor Tragedy, p. 117. Pantheon, 1961.

44. Scarisbrick, p. 429.

45. Smith, Henry VIII, p. 191.

46. Ibid., p. 195.

47. Ibid., p. 197.

48. Ibid., p. 259.

49. Ibid., p. 258.

50. Pollard, Henry VIII, p. 486.

51. Smith, Henry VIII, p. 192.

52. Brinch, p. 357.

53. The Hamilton Papers. Vol. II, p. 326-27. Edited by J. Bain. Quoted in Morris, p. 93.

54. Saccio, p. 228.

55. Smith, Henry VIII, p. 21.

56. Fraser, p. 156.

57. W. K. Jordan. Edward VI: The Threshold of Power, p. 532. Belknap Press/Harvard University, 1969.

58. Ibid., p. 423.

59. Ibid., p. 19.

60. Morris, p. 98.

61. Chapman, p. 223.

62. Ibid., p. 96.

63. Morris, p. 100.

64. Jordan, p. 514.

65. Morris, p. 114.

66. Ibid.

67. Chapman, p. 284

68. H. F. M. Prescott. A Spanish Tudor, p. 252. Columbia University Press, 1940.

69. Ibid.

70. J. M. Stone. The History of Mary I, Queen of England, p. 29. Sands and Company, 1901.

71. Ibid., p. 255.

72. Ibid., p. 251.

73. Fraser, p. 129.

74. Prescott, p. 354.

75. Fraser, p. 129.

76. Prescott, p. 353.

77. Ibid.

78. Calendar of State Papers--Spanish. Vol. XIII, 61.

79. Calendar of State Papers--Venetian. Vol. VI, 884 and 1056.

80. Fraser, p. 137.

81. Prescott, p. 368.

82. Calendar of State Papers--Spanish. Vol. XIII, 22.

83. Prescott, p. 397.

84. Carolly Erickson. Bloody Mary, p. 414. Doubleday, 1978.

85. Calendar of State Papers--Spanish. Vol. XIII, 378.

86. Calendar of State Papers--Venetian. Vol. VI, 884, 1056.

87. Fraser, p. 134.

88. From a letter written by Pedro Enriquez. Quoted in M. A. S. Hume. "The Coming of Philip the Pru-

dent. " In The Year After the Armada and Other
Historical Studies, p. 169. N. p., 1896.

89. Elizabeth Jenkins. Elizabeth the Great, p. 44.
Coward-McCann, 1958.

90. Ibid., p. 45.

91. Neville Williams. Elizabeth I, p. 7. Dutton, 1968.

92. Ibid., p. 20.

93. Frederick Chamberlain. The Private Character of
Elizabeth I, p. 295. Dodd, Mead, and Co., 1922.

94. Paul Johnson. Elizabeth I, p. 13. Holt, Rinehart,
and Winston, 1974.

95. Jenkins, p. 88.

96. Ibid., p. 258.

97. Sir James Perrot, quoted in Morris, p. 153.

98. Williams, Elizabeth I, p. 127.

99. Jenkins, p. 85.

100. Fraser, p. 143.

101. Tempersley, p. 100.

102. Johnson, p. 111.

103. Antonia Fraser. Mary Queen of Scots, p. 64. Dela-
corte, 1970. Originally published by Weidenfeld
and Nicolson, 1969.

104. Ibid.

105. Ian MacInnes. Arabella; The Life and Times of Lady
Arabella Seymour, p. 103. Allen, 1968.

106. Morris, p. 155.

107. Jenkins, p. 323.

108. A. M. MacKenzie. The Rise of the Stuarts, p. 94. Oliver and Boyd, 1957.

109. N. L. Harvey. The Rose and the Thorn, p. 224. Macmillan, 1975.

110. W. C. Richardson. Mary Tudor: The White Queen, p. 131. University of Washington Press, 1970.

111. H. W. Chapman. The Sisters of Henry VIII, p. 165. Cape, 1969.

112. Ibid., p. 172.

113. Ibid., p. 169.

114. Ibid., p. 190.

115. Williams, Elizabeth I, p. 99.

The Stewarts

1. Fraser, Mary Queen of Scots, p. 22.

2. Ibid., p. 149.

3. Ibid., p. 150.

4. Caroline Bingham. James V, King of Scots, p. 90. Collins, 1971.

5. Calendar of State Papers--Scotland. Vol. I, 205. Estiene's critique.

6. Fraser, Mary Queen of Scots, p. 143.

7. Caroline Bingham. The Stuart Kingdom of Scotland, p. 121. St. Martin's, 1974.

8. Ibid., p. 152.

9. R. L. Mackie. King James IV of Scotland, p. 2. Oliver and Boyd, 1958.

10. I. A. Taylor. The Life of James IV, p. 10. Hutchinson, 1913.

11. Agnes Strickland. Lives of the Queens of Scotland and English Princesses, p. 20. Four volumes. Harper, 1859.

12. G. Donaldson. Scottish Kings, p. 134. Wiley and Sons, 1967.

13. Taylor, p. 156.

14. Pollard, Reign of Henry VII from Contemporary Sources, p. 198.

15. Mackie, p. 113.

16. Bingham, Stuart Kingdom, p. 142.

17. J. Prebble. The Lion in the North, p. 105. Secker and Warburg, 1971.

18. Donaldson, p. 113.

19. Mackie, p. 104.

20. Strickland, p. 58.

21. Ibid., p. 114.

22. Chapman, The Sisters of Henry VIII, p. 61.

23. R. Nicholson. Scotland: The Later Middle Ages, p. 595. Barnes and Noble, 1974.

24. Prebble, p. 155.

25. Chapman, Sisters of Henry VIII, p. 84.

26. Strickland, p. 147.

27. Ibid., 148-49.

28. Chapman, The Sisters of Henry VIII, p. 121.

29. Morris, The Tudors, p. 83.

30. Chapman, The Sisters of Henry VIII, p. 102.

31. Harvey, p. 249.

32. Strickland, p. 155.

33. Ibid., p. 156.

34. Ibid., p. 364.

35. Bingham, James V, p. 27.

36. Ibid., p. 51.

37. Ibid., p. 70.

38. Ibid.

39. Ibid., p. 71.

40. Ibid., p. 81.

41. Ibid., p. 11.

42. Ibid., p. 75.

43. Fraser, Mary Queen of Scots, p. 4.

44. Bingham, James V, p. 98.

45. Ibid.

46. Ibid., p. 114.

47. Strickland, p. 261.

48. Ibid., p. 274.

49. Ibid., p. 299.

50. Ibid., p. 335.

51. Fraser, Mary Queen of Scots, p. 8.

52. Strickland, p. 340.

53. Ibid., p. 349.

54. Ibid., p. 363.

55. Bingham, James V, p. 174.

56. Strickland, p. 268.

57. Ibid., p. 361.

58. Ibid., p. 371.

59. Bingham, James V, p. 190.

60. Ibid., p. 190-92.

61. A. Mackinson. "Solway Moss and the Death of James V." In History Today, vol. X, no. 2 (1976), p. 115.

62. Bingham, James V, p. 176.

63. Fraser, Mary Queen of Scots, p. 1.

64. Ibid., p. 15.

65. Ibid., p. 36.

66. Ibid., p. 81.

67. Ibid.

68. Ibid., p. 67.

69. Ibid., p. 209.

70. Ibid., p. 157.

71. Ibid., p. 117.

72. Melville, quoted in Ibid., p. 220.

73. Ibid., p. 227.

74. Ibid., p. 223.

75. Ibid., p. 228.

76. Ibid., p. 251.

77. Ibid., p. 207.

78. Ibid., p. 247.

79. Ibid., p. 241.

80. Ibid., p. 259.

81. Ibid., p. 246.

82. Ibid., p. 271.

83. Ibid., p. 276.

84. Ibid., p. 277.

85. Ibid., p. 311.

86. Ibid., p. 316.

87. Ibid.

88. Ibid., p. 322.

89. Ibid., p. 324.

90. C. B. Harrison. Letters of Queen Elizabeth, p. 53. Cassell, 1935.

91. Fraser, Mary Queen of Scots, p. 538.

92. Harrison, op. cit., p. 185.

93. Fraser, Mary Queen of Scots, p. 324.

94. Caroline Bingham. The Making of a King, p. 84. Collins, 1968.

95. J. P. Kenyon. The Stuarts, p. 32-3. Fontana, 1976. First published by B. T. Batsford, 1958.

96. Antonia Fraser. King James, p. 63. Weidenfeld and Nicolson, 1974.

97. Kenyon, p. 42.

98. Ibid., p. 33.

99. Ibid.

100. D. Matthew. James I, p. 293. Eyre and Spotswood, 1967.

101. Kenyon, p. 36.

102. Calendar of State Papers--Scotland. For the year 1586, 656.

103. Fraser, King James, p. 52.

104. G. C. Williams. Anne of Denmark, p. 9. Longmans, 1970.

105. Ibid. , p. 15.

106. Kenyon, p. 55.

107. I. MacAlpine and R. Hunter. George III and the Mad Business, p. 203. Pantheon, 1969.

108. Kenyon, p. 48.

109. Bingham, The Making of a King, p. 197.

110. Kenyon, p. 61.

111. Bingham, The Making of a King, p. 197.

112. Kenyon, p. 49.

113. Fraser, King James, p. 48.

114. Kenyon, p. 57.

115. Ibid. , p. 55.

116. Ibid. , p. 57.

117. Fraser, King James, p. 199.

The Valois

1. Calendar of State Papers--Venetian. Vol. VI, 882.

2. L. B. Smith, Henry VIII, p. 22.

3. Niccolo Machiavelli. The Prince, Ch. 4. Edited by Lester Crocker. Washington Square Press, 1963.

4. Desmond Seward. Prince of the Renaissance, p. 17. Constable, 1973.

5. Will Durant. The Reformation: A History of European Civilization from Wyclif to Calvin: 1300-1564, p. 93. Volume VI in Durant, The Story of Civilization. Simon and Schuster, 1957.

6. E. R. Chamberlain. The Bad Popes, p. 183. Signet Books, 1971. Originally published by the Dial Press, 1969.

7. Durant, p. 93.

8. Francis Hackett. Francis I, p. 16. New York, Literary Guild, 1934.

9. J. S. C. Bridge. The History of France, Vol. III, p. 33. Five volumes. Oxford, 1930.

10. Phillipe de Commynes. The Memoirs of Phillipe de Commynes, Vol. II, p. 453. Edited by S. Kinser, University of South Carolina Press, 1973.

11. Hackett, p. 10.

12. Ibid., p. 72.

13. Bridge, p. 4.

14. Marjorie Bowen. Sundry Great Gentlemen, p. 64. Dodd, Mead, and Co., 1928.

15. Ibid., p. 67.

16. J. R. Hale. Renaissance Europe, p. 73. Collins, 1971.

17. Bridge, p. 23.

18. Constance, Countess de la Warr. A Twice Crowned Queen, p. 86. Everleigh Nash, 1906.

19. Bridge, p. 27.

20. M. B. Ryley. Queens of the Renaissance, p. 141. Methuen, 1906.

21. Bridge, p. 243.

22. Bowen, p. 88.

23. Durant, p. 95.

24. Bridge, p. 23.

25. Ibid., p. 243.

26. Bowen, p. 108.

27. Calendar of State Papers--Venetian. Vol. II, 553.

28. Chapman, The Sisters of Henry VIII, p. 172.

29. Seward, p. 33.

30. Bowen, p. 107.

31. Seward, p. 33.

32. Baldesar Castiglione. The Book of the Courtier, p. 68. Translated by Charles Singleton. Anchor Books (Doubleday), 1959.

33. Calendar of State Papers--Venetian. Vol. II, 600.

34. Ibid., p. 697.

35. A. C. P. Haggard. Two Great Rivals, p. 46. Hutchinson, 1910.

36. Smith, Henry VIII, p. 222.

37. Calendar of State Papers--Venetian. Vol. III, 1066.

38. Seward, p. 228.

39. Durant, p. 496.

40. Calendar of State Papers--Spanish. Vol. VI, 255.

41. Hackett, p. 88.

42. Ibid., p. 127.

43. Seward, p. 128.

44. Durant, p. 496.

45. Seward, p. 174.

46. Durant, p. 513.

47. Calendar of State Papers--Venetian. Vol. III, 811.

48. Seward, p. 240.

49. Calendar of State Papers--Spanish. Vol. III, pt. 1, 748.

50. Smith, Henry VIII, p. 220.

51. Calendar of State Papers--Spanish. Vol. VIII, 78.

52. Calendar of State Papers--Venetian. Vol. III, 60.

53. Seward, p. 246.

54. H. Noel Williams. Henry II, p. 62. Methuen, 1910.

55. Ibid.

56. Hackett, p. 424.

57. H. R. Williamson. Catherine de Medicis, p. 31. Viking, 1973.

58. Seward, p. 232.

59. Noel Williams, p. 85.

60. Ibid. , p. 38.

61. Ibid. , p. 176.

62. Ibid. , p. 234.

63. Ibid.

64. Ibid. , p. 177.

65. Ibid.

66. Ibid., p. 136.

67. Jean Heritier. Catherine de Medici, p. 42. Allen, 1963.

68. Fraser, Mary Queen of Scots, p. 41.

69. Williamson, p. 38.

70. Noel Williams, p. 258.

71. Williamson, p. 64.

72. Brantome, quoted in Noel Williams, p. 258.

73. Heritier, p. 70.

74. A. Mackinson, p. 16.

75. N. M. Sutherland. The French Secretaries of State in the Era of Catherine de Medici, p. 57. Athlone Press, 1962.

76. Ibid., p. 58.

77. Fraser, Mary Queen of Scots, p. 65.

78. Calendar of State Papers--Spanish. Vol. VI, pt. 3, 1216. Quoted in Fraser, Mary Queen of Scots, p. 65.

79. Heritier, p. 78.

80. Fraser, Mary Queen of Scots, p. 105.

81. Ibid.

82. Sutherland, p. 97.

83. Will Durant. The Age of Reason Begins, p. 334. Volume VII in Durant, The Story of Civilization. Simon and Schuster, 1961.

84. Calendar of State Papers--Venetian. Vol. VII, 270.

85. Ibid.

86. Ibid.

87. Ibid., p. 216.

88. Philipe Erlanger. St. Bartholomew's Night, p. 59. Pantheon, 1962.

89. Ibid., p. 71.

90. Williamson, p. 198.

91. James Davis, editor. Pursuit of Power; Venetian Ambassadors' reports on Spain, Turkey, and France in the Age of Philip II, 1560-1600, p. 197. Harper Torchbooks, 1970.

92. Heritier, p. 266.

93. Davis, p. 210.

94. Henri Noguerés. The Massacre of St. Bartholomew, p. 30. Macmillan, 1962.

95. E. Sichel. The Later Years of Catherine de Medici, p. 100. Constable, 1908.

96. Williamson, p. 196.

97. Durant, The Age of Reason, p. 348.

98. Erlanger, p. 148.

99. Ibid., p. 240.

100. Alfred Solman, editor. The Massacre of St. Bartholomew, p. 78. The Hague, Nijhoff, 1974.

101. Durant, The Age of Reason, p. 355.

102. Noguerés, p. 27.

103. Calendar of State Papers--Venetian. Vol. VII, 584.

104. Ibid.

105. Ibid., p. 591.

106. Davis, p. 211.

107. Durant, The Age of Reason, p. 361.

108. Erlanger, p. 240.

109. W. L. Wiley. The Gentlemen of Renaissance France, p. 81. Harvard University Press, 1954.

110. Sutherland, p. 431.

111. Ibid., p. 352.

112. Williamson, p. 251.

113. A. L. Martin. Henry III and the Jesuit Politicians, p. 78. Geneva, Libraire Droz, 1973.

114. Sichel, p. 423.

115. Sutherland, p. 346.

116. Williamson, p. 254.

117. Ibid.

118. Calendar of State Papers--Venetian. Vol. VII, 646.

119. Williamson, p. 255.

120. Heritier, p. 253.

121. Erlanger, p. 89.

122. Davis, p. 251.

123. Durant, The Age of Reason, p. 360.

124. Martin, p. 143.

125. Erlanger, p. 62.

126. Sutherland, p. 191.

127. Williamson, p. 65.

The Habsburgs

1. Garrett Mattingly. The Armada, p. 10. Houghton
    Mifflin, 1959.

2. Ralph Davis. The Rise of the Atlantic Economies, p.
    90. Cornell University Press, 1973.

3. Miguel de Cervantes. Don Quixote, Book I, Ch. 21.
    Translated by S. Putnam. Viking, 1972. Quoted
    in Henry Kamen. The Spanish Inquisition, p. 11.
    Plume Books, 1971. Originally published by the
    New American Library, 1965.

4. Kamen, p. 14.

5. Ibid.

6. Townsend Miller. Henry IV of Castile, 1425-1474,
    p. 60. Lippincott, 1972.

7. I. T. Plunkett. Isabella of Castile, p. 34. Putnam,
    1915.

8. W. H. Prescott. The History of the Reign of Ferdi-
    nand and Isabella, p. 98. Volume I. American
    Stationer's Co., 1838.

9. Felipe Fernández y Armesto. Ferdinand and Isabella,
    p. 42. Taplinger, 1975.

10. Amarie Dennis. Seek the Darkness, p. 5. Madrid,
    1961.

11. Fernández y Armesto, p. 33.

12. W. T. Walsh. Isabella the Crusader, p. 92. Sheed
    and Ward, 1935.

13. Fernández y Armesto, p. 118.

14. Prescott, p. 34.

15. Fernández y Armesto, p. 12.

16. Ibid., p. 108.

17. Miller, p 260.

18. Machiavelli, Ch. 21, p. 98.

19. Fernández y Armesto, p. 48.

20. Prescott, p. 172.

21. Ibid. , p. 173.

22. Fernández y Armesto, p. 12. , and Plunkett, p. 329.

23. Fernández y Armesto, p. 122.

24. Kamen, p. 233-34.

25. Prescott, p. 373.

26. Walsh, p. 223.

27. Tarciscio de Azcona. Isabel la Catolica, p. 113. Madrid, Biblioteca de Autores Cristianos, 1964.

28. Fernández y Armesto, p. 121.

29. Prescott, p. 95.

30. Plunkett, p. 344.

31. Prescott, p. 75.

32. Fernández y Armesto, p. 118.

33. Townsend Miller. The Castles and the Crown, p. 158. Coward, McCann and Co. , 1963.

34. V. de Braganca Cunha. Eight Centuries of Portuguese Monarchy, p. 42. Swift, 1917.

35. Miller, The Castles and the Crown, p. 17.

36. Ibid. , p. 185.

37. Fernández y Armesto, p. 34.

38. Dennis, p. 140.

39. Fernández y Armesto, p. 105.

40. Ibid., p. 126.

41. Ibid., p. 48.

42. Ibid., p. 45.

43. Ibid., p. 92.

44. Ibid., p. 89.

45. Ibid., p. 90.

46. Ibid., p. 108.

47. Dennis, p. 71.

48. Ibid., p. 187.

49. Ibid., p. 211.

50. Seward, p. 174.

51. Calendar of State Papers--Venetian. Vol. III, 613.

52. Royall Tyler. The Emperor Charles V, p. 61. Essential Books, 1956.

53. Ibid.

54. Karl Brandi. The Emperor Charles V: The Growth and Destiny of a Man and of a World Empire, p. 54. Translated by C. V. Wedgewood. Jonathan Cape Paperbacks, 1970. Originally published in 1939.

55. D. McGuigan. The Habsburgs, p. 52. Doubleday, 1966.

56. Durant, The Reformation, p. 628.

57. William Bradford, editor. The Correspondence of the Emperor Charles V, p. 237. Bentley, 1850.

58. McGuigan, p. 125.

59. Tyler, p. 61.

60. McGuigan, p. 77.

61. Ibid., p. 120.

62. Ibid., p. 121.

63. Ibid.

64. Calendar of State Papers--Venetian. Vol. VI, pt. 2, dispatch of 12 Dec. 1556.

65. McGuigan, p. 77.

66. Tyler, p. 279.

67. Chamberlain, p. 254.

68. Otto von Habsburg. Charles V, p. 30. Praeger, 1919.

69. Christopher Hare. A Great Emperor: Charles V, p. 36. Scribners, 1917.

70. A. Thomas. Felipe II: Estudio Medico Historico, p. 30. Madrid, Aguilar, 1956.

71. M. Gachard. Retrait et Mort de Charles Quint, p. 6. Bruxelles, M. Hayea, 1854.

72. von Habsburg, p. 31.

73. Ibid., p. 231.

74. Manuel F. Alvarez. Charles V, Elected Emperor and Hereditary Ruler, p. 50. Thames and Hudson, 1975.

75. Durant, The Reformation, p. 358.

76. Brandi, p. 220.

77. Ibid., p. 94.

78. Ibid., p. 214.

79. The Turks--Suleiman the Great in particular--employed a similar system of learned secretaries.

80. See, among others, Brandi and Tyler.

81. Alvarez, p. 63.

82. Correspondence of Charles V, p. 243.

83. Baltesar Porreneo. Dichos y Hechos de la Rey Don Felipe II. Madrid, n. p. , 1942.

84. Thomas, p. 28. Freely translated.

85. Ibid. , p. 201.

86. Tyler, p. 58.

87. Gachard, p. 7.

88. Ibid. , p. 8.

89. Durant, The Reformation, p. 641.

90. Alvarez, p. 95.

91. Correspondence of Charles V, p. 336.

92. Gachard, p. 18.

93. Durant, The Reformation, p. 636.

94. Gregorio Maranon. Antonio Perez, Spanish Traitor, p. 1. Roy, 1956. Originally published in Madrid, 1947.

95. Thomas, p. 37.

96. Garett Parker. Philip II, p. 112. Unpublished manuscript. Now available from Little, Brown, 1979.

97. Thomas, p. 18.

98. Ibid. , p. 45. Freely translated.

99. Ibid. , p. 111.

100. Parker, p. 14.

101. Ibid. , p. 17.

102. Ibid. , p. 18.

103. Ibid.

104. Ibid., p. 36.

105. Prescott, A Spanish Tudor, p. 354.

106. Parker, p. 118.

107. Ibid., p. 218.

108. McGuigan, p. 155.

109. Thomas, p. 111.

110. See Erik Erickson. Young Man Luther; A Study in
     Psychoanalysis and History. Norton, 1958.

111. Parker, p. 38.

112. Ibid.

113. Ibid., p. 265.

114. Pollard, The Reign of Henry VII from Contemporary
     Sources, p. 243.

115. John Lynch. Spain Under the Habsburgs, p. 176.
     Oxford, 1964.

116. G. Grierson. Fatal Inheritance, p. 143. Doubleday,
     1969.

117. Lynch, p. 177.

118. Ibid., p. 179.

119. Erika Spivakosky. Son of the Alhambra: Don Ber-
     nardino de Mendoza, p. 360. University of Texas
     Press, 1970.

120. Lynch, p. 179.

121. G. W. Bovill. The Battle of the Alcazar, p. 15.
     Batchworth, 1952.

122. Ibid., p. 131.

123. Hans Holzer. Rudolf II: The Alchemist and the Secret Magical Life of Rudolf von Habsburg, p. 57. Stein and Day, 1974.

124. Ibid., p. 140.

PART II

Birth

1. Calendar of State Papers--Spanish. Vol. XIII, 51.

2. Ibid.

3. S. Guistinian. Four Years at the Court of Henry VIII, Vol. II, p. 237. Smith-Elder, 1854.

4. Calendar of State Papers--Venetian. Vol. VI, 1081.

5. The Tudors and the Valois perished entirely, at least the ruling branch of those families vanished, and the Stewarts and Habsburgs came close to extinction as well.

6. Only a third of the ruling Tudors' live births lived to the age of fifteen.

7. Jenkins, Elizabeth the Great, p. 111.

8. Fraser, Mary Queen of Scots, p. 58.

9. Chapman, The Last Tudor King, p. 27.

10. Pollard, The Reign of Henry VII from Contemporary Sources, p. 237.

11. Hackett, Francis I, p. 182.

12. Giustinian, p. 180.

13. Williams, Anne of Denmark, p. 1.

14. Giustinian, p. 240.

15. Fraser, Mary Queen of Scots, p. 250.

16. Seward, p. 66.

17. Fernández y Armesto, p. 92.

18. Heritier, p. 48.

19. Chapman, The Last Tudor King, p. 30.

20. Bradford, Correspondence of Charles V, p. 15.

21. Strickland, p. 114.

22. Fraser, Mary Queen of Scots, p. 267.

23. Ibid.

24. Ibid., p. 276.

25. Harvey, p. 147.

26. Miller, The Castles and the Crown, p. 175.

27. Nancy Mitford. The Sun King: Louis XIV at Versailles, p. 111-12. Harper and Row, 1966.

28. A. Gonzalez de Amueza y Mayo. Isabel de Valois, vol. IV, appendice CXXXV. Four volumes. Madrid, 1949.

29. Ibid.

30. Ibid.

31. Amueza y Mayo, vol. III, appendice LXXXIII.

32. Ibid.

33. Amueza y Mayo, vol. IV, appendice CXLVI.

34. Pollard, The Reign of Henry VII from Contemporary Sources, p. 261.

35. Raynalde, ch. 7.

36. Ibid.

37. A. J. Rongy. Childbirth Yesterday and Today, p. 53. Emerson, 1937.

38. DeMause, p. 238.

39. Thomas, Estudio Medico-Historico, p. 28.

40. Thomas, p. 210.

Childhood and Adolescence

1. The Habsburgs produced on the average about four live births per marriage, while the other three major sixteenth-century royal houses struggled to produce two.

2. Fraser, Mary Queen of Scots, p. 22.

3. Richardson, Mary Tudor: The White Queen, p. 13.

4. MacInnes, Arabella, p. 65.

5. C. Bingham, The Making of a King, p. 84.

6. MacInnes, p. 65.

7. The Italian described Francis as "so great a majesty, accompanied nonetheless by a certain lovely courtesy." Castiglione, p. 68.

8. Seward, p. 22.

9. Hare, A Great Emperor, p. 26.

10. Keith Thomas. Religion and the Decline of Magic, p. 506. Scribners, 1971.

11. Scarisbrick, Henry VIII, p. 6.

12. Sichel, Catherine de Medici, p. 7.

13. Heritier, Catherine de Medici, p. 236.

14. Williamson, Catherine de Medici, p. 65.

15. Desiderius Erasmus. The Education of a Christian Prince, p. 142. Edited by L. K. Born. Columbia University Press, 1936.

16. Eucharius Roesslin. Rosengarten. Translated into English by Thomas Raynalde as The Birth of Mankynde, p. 116. London, 1545.

17. S. Byman. "Tudor Child Raising, " p. 75. Journal of Psychohistory, vol. VI, no. 1, summer 1978.

18. Ibid. , p. 76.

19. L. E. Pearson. Elizabethans at Home, p. 188. Stanford University Press, 1957.

20. Ibid. , p. 189.

21. G. E. Waas. The Legendary Character of Kaiser Maximilian, p. 5. Columbia University Press, 1941.

22. M. Marples. Princes in the Making; A Study of Royal Education, p. 61. Faber, 1962.

23. Ibid. , p. 75.

24. Smith, Henry VIII, p. 21.

25. Ibid. , p. 262.

26. Henry reportedly uttered the oft-repeated prophecy "If it is a daughter this time, by God, sons will follow. " Still, he was notably displeased.

27. Smith, Henry VIII, p. 261.

28. Thomas, p. 426.

29. Michiel reported that Mary suffered with a "menstrous retention, " or a "suffocation of the matrix. "

30. Pearson, p. 188.

31. T. Miller, The Castles and the Crown, p. 158.

32. R. Ascham. The Scholemaster. Quoted in Byman, p. 78.

33. N. Williams, Henry VII, p. 88.

34. Ibid.

35. Lloyd K. DeMause. The History of Childhood, p. 23. Harper Torchbooks, 1974.

36. Ibid.

37. Scarisbrick, p. 188.

38. Fraser, Mary Queen of Scots, p. 95.

39. Each Stewart monarch left only one surviving child for posterity in the sixteenth century, a result of infant mortality and the abbreviated marriages occasioned by the monarchs' early deaths.

40. The Frenchman Fontenay described him as "un vieulx jeune homme," an old young man. Quoted in Bingham, The Making of a King, p. 199.

41. Parker, p. 14.

42. McGuigan, p. 131.

43. Philip, after they were married and sent away, kept them informed of everything, including the state of the fruit in the royal gardens.

44. Seward, p. 69.

Marriage

1. According to the Cambridge Population Study Group, the average completed family size in Colyton England during this period was six. Yet only the Habsburgs approached this level among royal families in the sixteenth century.

2. Chamberlain, The Private Character of Queen Elizabeth, p. 54.

3. E. Sanceau. The Reign of the Fortunate King, p. 24. Archon, 1969.

4. C. Williams. England Under the Early Tudors, p. 63. Longmans, 1925.

5. Jenkins, Elizabeth the Great, p. 69.

6. Michael Prawdin. The Mad Queen of Spain, p. 199. Houghton Mifflin, 1939.

7. Jenkins, p. 102.

8. MacInnes, Arabella, p. 164.

9. Ibid., p. 193. P. M. Handover. Arabella Stuart, p. 32. Eyre and Spotswood, 1957.

10. Chapman, The Sisters of Henry VIII, p. 142.

11. Erasmus, The Education of a Christian Prince, p. 241.

12. Ibid., p. 243.

13. T. Maynard. Bloody Mary, p. 29. Bruce, 1955.

14. Richardson, Mary Tudor, p. 46.

15. Along with the marriage of Francis and Eleanor, Marguerite Valois was wedded to Emanuel Philibert of Savoy and Philip II espoused Elizabeth Valois.

16. Fernández y Armesto, Ferdinand and Isabella, p. 75.

17. Noel Williams, Henry II, p. 86.

18. Leland, Vol. IV, cited in Strickland, Lives of the Queens, p. 10.

19. David Herlihy. "The Natural History of Medieval Women, " p. 60. Natural History, vol. LXXXVII, no. 3 (March 1978).

20. Paul LaCroix. The History of Prostitution, vol. I, p. 188. Lorici, 1926. Originally published in France.

21. Ibid., p. 189.

22. Ibid.

23. McGuigan, The Habsburgs, p. 122.

24. Heritier, Catherine de Medici, p. 27.

25. Fraser, Mary Queen of Scots, p. 226.

26. Hackett, Francis I, p. 196.

27. LaCroix, p. 265.

28. M. E. Brooks. A King for Portugal, p. 17, endnote
    #6. University of Wisconsin Press, 1964.

29. Pollard, Henry VIII, p. 432.

30. LaCroix, p. 191.

31. Ibid., p. 312.

32. W. Nicholson. The Remains of Archbishop Grindal,
    p. 17. Parker Society, 1843.

33. Ibid., p. 18.

34. G. Donaldson. Scottish Kings, p. 134. Wiley and
    Sons, 1967.

35. Noel Williams, p. 258.

36. Williamson, Catherine de Medici, p. 64.

37. LaCroix, p. 267.

38. Ibid., p. 394.

39. Ibid., p. 395.

40. Ibid., p. 429.

41. Ibid., p. 406.

42. Ibid., p. 435.

43. Pollard, The Reign of Henry VII from Contemporary
    Sources, p. 358.

44. H. D. Sedgewick. Henry of Navarre, p. 337. Cam-
    bridge University Press, 1914.

45. F. W. Bain. Christina, Queen of Sweden, p. 8.
    Allen, 1890.

46. Bowen, Sundry Great Gentlemen, p. 109.

47. Spivakosky, Son of the Alhambra, p. 190.

48. Ibid.

49. Calendar of State Papers--Spanish. Vol. XIII, 302.

50. E. Noyes. The Story of Ferrara, p. 215. Dent, 1904.

51. Smith, Henry VIII, p. 33.

52. MacInnes, p. 164.

53. Peter Laslett. Family Life and Illicit Love in Earlier Generations, p. 99. Cambridge University Press, 1978.

54. W. L. Wiley. The Gentlemen of Renaissance France, p. 146. Harvard University Press, 1954.

55. J. M. Stone. The History of Mary I, Queen of England, p. 29. Sands, 1901.

56. N. B. Morrison. The Private Life of Henry VIII, p. 79.

57. Richardson, p. 46.

58. Smith, Henry VIII, p. 17.

59. Fraser, Mary Queen of Scots, p. 336.

60. Calendar of State Papers--Scottish. For the years 1593-95, 670.

61. McGuigan, p. 122.

62. Ferdinand's policy called for alliances with England as well as with other continental powers to forge a ring around dangerous France.

63. Parker, Philip II, p. 18.

64. John Nada. Carlos the Bewitched, p. 16. Cape, 1962.

Sex

1. Michel de Montaigne. Essays, p. 371. Translated by J. M. Cohen. Penguin Books, 1958.

2. Nada, Carlos the Bewitched, p. 19.

3. Richardson, Mary Tudor, p. 46.

4. Smith, Catherine Howard, p. 123.

5. Thomas, Religion and the Decline of Magic, p. 107.

6. N. E. Himes. The Medical History of Contraception, p. 172. Williams and Wilkenson, 1936.

7. Nada, p. 20.

8. Thomas, p. 539.

9. Montaigne, p. 368.

10. Jenkins, Elizabeth the Great, p. 298.

11. M. L. Bruce. Anne Boleyn, p. 318. Coward, Mc-Cann, 1972.

12. Smith, Catherine Howard, p. 59.

13. See I. Flugel. "The Character and Married Life of Henry VIII," in Men and Their Motives. Kegan Paul, 1934.

14. Durant, The Age of Reason Begins, p. 394.

15. J. A. Froude. The Reign of Elizabeth I, vol. iv, p. 120. Everyman's Library.

16. LaCroix, p. 270.

17. Ibid., p. 237.

18. Ibid., p. 414.

19. Ibid., p. 379.

20. Lynch, Spain Under the Habsburgs, p. 177.

21. David Lyndsay. "The Answer Sir David Lyndsay Made to The King's Flyting." In The Collected Works of Sir David Lyndsay, V. I. Edited by D. Hamer. Blackwood, 1931.

22. Smith, Henry VIII, p. 56. See also H. A. Kelley. The Matrimonial Trials of Henry VIII. Stanford University Press, 1978.

23. J. Aubrey. Brief Lives, p. 67. Edited by A. Powell. London, 1947.

24. From a MS in the Longford Castle, quoted in History Today, September 1978, p. 599.

25. Thornton, Table Talk from Ben Jonson to Leigh Hunt, p. 9.

26. LaCroix, p. 214.

27. Sedgewick, p. 282.

28. Hackett, Francis I, p. 43.

29. Ibid., p. 197.

30. LaCroix, p. 240.

31. Noel Williams, Henry II, p. 258.

32. Sutherland, p. 59.

33. Fraser, Mary Queen of Scots, p. 65.

34. Sutherland, p. 254.

35. LaCroix, p. 412.

36. Ibid., p. 432.

37. Durant, The Age of Reason Begins, p. 369.

38. Johannes Janssen. The History of the German People at the Close of the Middle Ages, vol. X, 439n. AMS Press, 1966.

39. Fraser, Mary Queen of Scots, p. 4.

40. Lyndsay, quoted in Bingham, James V, p. 98.

41. Bingham, The Making of a King, p. 197.

42. Bingham, James V, p. 90.

43. See Chapter Five for the reports of his early relations, unorthodox as they were, with his wife Juana.

44. McGuigan, p. 132.

45. Ibid., p. 131.

46. Parker, Philip II, p. 18.

47. Ibid.

48. Every male Habsburg of importance set down his philosophy on this issue at some length, and their relatives adhered for the most part to these standards.

49. McGuigan, p. 136.

50. Siegneur de Brantome. Oeuvres Completes, p. 33. Edited by Lalanne. Paris, Renouard, 1864.

51. Heritier, p. 81.

52. Richardson, Mary Tudor, p. 125.

53. LaCroix, p. 230.

54. Ibid., p. 279.

55. Ibid., p. 14.

56. Calendar of State Papers--Spanish. Vol. VIII, 76.

57. Sichel, p. 160.

58. Smith, Henry VIII, p. 71-72.

59. Prescott, A Spanish Tudor, p. 252.

60. Stone, The History of Mary I, p. 255.

61. Jenkins, p. 100.

62. Chapman, The Sisters of Henry VIII, p. 64.

63. Miller, Henry IV, p. 113.

64. Hackett, Francis I, p. 88.

65. Tyler, p. 61.

66. Nada, p. 24.

67. Sanceau, p. 8.

68. Brinch, p. 347.

69. Calendar of State Papers--Venetian. Vol. V, 1230.

70. M. Burke. Charles Brandon--Gentleman Adventurer,
    p. 179. Edinburgh Review, 1951.

71. MacInnes, p. 181.

72. Fraser, Mary Queen of Scots, p. 397.

73. Parker, p. 49.

74. Scarisbrick, p. 360.

75. MacInnes, p. 86.

76. LaCroix, p. 318.

Health

1. Noguerés, p. 27.

2. Erlanger, St. Bartholomew's Night, p. 215.

3. Sichel, p. 6.

4. LaCroix, p. 428.

5. Calendar of State Papers--Venetian. Vol. I, 845.

6. Thomas, p. 198.

7. Chamberlain, Private Character of Queen Elizabeth,
   p. 309.

8. Jenkins, Elizabeth the Great, p. 88.

9. Neville Williams, Elizabeth I, p. 58.

10. Jenkins, p. 258.

11. Ibid., p. 46.

12. Scarisbrick, p. 271.

13. Hackett, Francis I, p. 424.

14. Montaigne, "On Physiognomy," p. 313.

15. Durant, The Reformation, p. 758.

16. Hackett, Francis I, p. 406.

17. Durant, The Age of Reason Begins, p. 495-96.

18. Ibid., p. 545.

19. Ibid.

20. Ibid., p. 12.

21. Marchette Chute. Ben Jonson of Westminster, p. 164. Dutton, 1953.

22. Castiglione, The Courtier, p. 133-34.

23. Smith, Henry VIII, p. 91.

24. Ibid.

25. W. S. C. Copeman. Doctors and Disease in Tudor Times, p. 161. Dawson's, 1960.

26. Montaigne, vol. II, p. 12.

27. Pearson, p. 598.

28. Durant, The Age of Reason Begins, p. 368.

29. Pearson, p. 596.

30. Ibid., p. 56.

31. Nada, p. 18.

32. Juan also had an insatiable craving for sweets.

33. W. T. Walsh. Isabella the Crusader, p. 223. Sheed and Ward, 1935.

34. Miller, Henry IV, p. 344.

35. Heritier, p. 79.

36. Fraser, Mary Queen of Scots, p. 105.

37. Jordan, Edward VI, p. 514.

38. Discussed in The Journal of Family History, spring 1978.

39. Thomas, p. 259.

40. Ibid., p. 10.

41. Z. Cope. Sidelights on the History of Medicine, p. 82. Butterworth, 1957.

42. Ibid., p. 58.

43. Thomas, p. 316.

44. Ibid., p. 289.

45. Montaigne, "On Experience," op. cit., p. 361.

46. Copeman, p. 110.

47. R. Hunter and I. MacAlpine. Three Hundred Years of Psychiatry, p. 52. Oxford University Press, 1963.

48. Montaigne, "On Experience," op. cit., p. 361.

49. Aubrey, p. 251.

50. Thomas, p. 14.

51. Ibid., p. 9.

52. Ibid., p. 14.

53. Kenneth Dewhurst. Sir Thomas Sydenham, p. 116 and p. 163. Oxford University Press, 1966.

54. Smith, Henry VIII, p. 130.

55. Thomas, p. 210.

56. MacAlpine and Hunter, Three Hundred Years of Psychiatry, p. 52.

57. Pearson, p. 475.

58. Durant, The Age of Reason Begins, p. 593.

59. Copeman, p. 130.

60. W. S. C. Copeman. A Short History of the Gout, p. 57. University of California Press, 1964.

61. Ibid.

62. Noel Williams, Henry II, p. 343.

63. Jacques Boulenger. The Seventeenth Century, p. 37. Putnam, 1933.

64. Montaigne, vol. II, p. 212.

65. Lee, Edward VI, p. 239.

66. Ibid.

67. Hare, A Great Emperor, p. 239.

Death

1. Smith, Henry VIII, p. 255.

2. Ibid. , p. 268.

3. Ibid.

4. Ibid.

5. Nada, p. 20.

6. Ibid.

7. Smith, Henry VIII, p. 15.

8. Ibid.

9. C. V. Malfatti. The Accession, Coronation, and Marriage of Mary Tudor--As Related in Four Manuscripts of the Escorial, p. 246. Barcelona, 1956.

10. Miller, The Castles and the Crown, p. 353.

11. Fernández y Armesto.

12. Calendar of State Papers--Venetian. Vol. VII, 270.

13. Ibid., p. 216.

14. LaCroix, p. 232.

15. F. G. Lee. Edward VI, Supreme Head: An Historical Sketch, p. 240. Burns and Oates, 1899.

16. Scarisbrick, p. 334.

17. William Byron. Cervantes: A Biography. Doubleday, 1978.

18. Heritier, Catherine de Medici, p. 406.

19. Thomas, Estudio Medico Historico, p. 265.

20. Unacknowledged. "Some Royal Death Beds," p. 1303. British Medical Journal, 1910.

21. Spivakosky, p. 347.

22. Parker, p. 138.

Adrian of Utrecht 165, 166, 218
Alberi, Ambassador 123
Albert, Duke of Austria 134
Alfonso V of Portugal 139, 141
Allas, Ribas 145, 282
Alva, Duke of 185, 197, 210, 286, 298, 299
Angus, Earl of (Archibald Douglas) 48, 54, 55, 56, 268
Anne of Austria 183, 184, 213
Anne of Brittany 92, 93, 95
Anne of Cleves 22, 23, 262
Anne of Denmark 74, 75, 76, 206, 216, 243
Antoine of Navarre 111, 112
Aquinas, Thomas 205
Armada, Spanish 187
Arran, Earl of (James Hamilton) 63
Arthur (Tudor), Prince of Wales 13, 14, 15, 20, 151, 219, 223, 224, 241
Artificial insemination 138, 262
Assembly of Notables 114
Astrology 280
Austrian Dynasty (Habsburg) 133, 134, 135, 168, 196; accession to crowns of

Hungary and Bohemia 134

Bacon, Francis 281
Beaufort, Margaret 10, 12
Birth of Mankynde 213, 214, 220
Boccaccio 253
Boleyn, Anne 19, 20, 21, 205, 206, 211, 241, 248, 249, 250, 252, 261, 262, 270, 298; "The King's Great Matter" 27, 241
Book of the Courtier 97, 218, 273
Borgia 145
Borgia, Pope Alexander VI 92
Borgia, Cesare 92
Bosworth Field 6, 9, 11
Bothwell, Earl of (James Hepburn) 68, 69, 70, 243
Bourbon Line 111
Brandon, Charles 40, 41, 234
Brantome, Pierre 157, 235, 236, 251, 254, 259, 290
Buckingham, Earl of (George Villiers) 77, 78, 257
Burcot, Dr. 269
Burgogne, Duc de 208

Castiglione, Balthasar 97,

218, 273
Catalina, Princess 157, 161
Cateau-Cambresis, Treaty of
182, 189, 233
Catherine of Aragon 13, 14,
17, 18, 19, 20, 52, 146,
150, 151, 205, 206, 211,
224, 233, 240, 241, 250,
262, 290, 297, 298
"Catholic Kings" 137, 138,
139, 140, 141, 142, 143,
144, 145, 146, 147, 148,
149, 150, 151, 190, 208,
216, 277, 282, 302 (see
also Ferdinand of Aragon
and Isabella of Castile)
Cavalli, Ambassador 120
Cecil, William, Lord
Burghley 32, 33, 65,
66, 235
Cervantes, Miguel 136, 282,
291
"Chans Nuptial" 234, 235
Charles I 250, 301
Charles V 20, 21, 28, 101,
102, 103, 131, 132, 151,
154, 155, 157, 158, 159,
160, 161, 162, 163, 164,
165, 166, 167, 168, 169,
171, 172, 173, 174, 175,
176, 177, 178, 179, 180,
181, 182, 185, 189, 190,
195, 196, 197, 203, 216,
225, 233, 236, 239, 240,
243, 244, 254
Charles VIII 84, 87, 88,
92, 93, 219
Charles IX 81, 83, 86,
115, 116, 117, 118, 119,
120, 121, 128, 188, 191,
219, 238, 255, 261, 265,
277, 282, 296, 297
Charles, Grand Prior of
France 117
Charles, Prince of France
105, 106, 270
Childbirth 150, 151, 154,

155, 162, 169, 171, 183,
184, 203, 204, 205, 206,
207, 208, 209, 210, 211,
213, 214, 284
Childbirth, Rituals of 203,
204
Child-rearing 216, 218,
219, 220, 221, 222, 223,
225
Christian II 158, 159
Christina of Sweden 239
Claude, Princess 127
Claude, Queen of France
95, 98, 99, 100, 101,
205, 239
Coke, Edward 253
Coligny, Admiral 118, 119
Columbus, Christopher 129,
131, 142
Communeros Revolt 156,
167, 300
Commynes 148, 277
Condé, Louis Prince of 112
Confessions of St. Augustine
234
Contarini, Ambassador 165,
254
Correrro, Ambassador 123,
124
Cosmetics 263, 275
Criminal punishment 270,
271, 293

Daemonologie 283
Dandolo, Ambassador 112,
123
Dantiscus, Ambassador 261
Darnley, Lord (Henry Stewart) 36, 46, 47, 66, 67,
68, 241, 263
Debt: France 113; Spain
198
de Chateaubriant, Madame
99, 102
de Cisneros, Francisco
Ximenez 157, 166, 290

de Condé, Marie 122
de Cordoba, Cabrera 149
de Este, Hercules 240
d'Etampes, Duchesse 99,
    102
de Foix, Ambassador 261
de Guise, Marie 58, 59,
    60, 61, 63, 205
de Medici, Catherine 65,
    78, 83, 84, 85, 108,
    109, 111, 112, 113, 114,
    115, 116, 117, 118, 119,
    120, 121, 122, 125, 127,
    205, 206, 207, 219, 220,
    233, 234, 235, 237, 238,
    255, 259, 261, 266, 272
de Medici, Marie 189,
    208, 228
de Montmorency, Charlotte
    256
de Poitiers, Diane 83, 106,
    107, 108, 109, 110, 113,
    237, 250, 254, 255
de Vaudemont, Louise 122,
    123
Diet of Augsberg 172
Diet of Metz 134
Diet of Nuremberg 134
Dining and drinking habits
    271, 273, 274, 290
Don Carlos of Spain 65,
    181, 182, 186, 190, 191,
    194, 252, 277, 278, 282,
    286, 290, 299
Don Juan 172
Don Quixote 136, 282, 291
Donato, Ambassador 184
Douglas, Margaret 36, 37,
    268
Douglas Clan 56
Dudley, Guilford 240
du Laurens, Andre 280,
    283

Economic and political con-
    ditions: France 96,

101, 113, 121; England
    132; Italy 131
Education of a Christian
    Prince 220, 221, 227,
    231, 232, 233
Edward IV 11
Edward VI 24, 25, 26, 28,
    41, 63, 165, 205, 219,
    222, 278, 280, 285, 286,
    290, 300
Eleanor of Spain 102, 103,
    154, 155, 157, 158, 160,
    233, 262
Eleanor, Queen of France
    102, 103, 233
Elizabeth I 6, 7, 20, 30, 31,
    32, 33, 34, 35, 36, 42,
    62, 65, 70, 75, 88, 111,
    125, 182, 186, 190, 202,
    219, 223, 227, 229, 231,
    246, 253, 261, 262, 266,
    269, 272, 291, 295, 301
Elizabeth of Austria 117
Elizabeth of York 12, 13,
    14, 203, 213, 236
Erasmus of Rotterdam 48,
    86, 279
Erskine, Margaret 57

Farnese, Duke Ottavio 230,
    240
Ferdinand of Aragon 146,
    151, 152, 153, 154, 155,
    156, 157, 161, 213, 225,
    228, 229, 243, 249, 259,
    282, 291 (see also "Cath-
    olic Kings")
Ferdinand of Austria 155,
    157, 160, 161, 162, 163,
    169, 176, 188, 189, 195,
    225, 236, 237, 239, 243,
    246, 248, 254
Fernel, Jean 207
Fitzroy, Henry 19
Flodden Field 53, 54, 61
Francis I 18, 36, 40, 58,

59, 80, 81, 84, 85, 95,
96, 97, 98, 99, 100,
101, 102, 103, 104, 105,
106, 107, 108, 121, 127,
131, 158, 160, 172, 178,
195, 216, 224, 225, 233,
235, 237, 239, 241, 247,
249, 254, 288, 290, 301
Francis II 64, 83, 111,
112, 113, 114, 115, 121,
224, 228, 235, 255, 277,
278, 290, 291, 297
Francis, Prince 102, 105,
271, 291
Francis of Alençon 125,
127, 128
Franco-Scottish Alliance
("the auld alliance") 57,
58, 59, 63, 228
Frederick of Styria 134
Fugger bankers 197

Gattinara, Mercurio 131,
168
Geynes, John 279
"Golden Bull" 134
Grey, Lady Jane 25, 26,
27, 41, 221, 223, 240
Grey, Katherine 231
Grindal 236, 237
Guise, Charles (Cardinal of
Lorraine) 111, 114
Guise, Francis 111
Guise, Henry Duke of 125,
128, 183
Guise Family 113, 114,
115, 118, 122, 255, 297
Guistinian, Ambassador
200, 206

Habsburg Empire 28, 102,
129, 131, 132, 133, 134,
135, 136, 152, 154, 156,
157, 159, 161, 166, 168,
176, 299, 300

Hatton, Sir Christopher 251
Henrietta Maria 250
Henry II 64, 81, 85, 105,
106, 107, 108, 109, 110,
111, 113, 121, 219, 235,
237, 238, 240, 249, 250,
254, 255, 261, 262, 270,
277, 284, 296, 297, 300
Henry III (Henry of Anjou)
80, 81, 83, 84, 86, 118,
120, 121, 122, 123, 124,
125, 128, 159, 203, 219,
238, 247, 252, 255, 261,
266, 280, 287
Henry IV (Henry of Navarre)
73, 83, 118, 125, 127,
128, 227, 228, 229, 237,
238, 239, 251, 252, 255,
256, 266, 274, 275, 280,
283
Henry IV of Castile ("Henry
the Impotent") 137, 138,
139, 140, 141, 261, 262
Henry VI 10
Henry VII (Earl of Richmond)
6, 9, 10, 11, 12, 13, 14,
15, 16, 17, 37, 42, 51,
86, 94, 95, 131, 137, 216,
223, 236, 254, 261, 280
Henry VIII 6, 13, 15, 16,
17, 18, 19, 20, 21, 22,
23, 24, 25, 27, 31, 37,
42, 48, 51, 52, 54, 57,
58, 59, 60, 62, 69, 83,
88, 98, 123, 129, 146,
151, 172, 182, 203, 206,
213, 219, 222, 223, 229,
231, 232, 236, 240, 241,
248, 249, 250, 252, 261,
262, 263, 270, 274, 280,
288, 291, 295, 297, 298
Hobbes, Thomas 281
Holy League 118, 125
Holy Roman Empire 129,
133, 134, 135, 147, 154,
155, 159, 161, 163, 176,
186, 271

Homer 132
Homosexuality in reigning
  families: James I 72,
  74, 75, 76, 77, 243, 257,
  301; Henry III 121, 122,
  123, 255
Howard, Catherine 22, 23,
  236, 250, 261
Huguenot Movement 112,
  114, 118, 119, 120, 122,
  124, 125, 296, 297
Hygiene 171, 183, 207,
  211, 212, 214, 218, 274,
  275

Iberian Peninsular Alliance
  161
Iberian peninsular regions:
  Aragon 132, 135, 136,
  137, 139, 141, 142, 146,
  150, 152, 155, 167, 168;
  Castile 132, 135, 136,
  137, 138, 139, 141, 142,
  146, 149, 150, 152, 154,
  155, 157, 167, 168, 169,
  228; Portugal 132, 135,
  136, 137, 139, 149, 150,
  176, 177; Catalonia 132,
  135; Navarre 132; Gra-
  nada 132
Iberian Peninsular Reunifi-
  cation 136, 139, 142,
  149, 161, 177, 228, 235
"Iconoclastic Fury" 185
Inbreeding among Habsburgs
  133, 183, 244
Inquisition: Spanish 136,
  145, 293; Portuguese 150;
  Low Countries 185
Insanity within reigning families: Carlos II 244;
  Charles IX 115, 116, 117,
  118, 119, 120, 128, 265,
  297; Don Carlos of Spain
  190, 191, 252, 282;
  Ferdinand of Austria 163;

Francis II 113; Henry III
  111, 120, 121, 122, 123,
  124, 125, 252; Juana of
  Castile ("la loca") 151,
  152, 153, 155, 156, 157,
  161, 163, 218, 229, 300;
  Maximilian I 277; Rudolf
  of Austria 193, 194;
  Tudor melancholia 220
Isabella of Castile 153, 154,
  155, 165, 228, 259, 282
  (see also "Catholic Kings")
Isabella of Portugal 168,
  169, 171, 207, 211, 213,
  236, 278
Isabella, Queen of Denmark
  157, 158, 159, 189
Isabella, Queen of Portugal
  141, 144, 148, 149, 150,
  151, 157, 166, 223, 228,
  300

Jagellon, Anne 162, 195,
  236, 243
Jagellon Family 160, 162,
  195
James I (Scotland) 45, 253
James II (Scotland) 45
James III 45, 49, 50
James IV 13, 14, 37, 45,
  46, 47, 48, 49, 50, 51,
  52, 53, 54, 61, 225, 232,
  234, 237, 241, 249, 251,
  268, 287
James V 36, 37, 45, 46,
  52, 54, 55, 56, 57, 58,
  59, 60, 61, 62, 63, 225,
  228, 241, 252, 257, 266,
  268
James VI (Scotland) 40, 43,
  45, 47, 67, 70, 71, 72,
  73, 74, 75, 207, 216,
  225, 243, 257; became
  James I (England) 75,
  76, 77, 78, 79, 206, 221,
  222, 231, 232, 246, 262,

268, 273, 275, 282, 283, 291, 295, 301
Jeanne, Queen of France 89, 91, 92, 262
Jews in Spain 136, 137, 145, 150
John of Gaunt 10
Jonson, Ben 253, 272
Juan, Prince of Asturias ("the prince who died of love") 141, 144, 146, 147, 148, 149, 150, 151, 157, 166, 179, 208, 233, 257, 277, 278, 300
Juana "la Beltraneja" 138, 141, 149
Juana of Castile ("la loca") 14, 144, 150, 151, 152, 153, 154, 155, 156, 161, 163, 166, 190, 196, 206, 229, 243, 244, 275, 277, 288, 289, 290, 291, 300
Juana, Princess of Brazil 176

Kird o' Field 68
Knox, John 57, 62, 66

Leicester, Earl of (Robert Dudley) 32, 33, 251, 266, 272
Lennox, Earl of 48, 71
Leo X 165
Lepanto, Battle of 172, 186
L'Estoile 238, 252, 291
Lewis of Bohemia 160, 195
Loaysa 171, 172
Louis XI 89, 287
Louis XII 84, 85, 88, 89, 91, 92, 93, 94, 95, 96, 99, 100, 123, 137, 234, 237, 259, 260, 262, 263, 267
Louis XIII 224, 285

Louis XIV 208
Louise of Savoy 97, 98, 99, 101, 102, 103, 178
Low Countries 125, 154, 155, 160, 163, 175, 177, 181, 182, 185, 186, 197, 198, 210, 286, 298, 299
Luther, Martin 24, 53, 131, 169, 187, 214, 272
Lyndsay, David 55, 56, 57, 216, 252, 257

Machiavelli, Niccolo 84, 129, 131, 142, 143, 145, 168
Maitland of Lethington, William 68, 69
Manuel, King of Portugal ("Manuel the Fortunate") 149, 150, 157, 158, 189, 228, 229, 262
Margaret of Austria 144, 147, 148, 151, 157, 165, 208, 218, 233
Margaret of Habsburg 239, 240
Margaret of Parma 172
Maria, daughter of Juana of Castile 157, 159, 160, 163
Maria, Empress of Austria 169, 176, 257
Maria Manuela of Portugal 179, 180, 181, 213, 214
Maria, Queen of Portugal 150, 151, 161, 189
Marot, Clement 234, 235
Mary I 18, 26, 27, 28, 29, 30, 41, 180, 181, 182, 216, 219, 221, 222, 223, 261, 263, 269, 279, 282
Mary of Burgundy 155
Maximilian I 119, 134, 151, 152, 154, 155, 157, 159, 160, 161, 166, 188, 190, 221, 225, 243, 248, 249, 277, 288, 289, 290

Maximilian II 176, 183, 188, 195, 225, 257, 258, 259, 261
Mayerne 214
Medical treatment of reigning families 211, 213, 214, 215, 236, 278, 279, 280, 281, 282, 283, 284, 285; Charles V 172, 173, 174, 286; Don Carlos 282; Edward VI 26, 285, 286; Elizabeth I 269; Ferdinand of Aragon 146; Francis I 104, 207, 260; Francis II 115, 290; Henry II 108; Henry IV of Castile 138; Henry VIII 288; Isabella of Spain 171, 207; James V 60; Louis XIII 285; Maria Manuela 181; Mary I 282; Catherine de Medici 207; Philip II 187; Jane Seymour 205; Mary Stewart 66, 207; Elizabeth Valois 183, 208, 211; Victoire of France 208
Meditations of Saint Matthew 79
Mercado, Ludovico 214
Michiel, Ambassador 112, 116, 121, 201
Montaigne, Michel 129, 247, 248, 250, 270, 274, 280, 281, 285, 297
Montguyon, Vincente 214
Moorish and Jewish Expulsion, Spain 142, 146, 150, 186, 228, 282
Moray, Earl of (James Stewart) 45, 46, 47
More, Sir Thomas 241
Morosini, Ambassador 123

New World 131, 146, 163, 172, 174, 177, 186, 197, 251
Northumberland, Earl of 25, 26, 27, 41
Nostradamus 112

"On Physiognomy" 270
Ottoman Empire 131, 132, 177, 298
Overbury, Sir Thomas, murder of 77

Paracelsus (Philippus Aureolus Theophrastus Bombast von Hohenheim) 279
Paré, Ambroise 214, 282
Parr, Katherine 23, 31, 240
Pavia, Battle of 85, 101, 158
Peace of La Rochelle 119
Pedro Martyr 144, 147, 148, 152, 155, 165, 208, 277
Philip II 28, 29, 30, 127, 133, 157, 161, 163, 164, 168, 169, 174, 175, 176, 177, 178, 179, 180, 181, 182, 183, 184, 185, 186, 187, 188, 190, 191, 195, 198, 214, 225, 233, 243, 244, 252, 257, 274, 282, 286, 291, 293, 298, 299
Philip IV 228
Philip of Burgundy (Philip the Handsome) 144, 151, 152, 153, 154, 155, 156, 196, 243, 257, 262, 290
Plague 133, 270
Porphyria 55, 62, 76, 211, 268
The Prince 142, 143, 168
Princes in the Tower (Edward V and Henry) 11
Pulgar 139, 140, 141

Quirini, Ambassador 267

Rabelais, François 253
Raleigh, Sir Walter 251
Randolph, Thomas 66, 67, 68
Reformation, English 240, 241, 297, 298
Regimen of Salerno 274
Renard, Simon, Ambassador 200, 261
Renée, Princess 241
Reproductive capabilities of reigning families 202, 203, 207, 211, 227; Habsburg 133, 154, 155, 162, 171, 183, 184, 207, 208, 227; Stewart 52, 55, 59, 67, 74, 206, 207, 249; Trastamara line 138, 141, 147, 148, 150; Tudor 6, 7, 13, 14, 18, 19, 25, 29, 32, 33, 182, 205, 207, 227, 249; Valois 85, 93, 100, 108, 109, 112, 123, 127, 206, 207
Riccio, David, murder of 46, 67
Richard II 9
Richard III 9, 10, 11
Robsart, Amy, Lady Dudley 251
Roesslin, Eucharius 213, 214, 220
"Rosengarten, " text on childbirth 213, 214, 220
Royal ailments and health: Anne Boleyn 211, 262; Catherine of Aragon 211; Charles V 164, 165, 173, 174, 175, 262, 266, 274, 286; Charles IX 117, 119, 120, 265; Edward VI 26; Eleanor of France 158, 262; Elizabeth I 30, 31, 32, 33, 35, 269; Elizabeth Valois 210, 211; Francis I 103, 104, 105, 260; Francis II 112, 113, 114, 115, 277; Henry II 255, 262; Henry III 123, 124, 266; Henry IV 256, 266, 274; Henry VIII 16, 17, 23, 274; Isabella of Castile 144; Isabella of Portugal 171, 211; Isabella of Spain 148, 149; James I 72, 75, 76, 79, 268; James V 268; Juan of Asturias 147, 148; Juana of Castile 151, 155, 156; Louis XII 93, 94, 95, 263; Margaret Tudor 268; Mary I 27, 30, 261; Mary Stewart 64, 65, 66, 67, 68, 69, 207, 211, 268; Philip II 177, 181, 187, 274; Philip of Burgundy 154, 262
Royal College of Physicians 278, 279, 282
Rudolf of Austria 193, 194, 275

Sacco, Ambassador 235
Safety Act 34
Sandoval, Ambassador 145, 164
Santa Cruz 165
Sauval 254
Savoy, Duke of (Emanuel Philibert) 189, 190, 205, 254
Sebastian of Portugal 191, 192, 194, 235, 277, 278, 299
Semmelweis, Ignaz, Dr. 214
Several Chirurgicall Treatises (1676) 281

Seymour, Edward 231
Seymour, Jane 21, 205,
 207, 213
Seymour, Thomas, Lord
 Admiral 30, 269
Shakespeare, William 203,
 295, 296
Sixtus V 122
Social Behavior 272, 273,
 274
Somerset, Earl of (Robert
 Carr) 77, 257
Somerset, Earl of (Edward
 Seymour) 25
Spanish reconquest 137
Stewart, Mary, Queen of
 Scotland 34, 36, 37,
 46, 47, 61, 62, 63, 64,
 65, 66, 67, 68, 69, 70,
 71, 83, 111, 112, 115,
 203, 206, 207, 223, 224,
 228, 235, 241, 263, 268,
 286, 287
"Stockholm Bath of Blood" 159
Stuart, Arabella 218, 231, 268
Sully 255, 256
Suriano, Ambassador 116, 117,
 120, 121, 123, 163, 290
Sydenham, Sir Thomas 281
Sydney, Sir Philip 251

Tavannes, Ambassador 116
Taxation and crown revenue
 57; Spain 133, 167,
 186, 197, 198; France
 113; England 133; Neth-
 erlands 185, 298
Throckmorton, Sir Nicholas
 111
Touchet, Marie 117, 122
Trastamara line 137, 140,
 144, 146, 151, 152
True Law of Free Mon-
 archies 75
Tudor, Margaret, Queen of
 Scotland 13, 14, 35, 36,

51, 52, 54, 55, 59, 60,
 207, 211, 231, 232, 234,
 241, 251, 268
Tudor, Mary, Queen of
 France 13, 15, 21, 35,
 37, 40, 41, 95, 96, 234
"Tumult at Amboise" 114

Union of Calmar 158
Union of the Crowns 142

Valois, Elizabeth 127, 182,
 183, 205, 208, 209, 210,
 211, 284, 286, 291, 299
Valois, Madeline 58, 241
Valois, Marguerite 118,
 127, 128, 183, 190, 205,
 219, 220, 227, 237, 238,
 239, 251, 263
Vasa Family of Sweden 159
Venereal disease 172, 239,
 240, 248, 259, 260, 261,
 263, 266, 288
Vesalius 282
Victoire, Princess 208
Villeroy 122
Voltaire 129

Walsingham, Sir Francis
 74, 266
War of the Roses 9, 132
Wars of Religion 86, 113,
 121, 238, 300
Witchcraft 207, 250, 252,
 262, 283, 290
Wittelsbach Family 134
Wolff, Caspar 236
Wolsey, Cardinal 16, 54,
 55, 83
Wyatt's Rebellion (1554) 27,
 30, 31, 269

Yanguas, Dr. 290